School Bullying in Different Cultures

School bullying is widely recognised as an international problem, but publications have focussed on the western tradition of research. A long tradition of research in Japan and South Korea and more recently in mainland China and Hong Kong, has had much less exposure. There are important and interesting differences in the nature of school bullying in eastern and western countries, as the first two parts of this book demonstrate. The third part examines possible reasons for these differences – methodological issues, school systems, societal values and linguistic issues. The final part looks at the implications for interventions to reduce school bullying and what we can learn from experiences in other countries. This is the first volume to bring together these perspectives on school bullying from a range of eastern as well as western countries.

PETER K. SMITH is Emeritus Professor of Psychology at the Unit for School and Family Studies in the Department of Psychology, Goldsmiths, University of London.

KEUMJOO KWAK is a professor in the Department of Psychology at Seoul National University, South Korea.

YUICHI TODA is a professor of Osaka Kyoiku University (Osaka University of Education), Japan.

School Bullying in Different Cultures

Eastern and Western Perspectives

Edited by

Peter K. Smith, Keumjoo Kwak and Yuichi Toda

CAMBRIDGE
UNIVERSITY PRESS

University Printing House, Cambridge CB2 8BS, United Kingdom

Cambridge University Press is part of the University of Cambridge.

It furthers the University's mission by disseminating knowledge in the pursuit of
education, learning and research at the highest international levels of excellence.

www.cambridge.org
Information on this title: www.cambridge.org/9781107031890

© Cambridge University Press 2016

First published 2016

A catalogue record for this publication is available from the British Library

Library of Congress Cataloguing in Publication Data
Smith, Peter K.
School bullying in different cultures : Eastern and Western perspectives / edited
by Peter K. Smith, Keumjoo Kwak and Yuichi Toda.
      pages   cm
Includes bibliographical references and index.
ISBN 978-1-107-03189-0 (Hardback : alk. paper)
1. Bullying in schools–Cross-cultural studies.   2. Bullying in schools–
Prevention–Cross-cultural studies.   3. Comparative education.   I. Title.
LB3013.3.S58 2016
371.7′82–dc23   2015033547

ISBN 978-1-107-03189-0 Hardback

Contents

Figures

Tables

Contributors

SHERI BAUMAN Director, Counseling and Mental Health Program, University of Arizona, USA

GUANGHUI CHEN Department of Psychology, Shandong Normal University, China

LIANG CHEN Department of Psychology, Shandong Normal University, China

HELEN COWIE Faculty of Health and Medical Sciences, University of Surrey, UK

WENDY CRAIG Psychology Department, Queen's University, Canada

DAVID FUNDER Department of Psychology, University of California at Riverside, USA

VANESSA A. GREEN School of Education, Victoria University of Wellington, New Zealand

ESTHER GUILLAUME Department of Psychology, University of California at Riverside, USA

RUBINA HANIF National Institute of Psychology, Quaid-i-Azam University, Pakistan

SUSIE HARCOURT School of Education, Victoria University of Wellington, New Zealand

IRENE HONG Psychology Department, Queen's University, Canada

ALANA JAMES Department of Psychology, Royal Holloway, University of London, UK

JOHN JESSEL Department of Education, Goldsmiths, University of London, UK

LINQIN JI Department of Psychology, Shandong Normal University, China

KEVIN JONES University of Worcester, UK

TOMOYUKI KANETSUNA Department of Modern Applied Psychology, Koshien University, Japan

KEUMJOO KWAK Department of Psychology, Seoul National University, South Korea

CHI LEUNG LAI Department of Special Education and Counselling, Hong Kong Institute of Education, Hong Kong

SEUNG-HA LEE Yeungnam University, Seoul, South Korea

SIU-FUNG LIN Child and Adolescent Development Research Centre, Hong Kong

TEGAN E. LYNCH School of Education, Victoria University of Wellington, New Zealand

JESS MAHDAVI Lansdowne Primary Academy, Gateway Learning Community Trust, London, UK

JULIAN MENDEZ Department of Educational Psychology, University of Arizona, USA

FAYE MISHNA Factor-Intwentash Faculty of Social Work, University of Toronto, Canada

RAGNAR OLAFSSON Educational Testing Institute, Iceland

PHILLIP SLEE School of Education, Flinders University, Australia

PETER K. SMITH Department of Psychology, Goldsmiths, University of London, UK

DAGMAR STROHMEIER School of Applied Health and Social Sciences, University of Applied Sciences Upper Austria, Linz, Austria

KEITH SULLIVAN Statutory Professor of Education, National University of Ireland at Galway, Ireland

FRAN THOMPSON Department of Psychology, Goldsmiths, University of London, UK

YUICHI TODA Faculty of Education, Osaka University of Education, Japan

ZEHRA UCANOK Department of Psychology, Hacettepe University, Turkey

TAKUYA YANAGIDA School of Applied Health and Social Sciences, University of Applied Sciences Upper Austria, Linz, Austria

WENXIN ZHANG Department of Psychology, Shandong Normal University, China

Preface

School bullying is a universal phenomenon, but most of the research in the last thirty years has been in western countries. For example, the *Handbook of Bullying in Schools: An International Perspective* (Jimerson, Swearer, & Espelage, 2010) has 41 chapters, only 2 of which represent perspectives outside Europe, North America and Australia (1 being comparative and 1 on Japan). A publication providing a systematic comparison of eastern and western approaches to the topic has been lacking; a gap which this book seeks to fill.

Over the last two decades, issues around school bullying and violence have come to take a major role in academic research, public debate and national policy. As part of a general movement internationally towards individual rights, the rights of pupils (and teachers and others in school) not to be attacked, abused or socially isolated has come to be recognised as a vital part of a democratic society and for pupil well-being, academic achievement and future functioning. Research on the topic has been reinvigorated and challenged in the last decade by the phenomenon of cyberbullying (via mobile phones and the Internet).

The study of school bullying has more than one origin (see Smith, 2014). It is conventionally seen as starting in Scandinavia (Sweden, Norway) with the writings of Heinemann and especially Olweus (see Chapter 1). The research topic spread through Western Europe, in the 1980s and 1990s. The European work also had an impact in some Commonwealth countries (especially Australia, New Zealand and Canada) since the 1980s and from the 1990s on, researchers in the United States have been explicitly researching school bullying (as opposed to earlier general research on aggression and school violence).

Quite separately, however, researchers and educators in Japan were concerned with the problems of *ijime*, a term very similar to bullying. Publications on *ijime* go back at least to the early 1980s and until the mid 1990s most Japanese researchers seemed unaware of the European research. There was, however, some contact with South Korean researchers, where there was also some older tradition of research

(Koo, 2007). These separate traditions began to come together in the early 1990s. International cooperation organised by Morita in Japan led to a four-country cross-national survey (Japan, England, Norway, Netherlands) and the publication of two books, a Japanese version (Morita et al., 1999) and an English-language version (Smith et al., 1999).

Since then research on bullying in schools has become a more truly international endeavour. This has been marked by more academic interchange and by the involvement of international organisations. This book stems from collaboration amongst the three editors. Smith and Kwak jointly held a grant under the PMI2/British Council initiative (2008–2009), which allowed their research teams to meet and share knowledge of bullying work in the United Kingdom and the corresponding *wang-ta* in South Korea. Smith and Kwak also co-supervised the doctoral thesis of Hyojin Koo at Goldsmiths, on the topic of South Korean bullying. Smith and Toda participated in a workshop in Kobe, Japan in 2003 which Smith helped organise, and Smith and Morita jointly supervised the doctoral thesis of Tomoyuki Kanetsuna at Goldsmiths, which systematically compared *bullying* and *ijime*. All three editors had a role in the doctoral thesis of Alana James on peer support systems in England, South Korea and Japan. These prior endeavours feature in this book.

The greater international dimension of school bullying raises opportunities and challenges. The eastern and western traditions have different origins; so are we talking about the same phenomena? How similar or different are *ijime*, *wang-ta* and *bullying*? Is there a danger of western ethnocentrism in assuming a general similarity and not respecting differences? Also, what about China? Early research in China used western models (e.g. the Olweus questionnaire), but how appropriate are western research tools for measuring a quite different cultural reality? Even the pioneering cross-national study organised by Morita (1999) is open to this same concern.

This rush for commonality and disregard of differences was probably expectable and even perhaps necessary at the beginnings of international cooperation, but a decade or so later we need to (and are able to) step back and look more objectively at how different cultural and religious/ philosophical traditions, recent history and the nature of school systems in different countries, can profoundly influence the nature of what may loosely be called 'bullying' phenomena. A recognition of diversity and difference may in fact help us to learn more effectively from each other, especially about practical measures to reduce 'bullying'. We can learn from each other's experiences, but not in simplistic ways; we need to more fully recognise cultural diversity than was done in the past. The rationale of this book is thus to explicitly confront and discuss such diversity.

The book is organised in four parts. Part I consists of chapters outlining the traditions of research on school bullying in major countries or blocks of countries: Europe, North America, Australasia, Japan, South Korea, mainland China and Hong Kong. In Part II we have examples of three studies where direct east/west comparisons are possible, using the same instruments or methodology. In Part III, four chapters discuss various issues involved in making cross-country comparisons – measurement issues, the nature of educational systems, societal values and characteristics and linguistic terms used. Part IV has contributions on the practical measures taken to combat school bullying in western countries, Japan, South Korea, mainland China and Hong Kong. A concluding editorial chapter reflects on what we have learnt on similarities and differences between bullying in eastern and western cultures, how we can explain these and their relevance for future research and practical action.

REFERENCES

Jimerson, S. R., Swearer, S. M., & Espelage, D. L. (Eds.). (2010). *Handbook of bullying in schools: An international perspective.* New York & London: Routledge.

Koo, H. (2007). A time line of the evolution of school bullying in differing social contexts. *Asia Pacific Education Review*, 8, 107-116.

Morita, Y., Smith, P. K., Junger-Tas, J., Olweus, D., Catalano, R., & Slee, P. (Eds.). (1999). *Sekai no ijime.* Kaneko Shobou: Tokyo.

Smith, P. K. (2014). *Understanding school bullying: It's nature and prevention strategies.* London: Sage.

Smith, P. K., Morita, Y, Junger-Tas, J., Olweus, D., Catalano, R., & Slee, P. (Eds.). (1999). *The nature of school bullying: A cross-national perspective.* London: Routledge.

Peter K Smith, Keumjoo Kwak, Yuichi Toda

Foreword

This exciting book finally brings together research done in the area of school bullying around the world – it is a much needed collection of insights and empirical findings based on studies many western researchers have not been very familiar with. Personally, I was very keen on getting to know better the work done in mainland China, Hong Kong, Japan and South Korea, and I believe that this volume is an inspiring read for anyone interested in the problem of bullying – especially for those interested in, or planning to do cross-cultural research on the topic.

To me, it is fascinating that researchers in eastern countries have paid attention to the group nature of bullying from early on, describing it as a 'disease of the classroom' (as mentioned by Toda in Chapter 4) rather than a problem of individual misbehaving children. Even the roles of students who witness bullying were of particular interest in a Japanese study by Morita and colleagues, before they truly entered the research agenda in the west. Also, many of the concepts used to refer to bullying in South Korea bear a strong connotation of abuse by the group rather than by an individual student. Whether this reflects a cultural understanding of the phenomenon or actual differences in how and by whom it is done (prevalence of different forms, for instance, does not always seem to tell the same story as perceptions of what kind of forms bullying involves) still leaves room for further research.

Overall, there seem to be many similarities in the understanding of bullying, the forms it takes, its correlates, as well as gender differences and developmental changes in it. Although also differences between eastern and western cultures are found, they often leave some doubt concerning equivalence in samples and measurement issues. Reading about prevalence differences makes one think about the large differences found in the prevalence of bullying and victimisation even within European countries. Taking this variation into account, the prevalence of bullying actually does not seem to differ much from east to west; to me, the similarities are perhaps more striking than the differences.

Having said that, as there are known variations across classrooms and (to a lesser extent) schools in the prevalence and dynamics of bullying (for instance, more bullying in hierarchical classrooms or in classrooms where teachers do not have strong antibullying attitudes or they do not express such attitudes to students), such differences probably exist across wider cultural contexts as well. The interesting question is, what are the proximal factors (perhaps at the school level, or at the teacher/classroom level) that mediate such cultural influences on the dynamics of bullying.

There are obviously many exciting avenues for future research on bullying in eastern and western cultures. Before taking too many steps forward, however, there is also a need for a step backward, a careful look at methodological issues, such as measurement properties of the constructs across cultures. Before that, there is no guarantee that possible cross-cultural differences found in the associations between bullying and other constructs are not merely artefacts of measurement invariance. The chapter by Guillaume and Funder (Chapter 11) nicely highlights this need, as well as other important issues that need consideration when making cross-cultural comparisons. It is actually surprising that neither confirmatory factor analyses with the basic questionnaires nor forced-choice measures such as Q-sort techniques have been utilised in studying bullying across cultures. Also the implicit association test (IAT) comes to mind as a possible approach when examining bullying-related emotions or attitudes. This volume certainly provides a wonderful overview of what has been done so far and a great inspiration for those intending to take the exciting next steps.

Christina Salmivalli
University of Turku, Finland

Foreword

The phenomenon of 'bullying' can be found in any society at any time. It can be described as 'the phenomenon that can sneak up on any human relationships and groups that we form, like a shadow'. Does this mean that bullying is something that we, as a human being, must accept, like 'karma'? Is it something we cannot do anything about, but just put up with? It is quite understandable that comparative ethologists, at a very early stage of bullying research, found the primordial aggression of human beings (considered as an animal species) as an underlying reason for this phenomenon.

However, even if we concede that bullying is an inevitable karma that lurks deep within human nature, whether it is developed or inhibited should still depend on our perception and behaviour towards the phenomenon, namely educational approaches in a broader sense by families, schools and society as a whole. In fact, when we look around the world, the occurrence of the phenomenon and the process by which it becomes a social problem varies by society, time, education and the type and level of measures taken against it by adults.

Because of such differences and variations, we should not conclude that the problem of bullying is an inevitable karma of human nature, and give up trying to reduce it. We do not reject examining the darker reaches of human nature, but by revealing the common and uncommon features of bullying in each society, we can consider how we can tackle the problem together, and develop educational approaches against it. This is the biggest implication of this book.

Almost all sorts of so-called social problems, including bullying, can be characterised as being socially built up; people's attention is drawn to them by claims that it is something bad, unforgivable, unacceptable, sick or extraordinary. Thus, the fact that the phenomenon of bullying exists in a particular society and the fact that bullying is regarded as a social problem in that society are two different things.

For example, *ijime* (the most similar concept to *bullying* in Japan) is often claimed to have a less visible structure, and because of that, we base our judgment of the occurrence of *ijime* on the subjective emotions of victims. In such a situation, whether or not *ijime* becomes a social problem in Japanese society depends on the level and diversity of people's attention to the problem. If people lack concern for the problem, they remain ignorant about it, and no measures are taken against it.

Varying levels of people's attention, in turn, make a difference as to how the problem would be perceived and what measures would be taken in a particular society as a whole. However, this is not merely the problem of a particular society. Instead, we can understand the diversity of the problem of bullying and derive the measures to tackle it through the kinds of social comparisons which this book aims for. For example, *iljinhoe* (school gangsters) in South Korea appears at a glance to be based on the local conditions and climate of schools in South Korea, but we can still learn about the basic nature of school gangsters, which many societies have similar problems with, and about how we should tackle such problems from these local cases.

Measures against *ijime* in Japan often place a disproportionate emphasis on saving victims, but measures and mechanisms targeted more on citizenship education by questioning perpetrators over the responsibility for their negative behaviours, as is often done in Western countries, could give us a new perspective on tackling *ijime* in Japan. Measures against school violence as well as a national debate on a code of student rights and authority of teachers in South Korea could be another example which can be used as a useful reference for considering human rights education at schools in Japan.

When we look at such local cases, we must be careful not to focus too much on unique characteristics of a particular cultural setting or society, and thus to ignore the hidden common features. Bullying can be found in any society or culture at any time, so even if it's manifestation appears as unique characteristics of a particular culture or society, it is important for us to continue research to find out common features and mechanisms, and to attempt to generalise scientific findings about it.

There have been studies of bullying in various countries all over the world, and some common features and characteristics of bullying have been found from such studies. One of these features is that the abuse of 'asymmetric power' is related to the mechanism of the occurrence of bullying. 'Asymmetric power' can be understood as a 'force' which is an essential element for us as we interact with others, manage groups and form a society. This element can also be found in the definition of bullying and can be considered as a premise of universality of bullying (Morita, 2010). Because it is an essential element for everyday life, it is deeply related to various socio-cultural elements such as our lifestyle, interpersonal- and group-relationships based on politics, economics, culture and religions, and this can be considered to be reflected in the occurrence of bullying, people's attention towards it and the diversity of approaches to the problems in a particular society.

If we understand the basic element of bullying as the 'abuse of power', bullying will not be limited to the problem of children. Social problems in adult society such as power harassment, sexual harassment, domestic violence, child abuse and so on can all be occurred under the same mechanism. In other words, tackling bullying involves facing the common problems for adults and children to form peaceful, secure and comfortable interpersonal relationships within society.

Comparing bullying in various countries, there are societies where bullying can be stopped more easily and societies where bullying can hardly be stopped at all. The differences between these societies reflect the differences in the sensibility and educational levels of schools, families and society as a whole and the levels of maturation of awareness of people, both adults and children, living in a particular society. I believe this book fills an important gap in bringing together perspectives on bullying from a range of eastern and western cultures. I hope it will contribute to the continuing endeavour for each country to train better citizens and to form better societies.

Yohji Morita
Naruto University of Education, Japan

Part I

Social awareness and research on bullying and cyberbullying

1 Research on bullying in schools in European countries

Peter K. Smith

One origin of school-bullying research is in Western Europe, and specifically in Scandinavia. This chapter will review how this research program originated, the early work, and how it spread to the United Kingdom and to other European countries during the 1990s and 2000s. It will mention relevant issues around definition, history of research, types of bullying and some main research findings. The chapter is necessarily quite selective, as a vast amount of research has been carried out, in a range of European countries. As examples, I give a fairly detailed description of how interest and concern about bullying has developed in the United Kingdom, and use a recent survey in Northern Ireland to illustrate some common findings about bullying.

Origins and definition

The English term *bullying* first came to prominence through Thomas Hughes' (1857) book *Tom Brown's School Days*, in which Tom and some of his friends are tormented by Flashman and his gang at Rugby school: 'Flashman was about 17 years old, and big and strong of his age ... a formidable enemy for small boys' (p.178). The Head of House says: '... there's a deal of bullying going on. ... Bullies are cowards ...' (p.123). This early literary example already emphasises the imbalance of power involved in bullying, here through physical strength.

However the scientific study of bullying in Europe has its main origins in Sweden and Norway. A school doctor, Heinemann, introduced the Swedish term *mobbning* in a book *Mobbning – Gruppvåld bland barn och vuxna* (1972). This was borrowed from the ethological term *mobbing*, or 'all against one', describing a collective attack by a group on an individual (here, often of another species). His work was taken up by Dan Olweus, a Swede who later and for most of his research career has worked in Norway at the University of Bergen. Olweus used the term in his book *Forskning om skolmobbning* (1973), translated into English as *Aggression in the Schools: Bullies and Whipping Boys* (1978). His later book

Mobbning – vad vi vet och vad vi kan göra (1986) uses the same term, and was the basis of his most well-known book *Mobbning i skolan* (Swedish version), *Mobbing i skolen* (Norwegian version) and *Bullying at School: What We Know and What We Can Do* (English version) (all 1992/1993), which has been translated into many languages.

Mobbing carries the connotation of the 'group vs. one'. However, Olweus soon rejected this: 'It is questionable how common all-against-one situations really are in a school setting . . . it is perhaps rather unusual for the whole class (the boys or the girls) to be united in an intense collective activity . . . mobbing by very small groups is the more frequent type in our schools' (1978, p.5); and later 'Data from our Bergen study . . . indicate that, in the majority of cases, the victim of bullying is harassed by a small group of two or three students, often with a negative leader. A considerable proportion of victims, some 25–40 percent, report, however, that they are mainly bullied by a single student' (1999a, p.10).

Olweus also designed a self-report questionnaire to assess bullying in schools. This included a definition which mentioned different kinds of bullying (such as being hit or threatened), and emphasised that 'these things can happen frequently and it is difficult for the young person being bullied to defend himself or herself'. Thus, besides intentional hurt, bullying was defined by the criteria of repetition and imbalance of power. Shorter but similar definitions at the time were: 'Bullying is repeated oppression of a less powerful person, physical or psychological, by a more powerful person' (Farrington, 1993); and 'The systematic abuse of power' (Smith and Sharp, 1994, p.2).

The earlier work on bullying (Olweus, 1978) only mentioned physical and verbal kinds of bullying (reflecting the main kinds of aggression described at the time). However contemporary definitions stress a broader range of forms that bullying can take. Only in the 1990s was attention drawn explicitly to indirect, psychological and relational forms of aggression, and also of bullying (Björkqvist, Lagerspetz and Kaukiainen, 1997). And in the 2000s, research on cyberbullying has developed rapidly, in Europe as elsewhere (Smith et al., 2008; Mora-Merchán and Jäger, 2010).

History of research in Europe: (1) Scandinavia, the Netherlands

Action in Norway on school bullying was accelerated by the publicity given to the suicides of three 10–14-year-old boys in late 1982, attributed in large part to their experiences of severe bullying. This, together with Olweus' existing research findings, helped bring about the first

Norwegian National Anti-Bullying campaign, starting in autumn 1983. This campaign (see also Chapter 15) involved a nationwide survey using the Olweus questionnaire, a video for use in schools and materials for teachers and parents (Olweus, 1999b). In parallel with this, Olweus developed a school-based intervention program. His evaluation of this original version of the Olweus Bullying Prevention Program (1983–1985), with reports of reductions in bullying of around 50 percent, encouraged researchers and inspired the next wave of research.

In 1988 there was a conference in Stavanger, Norway, organised by Erling Roland, which also helped bring the Scandinavian work to a wider audience. From around 1989, books and journal articles started to appear; and surveys in other countries beyond Scandinavia were beginning to be carried out. Besides self-report surveys, some studies started to use peer nominations methodology. Also, some intervention campaigns took place, partly inspired by the Norwegian campaign; in Europe, early large-scale interventions were in England (Smith and Sharp, 1994) and Flanders (Stevens and Van Oost, 1994; and see Chapter 15).

Intervention work in Norway has continued, with both Olweus, and Roland, coordinating interventions in schools (Olweus and Limber, 2010; Roland, 2011). In Sweden, there was also a significant input by Anatol Pikas (1989, 2002), who developed his Pikas method of working in a non-judgemental way with children who bully others; this and the similar Farsta method are used quite widely in Sweden, although its empirical research base is limited and it is criticised by some, including Olweus.

In Finland there has been a strong research tradition since the 1980s, started by a research group with the late Kirsti Lagerspetz. This was one of the first groups to develop the peer nominations approach to gather information. In a nomination procedure, an informant is asked to nominate self or others (e.g. classmates) for involvement in roles such as bully, or victim. A development of this technique by Christina Salmivalli and colleagues (1996) allows differentiation of participant roles such as ringleader bully, follower, reinforcer, outsider and defender, as well as victim. Salmivalli and colleagues have also developed a nationally based intervention, KiVa (Salmivalli, Kärnä and Poskiparta, 2010; and see Chapter 15).

In the Netherlands, Veenstra et al. (2007) have developed the methodology of peer nominations further by asking about dyadic relationships, with questions such as 'who do you bully?' and 'by whom are you bullied?'. Huitsing and Veenstra (2012) asked for dyadic information on all the main participant roles, as well as getting sociometric data, enabling them to carry out a social network analysis on a class basis.

History of research: (2) United Kingdom

School bullying remained a low-key issue in the whole of the United Kingdom well into the 1980s. Two early studies by Lowenstein (1978a,b), on characteristics of bullying and bullied children, relied mainly on teacher nominations. Arora and Thompson (1987) used a 'Life in School' booklet to define the nature of bullying in a secondary school in the north of England. However public and media attention became particularly focussed on the issue in 1989–1990.

Three books on bullying appeared in the United Kingdom in 1989, and in that year a Government report, the Elton Report on Discipline, mentioned school bullying, the work in Norway and the need for further research. The Gulbenkian Foundation supported several research initiatives, one being a survey service, based on an English-language version of the Olweus questionnaire (Ahmad, Whitney and Smith, 1991). Some early results from these surveys suggested that bullying in English schools was higher than the rates in Norway.

This period also saw an expansion of media interest in the issue. In 1992, the BBC *That's Life* program pursued the topic of school bullying vigorously, following the suicide of an adolescent girl due in part to bullying at school. Following questions in Parliament about what was being done about school bullying, the then Department for Education in London decided to fund a survey and intervention project in Sheffield from 1991–1994 (Smith and Sharp, 1994; and see Chapter 15). This resulted in a Pack for schools, *Don't Suffer in Silence*; the first (1994) edition was free to state schools and was requested by most schools; a second edition came out in 2000, and was available on the internet. The national charity Kidscape, with a long interest in child protection, produced materials and campaigned on the issue of school bullying. These varied support activities contributed to not only keeping bullying 'on the agenda', but also to providing sources of practical help for schools and teachers.

Research in the 1990s pointed to certain at-risk groups for being bullied, such as ethnic-minority children, children of different sexual orientation, and children with SEN. Family factors were also implicated in the likelihood of a child becoming a bully or a victim (Bowers, Smith and Binney, 1992). In addition several studies (mainly cross-sectional) illustrated negative correlates of involvement in bullying, such as psychosomatic symptoms for victims (Williams et al., 1996) and anxiety, depression and low self-esteem (Salmon, James and Smith, 1998).

Telephone help lines were promoted as one source of support, and a dedicated ChildLine bullying line obtained funding for seven months in 1994, and received a total of 58,530 calls; the majority of callers were within the age range 11 to 14 years, predominantly girls. A detailed analysis of the calls, and of an associated survey on bullying, was given by McLeod and Morris (1996).

Interest in peer-support and mediation approaches increased considerably. A survey of peer-support schemes by Cowie (1998; Naylor and Cowie, 1999) found that there were benefits to the peer helpers in terms of confidence and responsibility, and to the school atmosphere generally; but there were also problems due to some degree of hostility to peer helpers from other pupils, and to issues of power sharing with staff, and ensuring sufficient time and resources for proper implementation.

By the end of the century, the climate of knowledge and opinion on school bullying in England had changed radically from that prevailing ten years earlier. It was now widely acknowledged that any school was likely to have some issues regarding bullying; it was no longer really plausible or acceptable to say 'there is no bullying in this school'. In late 1999 it became a legal requirement for every state school to have some form of anti-bullying policy. Regular inspections of schools by OFSTED (Office for Standards in Education) now asked to what extent bullying was a problem in a school, and whether the school had taken measures to combat it, including having a policy. Many more materials were now available to schools and teachers in the United Kingdom.

A new and comprehensive package of materials, *Safe to Learn*, was issued from November 2007, and was available until 2011. The importance of having effective anti-bullying policies was reinforced by a Report of the House of Commons Education and Skills Committee on Bullying (House of Commons, 2007). The response by the Government, in June 2007, referred extensively to the forthcoming *Safe to Learn* guidance (DCSF, 2009), including that 'schools should undertake an audit of behaviour and review their policies as a result'; 'policies should be reviewed every two years'; 'anti-bullying policies must address all forms. This would include bullying related to race, religion and culture; homophobic bullying; sexist and sexual bullying; bullying related to special educational needs (SEN) and disability; and cyberbullying'; and that 'as well as dealing with the bullying of pupils by pupils, anti-bullying policies should cover the bullying of school staff, whether by pupils, parents or other staff'.

Following the new coalition government in 2010, the now DfE issued a *Schools White Paper, The Importance of Teaching*, in November 2010 (DfE, 2010). It stated (section 9) that head teachers are expected to 'take a strong stand against bullying – particularly prejudice-based racist, sexist and homophobic bullying'. It also stated (section 3.17) that 'It is important that head teachers are able to maintain a culture of good behaviour and respect by reinforcing the school's expectations beyond the school gates. Bullying can happen or continue outside school, and behaviour on the way to and from school affects the perception of the school in the wider community'. It signalled an intention (section 9) to 'focus Ofsted inspections more strongly on behaviour and safety, including bullying, as one of four key areas of inspection' (DfE, 2010). Revised guidance on preventing and tackling bullying (DfE, 2014) was issued, most recently in October 2014, covering legal requirements, stating that 'Teachers have the power to discipline pupils for misbehaving outside the school premises "to such an extent as is reasonable"' (p.5), and that 'Schools should apply disciplinary measures to pupils who bully in order to show clearly that their behaviour is wrong' (p.7).

The development of these requirements over the last fifteen years has obviously impacted on schools, and the proportion of schools having an anti-bullying policy has increased dramatically over this period. Surveys carried out in relation to use of the *Don't Suffer in Silence* pack indicate that from 1994–1996 about 55% of schools had an anti-bullying policy (either separately, or as part of a wider behaviour/discipline policy); this had risen to 91% in 2002, with 8% developing a policy, and 1% providing no information (Samara and Smith, 2008).

The Anti-Bullying Alliance (ABA; www.anti-bullyingalliance.org.uk/) was founded in 2002. This brought together over fifty national organisations in England, from the voluntary and private sectors, LEAs, professional associations and the research community into one network to work together to reduce bullying and create safer environments for children and young people to live, grow, play and learn. It supported regional seminars, the development of a portfolio of resources, and promoted Anti-Bullying Weeks which have been held annually since 2004. The charity Beatbullying (now dissolved) developed various initiatives, notably a cybermentors scheme to provide counselling and advice for victims of bullying or cyberbullying (Kaenel-Platt and Douglas, 2012). Childnet International (www.childnet.com) has been very active in the areas of e-safety and cyberbullying.

History of research: (3) other countries in Europe

Through the 1990s, research on school bullying developed in many European countries, and by now there is some history of research and interest in the topic throughout all the European Community (EC) countries and indeed most countries in Europe. A wide range of activities and research is documented in the books *The Nature of School Bullying: A Cross-National Perspective* (Smith et al., 1999) and *Violence in Schools: The response in Europe* (Smith, 2003). A number of European countries developed legal requirements concerning bullying, or violence, in schools (Ananiadou and Smith, 2002).

One major research initiative was an EC funded Training and Mobility of Researchers project (1997–2001), linking teams in England, Italy, Spain, Portugal and Germany. Other notable European initiatives in the early 2000s included national surveys and the Donegal intervention project in Ireland (O'Moore and Minton, 2004); the anti-bullying work in Seville and Andalucia (Ortega, del Rey and Mora-Merchán, 2004); work by Menesini and colleagues in Italy (Menesini et al., 2003); and intervention in kindergartens in Switzerland (Alsaker, 2004).

During the 2000s, cyberbullying started to attract attention. This started off as text message and email bullying, which increased through the mid-2000s; but since then, the development of cameras in mobile phones, smart phones, and increased internet use of instant messaging and social networking sites, have offered many new tools for those wishing to hurt others. A project financed by DAPHNE II Programme (promoted by the European Union for projects concerned with child and family safety), was coordinated by Maria Luisa Genta (University of Bologna) from 2007–2009 (see Genta, Brighi and Guarini, 2009); it developed a questionnaire and carried out surveys on traditional and cyberbullying in Italy, England, Spain, Bosnia-Herzegovina and Finland. This project also developed resources for teachers and educators. Some cross-sectional data from three countries (Italy, England and Spain) are reported in Genta et al. (2012) and Brighi et al. (2012).

A collation of reports on action and research on cyberbullying, mostly focussing on the European countries, was provided by Mora-Merchán and Jäger (eds.) (2010). A further project carried out under DAPHNE III financing (2010–2012), on investigation and intervention regarding cyberbullying in adolescence, was carried out in six European countries: Italy, Spain, Poland, United Kingdom, Greece and Germany (Genta, Brighi and Guarini, 2013; www.bullyingandcyber.net).

Analysis of cyberbullying in many European countries was facilitated by COST Action IS0801 (2008–2012). This was primarily a networking action, involving twenty-eight European countries, plus Australia. Its full title was *Cyberbullying: Coping with negative and enhancing positive uses of new technologies, in relationships in educational settings*. The project website is at http://sites.google.com/site/costis0801/. In addition to many journal articles and book chapters, an edited book on the work of the Action, Smith and Steffgen (2013), summarises the work done. This includes discussions on how cyberbullying has been defined by (see also Menesini et al., 2012); a systematic review of forty-four instruments used to assess cyberbullying (see also Berne et al., 2013); and current knowledge on coping with cyberbullying (see also Perren et al., 2012). Other topics investigated perspectives from the law, industry and the media; the role of Internet Service Providers and Mobile Phone Companies; and the amount of attention that media pay to cyberbullying, and how the way they frame the issue influences the general public and policymakers.

Another product of this Action was a booklet, *Guidelines for preventing cyber-bullying in the school environment: A review and recommendations*, which is available for download on the COST Action website. This was based on a review of already nationally published guidelines in twenty-seven different European countries. Criteria for assessing best practice were determined, according to school ethos, policies and programs, skills and collaborative partnerships, and they targeted parents, young people, schools and teachers. For each target group, the research evidence is reviewed, key findings presented from the content analysis and recommendations made.

Some research findings

Prevalence

Prevalence has usually been assessed by large-scale surveys using anonymous self-report questionnaires. There are a number of issues in designing questionnaires appropriately, and they are not always well used; but they have obvious advantages in allowing researchers to gather data quickly on large and representative samples. The Olweus anonymous self-report questionnaire is probably the most widely used; it incorporates a standard definition of bullying (Solberg and Olweus, 2003.

The actual incidence figures reported in a survey or research study can vary very greatly, independent of the actual phenomenon. Even considering just questionnaires, incidence figures will be influenced by: what time span is being asked about (e.g. last month, last term, last year, ever at school); what frequency is regarded as bullying (e.g. once/twice a term; once a month, once a week or more); what definition is used (e.g. whether it includes indirect as well as direct forms, and cyberbullying). The time of giving a questionnaire in the school or calendar year can be important, if a short time span (last month, or term) is taken. All these issues make it often difficult to compare across different studies.

Two large-scale sources of prevalence data that used the same methodology across different countries, come from the World Health

Organisation surveys on Health Behaviour in School-aged Children (HBSC); and the EU KidsOnline project.

The HBSC surveys The HBSC surveys collect data from 11-, 13- and 15- year olds from nationally representative samples, every 4 years, starting in 1993/1994; there is a minimum of 1,500 respondents per year group, in each participating country. These are classroom-based, anonymous self-report questionnaire surveys. The reports on bullying are based on a single victim item and a single bully item, adapted from the Olweus questionnaire, which asks about experiences over the past couple of months, with five response options. Victim or bully rates were calculated from, 'at least two or three times in the past couple of months' or more (so, ignoring 'it only happened once or twice').

Craig et al. (2009) provide findings from the 2005/2006 survey. This data set is from 40 countries, mostly European, but also including the United States, Canada, Russian Federation and Ukraine. The rates for being bullied (victims) average out at 12.6%, and for bullying others at 10.7%, with 3.6% scoring as bully/victims. Currie et al. (2012) provide data from the 2009/2010 HBSC survey. This data set is from 38 countries, again mostly European, but also including the United States, Canada, Russian Federation, Armenia and Ukraine. The rates for being bullied (victims) average out at 11.3%, and for bullying others at 10.3% (there was no separate category for bully/victims). It can be seen that there is a slight decrease in figures between the two surveys.

The EU Kids Online survey Livingstone et al. (2011) report findings on traditional bullying and cyberbullying from 25 European countries, from the EU Kids Online survey carried out in spring/summer 2010. The samples were based on random stratified sampling of some 1000 children, aged 9 to 16 years, in each country, with a total sample of 25,142. Self-report survey questionnaires were given face-to-face, in children's homes. The survey was on internet use, risks and safety. A section on bullying did not use the term 'bullying', but started with a statement:

Sometimes children or teenagers say or do hurtful or nasty things to someone and this can often be quite a few times on different days over a period of time. For example, this can include: teasing someone in a way this person does not like; hitting, kicking or pushing someone around; leaving someone out of things.

The interviewer explained that these activities could be face-to-face; or by mobile phone calls or texts; or on the internet. Thus a range of activities was covered, and the repetition criterion, although the imbalance of power criterion was not explicitly mentioned. Then the child or young person was asked whether someone had acted in this hurtful or nasty way to them in the past twelve months, for these three types of activities. Following that, they were asked if they themselves had acted in a hurtful or nasty way to others in the previous year. Responses were scored as more than once a week, once or twice a month, less often than that, or never.

Across the whole sample of European countries, victim rates averaged 19%. Only 5% said this had happened more than once a week, and another 4% once or twice a month, with 10% responding that it was less often. Victim rates were slightly higher in girls, and increased slightly with age. Again across the whole sample, perpetrator or bullying rates averaged 12%. Only 2% said this had happened more than once a week, and another 3% once or twice a month, with 7% responding that it was less often. There was very little gender differences (boys slightly higher at 3% in the more than once a week category), and bully rates increased somewhat with age.

If one disregards experiences that were less frequent than once or twice a month, then victim prevalence is 9% and bully prevalence is 5%. This is lower than the HBSC findings with a corresponding frequency cutoff. The HBSC figures are about 11% and 10% respectively, so the main discrepancy is the lower prevalence of bullying others in the EU Kids Online findings. This is unexplained, although one possible explanation could be a greater unwillingness to admit to bullying others in a face-to-face interview compared to an anonymous class-based questionnaire.

An example of findings from a recent survey: Northern Ireland This survey is chosen as an example, as it is fairly recent and large-scale. RSM McClure Watters (2011) surveyed a representative sample of 90,460 primary schools (904 pupils from Year 6, aged about 10 years) and 60 post-primary schools (1,297 pupils from Year 9, aged about 13 years) in Northern Ireland in March 2011. Pupils were given Olweus questionnaires (with the standard definition of bullying), and asked about their experiences in the previous two months. The percentages who reported being bullied, and bullying others, at various frequencies, are shown in Table 1.1. Taking the '2 or 3 times a month' frequency as a cutoff, at primary school, 17.2% had been bullied and 3.9% had bullied others; at post-primary, 11.1% had been bullied and 3.4% had bullied others. The prevalence rates for victims and bullies seem fairly typical of western studies, with victim rates higher than rates for bullying others. Findings from this survey will also be taken as illustration for some of the topics that follow.

Table 1.1 *Percentages of pupils bullying others and being bullied in Northern Ireland; adapted from RSN McClure Watters (2011).*

	Only once or twice	2 or 3 times a month	About once a week	Several times a week
	BEEN BULLIED			
Primary	22.1	7.7	4.6	4.9
	boys 22.7	boys 6.1	boys 4.3	boys 3.9
	girls 22.7	girls 9.3	girls 4.8	girls 5.9
Post-primary	18.4	4.3	3.3	3.5
	boys 19.5	boys 4.5	boys 3.5	boys 5.1
	girls 17.3	girls 4.1	girls 3.0	girls 2.0
	BULLIED OTHERS			
Primary	17.6	2.2	1.1	0.6
	boys 20.5	boys 3.4		
	girls 14.7	girls 1.1		
Post-primary	17.8	1.6	1.1	0.7
	boys 20.8		boys 1.1	
	girls 15.1		girls 1.1	

Types of bullying

While a number of typologies of aggression and of bullying exist, the main types used in western studies of bullying include:

> *Physical*: hit, kick, punch, take or damage belongings
> *Verbal*: tease, taunt, threaten
> *Social Exclusion*: systematic and direct exclusion from peer groups
> *Indirect*: spreading nasty rumours, telling others not to play with someone
> *Cyberbullying*: bullying using electronic devices; this can include Text message bullying; Picture/Video Clip bullying (via mobile phone cameras); Phone call bullying; Email bullying; Chat-room bullying; Bullying through instant messaging; and Bullying via social networks and other websites.

Another category (or group of categories) is 'bias bullying' or 'prejudice driven bullying'. This refers to bullying on the basis of group rather than individual characteristics, and would include racial harassment, faith-based bullying, sexual harassment, and homophobic bullying. This could take any of the various forms mentioned earlier, but is often included in questionnaires when pupils are asked what kinds of bullying they experienced.

Table 1.2 *Percentages of pupils in Northern Ireland who reported different types of bullying experienced, from Year 6 and Year 9; adapted from RSN McClure Watters (2011).*

Type of bullying	Year 6	Year 9
Called names or teased in a hurtful way	17.3	13.5
Left out of things on purpose, completely ignored	12.7	6.8
Lies or false rumours spread about me	11.1	8.2
Hit, kicked, pushed, locked indoors	8.3	3.8
Mean names or comments about my ability	8.1	5.1
Threatened or forced to do things I didn't want to do	5.6	1.9
Mean names or comments about my race or colour	4.7	3.0
Mean names or comments about my disability	3.2	1.6
Money or other things taken away from me or damaged	3.1	1.2
Mean names or comments about my religion	2.4	1.7
Bullied with the use of mobile phones	1.4	1.2
Bullied with the use of computers	1.1	1.4
Bullied in another way	7.2	4.1

Taking the Northern Ireland survey data, the most frequent types of bullying experienced are shown in Table 1.2, using the '2 or 3 times a month or more' criterion. As in most studies, verbal bullying comes out as the most frequent. Physical bullying is not so common, especially in older pupils. The incidence of cyberbullying (by mobile phones and computers) is quite low – at the lower end of reported studies; in other European studies, there is considerable variation in prevalence of cyberbullying, depending on factors such as definition and criteria used (e.g. Olweus, 2012). Noticeable in Table 1.2 is the absence of categories of bullying due to gender, and due to sexual orientation (although race and religion are included). This is probably because these are sensitive issues to ask about in Northern Ireland; other European studies show significant amounts of bullying of a sexual nature (Duncan, 1999) and of homophobic bullying (Rivers, 2011).

Age changes Self-reports of being bullied decline rather steadily over the eight- to sixteen-year period; self-reports of bullying others do not show this decline, and may peak in early adolescence. The Northern Ireland data, shown in Table 1.2, illustrates this; whereas victim rates decline with age, bully rates do not show any consistent decline. Possible reasons for the age decline in victim rates were discussed by Smith, Madsen and Moody (1999).

There tends to be some shift with age away from physical bullying and towards indirect and relational bullying (Bjorkqvist et al., 1997), which both may require more cognitive sophistication, and be less obvious to teachers, from the point of view of the perpetrators.

Gender differences In most surveys, there are more boys in the bully category, but the sexes are more equal in the victim category. The Northern Ireland data, shown in Table 1.2, illustrates this; gender differences are relatively small for victims, but boys are clearly more frequent as bullies.

It is generally found that boys practice/experience more physical bullying, girls more indirect and relational bullying (Besag, 2006). The situation is more varied in cyberbullying, with some studies showing relatively greater involvement by girls (Smith et al., 2008). Such differences are often explained in terms of how, if a bully wishes to hurt or put down someone, he or she can most effectively do this; with physical strength being more important for boys, and social reputation for girls.

Bullying and disability The Northern Ireland survey reported on the relationship between involvement in bully/victim problems and disability. Using a lenient criterion (including even 'once or twice', Table 1.1), the prevalence of being bullied for children with disabilities, compared to those without, was higher in primary school (44.3% vs. 38.6%) and post-primary school (44.9% vs. 28.2%). The prevalence of bullying others was also higher in primary school (27.8% vs. 20.8%) and post-primary school (29.1% vs. 20.5%) for those with a disability.

Many other studies in European countries have shown a greater risk of being involved (as victim, but also to some extent as bully) in children with disabilities (e.g. Van Roekel, Scholte and Didden, 2009). Children with special needs can be 2 to 3 times more at risk of being bullied; they are also more at risk of taking part in bullying others. Likely factors to explain this are that they may have particular characteristics which make them an obvious 'target'; in mainstream settings they are less well integrated socially and lack the protection against bullying that friendship gives; and, those with behavioural problems may act out in an aggressive way and become 'provocative victims'.

Who bullies who General findings are that for those bullied, most of the bullying is done by pupils in the same class as the victim (in primary schools) or the same year group (in secondary schools); few are bullied by pupils from years below them. Even for cyberbullying, much is done by pupils in the same school and often the same year group.

In addition, although a majority of bullying relationships involve several bullies, a significant minority involves one-to-one relationships. Boys tend to be bullied by other boys (rarely by girls), but girls experience bullying from both sexes.

Data from the Northern Ireland survey, shown in Table 1.3, illustrate such differences. Here, percentages are of all children, so the percentage who are bullied (Table 1.1) needs to be borne in mind. As in other western studies, about half of victims report being bullied mainly by one other pupil, and about half by more, usually just 2–3 pupils. Most commonly the bully(ies) are in the same class, or else in a higher year (primary) or another class in the same year group (post-primary).

Place and duration of bullying Generally, in school the majority of traditional bullying takes place in the playground (especially in primary schools), the classroom or corridors. Much cyberbullying is initiated out of school, due to school restrictions on mobile phone and internet use, but often involves others in the school (e.g. Smith et al., 2008). Also, much bullying is reported as being short-term, but with some cases being much more long-lasting.

Data from the Northern Ireland survey, shown in Table 1.3, illustrate these findings. The playground is the most frequent location for primary pupils, but with a much wider distribution of significant locations in post-primary. Most bullying just lasts one or two weeks, but a significant minority of victims report much longer durations.

Attitudes to victims Generally, although most pupils say they do not like bullying, a significant minority do say they could join in bullying. Also, these 'pro-bullying' or anti-victim' attitudes tend to increase with age up to 14 or 15 years, after which they may start to decline (Menesini et al., 1997).

Data from the Northern Ireland survey showed that 95% of primary, and 90% of post-primary pupils expressed some sympathy for victims; however only 48% of primary pupils and 29% of post-primary said they would actually try to help a bullied pupil.

Coping strategies, and telling someone about the bullying A study of 406 pupils aged 13–16 years in English schools with peer-support systems found the five most frequent coping strategies were talking to someone, ignoring it, sticking up for yourself, avoiding/staying away from bullies, and making more/different friends (Smith et al., 2004). Over a two-year period, those who had stopped being victims more often had talked to someone about it (67%) than those who had stayed victims

Table 1.3 *Number and year group of bullies (percentages of all children, based on lenient criterion); adapted from RSN McClure Watters (2011).*

	Year 6	Year 9
Number of bullies		
Mainly by one pupil	21.4	13.1
By a group of 2–3 pupils	15.7	11.2
By a group of 4–9 pupils	4.5	na
By a group of more than 9 pupils	na	na
By several different pupils or groups of pupils	na	2.2
Year group of bullies		
In my class	23.6	16.7
In a different class but same year	4.3	8.5
In a higher year	9.7	5.5
In a lower year	4.1	0.9
In different years	4.1	2.2
Duration of bullying		
One or two weeks	20.9	14.3
About a month	7.8	6.0
About 6 months	3.1	3.3
About a year	4.4	3.3
Several years	5.0	3.0
Main locations for being bullied		
Playground	32.6	12.9
Classroom (teacher absent)	13.6	13.1
Classroom (teacher present)	10.3	10.4
Lunch room	13.6	6.9
On way to/from school	10.8	6.6
Toilets	8.7	3.1
Hallways/stairwells	5.6	12.3
Changing room/shower	5.6	7.5
School bus	4.2	5.9
School bus stop	1.1	2.5
Somewhere else in school	9.0	4.0

na = data not available due to small numbers

(46%) or become victims (41%). Coping strategies can be complex and dependent on many factors; telling teachers can be successful, but needs a consistent and effective response from teaching staff.

Generally, a substantial proportion of self-reported victims say that they have not told a teacher, or someone at home, about the bullying. A consistent finding is that rates of telling a teacher are less in older pupils, and boys (Naylor, Cowie and del Rey, 2001; Hunter and Boyle, 2004). This may reflect the more serious nature of victimisation at older age groups.

Data from the Northern Ireland survey showed that, so far as victims were concerned, 76% primary and 72% post-primary had told someone about it; most usually a parent/guardian or a friend. Girls were more likely to tell someone, than boys. These are quite high levels of telling. The extent of pupils telling others may have increased in a number of European countries, due to anti-bullying efforts in schools (Smith et al., 2004).

Other findings from the Northern Ireland survey were that, so far as bullies were concerned, some 65% of primary pupils and 55% of post-primary said that a teacher had talked to them about it, and some 49% of primary and 38% of post-primary said that someone at home had talked to them about it. Overall, 65% (primary and post-primary) saw teachers as being often or almost always supportive of bullied pupils.

Coping with cyberbullying A thorough review of studies on coping with cyberbullying was reported by Perren et al. (2012) and McGuckin et al. (2013). As well as seeking support, retaliation and avoidant strategies, they also identified technical solution strategies such as using report abuse buttons or blocking an abusive sender.

When victims of cyberbullying do tell someone, it appears to be most often friends, followed by parents, with teachers told rather infrequently (Smith et al., 2008; Slonje and Smith, 2008). Given the generational gap in use and awareness of new technologies, young people may feel that teachers and parents are less aware of the issues involved.

McGuckin et al. (2013) found rather little good evidence on the effectiveness of different strategies. However the value of support seeking was pointed to in a longitudinal study in twelve Swiss schools by Machmutow et al., (2012). They examined depression in 13-year olds, in relation to both traditional and cyber victimisation, together with coping. Both traditional and cyber victimisation were associated with higher levels of depression, and cyber victimisation predicted increases in depression by the second time point. Coping strategies rated as helpless were associated with more depression. Longitudinally, support seeking from peers and family was associated with reduced depression; assertive coping strategies (such as finding and contacting the bully) were associated with increased depression.

Individual and personality factors

In England and Wales the Environmental Risk (E-Risk) Study of over 1,000 twin pairs found a strong genetic influence on children's victimisation status at 9–10 years (MZ [identical] twins had more similar victimisation experiences than DZ twins), and also on bullying behaviour (Ball et al., 2008). These genetic factors may operate through various mechanisms including personality disposition, emotion regulation or social cognition, many identified as individual risk factors in bullying.

One dimension of personality studied has been Machiavellianism, defined as thinking that other people are untrustworthy, and can be manipulated in interpersonal situations. In a Scottish sample of 9–12 year olds, Sutton and Keogh (2000) found that bullies held more Machiavellian attitudes than non-involved children. Andreou (2004) explored four components of Machiavellianism, in a Greek sample of 9–12 year olds. She found that lack of faith in human nature correlated with both bully and victim roles for boys, while manipulation correlated with bully role for girls. Distrust characterised both boy and girl victims. Bully/victim children were particularly characterised by lack of faith in human nature, as well as overall Machiavellianism.

Another important personality factor in terms of bullying others may be impulsivity. Jolliffe and Farrington (2011) found impulsivity to be the most important predictor from a range of factors examined in English adolescents.

Empathy tends to be negatively related to bullying, and also to being a bully/victim, but not to being a victim (only). The findings regarding bullying tend to be stronger for affective empathy. For example, Endresen and Olweus (2001) found bullying behaviour was related to low affective empathy for both boys and girls in Norwegian adolescents. However, according to Muñoz, Qualter and Padgett (2011), callous-unemotional (CU) traits and particularly the uncaring subscale of this, may be more important than empathic scores per se. In a sample of English 11–12 year olds, they found that an association between CU traits and bullying remained, even taking empathy deficits into account. They suggest that in predicting bullying, being uncaring is more important than recognising or even feeling other people's emotions.

A related concept is moral disengagement. In an Italian sample, Gini (2006) found that bullies showed significantly higher moral disengagement; and in another Italian sample, Renati, Berrone and Zanetti (2012) reported that cyber bullies, and also cyberbully-victims, scored significantly higher on moral disengagement than cyber victims or non-involved students.

Although some bullying children may lack certain social skills, ringleader bullies especially may have good 'theory of mind' abilities [understanding of others' mental states] and be skilled social manipulators (Sutton, Smith and Swettenham, 1999). The finding that some bullies scored highly in this domain was not exactly replicated by Gini (2006) in an Italian sample, but neither did bullies show any deficits (victims scored the lowest, and defenders the highest). Peeters, Cillessen and Scholte (2010), in a Dutch sample of 13-year olds, found a possible explanation for these discrepant results. A cluster analysis suggested three kinds of bullies: one group was popular and socially intelligent; a second group was relatively popular and with average social intelligence scores; a third group, the smallest numerically, was unpopular and had lower than average scores on social intelligence.

Peer group factors

In a longitudinal study of English children aged 9 to 11 years, Fox and Boulton (2006) found that children who lacked good social skills were at greater risk of increasing victimisation over time. However, this relationship was weaker if the child had many friends; or if he or she had one best friend who was popular in the peer group.

It will not always be easy for a victim, especially one who has a reputation as such, to have many friends or a popular, high-status friend. Boulton (2013), using hypothetical vignettes with English 11–13 year olds, found that pupils said they would be less likely to befriend a new pupil (or think that other pupils would do so) if they were told that this new pupil had been the victim of bullying in previous schools. He argued that this is probably because pupils would see such befriending as risky for their own status in the peer group, and their own chances of being victimised.

Bullying children tend to be peer rejected in infant/junior school, but less so in secondary school; towards adolescence, some aggressive and bullying children can have quite high status in peer groups. This does not necessarily mean they are well-liked; Caravita, DiBlasio and Salmivalli (2009) found that children who bullied others did not score particularly highly on social preference scores (not so many pupils actually liked them a lot), but they did score high on perceived popularity (many pupils thought that they were popular, or at least of high status in the peer group).

Salmivalli (2010) reviewed the general evidence for a dominance hypothesis, namely that some children who bully are driven by a desire for dominant status in the peer group. Ringleader bullies especially may be rewarded if followers and reinforcers support their bullying actions, and if many bystanders remain passive. Correspondingly, children with high popularity or peer-group status can be the most effective defenders (Caravita et al., 2009).

Family factors

A number of studies have examined family background factors. For example, in a qualitative study in Greece, Bibou-Nakou et al. (2012) used focus groups with 13–15-year-old pupils; they extracted material relating to family factors, and reported that three main themes emerged – a difficult home environment; issues around protection and control; and abuse.

In a now classic study of Swedish boys aged 13–16 years, Olweus (1978) found that mothers of victimised boys often treated their sons as younger than the boys' age and were over-controlling of the boys' spare time. A child's weak temperament (such as being shy and unassertive) predicted over-protectiveness in mothers, which in turn predicted victim status. A separate pathway was from father's negativism, which predicted lack of identification with father, which in turn predicted victim status.

Bowes et al. (2010) reported findings from the E-risk study in England and Wales. Children were assessed at 10 and 12 years. In terms of emotional and behavioural adjustment, children's resilience to victimisation was increased by maternal warmth, sibling warmth and a positive atmosphere at home.

Class and school factors

A number of studies have shown some influence of class factors and, perhaps to a lesser extent, school factors, in predicting levels of bullying. For example, Saarento et al. (2013) used data from the Finnish KiVa project (see Chapter 15) to study individual, classroom and school effects in 358 classrooms in 74 schools. Victimisation was assessed by both self- and peer reports; for peer-report data, 22% of the variance in victimisation was due to classroom differences, and an additional 3% just by school differences; for self-reports these figures were 6% and 2% respectively. Both the extent of anti-bullying attitudes in the class, and the norms for defending behaviour, had significant effects. In addition the general perception of the homeroom teacher's attitude to bullying was a significant predictor of classroom differences, and also contributed significantly to school differences.

In-group attitudes within the class or peer group may be influential, and can lead to ostracism of those perceived as different, but there is little evidence for a scapegoating theory, in the sense that one pupil is selected as the 'victim', labeled as such, and becomes a focus for any hostility. This was suggested by Schuster (1999), who found that in 29 of 34 classes in Germany, only one or two victims were identified. She posed the question, '... does every class have its whipping boy or "scapegoat"?' (p.178). However, two separate studies failed to confirm this hypothesis about number of victims. Mahdavi and Smith (2007) analysed data from 67 classes of 8 to 13 year olds in England; there were 1 or 2 victims in only 27 of them; and calculations indicated that this was what would be expected by a chance model of individual risk factors. In quite a number of classes there were no victims. In a study in Austrian schools, Atria, Strohmeier and Spiel (2007) analysed data from 86 different classes (in grades 4 to 9). Again there was great variability in the number of victims in each class; some had no victims, some had many. These studies were commented on (with a reply by Schuster) in a special issue of the *European Journal of Developmental Psychology*, 4(3), 2007.

There are large school variations in the incidence of bullying, but factors such as size of school, class size or rural versus big city setting are usually not related to this. The E-Risk study (Bowes et al., 2009) found that school factors were associated with victim risk, family factors with bully risk and neighbourhood factors with risk of bully/victim status; and that maternal and sibling warmth and positive home atmosphere contribute to resilience in coping with victimisation. The school ethos, school policies and anti-bullying strategies, attitudes of teachers in bullying situations and the degree of supervision of free activities appear to be of significance for the extent of bully/victim problems.

Consequences of involvement in bullying

As with research worldwide, many studies have shown that victims of school bullying are more at risk of a range of negative outcomes, particularly internalising problems. As an example, Arseneault et al. (2008) reported twin data from the E-risk study in England and Wales; they compared monozygotic twins where one had been bullied, and the other not. The bullied twin had significantly greater internalising problems; this was true at 10 years, even when controlling for pre-existing internalising problems at 7 years. The authors concluded (p.145) that 'Being bullied at a young age is an environmentally mediated contributing factor to children's internalizing problems'.

In further data from the E-risk study in England and Wales, Fisher et al. (2012) found that exposure to frequent bullying in 12-year-old children predicted higher rates of self-harm, even after taking account of prior emotional problems. Other strongly contributing factors to self-harm were a family history of attempted or completed suicide and maltreatment by an adult. Using the twin data available in this study, victimised twins were more likely to self-harm than their non-victimised co-twin (though sample numbers here were small), supporting some direct causal link between peer victimisation and suicidal ideation.

A longitudinal study by Zwierzynska, Wolke and Lereya (2013) used data from the ALSPAC study based around the Bristol area of England. Children were assessed for being a victim (of both direct and indirect bullying) at 8 and 10 years (from mother, teacher and self report), and for internalising problems (depression, emotional problems, well-being) between 11 and 14 years. In line with many studies, victimisation predicted later internalising symptoms; but this study also showed that the risks were especially high for severe depression, and increased if the victimisation involved multiple forms (direct and indirect) and was stable from 8 to 10 years.

Bullying does not only affect victims, of course. Children involved in bullying are more likely to be involved in other kinds of antisocial behaviour, both concurrently and later in life (Farrington et al., 2012). Also, if bullying is not dealt with effectively, the school climate will be affected in a negative way and bystanders to bullying will learn that such abuse of power is tolerated.

Summary

The tradition of research on bullying in Europe goes back some 30 or even 40 years, but has gathered pace particularly in the last 20 years. Much of the research has been quantitative, and used self-report questionnaires or peer nominations to obtain data.

Starting in Scandinavia, research picked up rapidly in the United Kingdom and other European countries, and by now there is a reasonable body of research across Europe. Although there are clear differences in prevalence, as shown by the HBSC and EU KidsOnline surveys, in general, it appears that the characteristics of bullying, and the risk factors associated with it, or the outcomes, do not vary greatly across countries; although this has yet to be systematically investigated. The body of research has contributed to a range of anti-bullying strategies and interventions, which are considered in Chapter 15.

REFERENCES

Ahmad, Y., Whitney, I. and Smith, P.K. (1991). A survey service for schools on bully/victim problems. In P.K. Smith and D.A. Thompson (eds.), *Practical approaches to bullying* (pp.103–111). London: David Fulton.

Alsaker, F.D. (2004). Bernese programme against victimisation in kindergarten and elementary school. In P.K. Smith, D. Pepler and K. Rigby (eds.),

Bullying in schools: How successful can interventions be? (pp.289–306). Cambridge: Cambridge University Press.

Ananiadou, K. and Smith, P.K. (2002). Legal requirements and nationally circulated materials against school bullying in European countries. *Criminal Justice*, 2, 471–491.

Andreou, E. (2004). Bully/victim problems and their association with Machiavellianism and self-efficacy in Greek primary school children. *British Journal of Educational Psychology*, 74, 297–309.

Arora, C.M.J. and Thompson, D.A. (1987). Defining bullying for a secondary school. *Education and Child Psychology*, 14, 110–120.

Arseneault, L., Milne, B.J., Taylor, A., Adams, F., Delgado, K., Caspi, A. and Moffitt, T.E. (2008). Being bullied as an environmentally mediated contributing factor to children's internalizing problems: A study of twins discordant for victimization. *Archives of Pediatrics and Adolescent Medicine*, 162, 145–150.

Atria, M., Strohmeier, D., and Spiel. C. (2007). The relevance of the school class as social unit for the prevalence of bullying and victimization. *European Journal of Developmental Psychology*, 4, 372–387.

Ball, H.A., Arseneault, L., Taylor, A., Maughan, B., Caspi, A. and Moffitt, T.E. (2008). Genetic and environmental influences on victims, bullies and bully-victims in childhood. *Journal of Child Psychiatry and Psychiatry* 49, 104–112.

Berne, S., Frisén, A., Schultze-Krumbholz, A., Scheithauer, H., Naruskov, K., Luik, P., Katzer, C., Erentaite, R. and Zukauskiene, R. (2013). Cyberbullying assessment instruments: A systematic review. *Aggression and Violent Behavior*, 18, 320–334.

Besag, V.E. (2006). *Understanding girls' friendships, fights and feuds: A practical approach to girls' bullying.* Maidenhead: Open University Press.

Bibou-Nakou, I., Tsiantis, J., Assimopoulos, H. and Chatzilambou, P. (2012). Bullying/victimization from a family perspective: a qualitative study of secondary school student' views. *European Journal of Psychology of Education*, 28, 53–71.

Björkqvist, K., Lagerspetz, K.M.J. and Kaukiainen, A. (1997). Do girls manipulate and boys fight? Developmental trends in regard to direct aggression. *Aggressive Behavior*, 18, 117–27.

Boulton M.J. (2013). The effects of victim of bullying reputation on adolescents' choice of friends: Mediation by fear of becoming a victim of bullying, moderation by victim status, and implications for befriending interventions. *Journal of Experimental Child Psychology*, 114, 146–160.

Bowes, L., Arseneault, L., Maughan, B., Taylor, A., Caspi, A. and Moffitt, T.E. (2009). School, neighborhood, and family factors are associated with children's bullying involvement: A nationally representative longitudinal study. *Journal of the American Academy of Child and Adolescent Psychiatry*, 48, 545–553.

Bowes, L., Maughan, B., Caspi, A., Moffitt, T.E. and Arseneault, L. (2010). Families promote emotional and behavioural resilience to bullying: Evidence of an environmental effect. *Journal of Child Psychology and Psychiatry*, 51, 809–817.

Bowers, L., Smith, P.K. and Binney, V. (1992). Family relationships as perceived by children involved in bully/victim problems at school. *Journal of Family Therapy*, 14, 371–387.

Brighi, A., Melotti, G., Guarini, A., Genta, M.L., Ortega, R., Mora- Merchán, J. A., Smith, P.K. and Thompson, F. (2012). Self-esteem and loneliness in relation to cyberbullying in three European countries. In Q. Li, D. Cross and P.K. Smith (eds.), *Cyberbullying in the global playground: Research from international perspectives* (pp.32–56). Chichester: Wiley-Blackwell.

Caravita, S., DiBlasio, P. and Salmivalli, C. (2009). Unique and interactive effects of empathy and social status on involvement in bullying. *Social Development*, 18, 140–163.

Cowie, H. (1998). Perspective of teachers and pupils on the experience of peer support against bullying. *Educational Research and Evaluation*, 4, 108–125.

Craig W., Harel-Fisch Y., Fogel-Grinvald H., Dostaler S., Hetland J., Simons-Morton B., Molcho B., Gaspar de Mato M., Overpeck M., Due P., Pickett W., HBSC Violence & Injuries Prevention Focus Group & HBSC Bullying Writing Group (2009). A cross-national profile of bullying and victimization among adolescents in 40 countries. *International Journal of Public Health*, 54 (Suppl 2), 216–224.

Currie, C. et al. (eds.). (2012). *Social determinants of health and well-being among young people. Health Behaviour in School-aged Children (HBSC) study: International report from the 2009/2010 survey*. Copenhagen: WHO Regional Office for Europe.

DCSF (2009). *Staying Safe Survey: Key findings: Bullying*. London: DCSF.

DfE (2010). *The Importance of Teaching: The Schools White Paper 2010*. www.education.gov.uk/publications/eOrderingDownload/CM-7980.pdf
  (2014). Preventing and tackling bullying: Advice for headteachers, staff and governing bodies. www.gov.uk/government/uploads/system/uploads/attachment_data/file/444862/Preventing_and_tackling_bullying_advice.pdf

Duncan, N. (1999). *Sexual bullying: Gender conflict and pupil culture in secondary schools*. London: Routledge.

Endresen, I.M. and Olweus, D. (2001). Self-reported empathy in Norwegian adolescents: Sex differences, age trends, and relationship to bullying. In A.C. Bohart, C. Arthur and D.J. Stipek (eds.), *Constructive and destructive behavior: Implications for family, school and society* (pp.147–165). Washington, D.C.: American Psychological Association.

Farrington, D. (1993). Understanding and preventing bullying. In M Tonry (ed.), *Crime and justice: A review of research*, vol. 17 (pp.381–458). Chicago: University of Chicago Press.

Farrington, D. P., Lösel, F., Ttofi, M.M. and Theodorakis, N. (2012). *School bullying, depression and offending behaviour later in life: An updated systematic review of longitudinal studies*. Stockholm: Swedish National Council for Crime Prevention.

Fisher, H.L., Moffitt, T.E., Houts, R.M., Belsky, D.W., Arseneault, L. and Caspi, A. (2012). Bullying victimisation and risk of self harm in early adolescence: longitudinal cohort study. *British Medical Journal*, 344, e2683.

Fox, C.L. and Boulton, M.J. (2006). Friendship as a moderator of the relationship between social skills problems and peer victimisation. *Aggressive Behavior*, 32, 110–121.

Genta, M.L., Brighi, A. and Guarini, A. (2009). *Bullying and cyberbullying in adolescence*. Rome: Carocci.

(eds.) (2013). *Cyberbullismo: Ricerche e strategie di intervento (Cyberbullying: research and intervention strategies)*. Milano: Franco Angeli.

Genta, M. L., Smith, P. K., Ortega, R., Brighi, A., Guarini, A., Thompson, F., Tippett, N., Mora-Merchan, J. and Calmaestra, J. (2012). Comparative aspects of cyberbullying in Italy, England and Spain: Findings from a DAPHNE project. In Q. Li, D. Cross and P.K. Smith (eds.), *Cyberbullying in the global playground: Research from international perspectives* (pp. 15–31). Chichester, England: Wiley-Blackwell.

Gini, G. (2006). Social cognition and moral cognition in bullying: What's wrong? *Aggressive Behavior*, 32, 528–539.

Heinemann, P.P. (1972). *Mobbning – Gruppvåld bland barn och vuxna*. Stockholm: Natur och Kultur.

House of Commons Education and Skills Committee (2007). *Bullying: Third report of Session 2006-07*. London: The Stationery Office.

Hughes, T. (1857). *Tom Brown's schooldays*. Cambridge: Macmillan.

Huitsing, G. and Veenstra, R. (2012). Bullying in classrooms: Participant roles from a social network perspective, *Aggressive Behavior*, 38, 494–509.

Hunter, S.C. and Boyle, J.M.E. (2004). Appraisal and coping strategy use of victims of school bullying. *British Journal of Educational Psychology*, 74, 83–107.

Jolliffe, D. and Farrington, D.P. (2011). Is low empathy related to bullying after controlling for individual and social background variables? *Journal of Adolescence*, 34, 59–71.

Kaenel-Platt, J van and Douglas, T. (2012). Cybermentoring. In A. Costabile and B.A. Spears (eds.), *The impact of technology on relationships in educational settings* (pp.151–157). London: Routledge.

Livingstone, S., Haddon, L., Görzig, A. and Ólafsson, K. (2011). *Risks and safety on the internet: The perspective of European children. Full findings*. LSE, London: EU Kids Online.

Lowenstein, L.F. (1978a). Who is the bully? *Bulletin of the British Psychological Society*, 31, 147–149.

(1978b). The bullied and non-bullied child. *Bulletin of the British Psychological Society*, 31, 316–318.

Machmutow, K., Perren, S., Sticca, F. and Alsaker, F.D. (2012). Peer victimisation and depressive symptoms: Can specific coping strategies buffer the negative impact of cybervictimisation? *Emotional and Behavioural Difficulties*, 17, 403–420.

Mahdavi, J. and Smith, P.K. (2007). Individual risk factors or group dynamics? An investigation of the scapegoat hypothesis of victimisation in school classes. *European Journal of Developmental Psychology*, 4, 353–371.

McGuckin, C., Perren, S., Corcoran, L., Cowie, H., Dehue, F., Ševčiková, A., Tsatsou, P. and Vollink, T. (2013). Coping with cyberbullying: How can we

prevent cyberbullying and how victims can cope with it. In Smith, P.K. and
Steffgen, G. (eds.), *Cyberbullying through the new media: Findings from an
international network* (pp.121–135). Hove: Psychology Press.

McLeod, M. and Morris, S. (1996). *Why me? Children talking to ChildLine
about bullying.* ChildLine, Royal Mail Building, Studd Street, London
N1 0QW.

Menesini, E., Codecasa, E., Benelli, B. and Cowie, H. (2003). Enhancing
children's responsibility to take action against bullying: evaluation of a
befriending intervention in Italian middle schools. *Aggressive Behavior*, 29,
1–14.

Menesini, E., Eslea, M., Smith, P.K., Genta, M.L., Giannetti, E., Fonzi, A.
and Costabile, A. (1997). A cross-national comparison of children's
attitudes towards bully/victim problems in school. *Aggressive Behavior*, 23,
245–257.

Menesini, E., Nocentini, A., Palladino, B. E., Frisén, A., Berne, S., Ortega Ruiz,
R., Calmaestra, J., Scheithauer, H., Schultze-Krumbholz, A., Luik, P.,
Naruskov, K., Blaya, C., Berthaud, J. and Smith P.K. (2012). Cyberbullying
definition among adolescents: A comparison across six European countries.
Cyberpsychology, Behavior and Social Networking, 15, 455–463.

Mora-Merchán, J. and Jäger, T. (eds.) (2010). *Cyberbullying: A cross-national
comparison.* Landau: Verlag Emprische Padagogik.

Muñoz, L.C., Qualter, P. and Padgett, G. (2011). Empathy and bullying:
Exploring the influence of callous-unemotional traits. *Child Psychiatry and
Human Development*, 42, 183–196.

Naylor, P. and Cowie, H. (1999). The effectiveness of peer support systems in
challenging school bullying: the perspectives and experiences of teachers and
pupils. *Journal of Adolescence*, 22, 467–479.

Naylor, P., Cowie, H. and del Rey, R. (2001). Coping strategies of secondary
school children in response to being bullied. *Child Psychology and Psychiatry
Review*, 6, 114–120.

Olweus, D. (1973). *Forskning om skolmobbning.* Stockholm, Sweden: Almqvist
and Wiksell.

  (1978). *Aggression in the schools: Bullies and whipping boys.* Washington,
  DC: Hemisphere.

  (1993). *Bullying at school: What we know and what we can do.* Oxford: Blackwell.

  (1999a). Sweden. In Smith, P.K., Morita, Y., Junger-Tas, J., Olweus, D.,
  Catalano, R. and Slee, P. (eds.) (1999). *The nature of school bullying:
  A cross-national perspective* (pp. 7–27). London and New York: Routledge.

  (1999b). Norway. In Smith, P.K., Morita, Y., Junger-Tas, J., Olweus, D.,
  Catalano, R. and Slee, P. (Eds.) (1999). *The nature of school bullying:
  A cross-national perspective* (pp. 28–48). London and New York: Routledge.

  (2012). Cyberbullying: an overrated phenomenon? *European Journal of
  Developmental Psychology*, 9, 520–538.

Olweus, D. and Limber, S. (2010). The Olweus Bullying Prevention Program:
Implementation and evaluation over two decades. In S. Jimerson, S. Swearer
and D. Espelage (eds.), *Handbook of bullying in schools: An international
perspective* (pp. 377–401). New York: Routledge.

O'Moore, M. and Minton, S.J. (2004). Ireland: the Donegal Primary Schools' anti-bullying project. In P.K. Smith, D. Pepler and K. Rigby (eds.), *Bullying in schools: How successful can interventions be?* (pp.275–287). Cambridge: Cambridge University Press.

Ortega, R., del Rey, R. and Mora-Merchan, J. (2004). SAVE model: An anti-bullying intervention in Spain. In P.K. Smith, D. Pepler and K. Rigby (eds.), *Bullying in schools: How successful can interventions be?* (pp.167–185). Cambridge: Cambridge University Press.

Peeters, M., Cillessen, A.H.N. and Scholte, R.H.J. (2010). Clueless or powerful? Identifying subtypes of bullies in adolescence. *Journal of Youth and Adolescence*, 39, 1041–1052.

Perren, S., Corcoran, L., Cowie, H., Dehue, F., Garcia, D., Mc Guckin, C., Ševčíková, A., Tsatsou, P. and Völlink, T. (2012). Tackling cyberbullying: Review of empirical evidence regarding successful responses by students, parents and schools. *International Journal of Conflict and Violence*, 6, 283–293.

Pikas, A. (1989). A pure concept of mobbing gives the best results for treatment. *School Psychology International*, 10, 95–104.

(2002). New developments of the Shared Concern Method. *School Psychology International*, 23, 307–336.

Renati, R., Berrone, C. and Zanetti, M.A. (2012). Morally disengaged and unempathic: Do cyberbullies fit these definitions? An exploratory study. *Cyberpsychology, Behavior, and Social Networking*, 15, 391–398.

Research and discussion on scapegoating and classroom dynamics (2007). *Special Section of European Journal of Developmental Psychology*, 4(4).

Rivers, I. (2011). *Homophobic bullying: Research and theoretical perspectives*. Oxford: Oxford University Press.

Roland, E. (2011). The broken curve: Norwegian manifesto against bullying. *International Journal of Behavioural Development*, 35, 383–388.

RSM McClure Watters (2011). *The nature and extent of pupil bullying in schools in the North of Ireland*, Volume 56, Bangor, UK: Department of Education for Northern Ireland.

Saarento, S., Kärnä, A., Hodges, E.V.E. and Salmivalli, C. (2013). Student-, classroom-, and school-level risk factors for victimization. *Journal of School Psychology*, 51, 421–434.

Salmivalli, C. (2010). Bullying and the peer group: A review. *Aggression and Violent Behavior*, 15, 112–120.

Salmivalli, C., Lagerspetz, K., Björkqvist, K., Österman, K. and Kaukiainen, A. (1996). Bullying as a group process: participant roles and their relations to social status within the group. *Aggressive Behavior*, 22, 1–15.

Salmivalli, C., Kärnä, A. and Poskiparta, E. (2010). From peer putdowns to peer support: A theoretical model and how it translated into a national anti-bullying program. In S. Jimerson, S. Swearer, and D. Espelage (eds.), *Handbook of bullying in schools: An international perspective* (pp. 441–454). New York: Routledge.

Salmon, G., James, A. and Smith, D.M. (1998). Bullying in schools: Self reported anxiety, depression, and self esteem in secondary school children. *British Medical Journal* 317, 924–925.

Schuster, B. (1999). Outsiders at school: The prevalence of bullying and its relation with social status. *Group Processes and Intergroup Relations*, 2, 175–190.

Slonje, R., and Smith, P.K. (2008). Cyberbullying: Another main type of bullying? *Scandinavian Journal of Psychology*, 49, 147–154.

Smith, P.K. (ed.) (2003). *Violence in schools: The response in Europe*. Routledge: London.

Smith P.K., Madsen K. and Moody, J. (1999). What causes the age decline in reports of being bullied at school? Towards a developmental analysis of risks of being bullied. *Educational Research*, 41, 267–85.

Smith, P.K., Mahdavi, J., Carvalho, M., Fisher, S., Russell, S. and Tippett, N. (2008). Cyberbullying: its nature and impact in secondary school pupils. *Journal of Child Psychology and Psychiatry*, 49, 376–385.

Smith, P.K., Morita, Y., Junger –Tas, J., Olweus, D., Catalano, R. and Slee, P. (eds) (1999). *The nature of school bullying: A cross-national perspective*. London: Routledge.

Smith, P.K. and Sharp, S. (eds.) (1994). *School bullying: Insights and perspectives*. London: Routledge.

Smith, P.K. and Steffgen, G. (eds.) (2013). *Cyberbullying through the new media: Findings from an international network*. Hove: Psychology Press.

Smith, P.K., Talamelli, L., Cowie, H., Naylor, P. and Chauhan, P. (2004). Profiles of non-victims, escaped victims, continuing victims and new victims of school bullying. *British Journal of Educational Psychology*, 74, 565–581.

Solberg, M.E. and Olweus, D. (2003). Prevalence estimation of school bullying with the Olweus Bully/Victim Questionnaire. *Aggressive Behavior*, 29, 239–268.

Stevens, V. and Van Oost, P. (1994). *Pesten op school: Een actieprogramma [Bullying at school: An action programme]*. Kessel-Lo: Garant Uitgevers.

Sutton, J. and Keogh, E. (2000). Social competition in school: Relationships with bullying, Machiavellianism and personality. *British Journal of Educational Psychology*, 70, 443–456.

Sutton, J., Smith, P.K. and Swettenham, J. (1999). Social cognition and bullying: Social inadequacy or skilled manipulation? *British Journal of Developmental Psychology*, 17, 435–450.

Van Roekel, E., Scholte, R.H.J. and Didden, R. (2009). Bullying among adolescents with autism spectrum disorders: Prevalence and perception. *Journal of Autism and Developmental Disorders*, 40, 63–73.

Veenstra, R., Lindenberg, S., Zijlstra, B.J.H., De Winter, A.F., Verhulst, F.C. and Ormel, J. (2007). The dyadic nature of bullying and victimization: Testing a dual-perspective theory. *Child Development*, 78, 1843–1854.

Williams, K., Chambers, M., Logan, S. and Robinson, D. (1996). Association of common health symptoms with bullying in primary school children. *British Medical Journal*, 313, 17–19.

Zwierzynska, K., Wolke, D. and Lereya, T.S. (2013). Peer victimization in childhood and internalizing problems in adolescence: A prospective longitudinal study. *Journal of Abnormal Child Psychology*, 41, 309–323.

Sheri Bauman, Julian Mendez,
Wendy Craig and Faye Mishna

In this chapter, we discuss the contributions to research on bullying and cyberbullying by North American researchers. We describe several seminal studies that marked the entry of North American researchers into this field of research. We continue by reviewing the contributions of researchers from this continent to the field: several methodological contributions (peer nomination and direct observation) were initiated by US and Canadian scholars. We then discuss contributions to knowledge of specific subgroups, such as students with disabilities, lesbian, gay, bisexual and transgender (LGBT) youth, and students of diverse racial and ethnic groups. We also note that the concept of bully/victims was described early on by researchers from this part of the world. A topic that has garnered particular attention here is that of teacher responses to bullying, which we review. Next we discuss the theoretical contributions from North America: relational bullying, social cognitive theory, and related theories such as social information processing and moral disengagement. We engage in a discussion of the social ecological model of Bronfenbrenner, which was applied to bullying research by Espelage and Swearer (2004). We then outline the contributions to research on cyberbullying provided by scholars in North America. We conclude with a summary of major work from the United States and Canada and some recommendations about future directions for research on this important topic.

Research on bullying in North America

North American researchers were relative latecomers to the field of bullying research, despite evidence that bullying was a serious problem in schools. Hoover and Hazler (1991) lamented the absence of research on this topic being published by US scholars, and stressed the need to investigate the problem of bullying in the North American context, which differs from that of Scandinavian and other European countries where much of the early research had been conducted. The definition of bullying used by North American scholars is derived from the work of Olweus (1993): bullying is defined as intentional, repetitive, aggressive behavior towards a target of lesser power. In this chapter, we use the terms *aggressors* and *perpetrators* to refer to those who commit aggressive acts, and *victim* refers to the recipients of those acts.

There is ample evidence that bullying is a problem in North America. Using data from the World Health Organization's Health Behavior in School-Aged Children (HBSC) international survey, forty countries were ranked according to prevalence of bullying behaviors (1 = lowest). For boys (ages 11, 13, and 15), the United States ranked #20 and Canada was #21; for girls the United States was #24 and Canada #26 (Craig et al., 2009). Little data were found on bullying in México; one Mexican researcher used data from a study of school violence (including bullying) modeled on the HBSC study and concluded that more students are involved in school violence in México than in Canada, but the United States has a higher rate of school violence than in México (Abundez, 2008). Because of the dearth of literature on this topic from México, we focus on the United States and Canada in this chapter.

Societal influences

As in other countries, suicides and tragedies related to school bullying in the United States and Canada that were publicized by the popular media increased attention to the problem by the public and researchers (Craig and Pepler, 2003). Researchers detected links between some of these incidents and victimization by bullying. For example, Leary et al. (2003) found that 12 of the 15 cases of school shootings included in their study involved an ongoing pattern of malicious teasing and bullying of the perpetrator. Also, in December 1997, 14-year-old Michael Carneal killed three classmates and wounded five others. Reports indicated that he had been bullied by many of his classmates. On April 20, 1999, Eric Harris and Dylan Klebold murdered twelve students and one teacher at Columbine High School, leaving many others wounded in the massacre, and eventually taking their own lives. Reports circulated that the sources of their anger were constant bullying and ridicule by their peers in school, particularly by athletes. These incidents appeared to spur researchers in North America to action, as numerous publications began to appear in the late 1990s and have proliferated in the twenty-first century.

Seminal studies

Although peer victimization had been studied in North America in the 1990s (e.g., Hodges et al., 1999; Hodges, Malone, and Perry, 1997; Hodges and Perry, 1999; Perry, Kusel, and Perry, 1998; Perry, Willard, and Perry, 1990), the emphasis on the broader phenomenon of bullying was to come later. One early study arguably launched a bullying research tradition in the United States (Hoover, Oliver, and Hazler, 1992). Data were collected from 207 middle school and high school students across 3 Midwestern states in the United States. Hoover et al., found that almost 77% of respondents had experienced being bullied at some time in their school careers, with about 14% of respondents indicating their experience was severe. Eighteen percent of males and 14% of females believed that their academic performance was negatively impacted by the victimization. Ages 10 through 14 were the period in which participants reported the most bullying occurs. The most common form of bullying was "ridicule and teasing" which was higher for females. Students reported that not fitting in with peers was the most common motivation for their victimization; another perceived reason was their appearance (e.g., overweight, physically weak, wearing unattractive clothes). Good grades were also mentioned as a reason for being victimized, while poor grades were not. Females tended to be more emotionally distressed by the victimization than males. Bullied students did not believe school personnel were helpful (66% rated their response as "poor"). The authors concluded, with some reservations, that bullying was a greater problem in the United States than in Europe.

Arguably the most cited study on bullying in the United States is that of Nansel et al.(2001) because it was the first to report on findings from a nationally representative sample of US youth. The researchers used the data from the 1998 HSBC survey of 15,686 students in grades 6 through 10. Overall, 13% admitted to being involved in moderate ("sometimes") or frequent ("once a week or more often") bullying; 10.6% were classified as targets, and 6.3% were both aggressors and targets, with a total of 29% of the sample involved in moderate or frequent bullying as bullies, victims, or both. Boys were bullied and bullied others more than girls, and middle school students (grades 6–8) were more involved in bullying than those in high school (grades 9–10). Hispanic participants reported slightly more bullying of others than other groups, and Black youth indicated they were targeted less often than others. Males reported being victimized by physical bullying while females reported verbal and relational bullying. Race and religion were mentioned least often as a motivation for being bullied, while appearance and speech were most often given as reasons. Poorer psychosocial adjustment was associated with all the involved groups compared to uninvolved students, with the poorest adjustment found for those who were the targets. Those who were classified as bullies were more likely to engage in problem behaviors such as drinking and smoking, and to report lower academic achievement. The findings from this study provided a baseline for understanding bullying among US youth.

In 1995, Charach, Pepler, and Ziegler reported results of the first study of bullying in Canada. The researchers addressed many questions that continue to be investigated today, which makes this study particularly important. Participants comprised 211 ethnically diverse students, 22 teachers, and 172 parents from Toronto schools (grades 4–8 with some grade 3 students). Results revealed that 49% of students reported being bullied during the two-month reference period, with 20% saying the bullying had occurred more than once or twice, and 8% saying they were bullied weekly or more often. Parents' estimates of bullying were lower than those reported by students. The researchers pointed out that these rates were about twice as prevalent as those reported in Norway, but similar to those reported in the United Kingdom. Regarding bullying others, 24% of students said they had bullied others once or twice, 15% admitted to doing so more often, and 2% acknowledged bullying others once a week or more often. Other data collected suggest that these rates are likely to be fairly accurate. This important initial study also examined gender and age (grade) differences, and found that while both genders were victimized at similar rates, significantly more boys than girls bullied others. Younger children were victimized significantly more often than older ones; the highest rates of bullying were found in grades five and six. Bullies and victims were found to be of the same age. Children in special needs classrooms reported more victimization than mainstreamed children (38% vs. 18% in regular education settings). This study also asked for respondents' perceptions of the reasons children bully others. Students most often mentioned the desire for power as a motive, and the desire to be "cool." The adult participants also saw power as a primary reason, but thought low self-esteem on the part of the bullies was involved.

Seeking to describe the characteristics of victims of bullying, Charach et al. (1995) observed that victims were frequently alone at recess and were lonely and less well-liked by their classmates. When asked how they felt when observing incidents of bullying, 61% of observers said they found the experience very unpleasant, 29% said it was somewhat unpleasant, and 10% were indifferent. Those who were indifferent were more likely to be classified as bullies. The researchers also inquired about how children respond when they see bullying happening. A large group (43%) indicated they attempt to help, and 33% said they believe they should help but do not do so. Only 24% said bullying was not their concern. One-third of respondents said they could join in the bullying, and this group included more boys than girls. Regarding what should be done in the event of victimization, most said the target should tell adults (parents and teachers), although those classified as bullies did not think so. Perpetrators chose fighting back as a recommended response to a greater extent than did victims or uninvolved students. Victims were more likely to recommend doing nothing, and indeed nearly a third of victims had not told an adult about their plight. The study also examined how students and teachers perceived adult responses to incidents of bullying; 75% of teachers said they intervene but only 25% of students thought they did. The study provided an initial view of the problem of bullying in Canadian youth, and identified aspects of the problem that are still being investigated.

Important contributions

Methods

Although most research on bullying utilizes self-report measures, there are other methods that have been developed by North American researchers to provide valid information. Pellegrini (1998) acknowledged the contribution of Perry and colleagues (1988, 1990) in the United States for using peer nomination in their work, and called for more studies to use observational methods, which were pioneered shortly thereafter by Canadian researchers.

Peer nomination. Concerned that the extant research had placed a disproportionate emphasis on the aggressor, Perry et al., (1988) sought to develop a valid tool for identifying children who are the targets of aggression in order to be able to learn more about them. They developed a peer nomination scale to determine the degree to which students were subjected to physical and verbal abuse by their peers. The measure included seven aggression items, seven victimization items, and twelve filler items. Participants marked the names of same-sex classmates who fit the description (e.g., he gets hit and pushed by other kids). Evidence of adequate reliability and validity was presented. Participants included 165 students in grades three through six who attended a university-affiliated school in a middle-class community. Results indicated that 10% of students could be classified as extreme or chronic victims of peer abuse. Researchers concluded that victims are often disliked by their peers and possess qualities predictive of peer rejection. Perry et al., (1990) then studied peer perceptions of victimized children in a group of 175 students in fourth through seventh grade in a southeastern state. Findings suggested students believe victimized children reinforce the bully's actions by showing signs of distress and not retaliating against their attackers.

Observational studies. In 1995, Pepler and Craig (1995) pioneered the use of naturalistic observations in the study of bullying. Recognizing that proximal observations have many limitations (the presence of the observer being the most obvious), they developed a methodology that utilized wireless microphones and video cameras to capture children's interactions. This allowed the researchers to capture the interactions in the naturally occurring context, which provided rich data for analysis. Since the researchers were interested in the most aggressive students and their targets, they used live microphones on those students and dummy microphones on other children to avoid differential reactivity to the equipment. Recordings were not available to school personnel.

Using this methodology, these researchers and their colleagues conducted a series of studies that provided increased understanding of bullying and victimization. Craig and Pepler (1997) used naturalistic observations to examine the rate, duration, and types of bullying occurring on school playgrounds. Researchers videotaped 41 aggressive and 41 socially competent children on the playgrounds of two elementary schools over a three-week period. This method allowed researchers to study students' behaviors in the context in which they occur, to examine bystanders' behaviors in addition to that of bullies and victims, and to capture spontaneous bullying behavior not normally witnessed by adults. Results showed bullying occurred regularly on the playground, approximately once every seven minutes, and was of short duration ($M = 38$ seconds) with verbal abuse being the most common type of bullying. Boys were more likely to be the perpetrators and victims in the bullying behavior; however, no gender differences were found in the types of bullying employed.

Atlas and Pepler (1998) reported on their observations of 27 children whose teachers selected them as either aggressive or non-aggressive; 28 hours of recorded classroom activities containing 60 bullying episodes were coded. An often-cited finding from this study is that in 85% of the bullying incidents, peers were present. Teachers intervened in 18% of episodes; when that figure included only the incidents in which the teacher was in close proximity, the rate was 37%. When the rate considered only those incidents in which the teacher was clearly aware of the incident, the rate of interventions was 73%. Other students were in the proximity of 51 incidents, and intervened in only 12%. Interestingly, the researchers determined that 65% of the incidents occurred when students were working independently, 23% when students were engaged in group activities, and 12% when the teacher was leading the class.

In their study comparing the frequency of bullying on the playground and in the classroom, Craig, Pepler, and Atlas (2000) also used naturalistic observations of 34 children identified as either aggressive or non-aggressive in a previous study. The researchers concluded bullying occurs much more frequently on the playground (4.5 times per hour) than in the classroom (2.4 times per hour); there were more opportunities to receive or initiate aggression on the playground. In addition, direct bullying was more prevalent on the playground and indirect bullying was more common in the classroom. Finally, nonaggressive children were more likely to bully on the playground and students deemed as aggressive were more likely to bully in the classroom.

Prevalence in subgroups

Researchers in North America have also contributed to the field by identifying at-risk groups or individuals that may be involved in bullying. Recognition of the increased risk of bullying involvement in these groups enhances prevention and targeted intervention efforts.

Students with disabilities. While evidence has suggested bullying occurs frequently in schools, few research studies in North America have investigated bullying within subpopulations such as students with disabilities. In 2003, Mishna reviewed the extant international literature on bullying and victimization among students with learning disabilities, and urged researchers to investigate this population in order to develop a knowledge base upon which to build effective prevention and intervention programs. Rose, Espelage, and Monda-Amaya (2009) studied 7,331 7th and 8th grade students in middle school and 14,315 students in grades 9 through 12 from a Midwestern US county across 18 different high schools. Among middle school participants, 9.7% received special education services part-time and 4.2% of participants received special education services full-time. For the high school sample, those rates were 6.4% and 4.1% respectively. These researchers found that students with disabilities reported significantly higher rates of victimization, aggression, bullying and fighting than general education students. Furthermore, victimization was more prevalent for younger students with disabilities than for older students receiving special education services. The study's findings were consistent with international research and emphasized the need to focus on victimization of students with disabilities in American schools. On the other hand, Bauman and Pero (2011) found no differences by hearing status on rates of traditional or cyberbullying or both forms of victimization in a sample of deaf secondary students and a control group of hearing students.

LGBT Poteat and Espelage (2005) explored the relations between homophobic verbal content and bullying among 191 students at a Central Illinois middle school. Researchers developed the *Homophobic Content Agent Target* scale to assess the extent to which students experience homophobic slurs during verbal exchanges. Results indicated that males reported more negative attitudes towards gays and lesbians than females, reacted more negatively to being called homophobic names, and were more likely to engage in relational aggression and physical aggression related to homophobia than females. In addition, while homophobic verbal exchanges were often directed toward individuals who were perceived as gay or lesbian, these homophobic epithets were directed towards other students as well. Finally, data revealed that students who were targets of homophobic slurs were more likely to be victims of bullying.

Espelage et al. (2008) examined the degree to which social support networks influence psychological outcomes for homosexual students and students questioning their sexuality. Participants included 13,921 high school students across eighteen high schools in a Midwestern American county. Findings indicated that LGB students experienced significantly higher rates of homophobic teasing than heterosexual students. In addition, students questioning their sexuality reported more teasing and general victimization than heterosexual students and LGB students. Sexual minority youth were more likely to report higher levels of depression, suicidal feelings, and alcohol and drug use. However, students with adequate social support networks were less likely to experience negative outcomes.

A large-scale study of 7,559 adolescents (ages 14–22) provided comparative data on rates of bullying and victimization among heterosexual and sexual minority groups (Berlan et al., 2010), including youth who identified as "mostly" (vs. exclusively) heterosexual. At greater risk for victimization than heterosexual males were participants who were mostly heterosexual males and gay males. The same pattern was found for females: mostly heterosexual, bisexual, and lesbian females were more likely to report victimization than were heterosexual females. For bullying others, gay males were less likely to report engaging in that behavior than were heterosexual males, while mostly homosexual and bisexual females were more likely to do so than their heterosexual peers.

Race and ethnicity. Race-related bullying was detected in early studies; 43% of students and 36% of teachers indicated this form of bullying was a frequent occurrence in their schools (Charach et al.,1995) with 20% of students indicating racially motivated bullying happened frequently in their schools; and 50% of participants from disadvantaged neighborhoods saying so. On the other hand, Nansel et al. (2001) found that verbal bullying through derogatory comments about one's race or ethnicity was infrequently reported by both male and female participants. However, Graham and Juvonen (2002) found different results in their study of peer harassment and its relation to ethnic majority/minority status. They surveyed 418 sixth and seventh graders from an ethnically diverse urban middle school. The majority of students who attended the school were from Hispanic and African American backgrounds. Minority groups included White, Persian, Asian or Pacific Islander, and Middle Eastern groups. Participants completed peer nomination procedures to identify aggressive and victimized students. Peer acceptance and rejection were also measured using peer nominations. Graham and Juvonen found that majority ethnic groups had more students with reputations as aggressors. Students from minority ethnic groups were more likely to be victims of peer harassment and to be rejected by their peers. Peer harassment refers to repeated targeting of someone based on their status group: gender, race, ethnicity, national origin, sexual orientation, disability, etc. Harassment is a type of bullying, so that all harassment is bullying but not all bullying is harassment. Those members of the majority group (African American) who were victims had higher levels of loneliness, lower self-esteem, and higher rates of peer rejection than victims in the other ethnic groups. The researchers suggested that because the group norm for African Americans in that school was aggressive, being a victim is contrary to that norm, and the psychosocial consequences are thus increased.

Recent research examined racially motivated bullying using the 2001/ 2002 HBSC data from Canada and investigated the influence of individual (race, sex, grade, SES, general bullying) and school-level factors (student and teacher diversity, school climate factors) on racial bullying (Larochette, Murphy, and Craig, 2010). General bullying in the sample was reported by 42.5% of participants; 38% reported general victimization. Racially motivated bullying of others was reported by 3.5% of the sample, while 4.4% reported being victimized for those reasons. Using multi-level modeling, the researchers discovered that school-level variables did not explain racial bullying and victimization. In the final model, only being African-Canadian, male, and being involved in general bullying were associated with racial victimization. Researchers also found that perceived school support was predictive of less racial bullying, which was particularly so when teacher diversity was high.

Bully/victims. North American researchers have included bully/victims, who have received less attention in the literature than bullies and victims (Haynie et al., 2001).This group of researchers focused on a wider range of variables than individual factors, including parenting practices, other problem behaviors, and school environment. Their sample consisted of students in all middle schools in a suburban school district (4,263 participants; 49% male, 69% White). Results indicated lower prevalence rates than the Nansel et al (2001) study: 7.4% reported bullying others three times or more in the previous year, and 31% indicated they had been victimized three or more times. As in other studies, prevalence was higher for boys, and rates increased with grade. Of interest is the finding that more than half those who reported bullying others also reporting being victimized. This group differed from pure bullies and pure victims on several variables, and was found to have higher rates of problem behaviors, more depressive symptoms, lower self-control, lower social competence, and poorer functioning in school. Following this study, other researchers have recognized that this group is high-risk, and deserving of research attention.

A final area of contribution from North American researchers is understanding the role that adults (i.e., educators) may play in bullying. Because bullying involves a power imbalance, adults are needed to right this power imbalance and to effectively address the problem.

Teacher responses. Several of the studies described earlier included data on the frequency with which teachers responded to bullying situations. Because the rates at which teachers respond are disappointing, some researchers have investigated this issue more closely. One of the earliest such studies was conducted in Canada (Craig, Henderson, and Murphy, 2000) with 116 pre-service teachers, most of whom reported having one to three months of teaching experience. The authors designed the *Bullying Attitude Questionnaire*, which used vignettes to inquire about how teachers would respond and how they thought about each situation, and a number of other measures. The scenarios varied according to whether or not the teacher personally observed the incident. Results showed that observing the event increased the teachers' perceived seriousness of the event and likelihood of intervening for all three types of bullying (physical, verbal, and social exclusion). These pre-service teachers were more likely to label the incident as bullying when it was physical aggression compared to social exclusion. Physical aggression was more likely to be considered serious than the other two types. Of all the individual variables explored, only empathy was a significant predictor of the outcomes. Sex (female) predicted a small amount of variance for several of the depending measures. The authors comment that the large amount of unexplained variance suggests caution in interpreting the results.

Interest in this paper prompted Yoon and Kerber (2003) to do a follow-up study with ninety-four elementary school teachers in the Midwestern US, modifying the questionnaire so that the vignettes all depicted situations in which the teacher witnessed the incident. Two vignettes of each type of bullying (physical, verbal, relational) were used, and respondents were asked to rate their seriousness, their level of empathy for the victim in the vignette, and their likelihood of intervening. In addition, participants were asked to say how they would respond to the perpetrators, which was then coded according to a rating system devised by the researchers. Findings revealed that teachers rated physical bullying as more serious than the other two types; seriousness, empathy, and likelihood of intervening were all lowest for social exclusion. In contrast to physical and verbal bullying, in which 50% of responses indicated there would be disciplinary consequences for the bully, only 10% would implement such consequences in cases of social exclusion.

Bauman and Del Rio (2006) and Jacobsen and Bauman (2007) replicated the study with pre-service teachers and school counselors respectively, also coding responses to the victim. As in the earlier studies, both samples rated physical bullying as the most serious, and relational bullying as least. They also had less empathy for the victims of relational bullying, and were least likely to intervene in those incidents. Pre-service teacher respondents chose the lowest level responses (least punitive) to perpetrators of relational bullying, as did the counselors. However, the counselors who had received anti-bullying training rated relational bullying as more serious than those who did not have the training, and also had greater empathy and more inclination to intervene in those scenarios than those without training. Female counselors rated the relational incident as more serious than did the males.

Theoretical contributions

Much of the research conducted in North America has utilized several theoretical works to frame their own research. As these contributions come from North American scholars, this chapter would be incomplete without acknowledging them. We follow with brief overviews of these influential lines of inquiry.

Relational bullying

Initially, bullying brought to mind an attack by a brutish thug on a defenseless weakling. As knowledge of bullying expanded, it was understood that verbal bullying also existed. It was only later, primarily through the seminal work of Nicki Crick and her colleagues, that relational bullying was included as a legitimate and harmful form of bullying. The seminal paper by Crick and Grotpeter (1995) noted that physical and verbal aggression are more typically male behaviors, which makes sense in the context of the goals of such behavior (instrumentality and physical dominance). For girls whose goals are more affiliative and focused on relationships, these researchers tested whether a relational form of aggression could be identified empirically. They used peer nominations because they believed that peers would be the most knowledgeable and reliable informants. Their sample included 491 students in third through sixth grade in the Midwestern US. Their scale, developed for this research, included measures of overt aggression, relational aggression, and prosocial behavior. In addition, each child selected three liked peers and three disliked peers from their class. Children were classified into aggressive and nonaggressive groups using cutoff scores of one standard deviation above and below the sample mean for each type of aggression. They also categorized children as popular, average, neglected, rejected, and controversial based on the sociometric nominations. They measured a number of outcomes that had previously been associated with victimization such as depression, social anxiety, and so forth. First, the researchers found their measure had four factors: prosocial, overt aggression, relational aggression, and isolation. Then, they examined gender differences and found that boys were over-represented in the overtly aggressive groups, and girls were over-represented in the relationally aggressive group. Further, relationally aggressive students were more disliked than those who were not. Relationally aggressive participants had significantly higher levels of depression. There were also associations with the sociometric groups. This study established relational aggression as a legitimate area of study.

Social cognitive theory

Bandura (1986) proposed a social cognitive theory to explain human functioning. This theory is based on reciprocal determinism, which proposes a multidirectional interaction between person (P), environment (E), and behavior (B). It is beyond the scope of this chapter to describe all the components of this theory, but a key contribution of the theory is a delineation of the cognitive processes that are part of the person (P) component. Bandura believed that thoughts and beliefs about the self are central to cognitive processes such as imparting meaning to events, planning, solving problems, reflecting, etc. Two important theories that are related to this theory are described next.

Social Information Processing (SIP). This theory describes a process by which one processes social information. First proposed by Dodge (1986), a revision in 1994 (Crick and Dodge, 1994) is most widely known. According to this theory, when faced with a social situation, children bring to bear their biological capacities and their memories of previous experiences. These memories are integrated to form more general cognitive structures (*schemata* or *scripts*) which provide templates for new social experiences. The crux of the theory is the series of discrete steps that are employed to determine an action to take in a social situation. Those steps are: (1) Encoding of sensory input. This involves selective attention to details in the situation, which is influenced by the emotional state of the actor. (2) The input is interpreted. The interpretation may include a decision about the cause of a situation, or an attribution of the intent of others. Also in this step, the interpretation may include an evaluation of the actor's self-efficacy for similar social situations, and a consideration of outcome expectations. (3) A goal is selected (e.g., gaining status, getting even). (4) A menu of possible responses is examined. (5) A decision is made regarding the best response given the goal and expected outcomes. (6) The decision is enacted.

This process happens at a subconscious level and is very rapid. The process appears linear, but may also be cyclical. This theory is the basis for much research that attempts to understand how this process differs among individuals who take different participant roles in bullying, and has been the basis of prevention and intervention strategies.

Moral disengagement

This theory was proposed by Bandura (1999, 2002a,b) and his colleagues as an outgrowth of social cognitive theory, and posits that people behave in ways that are satisfying and validate their self-worth. Once moral standards have been developed, people do not typically behave in ways that are contrary to those standards because that would lead to negative self-evaluation. However, the process of *moral disengagement* allows one to avoid that negative self-evaluation by employing a cognitive mechanism (or several) to deflect self-blame. Those mechanisms can be grouped into several types:

1 Cognitive restructuring: moral justification (invoking higher principles such as honor or loyalty), euphemistic language (using terms that mask the malicious nature of the behavior, such as calling aggression "fooling around"), and advantageous comparison (e.g., this isn't as bad as beating him up).
2 Denying responsibility: minimizing one's role (e.g., everyone was doing it), disregarding harmful consequences (I'm showing him how to be tough).
3 Transforming the actions so they are the victim's fault: Dehumanizing the victim, blaming the victim.

This theory has generated hypotheses about the role of moral disengagement in bullying. A study of 494 junior secondary students in Canada revealed that those students who frequently bullied others had the highest levels of moral disengagement, and the lowest levels were reported by those who indicated they never bullied others (Hymel, Rocke-Henderson and Bonanno, 2005). Moral disengagement accounted for 38% of the variance of bullying behavior, demonstrating its importance in understanding bullying. In a later longitudinal study of 871 adolescents in Toronto, Canada (Pepler et al., 2008) researchers found that the participants in the high-bullying trajectory had higher scores on moral disengagement than those in the never-bullied group. Bauman and Pero (2011) included a measure of moral disengagement in their study of deaf and hard of hearing secondary students and found that moral disengagement was positively correlated with bullying behaviors. Many other studies have been conducted in other parts of the world with similar findings.

Social ecological model

This perspective is based on Bronfenbrenner's (1979) ecological model, and was applied by Espelage and Swearer (2004) to provide a framework for viewing the phenomenon of bullying in a broader context. This theory views the individual (with all his/her traits, experiences, biological dispositions, etc.) as the center of a series of concentric circles, which then have layers of family and peers, school, communities, and society. These circles or systems interact to affect the individual. The microsystem refers to those with whom the individual has direct contact (family, peers, school); the mesosystem includes the interactions among the components of the microsystem, the exosystem involves relationships between other systems, and the macrosystem includes culture and society. Researchers have used this framework to examine contextual factors in bullying.

A recent study sought to examine bullying trajectories across the transition to middle school within a social-ecological framework. Increases in bullying were associated with contextual factors: diminished trust in primary caregivers, negative relationships with teachers, and especially declines in school belonging (Espelage et al., 2015). Hong and Espelage (2012) conducted a review of research in which they examined findings related to the levels of the system. First, they reported findings on the individual characteristics that are associated with bullying including age, gender, race/ethnicity, sexual orientation, health status, mental health, disabilities, and intelligence. In the microsystem, they cited studies of parent-youth relationships, family violence, peer relationships, school connectedness, and school environment. The mesosystem discussion focused on the role of teachers, while within the exosystem media violence, and neighborhood and community context, are discussed. Cultural norms and beliefs about bullying and aggression are part of the macrosystem, with few studies found that addressed these issues. This review affirms the importance of studying factors beyond the individual in order to gain a complete understanding of bullying. Recently, the term "techno-subsystem" (Johnson and Puplampu, 2008; Johnson, 2010) has been coined to expand this framework to include the cyber world.

Cyberbullying

North American researchers have engaged in research on cyberbullying from the inception of this line of inquiry. In 2010, Sheri Bauman received funding to convene a "think tank" of cyberbullying scholars from around the world to discuss issues related to definitions, measures, and methods for this new research field. The outcome of the meeting was a book, *Principles of Cyberbullying Research: Definition, Method, and Measures* (Bauman, Walker, and Cross, 2013) that sought to provide guidelines for research going forward, so that studies could use consistent approaches and build upon one another.

Similar to traditional bullying, electronic bullying (or cyberbullying) has been defined as "any behavior performed through electronic or digital media by individuals or groups that repeatedly communicates hostile or aggressive messages intended to inflict harm or discomfort on others," (Tokunaga, 2010, p. 278). Electronic bullying includes sending or posting embarrassing or private photos to an outside audience, insulting another individual through cell phone text messages or emails, and spreading gossip via the internet among other actions. In North America, the majority of studies have examined the prevalence, the overlap with traditional bullying, and short term outcomes associated with involvement in electronic bullying. For example, in a comprehensive review of the literature, Hinduja and Patchin (2012) found that approximately 24% of students had been bullied electronically, compared to 17% of students who admitted to engaging in electronic bullying perpetration. These statistics appear to be similar to the rates reported for involvement in traditional bullying. Research using a nationally representative sample of 1,200 youth aged 6–17 in the United States yielded somewhat different findings: 25% of the sample reported being bullied monthly or more often in person, 10% had experienced online bullying, 7% were bullied by phone, and 8% via text messages (Ybarra et al., 2012). Nevertheless, it is generally accepted that cyberbullying is a serious problem in most developed countries, including in North America.

Many academics have researched whether the bullying that occurs electronically is an extension of traditional bullying (e.g., Juvonen and Gross, 2008; Tokunaga, 2010) or a qualitatively different phenomenon. Canadian researchers used factor analysis to address that issue, and found that while there were separate perpetration and victimization factors for traditional bullying, there was only a single factor for cyberbullying that included both roles (Law et al., 2012). Findings suggested that the large overlap between cyberbullying and cybervictimization suggests that much of what researchers include as cyberbullying may be "reciprocal banter" (p. 239) among peers. They also observed that it is easier to retaliate in the digital environment than in traditional bullying. Their finding was supported by other research that noted that the proportion of participants who are both bullies and victims in the cyber-context is much greater than in traditional bullying (Mishna et al., 2012).

One common way to test this theory is to measure the overlap between involvement in traditional bullying and involvement in electronic bullying (e.g., Bauman and Newman, 2013; Beran and Li, 2007; Juvonen and Gross, 2008; Law et al., 2012; Li, 2007; Ybarra, Diener-West, and Leaf, 2007). But results from published studies have varied. For instance, Juvonen and Gross (2008) reported that 85% of those who were involved in online bullying were also involved in traditional forms of bullying. On the other hand, Ybarra et al. (2007) found that 64% of youth harassed online do not report being bullied at school. With such a wide range of results, it is not possible to conclude how intimately associated electronic and traditional forms of bullying and victimization are. This issue is critical because the magnitude of the overlap may reflect the distinctiveness of the two types of aggression.

Another approach to determining whether traditional and cyberbullying are different forms of aggression or variations of the same phenomenon was a mixed-method study that used factor analysis (and follow-up interviews) to determine whether proactive or reactive motives were behind their behavior. Whereas in traditional bullying, participants can be classified by roles (bully, victim, bystander, uninvolved), their participants could be grouped by method of cyber-aggression used. Furthermore, the motivation for the aggression varied according to the method used rather than the role. Adolescents who posted mean messages or photos were likely to have reactive motives (retaliation), while those who did such acts as creating a website to disparage someone else had proactive motives (Law et al., 2012).

One important component of electronic media is anonymity (Patchin and Hinduja, 2006), which can create a deindividuation effect (i.e., loss of self-awareness). According to Zimbardo (1969), a loss of self-awareness brings with it reduced feelings of accountability and can lead people to behave in ways they normally would not. This process was later described specifically for the digital world when Suler (2004) identified a phenomenon, *online disinhibition*, which is a tendency to say and do things in cyberspace that would not be said or done in person. This effect likely contributes to the increased cruelty that has been noted in content posted or transmitted digitally. Moreover, since many people who are victimized electronically do not know the identity of their aggressors (Ybarra and Mitchell, 2007), they may refrain from reporting the incident. Reporting an incident of electronic bullying (either to a peer or to an adult) has been shown to stop future instances of electronic bullying from occurring in at least 50% of cases (Holfeld and Grabe, 2012).

Another unique aspect of the electronic environment is that it lacks salient contextual cues. For instance, interactions occurring online can reduce obvious physical characteristics of power, and therefore an imagined power imbalance might be created (Blais, 2008). Another example of a cue that is less obvious in the electronic world is emotion. Espelage and Asiado (2001) examined the emotional responses of middle school students who had been involved in traditional bullying and found that when students can see the impact of their actions (e.g., seeing another student crying), they express remorse for what they have done. Removing emotional cues reduces the potential that somebody who is bullying will feel empathy for the person they are targeting, thereby increasing the chance that the bullying will continue (Dooley et al, 2009). Furthermore, observers who would intervene in instances of traditional bullying might be less inclined to do so electronically.

Results on gender differences in electronic bullying and victimization are mixed. For example, Li (2006) found that males were significantly more likely than females to engage in electronic bullying. However, Kowalski and Limber (2007) concluded that females were more likely to be victimized and to have dual status (i.e., to both bully others and be bullied), whereas males were more likely to not be involved in electronic bullying in any form. Furthermore, after a systematic review of the literature, Tokunaga (2010) concluded that neither gender is victimized more than the other (see also Beran and Li, 2007; Ybarra, 2004).

Some researchers have posited that given the unique features of the electronic environment (i.e., anonymity, lack of emotional cues, rapidity, increased accessibility, and a large audience), the consequences of electronic victimization might be more serious than those for traditional victimization. In the Tokunaga review (2010), a number of problems resulting from electronic victimization were identified in the literature, including a drop in academic performance, increased truancy, perceptions of school being unsafe, poor concentration, and increased incidence of weapons-carrying. Perpetrators of electronic bullying have been found to engage in increased rates of rule-breaking and delinquent behaviors (Ybarra and Mitchell, 2007). The findings from these studies show that electronic bullying and victimization are associated with the same internalizing and externalizing outcomes as traditional bullying and victimization, including depression and suicidal behaviors. The relations between depression and four forms of bullying (physical, verbal, relational, and cyber) was different for cyber-involvement than for the other forms. For cyberbullying, frequent victims had higher levels of depression than occasional victims, whereas in verbal and relational bullying, both victims and bully-victims had higher levels of depression than the occasional or frequent bullies (Wang, Nansel, and Ianotti, 2011).

Bonnano and Hymel (2013) found that involvement in cyberbullying and cybervictimization were associated with suicidal ideation, whereas no such association was found for physical or social bullying. Those who were both cyberbullies and cybervictims had increased levels of suicidal ideation. This outcome was also reported by Kowalski and Limber (2013), who noted that effects were statistically significant but small in magnitude.

Researchers have begun to focus on the readiness of schools to provide prevention and intervention strategies for cyberbullying. Several studies have reported disappointing findings (Cassidy, Brown, and Jackson, 2012; Ryan, Kariui and Yilmaz, 2011) showing that teachers are unprepared to deal with cyberbullying. Trachtenbroit (2011) surveyed educators and found that they underestimated the number of students affected by cyberbullying.

Future directions

North American researchers have begun to recognize the importance of incorporating a developmental perspective. Recent research has examined the developmental trajectories of those involved in bullying because these problems can start in early childhood and persist through the school years, peaking during school transitions (Pellegrini and Long, 2002; Pepler et al., 2008). When children enter adolescence, new forms of aggression, combined with power, emerge. As children develop cognitive and social skills, they become more aware of others' vulnerabilities and differences, and of their own power relative to others. Bullying becomes diversified into more sophisticated forms of verbal and social forms, along with electronic, sexually and racially based bullying. All of these forms of bullying are destructive and need to be actively addressed. The lessons of power and aggression learned in playground bullying can transfer to sexual harassment, dating aggression, and may extend to workplace harassment, as well as marital, child, and elder abuse (Pepler et al., 2006). Thus, by intervening in bullying early, we can prevent the development of more severe problem behaviors later.

Current research in North America has focused on the mechanisms underlying bullying and victimization. Specifically, recent research has identified neural correlates that are associated with bullying (Vaillancourt et al., 2010; Vaillancourt et al., 2008). Understanding these underlying mechanisms associated with bullying and victimization can help identify critical areas to target in our prevention efforts.

Summary and conclusion

Despite a later start than many researchers around the globe, researchers in North America have clearly produced a great deal of important work on bullying and have made significant contributions to the theoretical bases for empirical studies. North America now has a vital research tradition on bullying and researchers are engaged in studying this problem along with their international colleagues.

Early studies from North America have provided important research about the prevalence and the identification of specific at-risk groups for involvement. The majority of this research was atheoretical. As the field advanced, many theoretical frameworks were applied to understanding bullying. Some theories, such as social cognitive, social informational processing, and moral disengagement, have focused on the individual factors. This perspective is consistent with the early research that focused on the individual perspective, but now it is recognized that there are many levels of influence on bullying interactions. More recently, the social ecological framework has identified the role of the individual, peers, adults, and the classroom and school context, as well as the influences of communities and the larger society. We now recognize that it is the interaction between the individuals, their salient socialization influences, and the contexts in which they live, learn, play, and work that all contribute to bullying.

A significant contribution to the field from North American researchers was the development of new methodologies to further understand bullying. Peer nomination techniques enable researchers to move beyond self-report (and any associated biases in reporting), as well as adult report (since adults tend to underreport the problem compared to children). Further, observational research enabled the enhanced understanding of the role that others play in bullying, that is, peers and adults, as well as the relationship aspects of bullying. Both of these methodological advances also contributed to the need for a more theoretical framework to understand the complex dynamics involved in bullying interactions.

In conclusion, North American research on bullying has grown exponentially in the last twenty years. There is growing recognition that bullying is a serious public health issue that has potentially long term negative consequences. Research and theory have evolved to provide a more sophisticated understanding of this complex problem. Through longitudinal developmental research focused on the mechanisms (genetic, neurological, cognitive, social, psychological), new findings can inform current intervention efforts such that we can more effectively address this societal issue.

REFERENCES

Abundez, G.M. (2008). School violence in Mexico and other countries. *Revista Mexicana de Investigación Educativa*, 13, 1195–1228.

Atlas, R. S. and Pepler, D. J. (1998). Observations of bullying in the classroom. *The Journal of Educational Research*, 92, 86–99.

Bandura, A. (1986). *Social foundations of thought and action: A cognitive social theory*. Englewood Cliffs, New York: Prentice Hall.

(1999). Moral disengagement in the perpetration of inhumanities. *Personality and Social Psychology Review*, 3, 193–209.

(2002a). Social cognitive theory in cultural context. *Applied Psychology*, 51, 269–290.

(2002b). Social cognitive theory of mass communication. In J. Bryant, and D. Zillman (eds.), *Media effects: Advances in theory and research*, second edition (pp. 121–153). Hillsdale, NJ: Erlbaum.

Bauman, S., Walker, J., and Cross, D. (eds.) (2013). *Principles of cyberbullying research: Definition, methods, and measures.* NY: Routledge.

Bauman, S. and Del Rio, A. (2006). Preservice teachers' responses to bullying scenarios: Comparing physical, verbal, and relational bullying. *Journal of Educational Psychology*, 98, 219–231.

Bauman, S. and Newman, M. L. (2013). Testing assumptions about cyberbullying: Perceived distress associated with acts of conventional and cyberbullying. *Psychology of Violence*, 3, 27–38.

Bauman, S. and Pero, H. (2011). Bullying and cyberbullying among deaf students and their hearing peers: An exploratory study. *Journal of Deaf Studies and Deaf Education*, 16, 236–253.

Berlan, E. D., Corliss, H. L., Field, A. E., Goodman, E., and Bryn Austin, S. (2010). Sexual orientation and bullying among adolescents in the Growing Up Today Study. *Journal of Adolescent Health*, 46, 366–371.

Beran, T.T. and Li, Q. (2007). The relationship between cyberbullying and school bullying. *Journal of Student Wellbeing*, 1, 15–33.

Blais, J. (2008). *Chatting, befriending, and bullying: Adolescents' Internet experiences and associated psychosocial outcomes* (Unpublished doctoral dissertation). Kingston, Ontario: Queen's University.

Bonanno, R. A. and Hymel, S. (2013). Cyber bullying and internalizing difficulties: Above and beyond the impact of traditional forms of bullying. *Journal of Youth and Adolescence*, 42, 1–13.

Bronfenbrenner, U. (1979). Contexts of child rearing: Problems and prospects. *American Psychologist*, 34, 844–850.

Cassidy, W., Brown, K., and Jackson, M. (2012). "Under the radar": Educators and cyberbullying in schools. *School Psychology International*, 33, 520–532.

Charach, A., Pepler, D., and Ziegler, S. (1995). Bullying at school: A Canadian perspective. *Education Canada*, 35, 12–19.

Craig et al., (2009). A cross-national profile of bullying and victimization among adolescents in 40 countries. *International Journal of Public Health*, 54, 216–224.

Craig, W. M., Henderson, K., and Murphy, J. G. (2000). Prospective teachers' attitudes toward bullying and victimization. *School Psychology International*, 21, 5–21.

Craig, W. and Pepler, D. (1997). Naturalistic observations of bullying and victimization on the playground (unpublished report). York University, Toronto, Ontario: LaMarsh Research Centre on Violence and Conflict Resolution.

Craig, W. M. and Pepler, D. J. (2003). Identifying and targeting risk for involvement in bullying and victimization. *Canadian Journal of Psychiatry*, 48, 577–582.

Craig, W. M., Pepler, D., and Atlas, R. (2000). Observations of bullying in the playground and in the classroom. *School Psychology International*, 21, 22–36.

Craig, W. M., Pepler, D. J., Connolly, J., and Henderson, K. (2001).
Developmental context of peer harassment in early adolescence. In
J. Juvonen and S. Graham (eds.). *Peer harassment in school: The plight of the
vulnerable and victimized* (pp. 242–261). New York: Guilford.

Crick, N. R. and Dodge, K. A. (1994). A review and reformulation of social
information-processing mechanisms in children's social adjustment.
Psychological Bulletin, 115, 74–101.

Crick, N. R. and Grotpeter, J. K. (1995). Relational aggression, gender,
and social-psychological adjustment. *Child Development*, 66, 710–722.

Cullen, D. (2009). *Columbine*. New York: Hachette Digital, Inc.

Dodge, K. A. (1986). A social information processing model of social
competence in children. In M. Perlmutter (Ed.), *Minnesota symposium on
child psychology*, 18 (pp. 77–125). New York: Routledge

Dooley, J. J., Pyzalski, J., and Cross, D. (2009). Cyberbullying versus face-to-face
bullying: A theoretical and conceptual review. *Zeitschrift für Psychologie/
Journal of Psychology*, 217, 182–188.

Espelage, D. L., Aragon, S. R., Birkett, M., and Koenig, B. W. (2008).
Homophobic teasing, psychological outcomes, and sexual orientation
among high school students: What influence do parents and schools have?
School Psychology Review, 37, 202–216.

Espelage, D. L. and Asidao, C. S. (2001). Conversations with middle school
students about bullying and victimization: Should we be concerned?
Journal of Emotional Abuse, 2, 49–62.

Espelage, D. L., Hong, J. S., Rao, M. A., and Thornberg, R. (2015).
Understanding ecological factors associated with bullying across the
elementary to middle school transition in the United States. *Violence and
Victims*, 30, 470–487.

Espelage, D. L. and Swearer, S. (eds.) (2004). *Bullying in American schools*.
New York: Routledge.

Graham, S. and Juvonen, J. (2002). Ethnicity, peer harassment, and adjustment
in middle school: An exploratory study. *Journal of Early Adolescence*, 22,
173–199.

Haynie, D. L., Nansel, T., Eitel, P., Crump, A. D., Saylor, K., Yu, K.,
and Simons-Morton, B. (2001). Bullies, victims, and bully/victims:
Distinct groups of at-risk youth. *Journal of Early Adolescence*, 21,
29–49.

Hinduja, S. and Patchin, J. W. (2012). Cyberbullying: Neither an epidemic nor
a rarity. *European Journal of Developmental Psychology*, 9, 539–543.

Hodges, E. V. E., Boivin, M., Vitaro, F., and Bukowski, W. M. (1999).
The power of friendship: Protection against an escalating cycle of peer
victimization. *Developmental Psychology*, 35, 94–101.

Hodges, E. V. E., Malone, M., and Perry, D. (1997). Individual risk and social
risk as interacting determinants of victimization in the peer group.
Developmental Psychology, 33, 1032–1039.

Hodges, E. V. E. and Perry, D. G. (1999). Personal and interpersonal
antecedents and consequences of victimization by peers. *Journal of
Personality and Social Psychology*, 76, 677–685.

Holfeld, B. and Grabe, M. (2012). Middle school students' perceptions of and responses to cyberbullying. *Journal of Educational Computing Research*, 46, 395–413.

Hong, J. S. and Espelage, D. L. (2012). A review of research on bullying and peer victimization in school: An ecological system analysis. *Aggression and Violent Behavior*, 17, 311–322.

Hoover, J. H. and Hazler, R. J. (1991). Bullies and victims. *Elementary School Guidance and Counseling*, 25, 212–219.

Hoover, J. H., Oliver, R., and Hazler, R. J. (1992). Bullying: Perceptions of adolescent victims in the Midwestern USA. *School Psychology International*, 13, 5–16.

Hymel, S., Rocke-Henderson, N., and Bonanno, R. A. (2005). Moral disengagement: A framework for understanding bullying among adolescents. *Journal of Social Sciences*, 8, 1–11.

Jacobsen, K. E. and Bauman, S. (2007). Bullying in schools: School counselors' responses to three types of bullying incidents. *Professional School Counseling*, 11, 1–9.

Johnson, G. M. (2010). Internet use and child development: Validation of the ecological techno-subsystem. *Educational Technology and Society*, 13, 176–185.

Johnson, G. M. and Puplampu, P. (2008). A conceptual framework for understanding the effect of the Internet on child development: The ecological techno-subsystem. *Canadian Journal of Learning and Technology*, 34, 19–28.

Juvonen, J. and Gross, E. F. (2008). Extending the school grounds? Bullying experiences in cyberspace. *Journal of School Health*, 78, 496–502.

Kowalski, R. M. and Limber, S. P. (2007). Electronic bullying among middle school students. *Journal of Adolescent Health*, 41, S22–S30.

(2013). Psychological, physical, and academic correlates of cyberbullying and traditional bullying. *Journal of Adolescent Health*, 53, S13–S20.

Larochette, A. C., Murphy, A. N., and Craig, W. M. (2010). Racial bullying and victimization in Canadian school-aged children: Individual and school level effects. *School Psychology International*, 31, 389–408.

Law, D. M., Shapka, J. D., Domene, J. F., and Gagné, M. H. (2012). Are cyberbullies really bullies? An investigation of reactive and proactive online aggression. *Computers in Human Behavior*, 28, 664–672.

Law, D. M., Shapka, J. D., Hymel, S. S., Olson, B. F., and Waterhouse, T. (2012). The changing face of bullying: An empirical comparison between traditional and internet bullying and victimization. *Computers in Human Behavior*, 28, 226–232.

Leary, M. R., Kowalski, R. M., Smith, L., and Phillips, S. (2003). Teasing, rejection, and violence: Case studies of the school shootings. *Aggressive Behavior*, 29, 202–214.

Li, Q. (2006). Cyberbullying in schools: A research of gender differences. *School Psychology International*, 27, 157–170.

(2007). Bullying in the new playground: Research into cyberbullying and cyber victimisation. *Australasian Journal of Educational Technology*, 23, 435–454.

Mishna, F. (2003). Learning disabilities and bullying: Double jeopardy. *Journal of Learning Disabilities*, 36, 336–347.

Mishna, F., Khoury-Kassabri, M., Gadalla, T., and Daciuk, J. (2012). Risk factors for involvement in cyber bullying: Victims, bullies and bully-victims. *Children and Youth Services Review*, 34, 63–70.

Nansel, T. R., Overpeck, M., Pilla, R. S., Ruan, W. J., Simons-Morton, B., and Scheidt, P. (2001). Bullying behaviors among US youth. *JAMA: Journal of the American Medical Association*, 285, 2094–2100.

Olweus, D. (1993). *Bullying at school: What we know and what we can do.* Cambridge, MA: Blackwell.

Patchin, J. W. and Hinduja, S. (2006). Bullies move beyond the schoolyard: A preliminary look at cyberbullying. *Youth Violence and Juvenile Justice*, 4, 148–169.

Pellegrini, A. D. (1998). Bullies and victims in school: A review and call for research. *Journal of Applied Developmental Psychology*, 19, 165–176.

Pellegrini, A. D. and Long, J. D. (2002). A longitudinal study of bullying, dominance, and victimization during the transition from primary school through secondary school. *British Journal of Developmental Psychology*, 20, 259–280.

Pepler, D. J. and Craig, W. M. (1995). A peek behind the fence: Naturalistic observations of aggressive children with remote audiovisual recording. *Developmental Psychology*, 31, 548–553.

Pepler, D. J., Craig, W. M., Connolly, J. A., Yuile, A., McMaster, L., and Jiang, D. (2006). A developmental perspective on bullying. *Aggressive Behavior*, 32, 376–384.

Pepler, D., Jiang, D., Craig, W., and Connolly, J. (2008). Developmental trajectories of bullying and associated factors. *Child Development*, 79, 325–338.

Perry, D. C., Williard, J. C., and Perry, L. C. (1990). Peers' perceptions of the consequences that victimized children provide aggressors. *Child Development*, 61, 1310–1325.

Perry, D. G., Kusel, S. J., and Perry, L. C. (1988). Victims of peer aggression. *Developmental Psychology*, 24, 807–814.

Poteat, V. P. and Espelage, D. L. (2005). Exploring the relation between bullying and homophobic verbal content: The Homophobic Content Agent Target (HCAT) Scale. *Violence and Victims*, 20, 513–528.

Rose, C. A., Espelage, D. L., and Monda-Amaya, L. E. (2009). Bullying and victimisation rates among students in general and special education: A comparative analysis. *Educational Psychology*, 29, 761–776.

Ryan, T., Kariuki, M., and Yilmaz, H. (2011). A comparative analysis of cyberbullying perceptions of pre-service educators: Canada and Turkey. *Turkish Online Journal of Educational Technology*, 10, 1–10.

Suler, J. (2004). The online disinhibition effect. *Cyberpsychology and Behavior*, 7, 321–326.

Tokunaga, R. S. (2010). Following you home from school: A critical review and synthesis of research on cyberbullying victimization. *Computers in Human Behavior*, 26, 277–287.

Trachtenbroit, M. L. B. (2011). Cyberbullying, school violence, and youth suicide. *Dissertations.* Paper 879. Retrieved Nov 6, 2015 from http://aquila.usm.edu/theses_dissertations/879

Vaillancourt, T., Clinton, J., McDougall, P., Schmidt, L. A., and Hymel, S. (2010). The neurobiology of peer victimization and rejection. In S. Jimerson, S. M. Swearer and D. L. Espelage (eds.), *Handbook of bullying in schools: An international perspective* (pp. 293–327). New York: Routledge.

Vaillancourt, T., Duku, E., Decatanzara, D., MacMillan, H., Muir, C., and Schmidt, L. A. (2008). Variation in hypothalamic-pituitary-adrenal axis activity among bullied and non-bullied children. *Aggressive Behavior*, 34, 294–305.

Wang, J., Nansel, T. R., and Iannotti, R. J. (2011). Cyber bullying and traditional bullying: Differential association with depression. *Journal of Adolescent Health*, 45, 368–375.

Ybarra, M. L. (2004). Linkages between depressive symptomatology and Internet harassment among young regular Internet users. *CyberPsychology and Behavior*, 7, 247–257.

Ybarra, M. L., Boyd, D., Korchmaros, J. D., and Oppenheim, J. (2012). Definition and measuring cyberbullying within the larger context of bullying victimization. *Journal of Adolescent Health*, 51, 53–58.

Ybarra, M. L., Diener-West, M., and Leaf, P. J. (2007). Examining the overlap in Internet harassment and school bullying: Implications for school intervention. *Journal of Adolescent Health*, 41, S42–S50.

Ybarra, M. L. and Mitchell, K. J. (2007). Prevalence and frequency of Internet harassment instigation: Implications for adolescent health. *Journal of Adolescent Health*, 41, 189–195.

Yoon, J. S. and Kerber, K. (2003). Bullying: Elementary teachers' attitudes and intervention strategies. *Research in Education*, 69, 27–35.

Zimbardo, P. G. (1969). The human choice: Individuation, reason, and order versus deindividuation, impulse, and chaos. In W. J. Arnold and D. Levine (eds.), *Nebraska Symposium on Motivation, 17*, (pp. 237–307). Lincoln, NE: University of Nebraska Press.

3 Research on bullying in schools in Australasia

Phillip Slee, Keith Sullivan, Vanessa A. Green,
Susie Harcourt and Tegan E. Lynch

In this chapter, consideration is given to the issue of school bullying in the Australasian region, with a principal focus on Australia and New Zealand. Research has been undertaken in other countries in the Australasian region including Singapore, Thailand and Malaysia. The focus on Australia and New Zealand arises principally because of the long history of research and policy development into the topic in these two countries. It is important to note that while Australia and New Zealand might appear to share a good deal in common, there are important political, social, cultural and educational differences. For example, New Zealand has one governing body, which means that the party in power decides policy and practice throughout the country. This is particularly relevant when we consider that in New Zealand schools are self-governing and in relation to bullying, for example, can decide the nature of their policy (including not having a policy) without reference to central government. In contrast, although Australia has a central government, it also has a range of state governments and therefore many more venues for debate and the creation of policy and practice for issues such as school bullying. Another contrast between the two countries is that given its larger population, Australia also has more universities (39 as compared to 8 in New Zealand) from which significant and practical research-led responses have resulted in important contributions both locally and internationally (see Cross et al., 2012, for example). Although New Zealand may seem disadvantaged, having a smaller population-base and an innovative spirit can result in creative, pragmatic and accessible developments, as is often the case in terms of responding face-to-face and in terms of anti-bullying program development.

Australia

Australia is an island continent with a population of just over 23 million, including a current indigenous population estimated at over 400,000.

Since the 1980s, the patterns of immigration to Australia have changed and the diversity of the population has increased. Although most of the population was born in Australia, about one-quarter were born outside (mostly from the United Kingdom, New Zealand, other European countries, Vietnam, China and the Philippines). Some of the older migrant streams, such as people born in Italy, have been declining in absolute numbers.

A brief background to the education system in Australia

Children typically begin school in Reception at around five years of age although many have attended pre-school or kindergarten in the previous year. The primary school years embrace Reception to Year 7 and the secondary school years are from Years 8 to 12. The majority of students attend public schools although in 2013 a sizeable minority (over 35%) attend Catholic and Independent schools.

School bullying: a physically harmful, emotionally hurtful and socially isolating experience.

'*Where Humans Can't Leave and Musn't Complain*'

Where humans can't leave and mustn't complain there some will emerge who enjoy giving pain. Snide universal testing leads them to each one who will shrivel reliably, whom the rest will then shun. Some who might have been chosen, and natural police, do routine hurt, the catcalling, the giving-no-peace…:, Murray (2009), *Killing the Black Dog* (p. 50)

In Australia, the issue of school bullying is a significant concern of educators, students and their caregivers. While bullying at school has long been recognised as existing in Australian literature and poetry (e.g., Blacklock, 1995; Murray, 2009), the empirical study of the phenomenon really did not begin until 1989–90. An interesting question concerns just why school bullying has become the focus of so much research in Australia? Part of the answer is the impetus that early international research (Olweus, 1993; Smith and Sharp, 1994) has given to the Australian research effort. Further momentum arose from the 1994 Federal Government inquiry into violence in Australian schools which concluded that while violence was not a major problem in Australian schools, bullying was. A recommendation of the inquiry was for the development of intervention programs to reduce school bullying. There was also an urgent need for data regarding the extent and nature of the problem in Australian schools and in this regard some advances had already been made by Ken Rigby from the University of South Australia and Phillip Slee from Flinders University.

Traditional or offline bullying

Traditional or offline bullying may be physical, verbal or psychological. In the first national assessment, Rigby and Slee (1999) collated data regarding the extent of being victimised in Australian schools based on research involving approximately 25,500 primary and secondary students from over 60 Catholic, Independent and public schools around Australia. The data was collected using the Peer Relations Questionnaire (PRQ), which was developed by Rigby and Slee in response to teacher's requests for a standardised method for assessing the nature and extent of school bullying. In gathering data anonymously, care was taken to differentiate between bullying in which there was a perceived imbalance of power, and other aggressive acts such as fighting and quarrelling between equals.

Overall, in this first collated Australian database between one in five and one in seven students reported being bullied once a week or more. Self-reported victimization was more frequently reported by younger students, and girls generally reported less victimization than boys. In secondary school the amount of bullying was highest in Years 8 and 9 (students aged approximately 12–14 years of age).

In a later national study Slee (2001) also used the PRQ with 9,889 primary and secondary school students aged 5 to 16 years. Some 5% of students reported that they 'often' (once a week or more) bullied another child either in a group or by themselves; and some 23% of students reported they were victimised (once a week or more). Among both boys and girls, less than 20% saw school as a safe place for vulnerable students. Of the students who were bullied at school, 9% reported that they had truanted and 15% thought about staying away from school. Boys reported that they could 'join in' bullying another child more than girls, and secondary students were more likely to report that they could bully another child than primary school students.

Further Australian research by Owens, Shute and Slee, (2004) provided insight into the nature of girl's aggression and the damaging effects of indirect or relational aggression in peer relationships. Nonverbal behaviours were found to be an important aspect of social aggression, serving functions such as conveying dislike and excluding individuals from peer groups. In another study of adolescent boys' aggression toward girls (Owens, Shute and Slee, 2007), analyses revealed some common and some differing explanations across boys, girls and teachers. All agreed that boys were verbally aggressive to girls to impress other boys and/or for their own entertainment or fun (i.e., to get a laugh). Boys and teachers reported that boys' offensive behaviour to girls was sometimes an attempt to impress girls. However for some boys, the motive for hurting girls was revenge. Some teachers suggested that boys' hurtful behaviour may be explained by sexist attitudes learned at home. This study highlights the vital role of the peer group in motivating boys' aggressive behaviour toward girls.

More recently, the Australian Covert Bullying Prevalence Study (ACBPS) reported that just over one-quarter (27%) of school students aged 8 to 14 years were bullied and 9% bullied others on a frequent basis (every few weeks or more often) (Cross et al., 2009).

The national studies reported here provided valuable insight into the extent and nature of bullying in Australian schools, and a foundation for the development of intervention programs. This paved the way for the introduction of the National Safe Schools Framework (NSSF) discussed later. However, the research also highlighted the plight of those young people who were particularly 'at-risk' for school bullying. For example, in a state wide South Australian study, students with an Autism Spectrum Disorder (ASD), which includes Asperger's syndrome, were found to be more at risk than the general student population (Slee et al., 2013); 62% of students with ASD report being bullied 'once a week or more often', this being significantly higher than the 1 in 6 students of the general school population (Rigby and Slee, 1999).

Cyberbullying: a new manifestation of an old problem!

Researchers in Australia have drawn attention to the emergent forms of cyberbullying. Defined as repeated, harmful interactions which are deliberately offensive, humiliating, threatening and power-assertive, cyberbullying interactions are enacted using electronic equipment, such as cell (mobile) phones or the Internet, by one or more individuals towards another. Cyberbullying can take the form of instant or email messages, images, videos, calls, excluding or preventing someone from being part of a group or an online community (Spears et al., 2012; Cross et al., 2011; Smith and Steffgen, 2012). Furthermore, cyberbullying behaviours can change and assume new forms according to different interactional settings, highlighting both the overt and covert nature of these behaviours (Spears et al., 2008, 2009). For example, the 'happy slapping' phenomenon often targeted the most vulnerable; trolling and flaming in forums and chats are used to disturb and harass; social image is often manipulated and exploited in social networks; while abrupt and violent threats are often made using instant messages or malicious calls.

New understandings regarding definitional issues have arisen as a result of this research. For example, the notion that the act must be 'repeated' is called into question when, as part of cyberbullying, one incident can go viral. Indeed the latest technologies have shifted cyberbullying from computers in rooms, to a totally integrated, mobile platform (Campbell, 2005; Cross et al., 2009; Spears et al., 2008).

'Together, Australia's widespread access and use of ICT, the relatively recent occurrence of negative online behaviours, and a limited understanding of their manifestation and impact creates a 'perfect storm' of online risk for young people' (Cross et al., 2013, p. 223). However, there is some disparity in the findings regarding the frequency of cyberbullying. High figures were reported in a survey of adolescents in a number of countries (including the United States, Canada, United Kingdom as well as Australia), which found that almost 30% reported that they had been victims of online bullying, which was categorised as having been ignored, disrespected, called names, threatened, picked on, or made fun of or having had rumours spread by others (Patchin and Hinduja, 2006). But somewhat lower figures have come from other surveys specifically in Australia.

Data collected from over 7,500 students as part of the Australian Covert Bullying Prevalence Study (ACBPS) suggested that the average level of frequent cyberbullying (every few weeks or more often) across Australia was approximately 7% of students in Years 4 to 9, while 4% reported that they cyberbullied others frequently (Cross et al., 2009).

Campbell et al. (2012) reported data gathered in 2009 from 3112 students from 29 different schools, both government and non-government, in three Australian states. The age range was from 9 to 19 years (mean 14 years). Most students were able to access the Internet from their home (87.5%) and owned their own mobile (cell) phone (83.1%). Students self-reported whether they had been traditionally or cyberbullied, and whether they had traditionally or cyberbullied others, during that school year, by a filter question of yes or no. This resulted in six groups of victims: 16.1% (n = 500) classified as traditional victims only, 4.5% (n = 139) as cybervictims only, 4.5% (n = 140) as both cyber and traditional victims, 4.7% (n = 147) as traditional bully-victims, 1.5% (n = 48) as cyberbully-victims, and 5.4% (n = 169) as both cyber and traditional bully-victims. Overall 8.9% of students reported cyberbullying others; slightly more males than females. There was no significant difference between the ages of those who cyberbullied and those who were not engaged in any type of bullying. The Year 9 students

(13–14 years old) comprised the largest percentage (28.5%) who reported cyberbullying others; but there was no difference in age of those who cyberbullied and those who were not involved in bullying others.

The variations in the frequencies reported in different studies may partly be due to the tendency of some researchers to use definitions of cyberbullying that include all forms of cyber aggression and not just bullying per se. In addition, differences may be produced by some researchers asking global questions such as 'have you ever been cyberbullied?' while others have asked more specific questions, for example, whether a particular act, such as receiving a nasty email, had been experienced, in a particular time interval (Menesini and Nocentini, 2009).

It is important to note that while young people are often considered the masters of the cyber-world (especially the socialising aspects of it), they are the ones that are at greatest risk of being exposed to cyberbullying behaviours. In addition, they are often the ones responsible for engaging in cyberbullying and other inappropriate behaviours. Furthermore, there is evidence that a large proportion of those who engage in cyberbullying behaviours do so against those individuals who are considered friends. Spears et al. (2008, 2009) found that bullying behaviours cycled between school and online (cyber) and back again, suggesting a clear link with existing relationships.

In addition, research evidence is a little conflicting regarding the overlap between those who engage in traditional and cyberbullying, with Campbell et al. (2010) reporting that a large number of those engaged in cyberbullying behaviours or being cyber victimised were not involved in traditional bullying. Furthermore, the impact of cyberbullying on mental health and emotional response is only just beginning to be understood, though it has been posited that it may be greater, possibly due to its 24/7 nature, the anonymity aspects and the broader audience available, not to mention the power that the written and visual electronic media can have (Spears et al., 2008, 2009; Cross et al., 2009; Campbell et al., 2010).

School bullying and mental health in Australian schools

Research in Australian schools has found that both traditional and cyberbullying has harmful mental health outcomes for all those involved. Skrzypiec et al. (2011) reported findings from a study of 1,313 students aged 12–15 years. Pupils in secondary schools completed the Strengths and Difficulties Questionnaire (SDQ; Goodman, 2005) and the Peer Relations Questionnaire (PRQ; Rigby and Slee, 1993). Participants involved in bullying, particularly bully-victims, were more likely to be screened in the 'abnormal range' on the SDQ. Students in the bully-victim group were most likely to have an abnormal total SDQ score, with one-quarter (25.7%) of these students scoring above Goodman's suggested 'abnormal range' cut-off point. About one-third of students (36.7%) in the bully-victim group showed signs of conduct problems. A small proportion of students in the bully-victim group (15.6%) had high Peer Problems scores and over one-third (34.3%) obtained low prosocial scores. Mental health difficulties experienced by victims, bullies and bully-victims varied by gender, with female victims and bully-victims scoring higher on emotional symptoms than their male counterparts.

Campbell et al.'s (2012) study of 3,112 students from grades 6–12 in three Australian states reported the mental health correlates for students bullied by traditional means and those who were cyberbullied. While students reported that traditional bullying was considered to be more harmful, cybervictims reported more social difficulties, anxiety and depression than face-to-face victims.

Overall, the findings from Australian research, along with a raft of international studies, highlight the need for a significant focus on the mental health of all students who are caught up in school bullying.

Summary: Australia

In the Australian context school bullying, including emergent forms of cyberbullying, is an all too frequent aspect of young people's lives and it has a negative impact on the wellbeing of all those involved. Australia is one of the few countries in the world to have in place a national framework, the National Safe Schools Framework (http://bullyingnoway.gov.au/teachers/nssf/), within which to consider the matter of addressing and reducing bullying and enhancing the wellbeing of young people in our schools by providing a safe and secure learning environment. The 'Safe Schools Toolkit' (www.safeschoolshub.edu.au/safe-schools-toolkit/overview) is the latest component of the National Safe Schools Framework developed and designed to further assist schools address the issue of bullying in all its forms.

To continue to provide leadership in this field, it is very important to maintain a focus on evidence-based research to inform anti-bullying practice. Evidence with regard to translational research indicates that schools are a very obvious setting for wellbeing and health promotion activities such as anti-bullying programs, and that teachers can effectively deliver evidence-based programs that make a difference to the wellbeing of young people. In particular, the contemporary issue of cyberbullying is one that requires urgent attention to meet the needs of the young people affected, the families involved and the educational institutions which are at the forefront in addressing the matter at both a policy and practical level.

New Zealand

New Zealand, also known by its Maori name of Aotearoa (land of the long white cloud) is located in Southwest Polynesia. Of its 4.5 million people, 67.6% are European, 14.6% indigenous Maori, 9.2% Asian, 6.9% Pacifika and 2.1% other (some identify with more than one classification). Education in New Zealand is organised as follows: Early Childhood Education (from birth to 5 years); Years 1–8, primary/ intermediate school (ages 5–13 years); Years 9–13, secondary school (ages 13 years+); and Tertiary Education (optional – ages 16 years+).

Similar to its Australian neighbour, bullying is also a significant problem within New Zealand society and there is evidence to suggest that New Zealand schools are failing students and their families in relation to bullying. In particular, when bullying is positioned within the broader context of health and safety and youth suicide, New Zealand continues to perform very poorly. In the OECD's Doing Better for Children report (2009), for 'Comparative policy-focused well-being in 30 OECD countries', New Zealand ranked 29th for 'health and safety', and 24th for 'risk behaviours'. In terms of youth suicide amongst 15- to 19-year-old males and females, of all 30 OECD countries, New Zealand had the highest youth suicide rates for both males and females (20.8 per 100,000 for males, 10.9 per 100,000 for females; the OECD average was 10.2 for males and 3.4 for females). Given the close link between bullying and youth suicide, these are sobering statistics.

The nature of traditional bullying in New Zealand schools

Traditional bullying in New Zealand schools appears to be relatively common. In a recent national survey of 1,236 New Zealand primary and secondary teachers and principals, Green et al. (2013) found that 94% of respondents agreed that bullying did occur in their school, 70% identified social/relational bullying as a problem, 67% verbal bullying and 35% physical bullying. Despite the high recognition of bullying as an issue in schools, a very different picture emerges when teachers were asked how safe they believed their students felt at school. In particular, according to the 2011 TIMSS report (Mullis et al., 2012), teachers indicated that only 1% of Year 4 students and 5% of Year 8 students were in schools that were 'not safe and orderly'. These results suggest that according to teachers in this study, schools are essentially safe places for the vast majority of students.

However a different picture emerges when prevalence rates are reported. It appears that bullying is a particular problem amongst primary school aged children, as evidenced by the 2011 TIMSS report. Countries were ranked from best to worst on a scale of 1 to 50. The results for the New Zealand Year 4 cohorts (8- to 9-years-old) showed New Zealand ranked 46th with 31% of students reporting they had been bullied 'about weekly'; the international average for this age group was 20%. The rate of bullying, however, appears to drop dramatically from primary school to secondary, with 12% of 12- to 13-year-olds reporting being bullied 'about weekly'. Further evidence of a decreasing age-related trend in the prevalence of bullying can be found in two recent large-scale surveys of high school students (13–17 years). The Adolescent Health Research Group (2013) surveyed 8,435 high school students and found that on average 6.2% of students reported being bullied weekly or more often. A similar prevalence rate of 6% was reported by Denny et al. (2015) in a 2007 survey of 9,107 high school students. When specific age groups are assessed, there appears to be a continuation of the downward trend in prevalence across teenage years. The Adolescent Research Group found that approximately 8% of 13- to 14-year-olds reported being bullied weekly or more, compared to 2% of 17-year-olds. Denny and colleagues also found a decreasing trend from 7% of 13-year-olds to 3% of 17-year-olds reporting being bullied weekly or more often. Despite the decrease from primary to secondary school, when these figures are compared to the responses from teachers with regard to school safety, it is evident that many New Zealand teachers are seriously out of touch with the lived experiences of their students.

When less frequent occurrences of bullying are indicated, the prevalence figures increase dramatically. Carroll-Lind and Kearney (2004) found that 63% of 1,480 participants aged 7–17 years reported that they were bullied one or more times in the last year, and 50% were bullied 'once in a while', suggesting that a large number of New Zealand children and young people experience some form of bullying during the school year. Little recent research has been conducted in New Zealand with regard to prevalence of bullying amongst early primary and preschool populations. However, in their survey of teachers and principals, Green et al. (2013) found that the majority of respondents (68%) believed that bullying began before children were 8 years old and 24% believed that it began in preschool (3- to 5-year-olds).

Similar to Australia, bullying behaviours may be more common amongst boys in New Zealand. In a survey of 1,168 students in Years 4–8, Raskauskas et al. (2010) found that boys were more likely to be involved in bullying than girls. The Adolescent Health Research Group (2013) found that of the 6% who reported being bullied weekly or more, female students were less likely to be bullied than male students were. In addition, there was a higher prevalence of bullying others and being bullied in all male schools compared to all girl schools and co-educational schools.

In terms of seeking support when bullied, victims of traditional bullying have been found to tell both peers and adults about being bullied. According to Carroll-Lind and Kearney (2004), of approximately 1,370 students from both primary and secondary schools, 79% of victims told a friend they were being bullied, 38% told a parent or guardian, 17% told no-one, 13% told the duty teacher, 19% told their class teacher and 10% told other school staff. This indicates that victims of bullying do seek support, with some seeking support through multiple avenues.

When asked about the location of bullying, Carroll-Lind and Kearney found that the playground is the most common place in the school, particularly when teachers are not around. Furthermore, it is evident that a considerable number of students stay away from school because of bullying. The Adolescent Health Research Group found 6–7% of 13- to 14-year-old students reported that they had stayed away from school because of bullying at least once in the last month compared to 2% of 17-year-old students. Girls were more likely than boys to stay away from school, with 3.5% of male students and 6.8% of female students indicating they were absent because of bullying 'at least once in the last month'.

The nature of cyberbullying in New Zealand schools

Research in New Zealand has shown that there is a high correlation between traditional bullying and cyberbullying. An early study by Raskauskas (2007) found that most (95%) of text-bullying victims were also victims of traditional bullying. Similarly Marsh et al. (2010) and Jose et al. (2011) found that victims of cyberbullying were also likely to be victims of traditional bullying. In addition, perpetrators of traditional bullying were also likely to be perpetrators of cyberbullying (Jose et al., 2011). In contrast to the higher prevalence of traditional bullying experienced by younger students, Raskauskas (2010) found that students in Years 7 to 9 (aged 10–13) were less likely to be text-bullied than students in Years 10 to 13 (aged 14–18). A probable cause would be less independent access to electronic media amongst younger students. Overall,

Raskauskas (2010) found that 43% of 11- to 18-year-olds reported being text-bullied at least once a year and 23% at least 3 times. This is comparable to the traditional bullying figure of 50% of participants indicating they experienced bullying 'once in a while' (Carroll-Lind and Kearney, 2004).

Findings about gender differences in relation to cyberbullying are variable. NetSafe (2005) reported that 21% of boys and 7% of girls had text-bullied others and that 62% of text-victims were boys. However, in a study by Raskauskas, Carroll-Lind and Kearney (2005) of 96 12- to 16-year-olds, the gender breakdown was reversed. Of the 21% who admitted to text bullying others, 86% were girls. Furthermore, in her study of 565 10- to 13-year-olds, Raskauskas (2007) found 67% of text-bullying victims were girls. But more recently, Marsh et al. (2010) found virtually no differences in the gender of cyberbullies (6.9% of boys; 7% of girls) and Raskauskas (2010) in her study of 1,530 11- to 18-year-olds found no gender differences in the identification of text bully victims.

In terms of seeking support, Green et al. (2013) found cyberbullying was the type of bullying least reported to school staff. Only 14% were informed about cyberbullying at least once a week, and 55% had received no reports in the previous month. Verbal bullying, however, was reported to 47% of teachers and principals at least once a week. Only 14% received no reports of verbal bullying.

When location is considered, Raskauskas and Prochnow (2007, p. 97) found a significant proportion of text-bullying occurring 'outside of school around town', and Raskauskas (2010) suggested up to 87% of text-bullying was received at home.

With regard to the impact of cyberbullying, there is a general consensus amongst school staff and students; 94% of teachers and principals in the Green et al. (2013) study believed that students are affected by cyberbullying. Furthermore, Marsh et al. (2010) found that victims of text bullying were significantly more likely to feel unsafe at school than non-victims and were more likely to have missed school as a result of feeling unsafe. With regard to mental health issues, young people who experienced both traditional and cyberbullying showed more depressive symptoms, low self-esteem and negative affect than those experiencing just one form of bullying (Raskauskas, 2007; 2010; Raskauskas and Prochnow, 2007).

Despite acknowledging cyberbullying as a problem, there is a lack of clarity about who should be responsible for preventing, responding to, and assisting in coping with its effects. This complex issue of responsibility is a key theme in Green et al.'s (2013) research. Although more than 90% of teachers and principals agreed or strongly agreed with

general statements about cyberbullying (i.e., students who are cyberbullied need help to ensure the cyberbullying stops), agreement was less
clear about responsibility for dealing with it. For example, 61%
of respondents agreed or strongly agreed that 'Teachers should help
students to deal with cyberbullying outside of school', but only 41%
agreed or strongly agreed that 'Teachers should do more to prevent
cyberbullying from happening'. Several comments reflected respondents' uncertainty and frustration about the different roles to be played
by adults in assisting students being cyberbullied.

Fenaughty and Harré (2013) also found mixed opinions amongst
young people about who to approach for help dealing with cyberbullying.
They conducted focus groups with 36 pupils aged 13–15 and surveyed
1,673 pupils aged 12–19 about if they had experienced electronic harassment, how they had responded and whether it had been resolved.
Participants answered questions concerning measures of family support,
social self-efficacy and adult help-seeking self-efficacy. Over half of the
participants had used more than one strategy to try to resolve the abuse:
73% ignoring it, 47% confronting the bullies, and 30% seeking social
support from peers. Participants were unlikely to tell parents or other
adults (such as school staff), citing 'concerns of adult overreaction, being
blamed for the problem, and most significantly, having their access to the
technology restricted' (p. 244). Technical solutions, such as changing
online account names, were used infrequently. This is in contrast to the
38% of victims of traditional bullying that indicated they told a parent or
guardian that they were being bullied (Carroll-Lind and Kearney, 2004).

Although just over half of those who had experienced distressing
harassment reported a successful resolution, the only factor predicting
a positive resolution for both Internet and smartphone bullying was
participants' sense of self-efficacy in seeking help from adults, whereas
unassertively informing 'other adults' (e.g., school staff, adult family
members) predicted a negative resolution to the harassment. The
authors suggested that this finding may be explained by a combination
of lack of quality adult support in the sample, and that young people
could manage the challenges of harassment on their own. They concluded: 'a history of support from caregivers and other adults may
produce a young person more able to resolve difficult situations, but that
does not guarantee the adults concerned will be able to help with individual cases of harassment' (Fenaughty and Harré, 2013, p. 248).

It is evident that bullying starts early in a child's school life and affects a
considerable number of primary and secondary school children in
New Zealand. In addition, although traditional bullying does appear to
drop off during the adolescent years, there is some stability with regard

to the prevalence of bullying in New Zealand high schools, with no significant change between 2007 and 2013. Although the vast majority of traditional bullies and victims appear to also be represented in the cyberbullying population, there appear to be some important differences, particularly with regard to gender, age and prevalence. Although it goes without saying that it is the duty of schools to provide a safe environment, it is evident that in the case of cyberbullying the lines of responsibility are not as clear.

School policies on bullying

Given the considerable time, effort and money from a large number of organisations and government departments that has been poured into addressing this issue in New Zealand (see also Chapter 15), it is evident from the TIMSS (2011) reports that New Zealand is continuing to fail a number of its students by not providing a safe school environment. One startling example of this is a series of violent incidents at Hutt Valley High School in 2007. The incidents, and subsequent handling of them, lead to a report by the Ombudsman to the House of Representatives in response to eighteen specific claims against several involved agencies (McGee, 2011). While this case was extreme, it is just one example of the ongoing ineffectiveness of many New Zealand schools to address bullying. It can be argued that this continued failure to provide a safe school environment is due in a large part to out-of-date policies in place in schools. As it is not mandatory for a school to have a bullying policy, it is therefore up to schools to decide how to deal with the problem. The resulting inefficiency has meant that bullying and student safety in general is badly handled and it is, of course, the children and young people who suffer.

A study by Marsh et al. (2011) highlighted the consequences of this independence, with regard to whether or not a school has a distinct anti-bullying policy. They compared the anti-bullying policies of 267 New Zealand schools with 93 schools in Victoria, Australia. All of the Victorian schools had an anti-bullying policy and for the majority of schools, this was not only distinct from other polices but had an emphasis on student engagement. In contrast, 14 New Zealand schools indicated that they had no anti-bullying policy and of the remaining 253 schools, only a third had anti-bullying policies that were distinct from other policies. New Zealand schools also tended to position their anti-bullying policies within behaviour management or discipline policies.

When the content of these policies were compared, overall the Victorian schools had more comprehensive anti-bullying policies than the New Zealand schools. However, both were lacking with regard to definitions and specific mention of bullying in relation to a range of minority groups. In addition, there was little information provided in the majority of policies of both Victorian and New Zealand schools about policy evaluation, follow-up procedures, preventative strategies and whether non-teaching staff has a responsibility to address bullying. Finally, although standard practice was to provide details of anti-bullying policies on Victorian school websites, such policies were rarely indicated on the websites of New Zealand schools (Marsh et al., 2011).

Green et al. (2013) found that 65% of teacher respondents agreed that the development of anti-bullying guidelines should be compulsory for all schools, while 17% were unsure. Furthermore, when these same respondents were asked about training or professional development, just under half indicated they had received any form of training in how to address bullying and for those that had it was out of date and wasn't focused at all on cyberbullying. Combined, these findings suggest that despite the good intentions of many stakeholders, not all schools and their governing bodies are taking the issue seriously enough.

Summary: New Zealand

The Education Act 1988 recently went through a highly contentious review and updating process. A debate raged around whether or not it should be mandatory for all New Zealand schools to have an anti-bullying policy. Contemporary research suggests that school bullying is frequent and detrimental to the health and safety of New Zealand children and that having an anti-bullying policy in every school should be enshrined in the law. This stance was supported by submissions from the powerful teachers and principals associations and by the Ombudsman's Office supported by the highly critical McGee Report (2011) in response to the extreme bullying incidents at Hutt Valley High School. The argument against this, and the stance of the Government, was that the cornerstone of New Zealand schools is that they are self-governing, and to make such a change would go against this principle. Furthermore, they argued that the National Administrative Guideline 5 (NAG5) that requires every school's board of trustees to provide a safe physical and emotional environment for students was an adequate vehicle for addressing school bullying. As a result, anti-bullying policies remain non-compulsory.

The educational policy of self-governance for every school is laudable to a certain extent, but in terms of addressing bullying effectively and safeguarding New Zealand's children against bullying, it is crucial to find a way that both safeguards the autonomy of our schools while also accessing the excellent resources that have been developed to solve the current bullying problem.

Overall summary

School bullying in Australia and New Zealand, including emergent forms of cyberbullying, is an all too frequent aspect of young people's lives and it has a negative impact on the wellbeing of all those involved. Evidence with regard to translational research indicates that schools are a very obvious setting for wellbeing and health promotion activities, and that teachers can effectively deliver evidence-based programs that make a difference to the wellbeing of young people. As noted at the beginning of the chapter, while there are apparent similarities between Australia and New Zealand, there are also significant political, cultural and educational differences, which lead to quite different approaches to addressing the issue of bullying in schools. A number of these different approaches have been highlighted in this chapter. Certainly a common understanding is that bullying is physically harmful, psychologically damaging and socially isolating, impacting on the health and wellbeing of those involved. What the two countries share in common relates to the issue of the new media and the challenges it presents to finding new ways to protect the health and wellbeing of young people. The new media are multimodal (text, image, video and sound), embracing messages, chats, photo albums, blogs and other applications. It is particularly attractive for children and young people and it is reshaping and reframing the presentation and management of young people's identity, lifestyle and social relations. At the same time, it presents new challenges for researchers regarding bullying related issues – definitional, measurement and legal amongst others. These issues present challenges for researchers internationally and are amply highlighted in Smith and Steffgen (2012). Findings regarding action and intervention to reduce bullying and cyberbullying in Australia and New Zealand are summarised in Chapter 15.

REFERENCES

Adolescent Health Research Group. (2013). *Youth'12: The health and wellbeing of secondary school students in New Zealand: Youth'12 prevalence tables.* Auckland: University of Auckland.

Blacklock, D. (1995). *Comet vomit.* Sydney, Australia: Allen and Unwin.

Campbell, M. A. (2005). Cyber bullying: An old problem in a new guise? *Australian Journal of Guidance and Counselling.* 15, 68–76.

Campbell, M. A., Cross, D., Spears, B. and Slee, P. (2010). *Cyberbullying: legal implications for schools*. CSE Occasional Paper, 118. Melbourne: Centre for Strategic Education.

Campbell, M., Spears, B., Slee, P. T., Butler, D. and Kift, S. (2012). Victims' perceptions of traditional and cyberbullying, and the psychosocial correlates of their victimisation. *Emotional and Behavioural Difficulties, 17,* 161–173.

Carroll-Lind, J. (2009). *School safety: An inquiry into the safety of students at school.* Wellington: Office of the Children's Commissioner.

Carroll-Lind, J. and Kearney, A. (2004). Bullying: What do students say? *Kairaranga, 5,* 19–24.

Cross, D., Campbell, M., Slee, P.T., Spears, B. and Barnes, A. (2012). Australian research to encourage school students' positive use of technology to reduce cyberbullying. In P. K. Smith and G. Steffgen (eds.), *Cyberbullying through the new media,* (pp. 222–243). Hove, UK: Psychology Press.

Cross, D., Epstein, M., Hearn, L., Slee, P. T., Shaw, T., Monks, H. and Schwartz, T. (2011). National safe schools framework: Policy and practice to reduce bullying in Australian schools. *International Journal of Behavioural Development, 35,* 398–404.

Cross, D., Shaw, T., Hearn, L., Epstein, M., Monks, H., Lester, L. and Thomas, L. (2009). *Australian covert bullying prevalence study* (ACBPS). Retrieved 4 June 2009, from www.deewr.gov.au/Schooling/ NationalSafeSchools/Pages/research.aspx.

Darlow, N. (2011). *Schools and the right to discipline: A guide for parents and caregivers.* 5th edition. Wellington: Wellington Community Law Centre

Denny, S., Peterson, E. R., Stuart, J., Utter, J., Bullen, P., Fleming, T., Ameratunga, S., Clark, T. and Milfont, T. (2015). Bystander intervention, bullying, and victimization: A multilevel analysis of New Zealand high schools. *Journal of School Violence, 14,* 245–272.

Fenaughty, J. and Harré, N. (2013). Factors associated with young people's successful resolution of distressing electronic harassment. *Computers and Education, 61,* 242–250.

Goodman, R. (2005). Strengths and Difficulties Questionnaire. Retrieved 7 August 2007, from www.sdqinfo.com/questionnaires/austral/aus10.pdf

Green, V. A., Harcourt, S. E., Mattioni, L. and Prior, T. (2013). *Bullying in New Zealand schools: A final report.* Wellington: Victoria University of Wellington.

Jose, P. E., Kljakovic, M., Scheib, E. and Notter, O. (2011). The joint development of traditional bullying and victimization with cyber bullying and victimization in adolescence. *Journal of Research on Adolescence, 22,* 301–309.

Marsh, L., McGee, R., Hemphill, S. A. and Williams, S. (2011). Content analysis of school anti-bullying policies: A comparison between New Zealand and Victoria, Australia. *Health Promotion Journal of Australia, 22,* 172–77.

Marsh, L., McGee, R., Nada-Raja, S. and Williams, S. (2010). Brief report: Text bullying and traditional bullying among New Zealand secondary school students. *Journal of Adolescence, 33,* 237–240.

McGee, D. (Ombudsman) (2011). Complaints arising out of bullying at Hutt Valley High School in December 2007. (*Presented to the House of*

Representatives, 2011). Retrieved 6 November 2015, from www.ombudsman
.parliament.nz/resources-and-publications/latest-reports

Menesini, E. and Nocentini, A. (2009). Cyberbullying definition and
measurement: Some critical considerations. *Zeitschrift für Psychologie/Journal
of Psychology*, 217, 230–232.

Mullis, I. V. S., Martin, M. O., Foy, P. and Arora, A. (2012). *TIMSS 2011
International results in mathematics*. Chestnut Hill, MA., USA: TIMSS and
PIRLS International Study Center, and Amsterdam, The Netherlands:
International Association for the Evaluation of Educational Achievement
(IEA).

Murray, L. (2009). *Killing the black dog*. New York, NY: Farrar, Straus and
Giroux.

Netsafe: The Internet Safety Group. (2005). *The text generation: Mobile phones and
New Zealand youth*. Auckland: Author.

OECD (2009) *Doing better for children: Comparative child well-being across the
OECD*. OECD: Paris.

Olweus D. (1993). *Bullying in schools: What we know and what we can do*. Oxford,
UK: Blackwell.

Owens, L., Shute, R. and Slee, P.T. (2004). 'You just stare at them and give
them daggers': Nonverbal expressions of social aggression in teenage girls.
International Journal of Adolescence and Youth, 10, 353–372.

Owens, L., Shute, R and Slee, P.T (2007). 'They do it just to show off.' Year 9
girls', boys' and their teachers' explanations for boys' aggression to girls.
International Journal of Adolescence and Youth, 13, 343–360.

Patchin, J. W. and Hinduja, S. (2006). Bullies move beyond the schoolyard:
A preliminary look at cyberbullying. *Youth Violence and Juvenile Justice*, 4,
148–169.

Raskauskas, J. (2007). Text bullying among early adolescents. *Kairaranga*, 8,
17–21.

(2010). Text-bullying: Associations with traditional bullying and depression
among New Zealand adolescents. *Journal of School Violence*, 9, 74–97.

Raskauskas, J., Carroll-Lind, J. and Kearney, A. (2005). Text-bullying: Is it
related to relational or verbal aggression? *SET: Research Information for
Teachers*, 3, 7–10.

Raskauskas, J., Gregory, J., Harvey, S. T., Rifshana, F. and Evans, E. (2010).
Bullying among primary school children in New Zealand: relationships
with prosocial behaviour and classroom climate. *Educational Research*,
52, 1–13.

Raskauskas, J. and Prochnow, J. E. (2007). Text-bullying in New Zealand:
A mobile twist on traditional bullying. *New Zealand Annual Review of
Education*, 16, 89–104.

Rigby, K. and Slee, P. T. (1993). Dimensions of interpersonal relations among
Australian children and implications for psychological well-being. *Journal of
Social Psychology*, 133, 33–42.

(1999). Australia. In P. K. Smith, Y. Morita, J. Junger-tas, D. Olweus, R.
Catalano and P. T. Slee (eds.), *The nature of school bullying. A cross-national
perspective* (pp. 324–440). London: Routledge.

Skrzypiec, G., Slee, P. T., Murray-Harvey, R. and Pereira, B. (2011). School bullying by one or more ways: Does it matter and how do students cope? *School Psychology International*, 32, 288–312.

Slee, P. T. (2001). *The P.E.A.C.E. Pack. A program for reducing bullying in our schools*. Adelaide: Flinders University.

Slee, P. T., Bottroff, V., Wotherspoon, A. and Martin, J. (2013). *Aspergers and bullying: An inclusive educational approach*. Adelaide: DVD, Flinders University. Retrieved Dec 3rd 2015 from http://ncab.org.au/aspergersbullying/

Smith, P. K and Sharp, S. (eds.) (1994). *School bullying: Insights and perspectives*. London: Routledge.

Smith, P. K. and Steffgen, G. (2012) (eds.) *Cyberbullying through the new media*. Hove: Psychology Press.

Spears, B. A, Kofoed, J., Bartolo, M. G., Palermiti, A. and Costabile, A. (2012). Positive uses of social networking sites: Youth voice perspectives. In A. Costabile and B. Spears (eds.), *The impact of technology on relationships in educational settings* (pp. 7–21). Routledge: London.

Spears, B. A., Slee, P. T., Owens, L. and Johnson, B. (2008). *Behind the scenes: Insights into the human dimension of covert bullying*. Report prepared for DEEWR: Canberra.

Spears, B., Slee, P., Owens, L. and Johnson, B. (2009). Behind the scenes and screens: Insights into the human dimension of covert and cyberbullying. *Zeitschrift für Psychologie/ Journal of Psychology*, 217, 189–196.

4 Bullying (*Ijime*) and related problems in Japan
History and research

Yuichi Toda

Bullying, or *ijime* in Japanese, has been one of the most problematic phenomena in Japanese schools in the last three decades. *Ijime* has not only affected the wellbeing and mental health of children, but has also led to some suicides. First, this chapter gives a short history of *ijime* as a context; it then explains the nature of *ijime* as a relationship-based problem, which requires interventions into not only individuals but also the quality of the relationship. Major research findings concerning *ijime* are then presented in line with the process of *ijime*; beginning moment, escalation, worst cases and long-term influence. Finally, three aspects of research concerns are discussed: cyberbullying and related problems, the relationship between bullying and school absenteeism, and an integrated understanding of bullying and child abuse.

A short history of *ijime*

The 1980s saw the peak of the Japanese economy in the period after World War II. Though the numbers of severely delinquent behaviours were then decreasing, following a chaotic post-war period, the media in the early 1980s focused on issues such as school violence toward teachers. To maintain order, some of the teachers controlled children by creating an aura of power and punishment, not only verbally but also sometimes physically. This was ineffective in reducing the problems, and growing problematic relationships among pupils were reported by some teachers. The problem was labelled as *ijime*, and some of the earliest books on *ijime* reported the suicide of children (e.g. Kin, 1980).

In 1986, Japanese society was shaken by the news of a suicide of a Japanese eighth-grade boy who had been bullied not only by peers but also by his three teachers. They bullied him, for example, by writing good-bye messages on a card and placing it on the boy's desk with a flower vase in the classroom, which indicated a mock funeral. It was followed by his real one. When he hung himself in the toilet of the department store near the station of his grandparents' prefecture, he had left the names of the perpetrators. The perpetrators were taken to the police and the case was brought to court, where the school was judged guilty.

In subsequent years, the amount of bullying reported by teachers decreased, and the media focus and people's interest turned to school absenteeism. Then most schools changed their policy from controlling pupils to listening to them carefully. However, *ijime* had just changed its visibility, and the second media focus on *ijime* occurred in 1994, when a 14-year-old boy hanged himself (Mainichi-shimbun shakaibu, 1995). It stemmed from crime rather than trouble in school, as the perpetrators had extorted more than one million Japanese Yen from the victim while severely harming him physically, and finally they were arrested. The tremendous efforts made to change schools seemed in vain. Introducing the Sheffield project (Sharp and Smith, 1994), the PEACE pack (Slee, 1996), and other programmes may have had some impact on Japanese schools, but unfortunately perhaps not enough, as a third wave of media focus happened in 2006–7, reporting sequential *ijime* suicides. Most media criticised schools and local educational committees, which created additional stresses for schools and teachers.

After the third media focus, by investigating opinions of responsible officers to supply training for teachers in local educational committees of Japanese prefectures and bigger cities, Sakane and Aoyama (2011) showed that more officials believe *ijime* problems are decreasing rather than 'stable or increasing'. This may influence whether they plan training to tackle school bullying and therefore, training is not supplied for teachers either in every year or at every place.

In short, in the past three decades, Japanese society has experienced three periods of media focus concerning *ijime* suicide at approximately ten-yearly intervals. This seemingly affected the number of presentations concerning *ijime* at the annual conferences of the Japanese Society of Educational Psychology, with three peaks coinciding with each media focus (Toda, 2010).

In 2011–12, an *ijime* suicide case of an eighth-grade boy in Otsu city, located in the Kansai area resulted in media focus and a big social issue. The school and the local educational committee were blamed for not dealing with the bullying incident appropriately and not reporting sufficiently. The blaming escalated and the superintendent of education in the local educational committee was attacked by a university student with a hammer and injured. Reacting to the enormous social concern, in June 2013 the Japanese government put forward an Act to require schools to be prepared for *ijime* incidents, the Bullying Prevention Promotion Act (Ijime Boushi Taisaku Suishin Hou); this was enforced from September 2013 (see Chapter 16 for details).

Some well-known cases of *ijime* suicide focused on by the media in the last three decades are shown in Figure 4.1, with the place and year of the death, and grade and gender of the victim. The places are widespread and the victims were all eighth grade boys except for the Hokkaido case. Regretfully, these are just a part of countless suicide cases.

The nature of *ijime*

The first academic description of *ijime* in English was published by Morita et al. (1999) among other chapters describing situations world-wide. Though the linguistic terms are different, the nature of *ijime* might be considered the same as *bullying*. However, the phenomenon differs due to the culture, history and the other factors. T. Naito and Gielen (2005) describe additionally the specific aspect of *ijime* as it may be interwoven with the collectivistic nature of Japanese society, its educational institutions and its child-rearing methods. They also argue in detail about the definition and frequency and some determinants of *ijime*.

Yoneyama and A. Naito (2003) attribute a major factor of bullying/ *ijime* to school climate (which means the level of bullying/*ijime* depends on each school), but they also argue for the necessity of abolishing the 'homeroom system' in Japan (which implies a common cause across every school). The latter proposition has the same logic and difficulties as saying that we should close the highway to avoid severe traffic accidents. Though such an argument was mostly ignored by *ijime* researchers and practitioners, A. Naito has appeared frequently in the Japanese media and got some enthusiastic supporters.

Ogura et al. (2012) reviewed the problem of *ijime* in Japan from a variety of perspectives. They discuss the existence of various definitions of *ijime* in Japanese and argue that it is necessary to study further the mechanisms and actual state of *ijime* accounting for the flow of the times, and compile research to enable the creation of more effective modes of prevention and intervention.

Ijime *as a disease of the classroom*

The first and most prevalent theory of *ijime* was presented in detail by Morita and Kiyonaga (1987). It was written in a book entitled 'Ijime – disease of the classroom'. Their Four Layer Structure model distinguishes bully, victim, onlooker and bystander, which is similar to the participant role model of Salmivalli (1999). Morita et al. (2001) also reported the results of cross-national research. In comparison with the Netherlands and Britain, fewer Japanese young teenagers answered

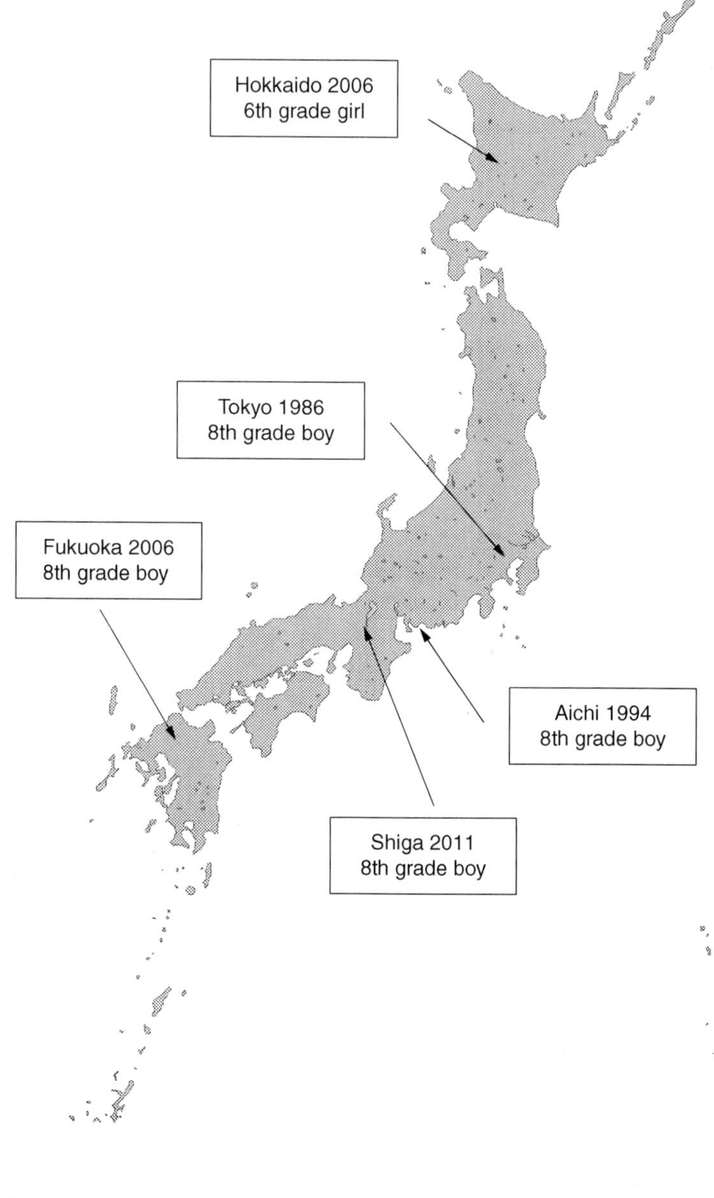

Figure 4.1 *Ijime* suicide and the media focus (prefecture, year and victim)

that they would try to stop bullying, thus this may have contributed to the lack of improvement. Actually, the 1986 suicide case was soon followed by the arrest of another student, due to bullying in the same school. Not only the individual students but also the school as a whole was problematic.

This would be true whether we consider bullying or *ijime*. Salmivalli, Kärnä and Poskiparta (2010, pp. 238, 239) note that there is a 'long research tradition on bullying as a group phenomenon', and 'there is something in individual children, but also something in the classroom context that drives the behaviour of children in bullying incidents'. For both *ijime* and bullying, we should not neglect the group nature of the problem.

In addition to *ijime* in classrooms, *ijime*-like phenomena do also occur in groups for extra-curricular activities. *Shigoki* is a Japanese word for a hard training regime that sometimes accompanies physical aggression toward younger members. *Shigoki* was not rare in extra-curricular activities in schools until some decades ago, but it looks out-of-date nowadays. Recently, *taibatsu*, physical punishment by sports instructors, is under media focus and social concern due to the suicide of a student who killed himself after severe physical punishment by an instructing teacher.

Ijime *as a relationship problem*

The importance of the context has been described by Smith and Sharp (1994, p. 2), pointing out that the nature of bullying is a 'systematic abuse of power'. Power is inevitable for human beings to survive in the world, but its use differs between individuals. Power can be used sometimes for dominating others, and sometimes for supporting others. The former may bring bullying and other problems, while the latter may provide care or empowerment. Pepler (2006) highlights bullying as a relationship problem, which explains why victims do not tell someone with power to stop the victimisation. Children can more readily inform adults or call the police, if the perpetrator is neither a peer nor a family member. In sum, the nature of bullying should be considered as a kind of relational problem due to the systematic abuse of power, which may have similarities with harassment, domestic violence, child abuse, and so forth. This notion was included in the Kandersteg Declaration, which described bullying as 'a form of aggression, involving the abuse of power in relationships' (www.kanderstegdeclaration.com/original-in-english-2007/).

In line with these notions, Toda, Strohmeier and Spiel (2008) depicted the core of bullying and of *ijime* as repetitive aggression in a relationship. 'In a relationship' implies its nature as a relationship problem, while 'repetitive' indicates a high frequency of showing aggression in a certain period of time; this accords with the frequency options for behaviours given in the traditional style of bullying questionnaires (none, seldom, sometimes, often, etc.). Just as typhoon and hurricane are local names for a certain low-pressure weather phenomenon, *ijime*, *bullying*, and so forth. should be local names for repetitive aggression in a relationship among peers. Of course, the local names bring detailed individual nuance in addition to their common meaning, as shown in detail by Smith et al. (2002).

A focus on process

Morita and Kiyonaga (1986) described *ijime* as a group-interaction process, in their definition. A Japanese psychiatrist, Nakai (1997), described three steps of such a process of victimisation, considering retrospectively his own experience of being victimised: isolation, helplessness and invisibility. The isolation begins with targeting to let others know who is marked out to be attacked, followed by spreading propaganda to justify the victimisation; pupils are ultra-sensitive to salient differences of behaviour or appearance. At the second step, the victim is forced to learn helplessness through violence, from which they are not protected, punishment for informing adults and punishment for psychological resistance. Due to this process, the victim comes to look as if they are obeying voluntarily, and the perpetrators have a sense of superiority in maintaining their dominant power. The completion of this process makes the victim surrender simply by being threatened. The last step is invisibility. The victims gradually lose their own pride and dignity. And with the conspiracy of the onlookers, the *ijime* then cannot be recognised. The perpetrators control the victims psychologically, for example, depriving them of their right to speak out against *ijime* by forcing them to join in with *ijime* toward other pupils. In addition, victims' money is wasted in a useless way and/or belongings are easily taken and damaged by the perpetrators, which harms the self-esteem of the victim. The weakened victim cannot escape from the relationship with the perpetrators.

Following such understandings of bullying and *ijime*, Toda et al., (2008) presented a process model of bullying (see Figure 4.2). The model explains the need to distinguish between aggression, bullying and crime. Practically, ignorance of their differences may lead to misunderstandings among parents and teachers, when they talk about bullying-related matters occurring in schools.Academically, the trends of aggression study and bullying study should be integrated using

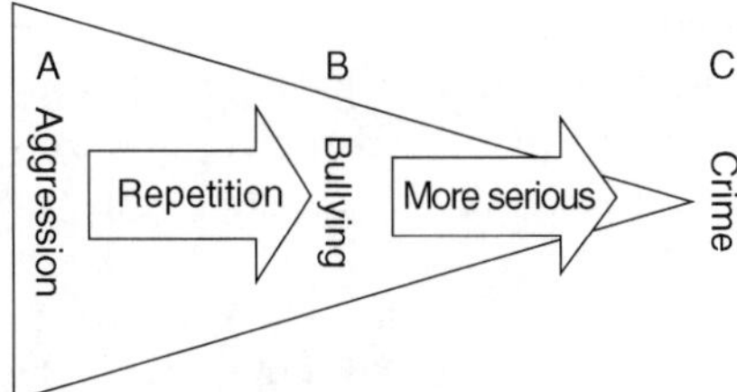

Figure 4.2 Process model of bullying (from Toda, Strohmeier and Spiel, 2008)

such models. However, the spectrum nature of the behaviours will evoke some definitional problems.

Ijime studies in Japan

In reviewing Japanese *ijime*-related studies in the last decades, most of them are focusing on a certain point of the process of the *ijime* phenomenon. They are presented below in line with the process of *ijime*: beginning moment, escalation, worst cases and long-term influence.

Beginning moment of ijime *and related factors*

Concerning the beginning of *ijime*, two kinds of focuses are possible. One is developmental focus and the other is chronological focus.

From a developmental perspective, Hatakeyama and Yamazaki (2003) examined whether preschoolers' aggressive and rejecting behaviours had three properties of bullying: number of assailants, continuation of aggressive and rejecting behaviours, and distress of victims. Four- and five-year-old preschoolers (16 boys and 18 girls) were studied in natural settings over a period of one year, using episode analysis and network analysis. Aggressive and rejecting behaviours towards one girl were observed in 20 episodes, and fulfilled the three properties of bullying.

The behaviour and the difference of roles of young children is conceptualised as a structure by their teachers. Hayashi and Tobin (2011) examined Japanese preschool teachers' beliefs about children's peripheral participation in fights (not *ijime* but probably including *ijime*) in the classroom. This emic perspective showed that Japanese teachers had a cultural vocabulary for conceptualising such peripheral participation, including the terms *gyarari* (gallery), *gaiya* (outfielders), *seken* (the generalized audience) and *mawari no ko* (the children around). They suggest that Japanese preschool teachers believe that in responding to children's fights, their goal should be not only for the protagonists but also for the whole class to have opportunities to experience emotions and to cultivate a sense of collective responsibility for events in their classroom community.

If *ijime* can be seen even from young childhood, why have the media focused mostly on *ijime* suicide incidents in 8th grade boys? To answer this question, we should see the age trends of *ijime* prevalence and suicide ratio separately.

Concerning age trends, M. Toda and Watanabe (2012) investigated 699 Japanese students from 5th to 11th grades, who responded to hypothetical vignettes based on social information processing (SIP) assessments, and found a decrease of hostile attributions and aggressive responses between grades 5 and 11, while evoked negative emotions peaked in grade 7 (1st grade of junior high school). The results indicate that early adolescents tend to have more negative emotions toward a target person than other age groups when they suffer mild harm, even if they understand intellectually that the target person could be blameless.

In the process of age trends, we should also consider the school system (see also Chapter 12). Japanese elementary school begins when children are 6 years old, and junior high school at 12 years old. Hashimoto (1999) depicts a developmental change of *ijime* from types in elementary schools to those of junior high schools. The classification has not been applied to the process of each *ijime* phenomenon but to the change of the *ijime* phenomenon itself alongside the development of children. This suggests the qualitative difference of *ijime* phenomenon, which may explain the problematic nature of *ijime* in junior high schools or in early adolescence.

Kasai (1998) examined the effects of four situational factors related to bullying (*ijime*), that is, the number of attackers, the relationship between the attacker and the attacked, the background of the act and the type of the act, on children's cognition of an incident as *ijime*. In all, 468 primary school students and 318 secondary school students rated the degree to which they agreed that the incidents, each of which was made by combining the four factors, was *ijime*. Three factors affected primary school student's cognition, and all the factors affected secondary school students; there were also some interactions, suggesting that pupils' cognition of *ijime* was affected by a combination of these factors. Although primary school students considered the incidents as *ijime* more often than secondary school students, a particular type of act, neglect, was considered to be *ijime* by secondary school students more often than primary school students.

As for the chronological beginning of the *ijime* process, jokes can be turned into aggression. Hayama and Sakurai (2010) examined a personality factor and situational factors as determinants of listeners' reactions to aversive jokes. Some reactions may evoke more aversive jokes and furthermore bullying.

Ono and Hasegawa (2001) investigated physical stereotypes of victims of *ijime*. Undergraduates were asked to identify *ijime* victims from facial photographs of 49 middle school students. Their judgments were concentrated on a handful of photographs, and one particular photograph was judged to be an *ijime* victim by about 70% of them, which was reported true after the experiment. This may mean that some facial cues are evoking *ijime*, or that the duration of *ijime* will alter the facial appearance to be identified as a victim.

Escalation of ijime

In a school class full of aggressive behaviours, somewhere imbalance of power may emerge and that can be the beginning of bullying. However, without any factors to maintain the aggression and power imbalance, there should be no escalation of violence. That should be also the case for *ijime* in Japan, and researchers have been investigating several factors to affect the escalation. Here, studies on justification of aggressive behaviour, group process and victim's attempts to cope with it, and other factors are summarised.

***Justification*:** Justification is necessary to avoid self-punishment when we commit or continue prohibited behaviours. Bandura (1986) theorised this process as dysfunctional mechanism of self-regulation process and later, Moral Disengagement (e.g., Osofsky, Bandura and Zimbardo, 2005).

As for *ijime*, from questionnaire research on junior high school students, Inoue, Y. Toda and Nakamatsu (1986) elicited three reasoning factors to justify bullying: sanctions, heterogeneity exclusion and enjoyment. Using the same items, Onishi, Kurokawa and Yoshida (2009) found two factors, where heterogeneity exclusion and enjoyment appeared in one factor. Hara (2002) also looked at justifications for bullying among Japanese schoolchildren of 12–14 years old (54 boys and 46 girls). Children with different types of involvement in bullying showed different justification strategies. In particular, bullies were more likely to blame the victims than were children assuming other roles.

Matsumoto, Yamamoto and Hayamizu (2009) focused on the assumed-competence of self, which evaluates own competence exaggeratedly and coincides with the degree of undervaluing others. Participants were 1,062 high school students and both scores of bullying and victimised scales were positively related to their assumed-competence.

Furthermore, Onishi et al. (2012) examined some factors that influenced the justification of bullying among 240 fifth and sixth grade students and 307 seventh to ninth grade students. Results of structural equation modelling demonstrated that narcissistic rage was positively associated with relational aggression (punishment type). Moreover, interpersonal exploitation was related to more relational aggression (self-satisfactory and punishment type); however, guilt feelings toward and perceived classroom norms against relational aggression mediated this association.

Among mechanisms of moral disengagement, 'diffusion of responsibility' brings collective harmfulness without attributing responsibility to a single person. If the number of perpetrators is growing, the process of 'diffusion of responsibility' works more and the violence may escalate.

Group process: The increase of the number of the perpetrators should be explained mainly by conformity. Some studies have looked in detail concerning the process of conformity.

Masataka (1998) explained the process of bullying using the analogy of a nuclear reaction, comparing the acceleration of conformity from a certain point with that of nuclear reaction speed. This may indicate a need to intervene in the scene before the acceleration point. Toda et al., (2008) showed a contingency between group size and frequency of victimisation: when the aggression was not frequent, in half of the cases the number of perpetrators was one or two; on the other hand, when the aggression was frequent, in half of the cases in Austria and 80% of the cases in Japan, the perpetrators were a group (see Chapter 13 for details). Kubota (2004) also showed that the number of assistants of bullying and the kinds of bullying affect the duration of bullying.

Takemura and Takagi (1988) investigated differences of negative attitude toward a deviator and conformity to majority. Their participants, 195 junior high school students, responded to a questionnaire, which measured (a) negative attitude toward a deviator and (b) conformity to the group in various situations. They found that the conformity level of assailants was higher than that of mediators.

Sometimes, the bully-victim relationship is concealed as if it were a close friendship. Mishima (2003) investigated bullying amongst close friends in elementary schools to examine for any relationships between 'bullying among close friends' and their social skills and exclusiveness. More than 400 participants who were 10- to 12-year-olds filled in a questionnaire. Path-analysis was conducted to determine if social skills and exclusiveness might predict victimisation as well as bullying. The path model fitted better for boys than girls. For boys, social skills and exclusiveness showed significant paths to victimisation and bullying; for girls, only exclusiveness was predictive of these factors.

Attempts to cope and other factors: Though justification by perpetrators and group nature of bullying may escalate, victims are not just watching the on-going of tragedy. They try to change, but sometimes in vain. Also, there are some important factors to bring the process to a certain direction.

Kubota (2004) examined whether the coping behaviours of bullied children can provide effective alternatives to bullying. Participants for the questionnaire were 625 pupils in 4th to 6th grade. The results showed that the majority of bullied children take actions to cope with bullying in some way, and there was a close relationship between their coping behaviours and the reasons why the bullying ended up. The coping behaviours of bullied children could bring an opportunity to end bullying, but did not contribute to an early solution to bullying.

However, such coping would not be applied, if the victims did not admit themselves as victims. Takenoyama and Haraoka (2003) compared children's judgements concerning bullying scenarios by the difference of their viewpoint (victim, assailant or bystander), finding that bystanders labelled the situation as bullying more than victims. They suggest that the reason why the victims tended to deny being bullied is to maintain self-esteem by not labelling themselves as victims.

Various psychological factors may be related to the escalation of *ijime*. Kurokawa (2010) explored the relationships between victimisation and psychological stress, peer relationships, and enjoyment of school life. A total of 1,271 junior high school students responded to questionnaires. Seven groups were identified by hierarchical cluster analysis. 'Traditional-indirect victims' reported a lower level of enjoyment of school life and higher levels of irritated-angry affect, depressive-anxious and physical responses than did 'low victims' (victims who experienced relatively low levels of all the subtypes of victimisation). 'Cyber-indirect victims' reported a higher level of depressive-anxious feelings than did 'low victims'. 'Traditional-direct victims' reported a higher level of depressive-anxious feelings, and cognition-thoughts of helplessness than did 'low victims'. 'High victims' (the opposite of 'low-victims') reported higher levels of irritated-angry affect, depressive-anxious feeling, and cognition-thoughts of helplessness than did 'low victims'. 'Internet victims' reported a higher level of depressive-anxious feeling and had fewer friends in their classes than did 'low victims'.

Okayasu and Takayama (2000) investigated the psychological stress of victims and bullies in junior high school, asking about involvement in bully/victim problems, together with a stress response scale, and a school stressor scale. The participants were categorised as 'relational victims', 'relational and overt victims', 'relational bullies', 'relational and overt bullies' and 'other'. 'Relational and overt victims' reported the highest stress symptoms; 'relational victims' showed especially depressive-anxious moods, and both types of victims experienced stressful events most frequently in relation to their academic achievement, and felt that these events were aversive. Most of the 'relational and overt bullies' complained that they had extremely irritable-angry and helpless moods, and they were dissatisfied with their relations with their teachers.

Apart from those studies focusing on escalating factors, Honma (2003) tried to clarify characteristics and factors relating to the cessation of *ijime*, suggesting that intervention with students belonging to 'bullying-maintaining groups' should involve not only individual bullies but also the bullying groups and other classroom members.

Worst cases and long-term influence of ijime

The worst cases of *ijime* in Japan so far should be countless *ijime* suicides, some revenge murders of perpetrators by victims, and a few cases of murder of victims by perpetrators. Mayama (2002) argued that '*ijime* suicide' (or suicide caused by bullying) was 'one of the most serious problems in Japanese primary and secondary schools since the late 1970s'. Though there have been many revenge rampage shootings by ex-victims of bullying in the United States (Larkin, 2013), until 2013, Japanese society has not experienced any rampage shooting case in a school. However, there is no guarantee or reason to say such rampage shooting will never happen in Japan.

Not only prevention and intervention against *ijime*, but also recuperation would be necessary to compensate the damage of victims and to prevent the possibility of a very few but terrible fight-back cases by ex-victims against perpetrators, teachers or schools.

Ishibashi et al. (1999) clarified the lasting effects of past victimisation experiences (being bullied by peers) and its relationship to their tendencies of feeling fear of people among college students. The long-lasting effects were to suffer from various physical, behavioural, social and psychological symptoms. However, those students who regarded themselves as having become more patient by having been bullied did not have stronger tendencies of fearing others. Also, Miyake (2004) suggested a relationship between pre-adolescent bullied experiences with the attachment of college students. Their results suggest that experiences of being bullied can have lasting effects which continue after graduation from high schools.

Mishima (2008) also investigated the long-term influence of bullying received from intimate friends during upper elementary school grades (5th and 6th grades). Among about 2,000 high school students, those who reported victimisation in the questionnaire tended to show subsequent school maladjustment in high school, as well as feeling more anxiety toward interpersonal relationships than others.

Some studies have focussed on buffering effects of recuperation. Kameda and Sagara (2011) examined the factors that enhanced the sense of self-growth among ex-victims, giving a semi-structured interview to seventeen young adults. They found that a supportive relationship might help in the recuperation of victims. In addition to support from others, victim's own initiative to cope with the negative experience appeared to be important to have a feeling of self-growth.

As for personal factors that buffer the negative effects of victimisation, Araki (2005) investigated whether resilience contributes to victims' adjustment in young adulthood. Participants for the questionnaire research were 301 Japanese young adults (mean age = about 20 years). Compared with non-victimised controls, young adults who were peer-victimised during childhood had more distress and anxiety, although no difference was found in the levels of exposure to current interpersonal stressful events. The distress and anxiety were stronger for men than women, and the starting age of victimisation made no difference in the problems. Both problem-focused and support-seeking coping as a protective factor had a compensatory effect for long-term negative outcomes of victimisation by peers during childhood.

Important research concerns

Among various related issues, three aspects of research concerning *ijime* are discussed: cyberbullying and related problems, relationship between bullying and school absenteeism, and integrated understanding of bullying and child abuse.

Cyberbullying and related problems

In recent years, cyberbullying and related problems (Internet addiction, inadequate use of the Internet, etc.) have become among the most concerned topics in Japan as in other countries. In particular, the smartphone is now a new gateway to cyber-problems (Takeuchi et al., 2012).

Takeuchi et al. (2012) distinguished Internet problems into Internet delinquency and risky behaviour. Among Internet delinquency is forcible obstruction of business, insulting someone, defamation, threatening and unauthorised access to the Internet. Risky behaviour via the Internet includes GAME: spending much money in online game, PRIVACY: disclosure of personal information to the Internet, NIGHT: staying up late at night doing online game and so forth, and DEAI-KEI: introduction to adults with evil intent. Cyberbullying itself is problematic; however, it may be related to other problems, based on the frequent and free use of the Internet.

As for the prevalence of cyberbullying in Japan, Utsumi (2010) reported that among 487 students at 5 middle schools, 67% of regular Internet users were not involved in cyberbullying; 8% were cyberbullies; 7% cybervictims, and 18% cyberbully-victims. As those who were bullies and/or victims showed longer use of the Internet than non-involved students, this tendency may be related with the Internet addiction. In addition, Utsumi (2010) investigated whether parental controls were associated with youth's Internet-related behaviour. Although perceived parental controls did not directly predict cyberbullying, parental regulation was an indirect predictor of the students' Internet use, and both parental knowledge and free access were direct predictors of Internet use. Both Internet use and relational aggression were found to be direct predictors of cyberbullying and being cyber-bullied.

Ono and Saito (2008) depicted three aspects of the nature of cyberbullying: anonymity, wide-audience and accessibility. The anonymity may be due to the difficulty of tracing the perpetrating tracks by ordinary people, which may conceal the identity of the bullies. Wide-audience refers to gathering audience to the bulletin board system (BBS) with bullying writings, and accessibility is due to the borderless and wide spreading of the derogation and that victims are not able to escape this even after coming back home.

Relationship between bullying and school absenteeism

In Japanese schools, besides school bullying, the problem of most concern is school absenteeism (sometimes named 'school refusal'). It is also associated with *ijime* (Ogura et al., 2012). T. Naito and Gielen (2005) depicted *ijime* and school refusal as 'twin problems'.

The Japanese Ministry of Education, Culture, Sports, Science and Technology asks schools to report the number of school absenteeism by counting the days a child is absent. If a child is absent from school for more than 30 days per school year, it is considered to be school absenteeism. Among various reasons of school absenteeism, not only being the victim of bullying but also witnessing the bullying should be considered. Some western researches have reported depression of both victims and perpetrators (Kaltiala-Heino et al., 1999; Kaltiala-Heino et al., Roland, 2002; 2000; Brunstein et al., 2007), and also depression among pupils who witness bullying (Rivers et al., 2009). A similar psychological process might be happening for some pupils who are absent from schools in Japan.

Kawabata (2001) described two cases of *ijime* and school refusal. The two related cases were of junior high school students (aged 13 and 14 years), both of whom suffered from *ijime* and started refusing to attend school. *Ijime* in these cases did not take the form of exclusion, though consequently they were apart from schools and peers. Kano and Arisaka (2006) reported that 15 cases among 65 school absenteeism children (7–15 years old) related to *ijime* and some of them showed a high level of stress response. In comparison to the accumulation of case studies concerning bullying and school absenteeism, there are few research results on this topic.

As Sutton, Smith, and Swettenham (1999) showed in England, ring-leaders of *ijime* also should be coldly reading the other's mind and mostly finding fun with other's distress. On the other hand, some pupils who are absent from schools are much more emotionally empathic than others and probably cannot stand the situation where *ijime* happens daily. If this explains the situation in Japanese classrooms, not only individual traits but also classroom ethos could be problematic. The classroom where cold mind reading works well to get power will be controlled by the ringleader of *ijime* and may exclude emotionally empathic pupils. Peer support practice could give a positive role to those who are emotionally empathic with others but could not find a way to utilise their trait.

Integrated understanding of bullying and child abuse

As recent arguments suggest, we should consider bullying-like problems in different contexts. Especially, child abuse at home should be an important issue to be concerned about (Meyer, 2008; Monks and Coyne, 2011).

The SIP study by M. Toda and Watanabe (2012) suggested that negatively distorted SIP could be related to undesirable family inter-actions rather than to school life. Though this result may be plausible due to the bigger diversity of family backgrounds rather than that of school, we should not underestimate the influence of school life.

Sugawara et al. (2003) focused on the relationship between dating violence, bullying at school and family-of-origin violence. Among 166 Japanese college students, about 77% reported the use of psychological aggression and 40% have used some forms of minor or severe physical abuse. A positive relationship was found between psychological and physical aggression in dating relationships and bullying experiences. Experiences of parental aggression at home including witnessing parental arguing and fighting were also associated with psychological and physical aggression in dating relationships.

Inosaki and Nosaka (2010) examined perpetrations of bullying/dating violence among 352 boys and 385 girls aged 12–16. They found that such perpetrations were positively related to the experience of being abused by adults and of being victimised by peers. However, the relations were complex according to the subtype of perpetration/victimisation.

Such results imply not only the existence of victimised perpetrators but also the existence of poly-victims (Finkelhor et al., 2011) who are victimised in various contexts. If child abuse at home is related to victimisation in school, intervention against child abuse may help prevent such poly-victimisation. However, usually Japanese school teachers are not trained in the area of social welfare, and their knowledge on child abuse is not sufficient. For any future prevention scheme which covers family-originated violence and school bullying together, trainee-teachers should be informed concerning family-related problems.

Future directions

Japanese researches on *ijime* have been conducted widely and for a considerable time, but they are not sufficient and have drawbacks. Some of these drawbacks are a lack of research on *ijime* with participants aged 7–10 years, a lack of longitudinal studies of *ijime* and over-reliance on using self-report questionnaires. Concerning the long-term influence of *ijime*, case studies have been dominant, but no meta-synthesis study has appeared yet. A challenge to the next generation of researchers is to cover these lacks and contribute to the decreasing of *ijime* problems and prevention of related suicides of children.

REFERENCES

Araki, T. (2005). Resilience in a personal history of peer victimization : What factors contribute to victims' adjustment in young adulthood? *Japanese Journal of Personality*, 14, 54–68 (in Japanese).

Bandura, A. (1986). *Social foundations of thought and action: A social cognitive theory*. Englewood Cliffs, NJ: Prentice-Hall.

Brunstein-Klomek, A., Marrocco, F., Kleinman, M., Schonfeld, I. S. and Gould, M. S. (2007). Bullying, depression, and suicidality in adolescents. *Journal of the American Academy of Child and Adolescent Psychiatry*, 46, 40–49.

Finkelhor, D., Turner, D., Hamby, S. and Ormrod, R. (2011). Polyvictimization: Children's exposure to multiple types of violence, crime, and abuse. *Juvenile Justice Bulletin*, US Department of Justice. www.ncjrs .gov/pdffiles1/ojjdp/235504.pdf

Hara, H. (2002). Justifications for bullying among Japanese schoolchildren. *Asian Journal of Social Psychology*, 5, 197–204.

Hashimoto, S. (1999). The dynamic process in 'ijime' situations: Focusing on the bystanders. *Journal of Educational Sociology*, 64, 123–142 (in Japanese).

Hatakeyama, M. and Yamazaki, A. (2003). Bullying in early childhood: Preschooler aggression, rejection behaviors, and teacher intervention. *Japanese Journal of Developmental Psychology*, 14, 284–293 (in Japanese).

Hayama, D. and Sakurai, S. (2010). Rejection sensitivity and situational factors as determinants of listeners' reactions to aversive jokes. *Japanese Journal of Educational Psychology*, 58, 393–403 (in Japanese).

Hayashi, A. and Tobin, J. (2011). The Japanese preschool's pedagogy of peripheral participation. *Ethos*, 39, 139–164.

Honma, T. (2003). Cessation of bullying and intervention with bullies: Junior High School students. *Japanese Journal of Educational Psychology*, 51, 390–400 (in Japanese).

Inosaki, A. and Nosaka, S. (2010). Perpetration experience of bullying and dating DV among junior high and high school students: victimisation, allowance for violence, and narcissism. *Japanese Association for Sex Education Proceedings*, 22, 40–51 (in Japanese).

Inoue, K., Toda, Y. and Nakamatsu, M. (1986). Roles in bullying situation. *Bulletin of the Faculty of Education, University of Tokyo*, 26, 89–106 (in Japanese).

Ishibashi, S., Wakabayashi, S., Naito, T. and Shikano, T. (1999). An investigation of the lasting effects of peer victimization in college students: Relationship to anthropophobic tendencies. *Bulletin of Christian Culture Studies, Kinjo Gakuin University*, 3, 11–19 (in Japanese).

Kaltiala-Heino, R., Rimpel, M., Marttunen, M., Rimpel, A. and Rantanen, P. (1999). Bullying, depression, and suicidal ideation in Finnish adolescents: School survey. *British Medical Journal*, 319, 348–351.

Kaltiala-Heino, R., Rimpel, M., Rantanen, P. and Rimpel, A. (2000). Bullying at school: An indicator of adolescents at risk for mental disorders. *Journal of Adolescence*, 23, 661–674.

Kameda, H. and Sagara, J. (2011). Effect of past bullied experiences and factors that help develop feelings of self-growth: Examination of the development process involving past bullied experiences and the current awareness of self-growth. *Japanese Journal of Counseling Science*, 44, 277–287 (in Japanese).

Kano, K. and Arisaka, O. (2006). Clinical application of the Stress Barometer in the field of pediatrics. *Dokkyo Journal of Medical Sciences*, 33, 249–254 (in Japanese).

Kasai, T. (1998). Cognition of bullying (ijime) by primary and secondary school pupils. *Japanese Journal of Educational Psychology*, 46, 77–85 (in Japanese).

Kawabata, N. (2001). Adolescent trauma in Japanese schools: Two case studies of Ijime (bullying) and school refusal. *Journal of the American Academy of Psychoanalysis*, 29, 85–103.

Kin, S. (1980). *Boku mou gaman dekinai yo: Aru 'ijimerarekko' no jisatsu [I cannot stand any more: Suicide of an ijime victim]*. Tokyo: Ikkoh-sha (in Japanese).

Kubota, M. (2004). Can the coping behaviors of bullied children provide effective alternatives to bullying? Attempts to modify the stigmatic labels given by gangs of bullies. *Journal of Educational Sociology*, 74, 249–268 (in Japanese).

Kurokawa, M. (2010). Relationships between victimization and psychological stress, peer relationships, and enjoyment of school life: Traditional and cyber bullying. *Japanese Journal of Counseling Science*, 43, 171–181 (in Japanese).

Larkin, R. W. (2013). Legitimated adolescent violence: Lessons from Columbine. In N. Böckler, T. Seeger, P. Sitzer and W. Heitmeyer (Eds.), *School shootings: International research, case studies, and concepts for prevention* (pp. 159–176). New York, US: Springer Science + Business Media.

Mainichi-shimbun shakaibu (1995). *Souryoku shuzai 'ijime' jiken [Team reports on the ijime incident]*. Tokyo: Mainichi-shimbun sha.

Masataka, N. (1998). *Ijime wo yurusu shinri (Psychology on allowing bullying)*. Tokyo: Iwanami Shoten (in Japanese).

Matsumoto, M., Yamamoto, M. and Hayamizu, T. (2009). Relation between assumed competence and bullying in High School students. *Japanese Journal of Educational Psychology*, 57, 432–441 (in Japanese).

Mayama, H. (2002). Discourse analysis as conceptual study: Toward the dismantling of ijime suicide. *Journal of Educational Sociology*, 70, 145–163 (in Japanese).

Meyer, E. J. (2008). Gendered harassment in secondary schools: Understanding teachers' (non) interventions. *Gender and Education*, 20, 555–570.

Mishima, K. (2008). Long-term influence of 'bullying' received from intimate friends during upper elementary school grades: Focusing on retrospect of high school students. *Japanese Journal of Experimental Social Psychology*, 47, 91–104 (in Japanese).

(2003). Bullying amongst close friends in elementary school. *Japanese Journal of Social Psychology*, 19, 41–50 (in Japanese).

Miyake, K. (2004). Adult attachment and victimization of bullying. *Journal of Kyushu University of Health and Welfare*, 5, 1–10 (in Japanese).

Monks, C. P. and Coyne, I. (Eds.) (2011). *Bullying in different contexts*. Cambridge: Cambridge University Press.

Morita, Y. and Kiyonaga K. (1986). *Ijime: Kyousitsu no yamai [Ijime: The disease of the classroom]*. Tokyo: Kaneko Shobo (in Japanese).

Morita, Y., Soeda, H., Soeda, K. and Taki, M. (1999). Japan. In P. K. Smith, Y. Morita, J., Junger-Tas, D. Olweus, R. Catalano and P. Slee (Eds.), *The nature of school bullying: A cross-national perspective* (pp. 309–323). London: Routledge.

Morita, Y., Soeda, H., Taki, M., Hoshino, K., Takemura, K., Matsu'ura, Y., Hata, M. Yonezato, S., Takekawa, I. and Soeda, K. (2001). *Cross-national studies on bullying*. Tokyo: Kaneko Shobo (in Japanese).

Naito, T. and Gielen, U. P. (2005). Bullying and ijime in Japanese schools: A sociocultural perspective. In F. L. Denmark, H. H. Krauss, R. W. Wesner, E. Midlarsky and U. P. Gielen (Eds.), *Violence in schools: Cross-national and cross-cultural perspectives.* (pp. 169–190). New York, NY, US: Springer Science + Business Media; US.

Nakai, H. (1997). *Ariadone kara no ito [Ariadne's thread]*. Tokyo: Misuzu Shobo.

Ogura, M., Okada, K., Hamada, S., Asaga, R. and Honjo, S. (2012). Ijime in Japan. *International Journal of Adolescent Medicine and Health*, 24, 69–76.

Okayasu, T. and Takayama, I. (2000). Psychological stress of victims and bullies in junior high school. *Japanese Journal of Educational Psychology*, 48, 410–421 (in Japanese).

Onishi, A., Kawabata, Y., Kurokawa, M. and Yoshida, T. (2012). A mediating model of relational aggression, narcissistic orientations, guilt feelings, and perceived classroom norms. *School Psychology International*, 33, 367–390.

Onishi, A., Kurokawa, M. and Yoshida, T. (2009). Influences of students' teacher recognition on abuse. *Japanese Journal of Educational Psychology*, 57, 324–335 (in Japanese).

Ono, A. and Saito, F. (2008). Educational psychological review about understanding and coping with cyber bullying. *Journal of Senri Kinran University*, 5, 35–47 (in Japanese).

Ono, T. and Hasegawa, Y. (2001). Physical stereotypes of ijime victims. *Japanese Journal of Experimental Social Psychology*, 40, 87–94 (in Japanese).

Osofsky, M. J., Bandura, A. and Zimbardo, P. G. (2005). The role of moral disengagement in the execution process. *Law and Human Behavior*, 29, 371–393.

Pepler, D. J. (2006). Bullying interventions: A binocular perspective. *Journal of the Canadian Academy of Child and Adolescent Psychiatry*, 15, 16–20.

Rivers, I., Poteat, V.P., Noret, N., and Ashurst, N. (2009). Observing bullying at school: The mental health implications of witness status. *School Psychology Quarterly*, 24, 211–223.

Roland, E. (2002). Bullying, depressive symptoms and suicidal thoughts. *Educational Research*, 44, 55–67.

Sakane, K. and Aoyama, I. (2011). Perceived prevalence of bullying incidents, teachers' training, and regional differences: Based on the survey from school districts. *The Japanese Journal of the Study of Guidance and Counseling*, 10, 47–56 (in Japanese).

Salmivalli, C. (1999). Participant role approach to school bullying: Implications for interventions. *Journal of Adolescence*, 22, 453–459.

Salmivalli, C., Kärnä, A. and Poskiparta, E. (2010). Development, evaluation, and diffusion of a national anti-bullying program, KiVa. In B. Doll, W. Pfohl and J. Yoon (Eds.) *Handbook of youth prevention science* (pp. 238–252). New York: Routledge.

Slee, P. T. (1996). The P.E.A.C.E. Pack: a programme for reducing bullying in our schools. *Australian Journal of Guidance and Counselling*, 6, 63–69.

Smith, P. K., Cowie, H., Olafsson, R. F., Liefooghe, A. P. D. et al. (2002). Definitions of bullying: A comparison of terms used, and age and gender differences, in a fourteen-country international comparison. *Child Development*, 73, 1119–1133.

Smith, P. K. and Sharp, S. (Eds.) (1994). *School bullying: Insights and perspectives*. London: Routledge.

Sugawara, Y., Katsurada, E., Sibata, S. and Terui, N. (2003). Dating violence, bullying at school and family-of-origin violence among Japanese college students. *Bulletin of the Center for Educational Research and Practice, Faculty of Education and Human Studies, Akita University*, 25, 83–87 (in Japanese).

Sutton, J., Smith, P. K. and Swettenham, J. (1999). Social cognition and bullying: Social inadequacy or skilled manipulation? *British Journal of Developmental Psychology*, 17, 435–450.

Takemura, K. and Takagi, O. (1988). Psychological factors of ijime phenomenon: Negative attitude toward deviant and conformity to majority. *Japanese Journal of Educational Psychology*, 36, 57–62 (in Japanese).

Takenoyama, K. and Haraoka, K. (2003). The comparison among the bullying judgements on the viewpoints when imagining a bullying situation. *Kurume University Psychological Research*, 2, 49–62 (in Japanese).

Takeuchi, K., Kanayama, K., Ogiso, M., Minemoto, K. and Toda, Y. (2012). Smartphone as a new gateway to cyberbullying and related problems: Collaborative views on problems and interventions by experts in Japan. *Joint Conference COST Action IS0801 on Cyberbullying, Austrian Federal Ministry for Education, the Arts and Culture, Vienna, Austria*, 19 October, 2012.

Toda, M. and Watanabe, K. (2012). Social information processing and development of interpretative and reactive behavior toward ambiguous attacks. *Japanese Journal of Developmental Psychology*, 23, 214–223 (in Japanese).

Toda, Y. (2010). Review of research trends on the development of school-age and adolescence and perspectives on ijime study. *Annual Report of Educational Psychology in Japan*, 49, 55–66 (in Japanese).

Toda, Y., Strohmeier, D. and Spiel, C. (2008). Hito wo oitsumeru ijime (Process model of bullying). In T. Katoh and H. Taniguchi (Eds.), *Taijin kankei no da'aku saido [Darkside of interpersonal relationships]* (pp.117–131). Kyoto: Kitaohji-Shobo (in Japanese).

Utsumi, S. (2010). Cyberbullying among middle-school students: Association with children's perception of parental control and relational aggression. *Japanese Journal of Educational Psychology*, 58, 12–22 (in Japanese).

Yoneyama, S. and Naito, A. (2003). Problems with the Paradigm: the school as a factor in understanding bullying (with special reference to Japan). *British Journal of Sociology of Education*, 24, 315–330.

5   The Korean research tradition on *wang-ta*

Keumjoo Kwak and Seung-ha Lee

Research about bullying in South Korea has increased rapidly since the late 1990s. A main factor in this was the alarm caused by a pupil committing suicide in 1996 after being bullied (see the following text). There were only a few studies about bullying before this. The number of studies about bullying increased greatly from the late 1990s to the early 2000s, and have remained steady or shown a little increase over the last ten years.

Recently, bullying in South Korea has become a national issue again, as three pupils consecutively committed suicide in 2011 after serious victimisation in their schools. On 6 February 2012, the South Korean Prime Minister announced countermeasures for eradication of *hakkyo-pokryuk* (school violence) and appealed to the people to consider *hakkyo-pokryuk* as a crime that will be treated seriously if it occurs.

Research on bullying in South Korea has been mainly conducted in four areas: prevalence, related factors, prevention programs, and perception of or attitudes towards bullying. A large number of studies on bullying have been conducted quantitatively using anonymous questionnaires, and a few studies have been conducted qualitatively to investigate the process or perception of bullying. This chapter introduces the concept of Korean bullying and explains its characteristics.

History of terms for bullying

In 1996, one high school pupil who had a heart disease committed suicide because of group harassment towards him over a period of one year. The Korean mass media called it *Korean ijime*, *gipdan-hakdae* (group abuse), or *gipdan-gorophim* (group harassment). Since then, phenomena similar to *ijime* in Japan have been an important social issue. The term *wang-ta* was introduced to the public in 1997 by a South Korean newspaper (*Dong-a ilbo*, 1997) when bullying became a serious social issue after the pupil's death. The report introduced several slang terms used by school pupils, and *wang-ta* was one of those; *wang-ta* was explained as being an abbreviation of the term *wang-ttadolim* (exclusion).

Wang is both a noun and a prefix meaning 'king' or 'big', and *ta* is a short version of *ttadolim* (isolation) or *tadolida* (to isolate). Thus, *wang-ta* means severe exclusion or an excluded person.

In 1999, the government recommended the use of the term *gipdan-ttadolim* (group isolation) and discouraged the term *wang-ta*; some scholars in South Korea suggested that the term *wang-ta* had negative connotations for the victimised person and meant that these behaviours would be taken less seriously (No et al., 1999).

Several terms have been used interchangeably for bullying-like phenomena; however, there are some differences among these terms. *Gipdan-ttadolim* (group isolation) and *gipdan-gorophim* (group harassment) imply group behaviours (rather than one-to-one), and *hakkyo-pokryuk* includes a wide range of hostile and violent behaviours which happen among pupils, within or around schools, such as physical attack, name calling, *gipdan-ttadolim*, extortion of money and sexual abuse. In addition, *hakkyo-pokryuk* is the term that has been most commonly used among studies in South Korea to indicate aggressive behaviour, corresponding to violence or bullying in western cultures. In spite of the government recommendations for usage of the terms, H. Koo (2005) reported that Korean pupils used *wang-ta* rather than other terms to describe bullying-like behaviours.

The meaning of wang-ta

B. Y. Koo (1997) defined *gipdan-ttadolim* or *wang-ta* as meaning verbal and physical behaviours which aim to ignore or attack one person or group of people by excluding them from a group, and which is carried out by more than two people. Kwon (1999) defined *wang-ta* as 'an excluding behaviour or an excluded person, it accompanies physical and verbal *gorophim* (harassment). An imbalance of power exists between aggressor(s) and victim(s) and the excluding process occurs constantly and repeatedly by negative labeling of the person in public' (p.62; translated from original Korean). He emphasised that a distinctive feature of *wang-ta* compared to *ijime* is stigmatization by public labeling.

No et al. (1999) emphasised the collective aspects of *wang-ta*; it is a phenomenon in which a whole class or most pupils in a class engage in excluding one or more pupils. It is intentional *gorophim*, which happens consistently and repeatedly. No (2001) suggested that *wang-ta* does not only simply mean teasing or harassing, but also ignoring a person's being. According to him, in Western *bullying* a person is being bullied when he/she is consistently exposed to aggressive behaviours, whereas a person is being *wang-ta* when all or majority of pupils in the class are engaged in the exclusion and therefore he/she does not have friends at all. Similarly, S-H. Lee (2011) reported that Korean school pupils aged 10–17 labeled group aggressive behavior as *wang-ta*: they used *wang-ta* to describe situations of social isolation first, followed by group physical aggression, and rumour spreading.

Some empirical findings

Prevalence

Depending on the terms used, as well as other factors, different prevalence rates of being bullied have been reported. Y. Kim and Park (1997), who used the term *ttadolim*, found a high incidence (30%). G. Park, Son and Song (1998) found up to 56% of pupils experiencing being a victim of *hakkyo-pokryuk*. This may have resulted from the types of behaviour or severity included in the study. Y. Kim and Park (1997) only included isolating or excluding behaviour but G. Park, Son and Song (1998) included a wider range of aggressive behaviour.

H. Koo, Kwak and Smith (2008) investigated 2,926 11- to16-year-olds using the term *wang-ta*; they modified the Olweus bullying questionnaire and found there were more aggressors than victims. Ten per cent of the pupils did *wang-ta* once in a month or more, 7% once or twice in a month and 3% once a week or several times a week; and 6% received it once in a month or more, 3% once or twice in a month and 3% once a week or several times a week. Therefore, half of the victims were bullied chronically during one academic term.

The Foundation for Preventing Youth Violence (FPYV) has been conducting annual surveys to investigate the incidence of *hakkyo-pokryuk* since 2006. They used self-report questionnaires administered to 5th and 6th grades (10–11 years) in elementary school, middle (12–14 years) and high school pupils (15–17 years), and asked about their experiences of *hakkyo-pokryuk* during the last year. This annual survey provides comprehensive information about *hakkyo-pokryuk* and has been particularly useful in tracking changes in its incidence. Table 5.1 shows the percentage of pupils who have experienced *hakkyo-pokryuk* from 2006 to 2010, based on samples of around 4,000 pupils at each time point.

FPYV used the term *hakkyo-pokryuk* and included verbal aggression, physical aggression, extorting money, *gipdan-gorophim* (*gipdan-ttadolim* and *wang-ta* were mentioned together with this), sexual abuse, joining gang and cyber aggression. The percentage of victims has decreased from 2006 until 2009, but then increased again; the percentage of aggressors has fluctuated up and down.

Table 5.1 *Percentage of pupils who experienced* hakkyo-pokryuk *in the last year, from Foundation for Preventing Youth Violence (FPYV) reports.*

Year of investigation	2006	2007	2008	2009	2010	2011	2012
Doing *hakkyo-pokryuk*	12.6	15.1	8.5	12.4	11.8	18.3	12.6
Receiving *hakkyo-pokryuk*	17.3	16.2	10.5	9.4	11.4	15.7	12.0

Table 5.2 *Percentage of cases of receiving* hakkyo-pokryuk *by type of behavior (FPYV, 2006; 2008)*

Type of *hakkyo-pokryuk*	2006	2007
Verbal (insulting, swearing)	24.4	21.5
Physical (hit)	22.6	24.6
Extortion (extorted money or belongings)	19.6	16.3
Ttadolim (isolated, ignored by one or more than one pupil)	7.1	8.6
Gorophim (forced errands or 'what I don't want to do')	11.7	7.2
Cyber (received a nasty or threatening email, texts or video-recorded in insulted way)	4.6	6.1
Sexual (received unwanted physical or sexual contact)	0	2.9
Threaten (e.g., 'I will hit you', 'Bring me money')	9.2	9.3
Other ways	0.8	3.5
Total	100	100

Regarding repetition of the behaviour, 54% of victims reported that they received *hakkyo-pokryuk* for less than two weeks, 16% of pupils reported that their victimisation lasted two weeks to three months, 16% of victims for three months to six months, and 14% for more than six months (FPYV, 2012). Thus, nearly half of victims experienced prolonged victimisation.

Table 5.2 shows the percentage of cases in which pupils received *hakkyo-pokryuk* in 2006 and 2007, by type of behaviour. Verbal and physical victimisation was most common, followed by extortion and threatening and *ttadolim* and *gorophim*. There were relative increases in physical aggression, *ttadolim,* cyber aggression and sexual harassment between the two years.

Age differences

FPYV (2008) specified the decrease in incidence by each grade. Table 5.3 shows the prevalence in each grade. After first grade in middle school,

Table 5.3 *Percentage of pupils doing/receiving* hakkyo-pokryuk *(from once to a lot of times) (FPYV, 2008).*

	Doing *hakkyo-pokryuk*	Receiving *hakkyo-pokryuk*
Fifth grade in elementary (10–11 years old)	20.1	22.0
Sixth grade in elementary (11–12 years old)	20.2	25.1
First grade in middle school (12–13 years old)	20.2	21.7
Second grade in middle school (13–14 years old)	14.1	18.2
Third grade in middle school (14–15 years old)	15.2	15.2
First grade in high school (15–16 years old)	8.2	6.5
Second grade in high school (16–17 years old)	9.7	7.0

the incidence of doing *hakkyo-pokryk* decreased; and in high school, the incidence of doing *hakkyo-pokryuk* was half of the level found in upper grades in elementary school. Victimisation (receiving *hakkyo-pokryuk*) decreased after first year in middle school and in high school years it decreased to one-third of the incidence reported in elementary school years.

Characteristics

Gender differences in victim/bully

Victims. Girls are usually more likely than boys to be victimised. Y. Kim and Park (1997) reported that girls (32%) were more likely to receive *ttadolim* than boys (26%). C. Lee and Kwak (2000) reported the gender difference by level of schools; female victims were more common in elementary school but there were more male victims in middle school. However, FPYV (2013) reported that boys (14%) were more likely than girls (11%) to receive *hakkyo-pokryuk*. Also, H. Koo et al. (2008) showed that more boys than girls had experience of being *wang-ta*. H. Park et al. (2006) showed that the gender differences may depend on the type of aggression investigated: they found that girls more often experienced social, relational victimisation than boys; physical victimisation happened more among boys than girls. FPYV (2013) showed that boys largely received 'hit' followed by 'verbally threatened' and 'extortion', while girls mainly received 'verbally abused', *gipdan-ttadolim* and 'verbally threatened' (see Table 5.4). Regardless of the type of *hakkyo-pokryuk*

Table 5.4 *Percentage of types of victims of* hakkyo-pokryuk *by gender (FPYV, 2013)*

Type of *hakkyo-pokryuk*	Boy	Girl
Hit	27.6	7.2
Extortion	8.8	6.4
Verbally threatened	15.4	12.1
Verbally abused or insulted	22.7	32.6
Gorophim	14.8	11.3
Gipdan-Ttadolim (group isolation)	6.4	19.4
Cyber abuse	2.4	6.8
Sexual abuse	1.9	4.3

that pupils received, they were often upset by it; 69% of girl victims and 61% of boy victims responded that they were distressed. Girls seemed to be more distressed than boys by *hakkyo-pokryuk* (FPYV, 2012).

Bullies. Boys are usually more likely than girls to be bullies: 0.7 % of boys responded that they bullied numerous times ('more than 6 times') compared to 0.4% of girls (FPYV, 2013). Moreover, 73% of boys responded that they 'never bullied' compared to 82% of girls (FPYV, 2012). Other research confirms boys more often being bullies (Nho and Lee, 2003). Boys tended to bully others using physical aggression, verbal abuse and *gorophim* whereas girls often bullied others through verbal abuse using *gipdan-ttadolim* and *gorophim* (FPYV, 2013). Similarly, among 5th and 6th graders, girls (12%) did *gipdan-ttadolim* (group isolation) more than boys (7%) (J. Park and Chae, 2011). This is partly consistent with some Western studies (Salmivalli and Kaukiainen, 2004; Scheithauer et al., 2006); if girls are aggressive, they tend to use indirect or relational aggression rather than direct or physical aggression.

The number of aggressors

The number of aggressors has often been investigated in South Korean studies. This may reflect the group characteristic of bullying behaviour in South Korea. H. Koo et al. (2008) reported that in elementary school, 34% of victims reported that they received *wang-ta* from more than 10 pupils, 47% of victims from 3 to 5 pupils and only 19% from just 1 pupil. FPYV reported an increase over time in the percentage of victims who reported being victimised by a group of aggressors (see Table 5.5). The number of pupils who are victimised by more than two pupils has tended to increase, from about 55% in 2006 to 70% in 2012

Table 5.5 *Percentage of victims who received* hakkyo-pokryuk *from more than two pupils, from Foundation for Preventing Youth Violence (FPYV) reports.*

Year of investigation	2006	2007	2008	2009	2010	2011	2012
Percentage	54.9	59.5	69.1	68.0	66.2	68.0	70.0

(FPYV, 2012, 2013). This suggests that the power imbalance between bully and victim is increasing, which may imply that a target child receives more severe aggressive behaviour.

Who bullied whom?

Studies have consistently reported that the majority of victims were victimised by classmates (FPYV, 2008, 2010, 2011; C. Lee and Kwak, 2000; Yang 2009). C. Lee and Kwak (2000) reported that 56% of victims received *gipdan-ttadolim* by classmates, 19% by other peers in the same grade and only 3% received it from older pupils. Similarly, FPYV (2008) reported that 46% of victims received *hakkyo-pokryuk* by classmates, 19% by different class in the same grade, 14% from different grade and 9% by other school pupils. Most *hakkyo-pokryuk* or *ttadolim* happened among pupils they knew, especially pupils in the same class.

Level of isolation

Korean pupils differentiate levels of isolation. They have made terms adding *ta* at the end of a word, related to meaning of isolation. The words keep being created and then may drop out of use again. For example, *eun-ta* means a victim isolated implicitly and only for few occasions, so the victim is often not aware of his/her victimisation, but other people may perceive the person was *eun-ta*. Another example is *jun-ta*. This means very severe victimisation: victimised by a whole school (*jun* means whole or completely) (H. Koo, 2005). This may reflect that the isolating phenomena themselves have evolved over time, as well as the terms used (S-H. Lee, Smith and Monks, 2012). It further suggests the need for intervention specifically to target this social isolation.

Perceptions of bullying

FPYV (2008) asked for pupils' perceptions of the reason for doing *hakkyo-pokryuk* ('why do you think some pupils do *hakkyo-pokryuk* to

Table 5.6 *Percentage of perceived reasons for doing/receiving* hakkyo-pokryuk *by school level (FPYV, 2008).*

School level (ages)	Reasons for doing *hakkyo-pokryuk*			Reasons for receiving *hakkyo-pokryuk*		
	No reason	For fun	Conflict	No reason	Aggressors look down on others	Victims are selfish
Elementary (11–12 years)	21	37	22	17	33	14
Middle (13–15 years)	31	40	16	22	40	8
High (16–18 years)	25	47	18	20	40	8

others?'). The majority of answers were 'for fun' (41%) or 'no reason' (27%). Table 5.6 shows this data, differentiated by school level. Many pupils responded 'for fun' across all school levels, but especially among older pupils. For the reason for receiving *hakkyo-pokryuk* ('why do you think some pupils receive *hakkyo-pokryuk*?'), there was an age decline in thinking of victims as selfish, and an age increase in aggressors looking down on others.

Blaming the victim

Y. Kim and Park (1997) found that attributional responsibility for *ttadolim* [isolation] differed by bullying/victimisation experiences. More than 83% of pupils who did or who witnessed *ttadolim* attributed the behaviour to the victims (i.e., she/he deserved it). Similarly, C. Lee and Kwak (2000) reported arrogance, selfishness and appearance of victim as reason for victimisation. In contrast, 42% of victims reported they did not know the reason, 27% of victims reported the reason is that they had no friend to protect them and 23% reported other pupils thought them as weak. S-H. Lee et al., (2011) also reported negative attitudes toward a victim: Korean pupils often viewed a victim as an abnormal, inept or maladjusted person, and this is the reason why the person is victimised. Given the findings across these studies, pupils' perception of victims seems often to be negative rather than empathising with him/her.

This blaming the victim attitude may be explained by group conformity. Some studies suggest pupils' conformity as a reason for *wang-ta* occurring (B. Y. Koo, 1997; H-K. Lee and Hong, 2002). H-K. Lee and Hong (2002) examined beliefs and rules which may lead pupils to make one person *wang-ta* among middle school pupils in Seoul. They found that perceived rules (i.e., 'Other pupils think that *wang-ta* deserves the victimisation') were more influential than personal attitudes towards *wang-ta* ('if I do *wang-ta*, I would feel guilty') in predicting doing *wang-ta*. This association was stronger among pupils who did *wang-ta* than pupils who did not. According to their study, perceived group value surpasses personal moral value in engaging in *wang-ta* behaviour, thus *wang-ta* behaviour needs to be viewed from the perspective of group conformity.

When they bully others

When bullies were asked 'what do you think of your *hakkyo-pokryuk* behaviour?' (FPYV, 2012), half of them (51%) said they felt sorry for the victim, and 29% admitted that they should have controlled their compulsive behaviour, whereas 21% reported it as justifiable behaviour or had no idea about this. Thus many of the bullies recognised it was wrong, but one-fifth did not show any responsibility about their behaviour. However, the perspective on bullying behaviour depended on the frequency of bullying behaviour; the more pupils bully others, the more they think of their bullying behaviours as justifiable, and the less they feel sorry for the victim (FPYV, 2012). When pupils who had previously done *hakkyo-pokryuk* were asked reasons for why they had stopped bullying, the highest response (65%) was 'because I realized that it was an unjustifiable behaviour' followed by 'because I got told off by my teacher' (12%), 'because I got told off by the parent of victimized student' (5%), and 'because my thoughts have changed after attending school violence prevention program' (3%) (FPYV, 2012).

When they are victimised

According to the FPYV (2010), the majority of victims (64%) did not report the incident or ask for help from others; only 36% of victims asked for help. Of those who did ask for help, 41% asked for help from their parents and 36% from teachers; victims tend to ask for help from parents and teachers rather than other pupils. These results are consistent with that of E. Lee (2007), and of FPYV (2008) which reported that students tend to ask for help from their parents. When the victims were asked for reasons for not asking for help, the highest response was 'because I thought the situation will get worse' (26%), followed by 'because I thought it is no use telling others about being bullied' (21%), and 'because I thought bullies will retaliate' (18%) (FPYV, 2012).

When they witness victimisation

According to the FPYV studies, pupils seem to be becoming more indifferent to bullying. Many pupils who witness bullying ignore it, the most frequent responses being 'as if nothing happened' or 'just watching'; this was 35% in 2007, rising to 57% in 2009 and 62% in 2011. Some pupils said that they intervened to stop it themselves or informed parents, teachers or police officers about it; these were 13% in 2007, 36% in 2009 and 31% in 2011.

The reason why pupils who witnessed bullying did not act to stop bullying was most often 'fear of being victimised' (28%) and 'indifference' (25%). Also, bullying or victimisation experiences were related to ignoring bullying behaviour when witnessed. Pupils who had victim experience were more likely to respond that 'intervention will not make a difference'. On the other hand, the more bullying experience a pupil had, the more they showed indifference toward the victim's situation. When the pupils were asked whether ignoring behaviour when they witness bullying is *hakkyo-pokryuk*, 56% of pupils replied 'I don't know', or 'no, it is not *hakkyo-pokryuk*'. Only 44% considered the situation as *hakkyo-pokryuk*. Therefore, many pupils do not recognise passive bystanding (i.e., ignoring) behaviour as *hakkyo-pokryuk*.

What they think about prevention

E. Lee (2007) investigated perceptions of important methods of preventing *hakkyo-pokryuk* among 4th, 5th, and 6th graders. Thirty-six per cent responded that 'recognizing and advising isolated or maladjusted students' was the most important, while 13% responded 'increase in parent and child conversation', 11% 'watching video for *hakkyo-pokryuk* prevention program in the beginning of semester', and 11% 'educating *hakkyo-pokryuk* prevention program quarterly in the class'. Pupils tended to think that the school plays an essential role for preventing *hakkyo-pokryuk*. When the pupils were asked which organisation/institution they think is striving to prevent *hakkyo-pokryuk*, 30% of students responded 'school', 20% said 'youth-related organisations' and 15% said 'home' (E. Lee, 2007). For the effectiveness of a prevention program for *hakkyo-pokryuk*, 32% replied 'it was helpful', 32% 'average', but 36% responded 'it was not helpful'. Thus, modifying or developing models for more practical *hakkyo-pokryuk* programs (FPYV, 2012) are very much needed.

Factors related to bullying involvement

Individual factors

Victims. A study on middle school students by H. Kim and Lee (2000) reported that victims of *gipdan-gorophim* (group harassment) had lower self-esteem than non-involved controls. Moreover, the victims were more distressed about interpersonal relationships than the bullies. Another study on middle school students by Jun (2008) showed that the self-concept (physical, moral, personality, social and general) of victims of *gipdan-ttadolim* (group isolation) was significantly lower than that of bullies. S. Lee (2006) studied personalities of middle school students who received *hakkyo-pokryuk*, and showed that victims often had sensitive and timid personality. J. Park and Chae's (2011) study on 5th and 6th graders showed that victims of *gipdan-ttadolim* (group isolation) tended to score poorly on communication and problem solving skills.

Bullies. Reporting on middle school students who had done *gipdan-gorophim* (group harassment) to others, H. Kim and Lee (2000) found that they had lower self-esteem than non-involved controls, although still higher than victims (see above). Also, these children doing *gipdan-gorophim* had lower empathy in interpersonal relationships than controls or victims. J. Park and Chae (2011) found that in 5th and 6th graders, those with more experience of doing *gipdan-gorophim* tended to score poorly on communication and problem solving skills. This result, however, is similar to that for victims (J. Park and Chae, 2011), with both victims and bullies having poor communication and problem solving skills.

Bullies' personality characteristics were also examined among middle school pupils, by H. Shin (2006). The probability of being in the bullying group became higher as anger level became higher. Also, according to S. Lee (2006), bullies were often (38%) characterised by an impulse-defiant personality type.

Bullies who are exposed to family trouble and dissatisfaction have tended to spend more time outside and relieve the dissatisfaction by bullying others with their friends, which reinforces and ascertains cohesiveness of their own group. Choi and Kim (2003) showed that family, moral and social self-concepts were significant predictors for doing *gipdan-ttadolim* (group isolation) among middle school pupils. Nho and Lee (2003) found that internal locus of control had a significant negative correlation with doing *hakkyo-pokryuk*. On the other hand, students who had a positive perception on school life had a lower level of doing *hakkyo-pokryuk*.

Bully-Victims. H. Kim and Lee (2000) found that bully-victims (those who were both bullies and victims) showed higher aggressiveness than those who were just bullies. Also, H. Shin (2006) found that youths having positive attitudes toward aggressiveness tended to be bullies and bully-victims. H. Kim and Lee (2000) found that the self-esteem of the bully-victims was even lower than that of the victims. Yom's (2011) study on adolescents found that the self-esteem of bully-victims partially mediated between self-control and externalising problems (e.g., aggressiveness); thus, self-control indirectly influenced externalising problems through self-esteem and also it directly affected the externalising problems.

Home environment factors

Victims. A child's attachment to his or her parent has been found to be related to victimisation. S. Kim (2007) found that a child's chance of being a victim of *hakkyo-pokryuk* was related to weaker attachment, low parental monitoring and conflicting family atmosphere. B. Lee's (2007) study on middle school students showed that coercive parenting behaviour significantly affected the students' experience of being a victim. Specifically, father's warm attitude was negatively correlated with 5th and 6th graders' experience of being a victim, whereas father's aggressive attitude, ignoring attitude and denial attitude were positively correlated with the child's experience of being a victim of *gipdan-ttadolim* (group isolation) (J. Park and Chae, 2011). In addition, mother's warm attitude, aggressive attitude, ignorance attitude and denial attitude all correlated with the children's experience as victims (J. Park and Chae, 2011).

Bullies. Similar to the relation between victim and parental attachment above, a child's attachment to his or her parent was related to the chance of being a bully of *hakkyo-pokryuk*. S. Kim (2007) found that when parental monitoring was low, and family atmosphere was conflicting, a child was more likely to be a bully. J. Park and Chae (2011) found that warm parenting behaviour was negatively correlated with 5th and 6th grader students' experience of doing *gipdan-ttadolim* (group isolation), and the father's denying parenting behaviour was positively correlated with the children's experience of bullying. Moreover, the mother's aggressive parenting behaviour, ignoring attitude and denying behaviour were positively correlated with the children's bullying experience. B. Lee (2007) showed that non-intervention parenting behaviour significantly increased middle school students' experience of doing *hakkyo-pokryuk*.

In addition to parenting behaviour, the parents' socio-economic status was another important factor; S. Lee (2006) found that students in low socio-economic status families tended to bully other students whose parents had a high socio-economic status. Moreover, Nho and Lee (2003) showed that middle school students who had experience of being abused by both their father and mother did more *hakkyo-pokryuk* than non-abused controls.

Bully-Victims. H. Kim and Lee (2000) found that bully-victims of *gipdan-gorophim* (group harassment) were more likely than victims or bullies to experience family violence. H. Shin (2006) showed that the more adolescents experienced parental violence, the more likely they were to be a bully-victim; the probability of being a bully-victim was significantly higher than that of being a bully or victim, which suggests that parental violence can be a factor differentiating bully-victims from other groups.

J-H. Shin et al. (2014) examined relationships between roles in bullying (aggressor, victim, aggressor-victim, uninvolved) and inter-parental conflict and parenting behaviour. They found more significant differences from self-report, than from peer report data. In peer reports, the bullying-involved subgroups were not very much different from each other, but did differ from the uninvolved group. From self-report, inter-parental conflict was higher in victims than in uninvolved pupils; maternal rejection and maternal neglect were higher in victims, aggressors and aggressor-victims, but the three groups were not different from each other in maternal rejection. In contrast, aggressors, victims and aggressor-victims were not different from uninvolved pupils in maternal overprotection and maternal affectionate/accepting behaviour; this is inconsistent with previous western studies (Bowers, Smith and Binney, 1994; Georgiou, 2008) in which victims tended to experience parents' overprotection.

School and peer factors

Victims. Concerning school factors, S. Kim (2007) found that elementary school students tended to receive *hakkyo-pokryuk* when they had high study pressure, low academic achievement and weak attachment to their teachers; as for peer factors, the more they contacted delinquent peers and the less they were attached to their friends, the more they received *hakkyo-pokryuk*. Similarly, H. Shin (2006) showed that middle school students have a high probability of being a victim when they have low academic achievement and were isolated in the peer group.

Bullies. Similar to the victims of *hakkyo-pokryuk*, S. Kim (2007) found that elementary school students had more bullying experience when they had higher study pressure, lower academic achievement and weaker attachment to the teachers. However, among middle school students, bullies were less satisfied with school life compared to non-involved pupils, suggesting that school dissatisfaction was expressed though maladjustment and bullying behaviours in/around school. Lastly, in adolescents, H. Shin (2006) found that being rejected by peers increased the probability of being a bully-victim.

Social and cultural factors

Victims. S. Lee (2006) reported that middle school students who were being *kakkyo-pokryuk* were more likely than non-bullies to be exposed to a harmful social environment where video arcades, pubs or karaoke bars are around. Moreover, victims were more likely than those having no experience of being bullied to imitate violent media than those who had suggesting that exposure to violent media could be one of the factors increasing the likelihood of being a victim. S. Kim's (2005) study indicated that vertical collectivism (i.e., a cultural belief emphasising hierarchical order, fidelity, obedience and submission) negatively predicted victimisation in young people.

Bullies. S. Lee (2006) reported that youths having had bullying experience were more exposed to harmful social environment around the house and school, and they also showed more imitation of violent media, than students having no experience of bullying. In another study, H. Kim and Lee (2000) found that bullies and bully-victims were more exposed to violent media than non-involved controls. C-H. Lee and Song (2009) demonstrated that levels of collectivism and social disorganisation negatively affected school climate, which in turn increased bullying behaviour.

Relative effects of related factors

Victims. S. Kim (2007) examined the relative effects of factors influencing children's victimisation of *hakkyo-pokryuk*. Five such factors in order of importance were having a delinquent peer, followed by attachment to friends, conflicting home atmosphere, study pressure and gender. J. Park and Chae (2011) showed that father's aggressive parenting behaviour was the greatest influencing factor for being a victim of *gipdan-ttadolim* (group isolation), followed by (all negatively) children's problem solving skills, communication skills, and father's warm parenting behaviour. D. Shin (2012) examined factors influencing children's experience of being a victim of *wang-ta* (*ttadolim* through insulting and ignoring) and found that children's defensive attitude, negative self-conception and inferiority were influencing factors. As for adolescents, H. Kim and Lee (2000) showed that harmful environment around schools, teachers' violence, one's self-esteem, teachers' support, fathers' jobs and peers' support predicted youths' experience of receiving *gipdan-gorophim* (group harassment). Among those six factors, the teachers' support was the greatest influencing factor, but interestingly, the more youths received the teachers' support, the more they received *gipdan-gorophim* (group harassment).

Bullies. The most influential factor for bullying varied in different studies. H. Kim and Lee (2000) found that aggressiveness and grades/school years were the most influential factors among seven variables (e.g., peer group's violence, aggressiveness, family violence, grades, media violence, father's job and harmful environment around school). J. Park and Chae (2011) showed that children's analytical communication skills was the most influential factor for bullying, and mother's denying parenting behaviour was the second most influential factor. D. Shin (2012) examined children doing *wang-ta* and showed that general antisocial behaviour was most influential, followed by aggressiveness, desire for controlling and emotional disorders. Nho and Lee (2003) reported that the most influential factor for youths' doing *hakkyo-pokryuk* was gender; boys did more *hakkyo-pokryuk* than girls. The next most influential factors were experience of being abused by father and by mother, followed by the youths' perception of school life.

Hwang, Shin and Park (2006) reported that individual and peer factors greatly influenced the youths' doing *hakkyo-pokryuk*, whereas family and school factors were less influential on bullying behaviour. They indicated that the relationship with parent and family conflict (family factors) indirectly influenced the youth's bullying behaviour through the youths' impulsiveness (an individual factor); and also that teachers' punishment and perception of school (school factors) indirectly influenced the youth's doing *hakkyo-pokryuk* through the youths' contact with delinquent peer (peer factors).

Conclusions

Bullying-like behaviour in South Korea has been investigated using several terms. The term *wang-ta* reflects some group aspects of bullying in South Korea (S-H. Lee et al., 2012). *Wang-ta* is used informally to describe bullying among pupils, especially those socially isolated by a group of pupils; and the term *hakkyo-pokryuk* tends to be used to indicate pupils' aggressive behaviour occurring in/around schools. Recent studies about bullying are more likely to use the term *hakkyo-pokryuk* than other terms, perhaps because bullying behaviour in school has become more diverse. For example, cyber aggression using mobile text and online message is increasing in recent years (Tippett and Kwak, 2012). Physical and verbal forms have been the most common types of *hakkyo-pokryuk* and group isolation was common particularly among girls.

An age decrease in prevalence of bullying, and gender differences in types of bullying, are consistent with western studies (e.g., Björkqvist, Lagerspetz and Kaukiainen, 1992; Smith, Madsen and Moody, 1999; and see Chapters 1, 2 and 3). However, the greater ratio of bullies to victim, an emphasis on isolating one person and sophisticated levels of isolation in bullying are different characteristics from those found in western studies. Collectivistic cultural characteristics of South Korea may be related to this. Although some studies provide negative correlations between collectivism and bullying (e.g., Georgiou et al., 2013; S. Kim, 2005), other studies showed positive relationships between them (e.g., C-H. Lee and Song, 2009; Nesdale and Naito, 2005).

In-group membership plays an important role for an individual to identify him- or herself, and reinforces a tendency to modify one's behaviour to fit the perceived in-group norms. However, the extent to which people identify themselves with a group may differ across cultures (Nesdale and Naito, 2005). Creation of positive in-group norms may be very influential in a collectivistic culture such as South Korea in which collective ostracism such as *wang-ta* is performed.

An important issue to consider in order to decrease bullying in South Korea is to change general pupils' perceptions. Pupils who bully, but also even non-bullies tend to think that bullying behaviour has been done for fun and that victims deserve it. Korean pupils are becoming indifferent to bullying and justifying bullying behaviour. Many victims tend not to ask for help, and many pupils who witness a bullying situation say that they have ignored it. There is a strong need for prevention programs which emphasise empathy and moral responsibility, together with educating bystanders that ignoring *hakkyo-pokryuk* can be considered as another kind of violence.

Individual, home, school and peer, and social and cultural factors have been examined in relation to *hakkyo-pokryuk*, *gipdan-ttadolim*, *gipdan-gorophim* or *wang-ta*. Those influential factors and relative effects were different across victim, bully and bully-victim groups. However, both victims and bullies have some similar influential factors such as poor communication and problem solving skills and high study pressure, low

academic achievement and weak attachment to the teachers. It is necessary to consider these factors thoroughly when developing prevention or
treatment programs and counselling victims and bullies effectively.

In sum, this chapter has reviewed the history of research on South
Korean bullying, and findings about its characteristics, prevalence and
related factors. The previous and recent South Korean studies have
suggested a need for persistent efforts by government, community,
school and home for reducing the incidence of *hakkyo-pokryuk*.
Throughout these efforts and future studies, various methods or practical
models should be provided for preventing Korean bullying.

REFERENCES

Björkqvist, K., Lagerspetz, K. M. and Kaukiainen, A. (1992). Do girls
  manipulate and boys fight? Developmental trends in regard to direct and
  indirect aggression. *Aggressive Behavior*, 18, 117–127.
Bowers, L., Smith, P.K. and Binney, V. (1994). Perceived family relationships of
  bullies, victims, and bully/victims in middle childhood. *Journal of Social and
  Personal Relationship*, 11, 215–232.
Choi, Y. and Kim, A. (2003). A study on middle school students' bullying
  behaviors in relations to self-concept and attribution style. *The Korean
  Journal of Educational Psychology*, 17, 149–166.
Dong-a ilbo (1997). 80% middle school pupils use slang, 52% use habitually.
  March 26th. Retrieved 10 November 2015, from http://news.donga.com/3/
  all/19970326/7242621/1.
FPYV (Foundation for Preventing Youth Violence) (2006). *2006 The national
  survey of hakkyo-pokryuk in Korea.* Seoul: Foundation for Preventing Youth
  Violence.
  (2008). *2007 The national survey on the state of school violence.* Seoul: Foundation
  for Preventing Youth Violence.
  (2010). *2009 The national survey report on school violence in Korea.* Seoul:
  Foundation for Preventing Youth Violence.
  (2011). *2010 Summary report of the national survey of school violence.* Retrieved
  10 November 2015, from www.edujikim.com/customercenter/board/
  default/view_b.asp?intBbsSeq=8&Page=1&intArticleSeq=8234.
  (2012). *2011 The national research on school violence.* Seoul: Foundation for
  Preventing Youth Violence.
  (2013). *2012 The national research of school violence.* Seoul: Foundation for
  Preventing Youth Violence.
Georgiou, S. N. (2008). Bullying and victimization at school: The role of
  mothers. *British Journal of Educational Psychology*, 78, 109–125.
Georgiou, S. N., Fousiani, K., Michaelides, M. and Stavrinides, P. (2013).
  Cultural value orientation and authoritarian parenting as parameters of
  bullying and victimisation at school. *International Journal of Psychology*, 48,
  69–78.

Hwang, H., Shin, J. and Park, H. (2006). The path analysis among selected eco-systemic factors on the school violence of Korean early adolescents. *Journal of Korean Council for Children's Rights*, 10, 497–526.

Jun, M. (2008). The comparison between the self-conception of group-bullying students and that of victimized students according to the subject of recognition. *Journal of Counseling Psychology*, 8, 71–89.

Kim, H. and Lee, H. (2000). Social and psychological variables affecting the behaviors of bullies and victims of school bullying. *Korean Journal of Social and Personality Psychology*, 14, 45–64.

Kim, S. (2005). Psychological and social factors influencing bullying and victim tendencies. *Korean Journal of Counseling*, 6, 359–371.

(2007). A study on the relationships among family, school, peers-related variables, and school violence. *Korean Journal of Youth Studies*, 14, 101–126.

Kim, Y. and Park, H. (1997). *Pupils who do ttadolim and pupils who received ttadolim*. Seoul: Youth Communication Plaza.

Koo, B. Y. (1997). Reason of gipdan-ttadolim in youths and instructions for prevention. *Korean Youth Counselling Institute, 29*, Seoul: Youth Communication Plaza.

Koo, H. (2005). *The nature of school bullying in South Korea*. Unpublished PhD thesis. London: Goldsmiths, University of London.

Koo, H., Kwak, K. and Smith, P. K. (2008). Victimisation in Korean schools: The nature, incidence and distinctive features of Korean bullying or wang-ta. *Journal of School Violence*, 7, 119–139.

Kwon, J. M. (1999). Conceptualization of wangtta in Korea and methodological review of wangtta researches. *Korean Journal of Psychology: Social Issues*, 5, 59–72.

Lee, B. (2007). The effects of parenting behavior on self-esteem, aggression, school violence experience, violence tolerance as perceived by adolescence. *Journal of School Social Work*, 13, 25–50.

Lee, C. and Kwak, K. (2000). *Gipdan-ttadolim at school: An actual condition and characteristics*. Seoul: Gipmoondang.

Lee, C-H. and Song, J. (2009). An ecological approach to bullying: A comparative study between South Korea and the United States. *Korean Criminology*, 3, 103–143.

Lee, E. (2007). Perceptions of children and parents toward school violence in elementary school. *Journal of Korean Council for Children's Rights*, 11, 291–318.

Lee, H-K. and Hong, Y-O. (2002). The characteristics of Korean wang-ta phenomena -the process of behavioral decision making of school violence: The application of Fishbein theory. *Studies in Victimology*, 10, 101–122.

Lee, S. (2006). A study on influence factor of juveniles school violence. *Korean Association for Public Security Administration*, 2, 53–78.

Lee, S-H. (2011). *Bullying-like behaviours in South Korea: Terms used, origins in early childhood and links to moral reasoning*. Unpublished PhD thesis. London: Goldsmiths, University of London.

Lee, S-H., Smith, P. K. and Monks. C. P. (2011). Perceptions of bullying-like phenomena in South Korea: A qualitative approach from a lifespan perspective. *Journal of Aggression, Conflict, and Peace Research*, 3, 209–221.

(2012). Meaning and usage of a term for bullying-like phenomena in South Korea: A lifespan perspective. *Journal of Language and Social Psychology*, 31, 342–349.

Nesdale, D. and Naito, M. (2005). Individualism-collectivism and the attitudes to school bullying of Japanese and Australian students. *Journal of Cross-Cultural Psychology*, 36, 537–556.

Nho, C. and Lee, S. (2003). A study on predictive factors for school violence among junior high school students: Focusing on intraparental violence, child abuse, internal locus of control, and perception of school life. *School Social Work*, 6, 1–35.

No, S. (2001). Harmful consequences of gipdan-ttadolim. *Victimology*, 9, 5–29.

No, S., Kim, S., Lee, D. and Kim, J. (1999). *A study of adolescents' gipdan-ttadolim.* Seoul: Korean Institute of Criminology.

Park, G., Son, H. and Song, H. (1998). *Study of pupils' wang-ta phenomenon (gipdan-ttadolim and gorophim). (RR 98-19).* Seoul: Korean Educational Development Institute.

Park, H., Jung, M., Park, J. and Han, S. (2006). *A study of hakkyo-pokryuk (RR 2006-08-04).* Seoul: Korean Educational Development Institute.

Park, J. and Chae, K. (2011). The role of parenting behaviors, child's communication and problem solving skills in bullying/being bullied. *The Korean Journal of Psychology*, 30, 45–67.

Salmivalli, C. and Kaukiainen, A. (2004). 'Female aggression' revisited: Variable and person-centered approaches to studying gender differences in different types of aggression. *Aggressive Behavior*, 30, 258–163.

Scheithauer, H., Hayer, T., Petermann, F. and Jugert, G. (2006). Physical, verbal, and relational forms of bullying among German students: age trends, gender differences, and correlates. *Aggressive Behavior*, 32, 261–275.

Shin, D. (2012). A study of psychological school violence in an elementary school child. *Association of Criminal Psychology*, 8, 105–138.

Shin, H. (2006). A study on the continual development of aggressive victims, passive victims, and bullies. *Studies on Korean Youth*, 17, 297–323.

Shin, J-H., Hong, J. S., Yoon, J. and Espelage, D. L. (2014). Interparental conflict, parenting behavior, and children's friendship quality as correlates of peer aggression and peer victimization among aggressor/victim subgroups in South Korea. *Journal of Interpersonal Violence*, XX, 1–20.

Smith, P. K., Madsen, K. C. and Moody, J. C. (1999). What causes the age decline in reports of being bullied at school? Towards a developmental analysis of risks of being bullied. *Educational Research*, 41, 267–285.

Tippett, N. and Kwak, K. (2012). Cyberbullying in South Korea. In Q. Li, D. Cross and P. K. Smith (Eds.), *Cyberbullying in the global playground:*

Research from international perspectives (pp. 202–219). Chichester, England: Wiley-Blackwell.

Yang, S. (2009). *Pupils awareness and prevalence of hakkyo-pokryuk.* Unpublished Master thesis, Gwangju, South Korea: Chonnam National University.

Yom, Y. (2011). A study on difference of school bullying and school bully-victim groups mediating effects of self-esteem. *Journal of Future Oriented Youth Society,* 8, 117–136.

6 Research on school bullying in mainland China

Wenxin Zhang, Liang Chen and Guanghui Chen

School bullying is a common phenomenon with relatively high prevalence in all countries investigated (Eslea et al., 2003; Craig et al., 2009), and China should not be an exception. Although the problem of bullying/victimization among children in Chinese schools has been a major concern for the government and the public, and bullying is prohibited in the *Regulations of Primary and Middle School Students* issued by the Ministry of Education, scientific research on school bullying in mainland China only has a very brief history.

In 1999, Zhang and colleagues published a review paper on *research on school bullying/victimization* in the Chinese Journal of *Advances of Psychology* (Zhang, Wu, and Cheng, 1999), introducing related concepts, theories, and important research findings of school bullying to Chinese readers, which was the first paper on school bullying published in Chinese scientific journals. Since then, there has been a growing interest in the topic of school bullying among researchers and school practitioners in mainland China. This chapter aims to review the major research findings on school bullying in mainland China.

Etymological research of *qifu*

The Chinese word that is most close in meaning to the English word *bullying* is *qifu* (欺负), and for the past decade, *qifu* was used as the counterpart of the behavior/phenomenon of bullying in Chinese publications. In Chinese dictionaries (i.e., *Modern Chinese Dictionary*, or *Ci Hai*, which is the most comprehensive and authoritative Chinese dictionary), *qifu* is defined as a kind of behavior to intimidate, oppress, or embarrass others with an arrogant attitude and in unreasonable ways. Obviously, this definition is similar to that of bullying, which was defined as "a student is being bullied or victimized when he or she is exposed repeatedly and over time, to negative actions on the part of one or more other students" (Olweus, 2001, p. 5–6) or "a systematic abuse of power" (Smith and Sharp, 1994, p. 2). As such, *qifu* is also a subtype of

113

aggressive behavior characterized by the harmful nature of the behaviors and the power imbalance between the bullies and victims.

Etymological research found that the phenomenon of *qifu* expressed in Chinese literary works can be traced back to *The Hut for Autumn Song* by Tu Fu, who lived from AD 712 to AD 770. Over a long period, *qifu* gradually became a commonly used Chinese word describing behaviors such as the stronger harming the weaker, the bigger harming the smaller, or the bigger group harming the smaller group. In Chinese culture, the distinct feature of *qifu* is the imbalance of power between perpetrators and victims, while repetition is not a necessary characteristic (G. H. Chen, 2010). In other words, it is also regarded as *qifu* even if the stronger person or group harms the weaker only once.

In English language, *bullying* has been broadened to include physical, verbal forms, and social exclusion. These three forms of bullying also exist in Chinese culture, but (using a cartoon task, see Chapter 14) only 68% of Chinese 14-year-olds agreed that social exclusion was *qifu*, compared to 94% and 85% for physical and verbal forms respectively (Smith et al., 2002; Zhang collected the data of Chinese students). However, it should be noted that *qifu* is not the unique Chinese word to describe this kind of behavior; *qiwu* (欺侮), *qiling* (欺凌), *qiya* (欺压), *qiru* (欺辱), *lingru* (凌辱), and *wuru* (侮辱) are also parasynonyms of *qifu*, and they are used in some special bullying contexts. For example, *wuru* is often used to express verbal bullying. Nonetheless, it is important to note that *qifu* in Chinese culture represents the closest counterpart of *bullying*.

Characteristics of school bullying and victimization in mainland China

Since the Olweus Bully/Victim Questionnaire was translated into a Chinese version (Zhang, Wu, and Jones, 1999), researchers have made major progress assessing school bullying. To date, a total of eight surveys have been conducted on the nature and characteristics of school bullying/victimization in mainland China, notably, four of which investigated more than 3,000 students separately (see Table 6.1). All of these studies have revealed the presence of bullying, the effect of age and gender on bullying, and children's attitude toward bullying.

Prevalence

Prevalence percentages reported in the literature appear to vary somewhat across studies. As can be seen in Table 6.1, about 25% of the primary school students and 15% of the middle school students were

Table 6.1 *Studies reporting prevalence of Chinese bullies and victims*

					Bullies (%)		Victims (%)	
Study	Sample characteristics	Age group	Sample size	Measure	Now and then	Once a week or more	Now and then	Once a week or more
Cao (2012)	Migrant children in urban areas of Guiyang City	Ages 10–13	600	Self-report Olweus (1991)	14.1	3.6	26.7	9.0
Chen and Yue (2002)	Urban areas in Tianjin City	Grades 1–6	1,185	Self-report Olweus (1991)	5.0	2.0	20.3	7.2
		Grades 7–9	1,190		4.3	1.0	11.8	2.7
		Grades 10–12	957		2.7	1.0	4.0	1.5
Chen and Zhang (2007)	Girls of vocational schools in Shandong Province	Ages 16–20	488	Self-report Olweus (1991, 1993)	7.8	1.2	11.7	3.4
Lei and Chang (2002)		Junior middle school students	3,061	Peer nomination	Not reported	Not reported	Not reported	Not reported
Tan (2010)	Migrant children in rural areas	Grades 5–9	758	Self-report Olweus (1991, 1993)	4.2		15.8	
Qu (2005)	Hunan Province	Ages 3–7	308	Teacher report; Olweus (1990)	5.5		9.4	
H. Wang et al. (2012)	Four cities in Guangdong Province	Middle school students	8,342	Self-report	8.6		18.99	
Zhang (2002)	Urban and rural areas in both Shandong and Hebei Province	Ages 7–12	3,957	Self-report Olweus (1989, 1997)	6.2	4.2	22.2	13.4
		Ages 12–16	5,248		2.6	1.5	12.4	7.1

involved in regular interactions as either bullies or victims, ranging from 1.5% to 13.4% being bullied and 1.5% to 4.2% bullying others once every week or more (S.P. Chen and Yue, 2002; Qu, 2005; H. Wang et al., 2012; Zhang, 2002). Studies on the migrant samples have yielded slightly higher rates of bullies, with about 20% (Tan, 2010) or 40% (Cao, 2012). Additionally, studies on a girl sample indicated that a considerable proportion of girls acknowledged being bullied or bullying others (bullies, 7.8%; victims, 11.7%) (X. Chen and Zhang, 2007).

Given that nearly all of these surveys adopted a Chinese version of the Olweus Bully/Victim questionnaire, the percentages reported in these studies are comparable. Geographically, the eight samples covered most provinces in east China; hence, Chinese students were well-represented in these studies. However, limitations should be noted. The prevalence estimates were derived mainly using a single source informant, namely self-report, which may underestimate the frequencies of bullies or the frequencies of victims. Studies have shown that other informants, such as peers, teachers, and parents, may provide valid and useful information. Anyway, with these advantages and limitations in mind, the profile of the prevalence of bullying in Chinese schools has been described reliably.

Compared to the results of some major studies in western cultures, the prevalence of bullies and victims in primary and junior middle school in mainland China were lower than that in both Italy (bullies, 29%; victims, 8%) (Genta et al., 1996) and Britain (primary school: bullies, 12%; victims, 27%; middle school: bullies, 6%; victims, 10%) (Whitney and Smith, 1993), but a little higher than that in Norway (bullies, 7%; victims, 9%) (Olweus, 1993). One reason for this can be that in a collectivist culture, children are disapproved of if they bully others. Another reason can be that school bullying is strongly condemned in Chinese moral systems. Hence, the prevalence of bullying may be underestimated via self-report because of children's concern about negative moral evaluations (Zhang, 2002).

Age differences

Research conducted in western cultures has fairly consistently indicated that the frequency of bullying decreases with age (Smith, Madsen, and Moody, 1999). Similar age differences were also found in Chinese samples. Zhang (2002) conducted a study with a sample of 9,205 primary and junior middle school students, finding that both bullying and victimization declined steadily from Grade 2 to Grade 9 (see Figure 6.1; see also Zhang et al., 2000; Zhan et al., 2001). Specifically, the percentages of bullies and victims in junior middle school were significantly lower than

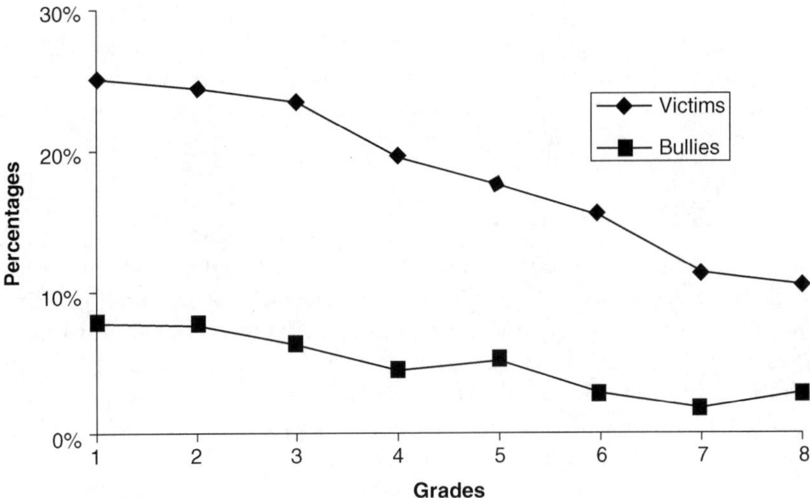

Figure 6.1 The prevalence of bullies and victims in primary and junior middle school

those in primary school. There are more bullies and victims in Grades 2, 3, and 4 than in Grades 5 and 6, and then the percentage of bullies and victims was the least in Grades 7, 8, and 9. A similar pattern of age differences between primary schools and secondary schools is also reported in other studies without examining year-to-year details (S. P. Chen and Yue, 2002). In contrast, the only study focused on preschool children found that the number of children involved in bullying incidents increased with age (Qu, 2005). In summary, the prevalence of bullying and victimization declined with age after primary school entrance.

Types of bullying and victimization

It has been accepted that there exists at least three main types of bullying/ victimization, including physical, verbal, and indirect forms. In Chinese primary and junior middle schools too, children were victimized by verbal bullying (35.1%), physical bullying (20.8%), and/or indirect bullying (18.3%) (Zhang, 2002; Zhang et al., 2001). Although children in both China and other cultures demonstrated the same forms of bullying, the prevalence of different types of bullying may vary across cultures. In a cross-cultural comparative research on Chinese and British children's bullying/victimization, the percentages of victims of verbal and indirect bullying were lower in China than that in Britain (Ji et al., 2004; and see Chapter 9). The most possible influencing factors for such culture differences may be the differential social context and culture values. For instance, Fujihara et al. (1999) concluded that oriental cultures, with an interdependent construal of self, seem to be more permissive of direct verbal aggression compared with Western cultures, but they have less tolerance for indirect verbal aggression.

Gender differences

Males are more often involved in bullying than females in all countries surveyed (see Felix and Green, 2010, for a review). Similar findings have also been reported in China. For example, Zhang (2002) found that a greater percentage of boys rated themselves as bullies than girls from Grade 2 through Grade 9 (see Table 6.2). However, the findings on gender of victims of bullying are not always consistent. As listed in Table 6.2, an equal number of boys and girls were identified as victims in primary school, whereas more boys were victims in junior/middle school. In another research, S. P. Chen and Yue (2002) reported similar findings on gender differences.

However, the gender differences in prevalence rates may not tell the whole story. Boys and girls may engage in different types of bullying. Western researchers have reported that boys tend to bully others or being bullied in overt ways, such as physical and verbal bullying, while girls are more likely to be involved in indirect bullying (Felix and Green, 2010). However, differential patterns of gender difference were consistently found in our studies (Ji et al., 2004; Zhang, 2002).

To illuminate the culture differences of bullying between Chinese and western students, we have conducted a cross-culture study (Ji et al.,

Table 6.2 *Percentages of bullies and victims in primary and junior middle school*

Roles	Primary students		Junior middle students	
	General	Severe	General	Severe
Victims				
Boys	22.2	14.3	13.9	7.2
Girls	22.1	12.2	10.8	7.0
Total	22.2	13.4	12.4	7.1
Bullies				
Boys	8.7	5.9	4.3	2.5
Girls	3.0	2.1	0.8	0.4
Total	6.2	4.2	2.6	1.5

2004; and see Chapter 9). We found that both in China and Britain, boys were more likely to experience physical victimization than girls. However, it is interesting to find that indirect victimization was more prevalent among Chinese boys than girls in both primary and junior middle schools, whereas in Britain, the case was reversed, that is, there were more girls experiencing indirect victimization than boys in both primary and junior middle schools.

In the western literature, indirect bullying has been considered as an easier way to harm girls because of their close and tight friendship networks (e.g., Lagerspetz and Björkqvist, 1994). Consequently, indirect bullying should be more prevalent among girls. However, in China, the cultural emphasis on interpersonal relationships, the policy of *the only child*, and the similarities of parenting style and educational mode may make both boys and girls tend to establish similar interpersonal networks.

Some other characteristics of bullying in mainland China

As stated earlier, bullying is characterized by the power imbalance between bullies and victims. Age may be one of the indexes of power imbalance, as Zhang et al. (2001) reported that victims were always bullied by the same age or older peers, with low probability of being bullied by younger peers.

Power imbalance may also be indexed by the number differences between the victims and the bullies and their supporters. In primary schools, the victims of physical and verbal bullying usually got bullied not only by a single boy or girl, but also by a group of boys or girls. However, the victims of indirect bullying generally got bullied by a group of bullies rather than by only one. In junior middle schools, most of the victims of all the three types of bullying got bullied by several bullies (Zhang et al., 2001).

With regard to places bullying occurred, classrooms (47.4%), playgrounds (21.6%), and passages (10.4%) were rated as the three main locations of bullying incidents in primary and junior middle schools (S. P. Chen and Yue, 2002). In addition, severe bullying incidents usually occurred in toilets or on the way to school and back home. It also should be noted that bullying generally occurs at undercover locations, which are unmonitored by adults, indicating that peer report information should be seriously considered in data collection.

Children's attitudes against bullying

Besides straightforward frequencies of bullying, attitudes of children against/towards bullying constitute an important aspect of the phenomenon. It is of great importance to understand children's attitudes towards bullying for the development of effective intervention programs. Although the research in this area on Chinese samples is insufficient, the essential feature of Chinese children's attitudes towards bullying has been provided (Ji et al., 2003; Zhang et al., 2002). This section summarizes the major findings.

Gender, grade, and role differences

In the studies conducted by Zhang and his colleagues (Ji et al., 2003; Zhang et al., 2002), children's attitudes were assessed and compared with that of British children. Findings indicated that the attitudes against bullying varied as a function of children's gender, grade, and participant roles in bullying. For example, girls were found to have more positive anti-bullying attitudes than boys. This is generally consistent with what has been reported in western studies, that girls have higher levels of empathy and are more prosocial than boys (Eisenberg, Fabes, and Spinrad, 2006).

In terms of grade or age differences, we found that pupils in primary schools were more supportive of victims than children in middle school. One possible reason may be that children become more familiar with the phenomenon of bullying with age, making them be indifferent with victims. It is interesting to find that children in Grade 6 and Grade 9 held the most negative attitudes against bullying. Given that Grade 6 and Grade 9 were the last year in primary and junior middle school respectively, these students were older than other schoolmates. Consequently, they were seldom bullied by others, and bullying seems to have nothing to do with these children.

With regard to the participant roles, bullies reported the most negative anti-bullying attitudes, implicating that practitioners should not only pay attention to the bullying behavior itself, but also to consider the bullies' attitude. In addition, we found that the outsiders had the most positive attitudes against bullying. Nevertheless, only in a few cases were bullying behaviors stopped by the outsiders, the reasons for which are discussed in the next section.

Dimensions of attitudes against bullying: feelings and action

Sympathetic feelings and action inclination are both necessary but different components of attitudes against bullying. As stated above, higher levels of attitudes against bullying do not mean an active inclination to intervene against victimization. Zhang et al. (2002) found that most of the students scored higher on sympathetic feeling than inclination to intervene. Furthermore, girls were more likely to show sympathy for victims than boys, but no significant differences were found between genders in daily school life. Primary school students have similar level of sympathetic feelings to middle school students. Primary school students, however, were more likely to intervene, maybe because the targets of children's prosocial behavior differentiated with age, with more prosocial behavior targeting their friends rather than stranger peers gradually.

Overall, these findings are in line with that of western studies (e.g., Menesini et al., 1997), albeit some culture differences exist. Our cross-culture comparison work found that Chinese children had higher levels of anti-bullying attitudes than British children (Ji et al., 2003). Furthermore, children in the two countries had similar level of sympathetic feelings towards victimization, whereas Chinese children showed greater willingness to act to help victims.

Besides others' active intervention, the victims' coping strategies were also of importance for the stopping of bullying. Research indicated that the mostly used strategy was to tell others and seek help. In junior middle school, about 25% to 65% of the victims tend to tell others, such as teachers, parents, classmates, or friends after being bullied. Furthermore, victims in junior middle school were more likely to tell their classmates or friends rather than their parents (S. P. Chen and Yue, 2002). Unfortunately, it's noteworthy that half of the victims tended to suffer in silence.

The socio-ecology of bullies and victims

According to the Social-Ecological Systems Perspective (Bronfenbrenner, 1979) and Developmental Contextualism (Lerner, 2002), school bullying does not occur in isolation. In fact, bullying/victimization are complicated social interactions among individuals, peer groups, and their broader social environment (Swearer and Espelage, 2004). As the macrosystem of child development, culture, such as the attitudes towards bullying behaviors, play a key role in school bullying. Chinese culture is always considered to be relatively collectivistic or group-oriented, rather than individualistic. Interpersonal harmony is strongly emphasized in Chinese society, which is reflected by the findings that Chinese children hold much more positive attitudes against school bullying than their British counterparts (Ji et al., 2003).

To the extent that the core values of Chinese culture are different from that of western cultures, the same contextual factors may have distinct function in different cultures. In this section, we introduce a series of indigenous Chinese studies on the correlates of bullying in China.

These studies have focused on children's individual characteristics, and their peer, family and school context. Both universal and culture-specific results have been found. Here we will discuss a number of culture-specific correlates of bullying.

Individual characteristics

Personality It has been well documented that personality factors are important for both bullies and victims, given the moderate to high stability of bullying roles. Both bullying and personality are associated with specific cultural context, thus the relationship between bullying and personality may not be consistent in different cultural systems.

In our studies, we found that primary school students' bullying behavior was positively associated with their neuroticism and psychoticism, with a bigger effect size for psychoticism (Gu and Zhang, 2003). Furthermore, children's experience of victimization positively correlated with their neuroticism. In other words, the instability of emotionality may be an important reason for victimization. These findings are consistent with that of western cultures, suggesting that the impact of neuroticism and psychoticism on bullying/victimization is universal across cultures.

We also found that both bullying and victimization negatively correlated with extraversion and self-esteem. In Chinese culture, introverted children were always timid and socially withdrawn, which made them easy targets of bullying. Interestingly, bullies were also found to be introverted in China, which is inconsistent with western findings that bullies were usually extroverted (Byrne, 1994; Mynard and Joseph, 1997). Chinese bullies' introversion may be caused by their academic failure. To a large extent, however, such inconsistency may also be due to the differences in cultural values. Traditionally, Chinese culture encourages children's restrained behavior, while Western cultures encourage children's self-expression.

Social behavior The definitive characteristic of bullying is the imbalance between bullies' and victims' power (Smith, 1991). The "power" here is not necessarily limited to physical strength (Lei and Chang, 2002). To a large extent, it refers to bullies' and victims' behavioral performance. Consistent with western studies, bullies in mainland China are also described as aggressive and rough, while victims are characterized as submissive-withdrawn, aggressive (as bully-victims), or having low levels of assertive behavior (Schwartz, Chang, and Farver, 2001).

Despite these social behaviors, shyness-sensitivity behavior emerges as an interesting correlate of bullying and victimization. Shyness-sensitivity behavior has different meanings in different cultures. In traditional Chinese culture, shy children were often regarded as socially matured and well-behaved; as a result, wariness and behavioral restraint are positively evaluated and encouraged in Chinese society. In this view, shy children would not be bullied. However, in one of our studies, we found that shyness-sensitivity behavior positively predicted 5-, 7-, and 10-grade children's physical victimization experiences (Zeng et al., 2010). As X. Chen et al. pointed out, the social functioning of shyness in urban Chinese adolescents has changed as China is undergoing dramatic social and economic changes (X. Chen et al., 2005; Liu et al., 2012).

Academic functioning There is some evidence in western cultures indicating that children's poor academic performance is related to peer victimization (e.g., Buhs and Ladd, 2001; Nakamoto and Schwartz, 2010). The case should be truer in mainland China to a greater extent. For one reason, academic achievement has been found to be positively correlated with children's social competence (X. Chen et al., 2010), which would protect children from peer conflict. For another reason, the Chinese school system is exam-oriented, and academic performance is the most important school evaluation standard. Students who do not work hard at school are devalued by their peers and teachers (Wentzel, 2009). As a result, children who perform poorly in school may be more likely to have lower peer status, fewer friends, and lower-quality friendships, making them easy targets of bullying. One empirical study in China did find that academic failure emerged as a powerful correlate of children's experience of peer victimization (Schwartz et al., 2001).

With regard to the academic performance of bullies, little evidence is available. However, it has been demonstrated that students' perceived academic pressure was a predictor of bullying (X. X. Zhu, 2005). When less academic pressure was perceived, low-self-controlled junior middle school students were more likely to bully others. One possible reason may be that students with less academic pressure were allowed to take part in more activities including bullying.

Peer context

School bullying generally occurs among peers. Therefore, the peer ecology is the most important context of bullying and victimization. Peer context is usually understood by referring to several levels of social complexity – individuals, interactions, relationships, and groups. As a special form of peer interaction, bullying and victimization correlates with other levels of peer relations. In this section, we review Chinese bullies' and victims' peer status and friendship.

Peer status Most of the studies on children's peer context involved children's sociometric status, that is peer rejection and peer acceptance. Consistent with findings from other cultures, victims in China were also found to be among the most rejected children. However there were sex differences in the relationship between victimization and social status, with male victims underrepresented in the popular group, relative to male non-victims, while for female victims this was not the case. In other words, victimization experiences indicate worse peer status for boys rather than girls. One possible reason may be that boys are expected to be strong enough to protect themselves, while girls are expected to be quiet and submissive.

Although bullies also had the highest score in peer rejection, they only show an average score in peer acceptance (M. F. Wang and Zhang, 2002). In other words, bullies are among the most rejected in a classroom, but they are also liked by some peers, which seem to be a contradictory thing. Generally, bullies acquire social dominance through bullying others; hence they are liked by some peers or friends. It probably does not matter that bullies are disliked by most of their classmates, because they have their own friends, and can get enough social support.

Friendship Children's friendship has received much attention in recent years. Friendship is also a complex relationship. In one of our studies, we discussed the effect of friendship on bullying and victimization in terms of the number of friends, friendship quality, and the characteristics of friends (G. H. Chen, 2010).

In our study, the number of friends children have, which represented an important friendship feature, positively correlated with bullying behavior. In the bully-victim dyads, having one or more friends becomes a kind of supporting power. However, the experiences of being bullied did not correlate with the number of friends. In other words, victims' status would not be improved even though they have many friends. One possible reason may be that, when victims do have friends, their friends tend to have similarly low peer status and behavior characteristics, making it difficult for the friends to protect them from being bullied.

In this study, we also found that friendship quality is not a direct predictor of bullying and victimization (G. H. Chen, 2010). Both bullies and victims can have intimate and high quality friendships. But in another study we conducted, we found that friendship quality moderated the relationship of shyness and victimization (Zeng, 2010).

An intimate and high quality friendship can protect shy children from being victimized.

In terms of friends' characteristics, we found that friends' positive characteristics (e.g., high achievement motivation, well-adjusted) did not necessarily lead someone to bullying others actively or being bullied by other peers because of envy. However, friends' externalizing problems positively correlated with bullying behavior. In other words, children who have friends with externalizing problems are more likely to be bullies rather than victims.

Family context

Only a few studies have focused on the family correlates of school bullying among Chinese children, including the family socioeconomic status, parenting, and family environment. As a basic family contextual factor, good economic status appeared to protect students from being bullied (H. Wang et al., 2012). Also, negative parenting was an antecedent of bullying and victimization. Students who were dissatisfied with parental caring were more likely to be either bullies or victims than those who were satisfied with parental caring (H. Wang et al., 2012). In addition, Chinese students who lived in a conflictual family environment were more likely to bully others than those experiencing harmonious family relations (Hazemba et al., 2008).

School context

In China, students usually stay at school for more than eight hours per day. Consequently, school life becomes a large part of a student's social ecology. Most of the bullying incidents happen in school or on the way going to school or back home. Studies on Chinese samples have demonstrated that teacher's attitude, class norms, and school climate served as predictors of bullying.

Teachers Teacher engagement and teacher's attitudes have been found to be vital for reducing bullying perpetration (Biggs et al., 2008). As significant others for Chinese children, the teachers in class, especially the head teacher, play an important role in intervening against bullying. Zhu has found that a good teacher-student relationship negatively predicted victimization, even after controlling for other risk factors (X. X. Zhu, 2005). Students disliked by their teachers were more likely to be bullied by peers (Lei and Chang, 2002), because teachers' negative attitude towards a student may turn into reasons for being bullied.

Teacher's attitude might also enhance the bullies' role and status. Low-self-controlled children were more likely to employ bullying strategies when they were perceived as being liked by their teachers (X. X. Zhu, 2005).

Class norms China possesses a group-oriented culture. Correspondingly, one's behavior performance and relationship experiences would be impacted by the groups' norms and attitudes to a great extent. Specifically, bullies usually choose their targets according to the group norms. Lei and colleagues (Lei, Wang, Guo, and Zhang, 2004) reported that the class norms moderated the relationship between children's social behavior and peer victimization. In classes with high levels of aggression, the relationship between aggression and victimization would be attenuated, while the relationship between social withdrawal and victimization would be strengthened. In classes with high levels of social withdrawal, the situation will be inversed.

School climate Besides the class- and teacher-level variables, the institutional supervision and control of students' behavior that the schools implement is still a significant influencing factor. Strict institutional monitoring and control serve as protective factors against school bullying (X. X. Zhu, 2005). Such a situation is particularly true for low-self-controlling students.

Adjustment of bullies and victims

In western studies, it has been well documented that victims are likely to experience many kinds of maladjustment (Berger, 2007). Do the cultural features of China exert influence on the functional meanings of peer victimization on children's psychosocial adjustment? On the one hand, given the strong emphasis on interpersonal harmony in Chinese society, children who were targets of bullying may get sympathy and help from other peers or teachers, which in turn may be expected to moderate the negative effect of peer victimization on psychosocial adjustment. However, on the other hand, the same situation may show another aspect. Children victimized by peers may be viewed as unsociable, and unable to maintain harmonious relationships with other peers in Chinese culture. With such kind of views in mind, it's reasonable to assume that peer victimization would lead to psychosocial maladjustment, which is similar to what is found in the West.

We have implemented a series of studies, and found that victims in China are also confronted with a series of maladjustment issues, such as loneliness, depression, externalizing problems, poor academic achievement, and poor peer relations (Ji et al., 2011; Zhang et al., 2009). A study by Cheng et al. (2010) also reported that victims were at risk of committing suicide. In addition, the victimization experiences often have long-term negative effects. In one study, we found that children's externalizing problems and peer rejection at age eleven were significantly predicted from their victimization experiences at age nine (Ji et al., 2011). However, victimization and emotional maladjustment was only concurrently associated (Ji et al., 2011).

With regard to the situation of bullies, only a little evidence is available. Given the strong emphasis on interpersonal harmony in Chinese society, bullies are expected to be more likely to be condemned. Therefore, bullies are also faced with maladjustment issues. In a study on primary school children, S. P. Chen (2003) reported that bullies tended to express impulsive, learning disorder, and teacher-student relationship problems. Additionally, to the extent that bullies were rejected and devalued by their peers and teachers, they may also report internalizing problems; H. Wang et al. (2012) have found that bullies were more likely to consider suicide or running away from home.

Bullying or *qifu* and Chinese culture

In the above sections, we have reviewed the research on bullying in mainland China. Findings were broadly similar to that of western studies in most respects, including the definitive feature of bullying in English and *qifu* in Chinese, except the repetition nature of bullying. At the same time, the particular effect of Chinese culture on bullying was clarified. In summary, the effects of Chinese culture are emphasized in three areas: the anti-bullying attitudes, gender differences in indirect bullying, and the role of school context, especially the teacher and children's academic performance.

In traditional Chinese culture, the morality of benevolence, righteousness, and propriety was extremely emphasized, and violation to others was restricted. As a result, anti-violence attitudes were emphasized all through life, which is reflected in the finding of Chinese children reporting more positive attitudes against bullying than British children.

A second important feature of Chinese culture is the emphasis on interpersonal relationship, or *guanxi* (关系) in Chinese. A series of complex relationships persist over one's lifetime, including relationship between parent and child, teacher and student, peer and peer, and so on. Destroying others' interpersonal relationship would achieve the aim of harming others to a great extent. Both boys and girls in China catch these ideas as early as they understand the meaning of relationship. Consequently, Chinese boys might use more relational bullying than girls.

Another keyword is authority or *quanwei* (权威) in Chinese. The traditional Chinese culture has an authority-minded way of thinking. In other words, the authority plays important roles in children's daily life. In school life, the teacher, especially the head teacher in class, is the one who plays the role of authority. As a result, teachers' attitudes have impact on the occurrence and prevention of bullying. To a great extent, teachers' attitudes are influenced by the students' academic and behavioral performance. Children's academic achievement is particularly important given the exam-oriented education both in traditional and modern China.

Despite these cultural differences, bullying is prevalent in mainland China, and exerts a negative impact on children's adjustment.

Conclusions

Since the 1990s, bullying became an important research issue in mainland China. The negative effects of victimization on bullies, and particularly the victims, make it a serious risk factor for school students. A number of investigations have been conducted, and the picture of school bullying among Chinese school students has been described.

Although many studies have been conducted to examine the phenomenon of *qifu* in mainland China, limitations should also be mentioned. First, the definition, questionnaires, and theories of bullying used in China are mainly derived from western literatures. Even though the hypothesis that the term *qifu* is the counterpart of bullying was supported by etymological research, we cannot exclude the possibility that Chinese students may perceive *qifu* differently from bullying in some details. Especially, repetition is not a necessary characteristic of *qifu*. Second, qualitative research about *qifu* is scarce. The studies of qualitative research about *qifu* like Olweus conducted in Sweden may be necessary among Chinese school children.

REFERENCES

Berger, K. S. (2007). Update on bullying at school: Science forgotten? *Developmental Review*, 27, 90–126.

Biggs, B. K., Vernberg, E. M., Twemlow, S. W., Fonagy, P., and Dill, E. J. (2008). Teacher adherence and its relation to teacher attitudes and student outcomes in an elementary school-based violence prevention program. *School Psychology Review*, 37, 533–549.

Bronfenbrenner, U. (1979). *The ecology of human development: Experiments by nature and design.* Cambridge, MA: Harvard University Press.

Buhs, E. S. and Ladd, G. W. (2001). Peer rejection in kindergarten as an antecedent of young childen's school adjustment: An examination of mediating processes. *Developmental Psychology,* 37, 550–560.

Byrne, B. J. (1994). Bullies and victims in a school setting with reference to some Dublin schools. *Irish Journal of Psychology,* 15, 574–586.

Cao, W. (2012). Investigation on parenting style to students of senior high schools (in Chinese). *Journal of Guizhou Normal University (Nature Sciences),* 30(6), 45–49.

Chen, G. H. (2010). *The definition and foundamental features of qifu/suffering qifu and its relationship with peer context in indigenous perspective* (in Chinese). Shandong: Unpublished Doctor's thesis, Shandong Normal University.

Chen, S. P. (2003). The relationship between school children's bully behavior and their personality traits (in Chinese). *Psychological Exploration,* 23, 55–58.

Chen, S. P. and Yue, G. A. (2002). A survey of bullying in primary and junior middle schools (in Chinese). *Psychological Science,* 25, 355–356.

Chen, X. Y. and Zhang, R. B. (2007). The current situation of bullying among the vocational college girls and its intervention strategies (in Chinese). *China Adult Education,* 16, 107–108.

Chen, X., Cen, G., Li, D., and He, Y. (2005). Social functioning and adjustment in Chinese children: The imprint of historical time. *Child Development,* 76, 182–195.

Chen, X., Huang, X., Chang, L., Wang, L., and Li. D. (2010). Aggression, social competence, and academic achievement in Chinese children: A 5-year longitudinal study. *Development and Psychopathology,* 22, 583–592.

Cheng, Y., Newman, I. M., Qu, M., Mbulo, L., Chai, Y., Chen, Y., and Shell, D. F. (2010). Being bullied and psychosocial adjustment among middle school students in China. *Journal of School Health,* 80, 193–199.

Craig, W., Harel-Fisch,Y., Fogel-Grinvald, H., Dostaler, S., Hetland, J., Simons-Morton, B., Molcho, B., Gaspar de Mato, M., Overpeck, M., Due, P., Pickett, W., HBSC Violence and Injuries Prevention Focus Group, and HBSC Bullying Writing Group (2009). A cross-national profile of bullying and victimization among adolescents in 40 countries. *International Journal of Public Health,* 54 (Suppl 2), 216–224.

Eisenberg, N., Fabes, R. A., and Spinrad, T. L. (2006). Prosocial behavior. In N. Eisenberg (Vol. Ed.) and W. Damon and R. M. Lerner (Series Eds.), *Handbook of child psychology, Vol. 3: Social, emotional, and personality development* (6th edn.; pp. 646–718). Hoboken, NJ: John Wiley and Sons.

Eslea, M., Menesini, E., Morita, Y., O'Moore, M., Mora-Merchán, J. A., Pereira, B., Smith, P. K., and Zhang, W. X. (2003). Friendship and loneliness among bullies and victims: Data from seven countries. *Aggressive Behavior,* 30, 71–83.

Felix, E. D. and Green, J. G. (2010). Popular girls and brawny boys: The role of gender in bullying and victimization experiences. In S. R. Jimerson,

S. M. Swearer and D. L. Espelage (Eds.), *Handbook of bullying in schools: An international perspective* (pp. 173–186). London: Routledge.

Fujihara, T., Kohyama, T., Andreu, J. M., and Ramirez, J. M. (1999). Justification of interpersonal aggression in Japanese, American, and Spanish students. *Aggressive Behavior, 25*, 185–195.

Genta, M. L., Menesini, E., Fonz, A., Costablile, A., Smith, P. K. (1996). Bullies and victims in schools in central and southern Italy. *European Journal of Psychology of Education, 11*, 97–110.

Gu, C. H. and Zhang, W. X. (2003). A survey on the relations of the bullying problem among primary school children to their personality (in Chinese). *Acta Psychologica Sinica, 35*, 101–105.

Hazemba, A., Siziya, S., Muula, A. S., and Rudatsikira, E. (2008). Prevalence and correlates of being bullied among in-school adolescents in Beijing: results from the 2003 Beijing Global School-Based Health Survey. *Annals of General Psychiatry, 7*, 1–6.

Ji, L. Q., Chen, L., Xu, F. Z., Zhao, S. Y., and Zhang, W. X. (2011). A longitudinal analysis of the association between peer victimization and patterns of psychosocial adjustment during middle and late childhood (in Chinese). *Acta Psychologica Sinica, 43*, 1151–1162.

Ji, L., Zhang, W., Jones, K., and Smith, N. (2003). A comparison of children's attitudes towards bullying between Chinese and British children (in Chinese). *Studies of Psychology and Behavior, 1*, 122–127.

(2004). Gender differences of physical, verbal , and indirect bullying among primary and secondary school children : A cross-cultural comparison between China and Britain (in Chinese). *Journal of Shandong Nnormal University (Humanities and Social Sciences), 49*, 21–24.

Juvonen, J., Nishina, A., and Graham, S. (2000). Peer harassment, psychological adjustment, and school functioning in early adolescence. *Journal of Educational Psychology, 92*, 349–359.

Lagerspetz, K. M. J. and Björkqvist, K. (1994). Indirect aggression in boys and girls. In Huesmann, L. R. (Ed.), *Aggressive behavior: Current perspectives* (pp. 131–150). New York: Plenum.

Lei, L. and Chang, L. (2002). Adolescent victims in school bullying: Some predictors (in Chinese). *Exploration of Psychology, 22*, 38–43.

Lei, L., Wang, Y., Guo, B. L., and Chang, L. (2004). The influence of classroom norms on the relations between social behaviors and peer victimization (in Chinese). *Acta Psychologica Sinica, 36*, 563–567.

Lerner, R. M. (2002). *Concepts and theories of human development.* London: Lawrence Erlbaum Associates.

Liu, J. S., Chen, X. Y., Li, D., and French, D. (2012). Shyness-sensitivity, aggression, and adjustment in urban Chinese adolescents at different historical times. *Journal of Research on Adolescence, 22*, 393–399.

Mynard, H. and Joseph, S. (1997). Bully/ victim problems and their association with Eysenck's personality dimensions in 8 to 13 year-olds. *British Journal of Educational Psychology, 67*, 51–54.

Menesini, E., Eslea, M., Smith, P. K., Genta, M. L., Giannetti, E., Fonzi, A., and Costabile, A. (1997). Cross-national comparison of children's attitudes towards bully/victim problems in school. *Aggressive Behavior*, 23, 245–257.

Nakamoto, J. and Schwartz, D. (2010). Is peer victimization associated with academic achievement? A meta-analytic review. *Social Development*, 19, 221–241.

Olweus, D. (1991). Bullying/Victim problems among school children: Basic facts and effects of a school based intervention programme. In: Pepler, D. J., Rubin, K. H. (Eds.), *The development and treatment of childhood aggression* (pp. 411–448). Hillsdale, NJ: Erlbaum.

(1993). *Bullying at school: What we know and what we can do.* Oxford: Blackwell.

(2001). Peer harassment: A critical analysis and some important issues. In J. Juvonen and S. Graham (Eds.), *Peer harassment in schools: The plight of the vulnerable and victimized* (pp. 3-20). New York: Guilford.

Qu, W. (2005). Investigation and remedy of young children's bullying behavior (in Chinese). *Studies in Preschool Education*, 29, 1–3.

Rigby, K. and Slee, P. T. (1991). Bullying among Australian school children: Reported behavior and attitudes towards victims. *Journal of Social Psychology*, 131, 615–627.

Schwartz, D., Chang, L., and Farver, J. M. (2001). Correlates of victimization in Chinese children's peer groups. *Developmental Psychology*, 37, 520–532.

Smith, P. K. (1991). The silent nightmare: Bullying and victimization in school peer groups. *The Psychologist*, 4, 243–248.

Smith, P. K., Cowie, H., Olafsson, R. F., and Liefooghe, A. (2002). Definitions of bullying: A comparison of terms used, and age gender differences, in a fourteen-country international comparison. *Child Development*, 73, 1119–1133.

Smith, P. K., Madsen, K., and Moddy, J. (1999). What causes the age decline in reports of being bullied at school? Towards a developmental analysis of risks of being bullied. *Educational Research*, 41, 267–285.

Smith P. K. and Sharp, S. (1994). The problem of school bullying. In P. K. Smith and S. Sharp (Eds.), *School bullying: Insights and perspectives.* London: Routledge.

Smith, P. K. and Shu, S. (2000). What good school can do about bullying: Findings from a survey in English schools after a decade of research and action? *Childhood*, 7, 193–212.

Swearer, S. M. and Espelage, D. L. (2004). A social-ecological framework of bullying among youth. In D. L. Espelage and S. M. Swearer (Eds.), *Bullying in American schools: A social-ecological perspective on prevention and intervention* (pp. 1–12). Mahwah, NJ: Erlbaum.

Tan, Q. (2010). The relationship between school bullying and adjustment among urban migrant children (in Chinese). *Theory and Practice of Contemporary Education*, 2, 94–96.

Wang, M. F. and Zhang, W. X. (2002). Peer relationships of bullies, victims and bully/victims in primary and junior middle schools (in Chinese). *Psychological Development and Education*, 18, 1–5.

Wang, H., Zhou, X., Lu, C., Wu, J., Deng, X., Hong, L., Gao, X., and He, Y. (2012). Adolescent bullying involvement and psychosocial aspects of family and school life: A cross-sectional study from Guangdong province in China. *PLoS One*, 7: e38619.

Wentzel, K. R. (2009). Peers relationships and motivation at school. In K. H. Rubin, W. M. Bukowski and B. P. Laursen (Eds.), *Handbook of peer interactions, relationships, and groups* (pp. 531–547). New York: Guilford.

Whitney, I. and Smith, P. K. (1993). A survey of the nature and extent of bullying in junior/middle and secondary schools. *Educational Research*, 35, 3–25.

Zeng, Y. (2010). *Social Behaviors and Academic Achievement as Correlates of Peer Victimization among Chinese Adolescents: Peer Relationships as Mediators and Moderators* (in Chinese). Shandong: Unpublished Master's thesis, Shandong Normal University.

Zeng, Y., Chen, L., Tian, L. M., and Zhang, W. X. (2010). Shyness-sensitivity, social preference and adolescents' physical victimization (in Chinese). *Psychological Science*, 33, 689–700.

Zhang, W. X. (2002). Prevalence and major characteristics of bullying/victimization among primary and junior middle school children (in Chinese). *Acta Psychologica Sinica*, 34, 387–394.

Zhang, W. X., Chen, L., Ji, L. Q., and Zhang, L. L. (2009). Physical and relational victimization, and children's emotional adjustment in middle childhood (in Chinese). *Acta Psychologica Sinica*, 41, 433–443.

Zhang, W. X., Gu, C. H., Wang, M. P., and Wang, Y. W., Jones, K. (2000). Gender differences in the bully/victim problem among primary and junior middle school students (in Chinese). *Psychological Science*, 23, 435–511.

Zhang, W. X. and Ju, Y. C. (2008). Intervention research on bullying of pupils in primary schools. *Educational Research (in Chinese)*, 2, 95–99.

Zhang, W. X., Wang, L. P., Gong, X. L., Wu, J. F., and Zhang, K. (2002). Children's attitude toward bullying in school (in Chinese). *Psychological Science*, 25, 226–227.

Zhang, W. X., Wang, Y. W., Ju, Y. C., and Lin, C. D. (2001). Types of bullying behavior and its correlates (in Chinese). *Psychological Development and Education*, 17, 12–17.

Zhang, W. X., Wu, J. F., and Cheng, X. (1999). The review of child bullying research in foreign countries (in Chinese). *Journal of Developments in Psychology*, 7, 37–42.

Zhang, W. X., Wu, J. F., and Jones, K. (1999). The modification of a Chinese version of the Olweus Bully/Victim Questionnaire (in Chinese). *Psychological Development and Education*, 15, 7–11.

Zhu, B. and Lei, L. (2005). The relationship between perceptions of control and victimization of adolescents (in Chinese). *Psychological Development and Education*, 21, 91–95.

Zhu, X. X. (2005). *The relationship between school climate and bullying perceived by junior middle school students* (in Chinese). Shandong: Unpublished Master's thesis, Shandong Normal University.

7   Bullying in Hong Kong schools

Siu-Fung Lin and Chi Leung Lai

In this chapter, the terms *school bullying* and *cyberbullying* will be explained in a distinctive culture and a language, Cantonese, used locally in Hong Kong, SAR. Behaviours related to these concepts will be exemplified in terms of prevalence in schools and amongst school children at both primary and secondary levels. Characteristics and patterns of bullying behaviours, consequences for children and responses from the media, schools and government will be discussed.

Hong Kong is a city that lies on the southern coast of China; it has an international reputation as a financial centre, business centre and shopping paradise, a city that has become a world leader in economic growth, historical and cultural heritage. With a 100-year long history of British colonialism and education, and a deeply entrenched Confucian culture being challenged by global exposure, Hong Kong's character is more one of 'Fusion' than Chinese or Far Eastern. However, any exploration of Eastern culture, including attitudes and behaviour, cannot skip this city as it still keeps the deeply entrenched Chinese culture in the heart. Hong Kong, together with South Korea, Taiwan and Singapore were named the 'four little dragons' after an economic growth spurt and technological advancement in the 1980s.

The education system in Hong Kong was influenced by the British during the colonial period. It consists of a 6-year primary education, a 3-year junior secondary education and a 3-year senior secondary education. Usually, when children reach 6 years old they enter Primary One, and when they reach 12 years old they enter Secondary One in secondary school. There is compulsory and free education for the first 9 years, that is from Primary One to Secondary Three.

How do our school children's bullying behaviours compare to neighbouring countries in the Far East, such as Japan and South Korea? And to countries in the West, such as the United States, the United Kingdom and Sweden, so widely studied for over two decades?

What is school bullying in Hong Kong?

Regarding language, there is a dual use of Chinese, with Cantonese speaking preserved in everyday life while writing is in Mandarin style. The Chinese way of writing 'bullying' is 欺凌 (read 'hei-ling' in Cantonese). '欺' means 'to deceive or insult', 凌 means 'overbearing'. Both characters carry negative meanings; there is a discourse of power and intent, and an implication of an imbalance of power between persons or parties. There is no specification of context and this combination of characters is used for all kinds of bullying and aggression, at least amongst Cantonese speakers in Hong Kong and Macau. The comparative term used in Taiwan in Mandarin, 霸凌 (read 'Ba Ling') is more on the side of taking advantage of the victim, such as with respect to the physical size and strength or a group of people towards individuals, without 'lording it over' or dominating the individual.

According to the Education Bureau (EDB) of Hong Kong (2012), school bullying is defined as: (1) a repetitive aggressive act, (2) the dominance of the powerful over the powerless and (3) a malicious behaviour. School bullying can be in the form of physical attacks, verbal attacks, isolation and coercive demands repeatedly and with ill-intention. Three major roles are considered in bullying behaviour: bully, victim and bystander. These conceptual and definitional matters have been introduced to all schools and teachers for operational purposes since 2004 (Education and Manpower Bureau, 2004; Education Bureau of Hong Kong; 2008; 2012). The EDB's approach developed from ideas and studies done in the West (see, for instance, Olweus, 1991; Beane, 1999; Department for Education and Skills (DFES), 2002).

Background of interest in the topic

Unlike in South Korea and Japan, bullying has never been properly and systematically addressed by the government or funded by government research and intervention (Lin, Kanetsuna and Lee, 2012). Although school teachers recognise the existence of school bullying, they may have little idea how serious it could be and what it concerns. It is still considered a kind of 'taboo' topic, and this renders it difficult to investigate thoroughly. This problem had been raised by many researchers including the current authors (see also Lam and Liu, 2007; Ng and Tsang, 2008).

This avoidance of the real situation was brought sharply into focus by the death of a 10-year-old girl who had been bullied in December 2013 (*Apple Daily*, 10 December 2013). After this girl had jumped from a balcony in front of her classmates, the head teacher announced that she had fainted. Instead of calling police and sending her to A&E immediately, the head teacher reportedly tried to cover it up by using a private medical order, thus delaying the rescue of a bullied girl who in fact had committed suicide without any warning symptoms being obvious to the teacher.

Going back a decade, in 2001, an association for the Hong Kong School Disciplinary staff had already declared that bullying was one of the top three misbehaviours in Hong Kong secondary schools (香港教育專業人員協會, 2001). Notwithstanding this claim, school bullying was not addressed as a serious issue in Hong Kong until the outbreak of some brutal cases in 2003–4. In November 2003, an appalling incident was found on the Internet, in which a boy in Secondary 5 was severely beaten up five times within 10 days in the classroom and changing room. The police arrested a group of 11 of his classmates and 10 of them pleaded guilty. A video was taped by a bystander who intended to disclose what had happened when it had failed to attract the school's attention and involvement (*Apple Daily*, 20 February 2004). In another case, a video was made of a skinny boy being beaten up at school and seriously hurt by over 10 people, and it was sent to the media. Passers-by watched with smiles on their faces and just walked away. In one of the attacks, a teacher got involved. The school refused to disclose anything to the media, and rejected help from the police. Five young men aged 17–18 were arrested; they were old boys of the same school (*Sing Tao Daily*, 11 February 2003). At around the same time, a Secondary 4 girl's hair was forcibly cut by two of her schoolmates, her arms were bitten and she was threatened with being covered with urine and faeces (*Apple Daily*, 15 February 2003). She was taken to A&E for medical advice by her parents and only then the school advised the parents to report to the police.

Long-term bullying has happened too: a boy was found forced to give up his own lunch box, being teased, smacked and scratched on his arms for over 5 months (*Sing Tao Daily*, 16 February 2004). He was psychologically affected, failed to attend school and subsequently left the school. One 15-year-old boy was arrested. The school explained that it was considered 'play' amongst students and did not take it seriously. Another wave of bullying was reported in the media in 2008–9, when some school boys and girls were found guilty of bullying by the Magistrates Courts; their sentences included months in juvenile detention or probationary periods of some two years.

Despite this, there is little evidence that schools and teachers pay any more attention to bullying in schools (*China Daily*, Hong Kong Edition, 9 November 2009). First, school teachers are already overwhelmed by teaching loads and administrative work and they feel that they are far too busy to do anything else or spend time with school children and their psycho-social needs. Second, schools set priorities on academic achievement, and this is approved of strongly by parents and society at large. These demands include performance both at school and in public examinations. Magistrates blame the bullying on neglect of moral values teaching in education and insufficient attention to the teaching of moral values by parents. Victims are usually threatened against any further reporting to the authority after being harassed violently (including physically and psychologically).

Prevalence of school bullying in Hong Kong

All primary and secondary schools were required to report to the EDB about schools' involvement in bullying interventions between September 2003 and February 2004. Seventy-two per cent of schools reported having had no cases, while 23% reported 1–3 cases and only 5% reported 4+ cases (Legislative Council, 2004). These figures announced by the EDB suggested that school bullying was a rare phenomenon in Hong Kong, and that there were no cases in most schools.

Compared with this teacher-reported data, a number of research studies have used pupil self-report surveys over the last decade. These paint a much more alarming picture. For example, Wong and colleagues surveyed pupils in 47 primary schools (5% of primary schools in Hong Kong) in 2001; 7,025 children aged 10–14 years returned questionnaires (see Wong, 2004; Wong et al., 2008). Bullying was defined and categorised into 4 types: physical, verbal, social and extortion. The children were asked about their experiences in the past 6 months, as bullies, victims and witnesses, quantified as 'never', '1 to 5 times', '6 to 10 times', or '11 times and above'. Table 7.1 gives a summary of the findings. Percentages are generally high in the 1–5 times frequency category, but (for bullies and victims at least) much lower for the 6–10 or 11+ categories. Verbal bullying was the most frequent type, but nearly 20% of them had experienced 3–4 types of verbal bullying as victims. Overall, 67% of victims said they did not report their experiences to teachers; of these, 58% believed that they were able to resolve the problem(s), while only 20% tried to stop the bullying.

In this study, participants were also asked about their attitudes towards bullying. It is interesting to compare the differences between attitudes and behaviours. Altogether 88% of participants said that they found physical bullying unacceptable; but nevertheless 24% had bullied others physically at least occasionally, while 68% had witnessed physical

Table 7.1 *Frequency of experiences as bullies, victims and bystanders over a 6-month period; data from Wong et al., 2008.*

Frequency/ % of total participants	Bullies				Victims				Bystanders			
	Physical	Verbal	Exclusion	Extortion	Physical	Verbal	Exclusion	Extortion	Physical	Verbal	Exclusion	Extortion
never	76%	48%	76%	90%	68%	38%	72%	87%	33%	13%	34%	60%
1–5	19%	39%	19%	7%	24%	41%	21%	9%	46%	38%	42%	27%
6–10	2%	6%	2%	1%	3%	9%	3%	1%	8%	20%	12%	6%
11+	3%	7%	3%	2%	5%	12%	4%	2%	14%	30%	12%	7%

bullying. Similarly, 66% claimed that social exclusion was unacceptable, yet 28% had experienced it; and 46% reported that verbal bullying was unacceptable, and yet 87% claimed to have witnessed some verbal bullying, and 30% had witnessed it 11+ times.

According to the definition of EBD in Hong Kong and worldwide, behaviour is bullying only when it is repeated and hurts people psychologically and/or physically. Therefore, in this study using the 1–5 frequency criterion might give inflated percentages if students had actually only witnessed or experienced a one-off incident. Also, different experiences (physical, verbal, isolation and extortion) were counted separately; hence, the occurrence of bullying reported (a summation of all types) was not necessarily the true percentage of the number of students involved.

Ng and Tsang (2008) conducted a self-report survey in 2003 with 366 secondary school students. Following the scale developed by Wong in 2001, this survey looked into the same 4 types of bullying behaviours (physical, verbal, exclusion and extortion), this time with 4 roles defined (bullies, bully-victims, victims and witnesses), measured by 4 response categories (never, at least once a month, about once a week, everyday), and over a 4-month period. Though primarily examining the correlation between bullying experiences and mental health, this study gave a profile of school bullying in Hong Kong as a background. Altogether 8% of students reported themselves as bullies, 9% as victims and 15% as bully-victims, at least once a week. Of the victims, 18% were bullied physically, 50% verbally, 18% were relationally excluded and 7% experienced extortion. Comparing boys and girls, boys were involved in committing bullying, being bullied and witnessing bullying more than girls, in all subtypes except relational bullying. As regards the mental health outcomes, girl victims and boy bully-victims were found to be the poorest on measures including depression, anxiety, coping and school adjustment.

In February 2004, a legislative council member together with the Ngau Tau Kok neighbourhood Social Services Centre jointly conducted a survey (Ming Pao, 16 February 2004). In total 3,005 questionnaires were collected from Primary 5–6 and Secondary 3–4 students from 23 schools in 5 districts in Hong Kong (Kowloon East and Kowloon West, New Territories East and New Territories West, Hong Kong Island). Altogether 31% of respondents had experience of bullying others; of these, 74% used verbal assault, 24% physical and 10% extortion within 6 months. Those who bullied others said that they did so because they wanted to retaliate (32%), attract attention (27%), were unable to deal with negative emotions (18%) or were following the gang (16%). Altogether 49% of the sample reported being victims; of these,

58% experienced verbal bullying, 28% physical and 14% extortion. Regarding coping strategies, 50% of victims remained silent, 24% retaliated and 19% told teachers. Altogether 78% of respondents had witnessed bullying; of these, 99% had seen verbal bullying, 63% physical and 39% extortion. Regarding what they did, 48% of these bystanders stayed away from the incident, 30% told teachers and 15% tried to stop the bullying; but 7% joined in the bullying. The generally high incidence figures in this study are because participants were asked if an experience had 'ever' happened (thus, perhaps just once), over a 6-month period.

These few studies may have been undertaken in response to the series of incidents reported in the media between 2003 and early 2004. Thereafter, research became quiet for two years until the second tide of bullying reports arrived in 2008–9.

In 2008, a survey was conducted involving 2,918 students from Hong Kong, Guangzhou and Macau, of which 1,552 were Hong Kong students in Forms 1–3 (TaKung Pao, 12 December, 2008;). This survey adopted the same four types of bullying as in Wong et al. (2008), therefore data collected were comparable with this earlier survey conducted in 2001. Participants were asked about their experiences in the past month on a scale '0–10' (0 = never, 2–5 times = seldom, 5 times = average, 7.5 times = many, 10 = a lot). The results are not reported in a scientific format, but it appears that of those in Hong Kong who bullied others, 77% used verbal bullying, 48% used physical assault, 47% used social exclusion, and 49% used extortion. The full results are given in a report prepared by four organizations (Hong Kong Playground Association, Youth Studies Room at City University of Hong Kong, Macau Neighbourhood Joint Community, Guangzhou Youth Alliance, Guangzhou, Macau and Hong Kong Youth Studies Association, 2008).

In a survey done in Hong Kong and Macau (Hong Kong Playground Association, 2008), 1,108 questionnaires were collected, of which 883 were from 6- to 24-year-olds from Hong Kong. Participants were asked about experiences of bullying 'at least once' in the past three months and the reasons for the act. Again the results are not reported in a scientific format, but it appears that over 45% of participants admitted having bullied peers (22% admitted physical bullying and 24% social exclusion). Among the Hong Kong bullies the top reason for bullying others was retaliation (39%), followed by anger and not controlling oneself properly (36%), and it being a habitual act (27%). Overall, 60% of the Hong Kong participants reported themselves to be victims in the past three months (51% reported being bullied verbally and 26% being bullied physically). Overall, 91% had been bystanders of at least one type of bullying behaviour (87% had seen verbal bullying, 74% social exclusion, 61% physical bullying and 41% extortion); 50% had witnessed 3 or 4 of these types of bullying. About two-thirds of respondents said they might help a victim, but one third would not.

The prevalence of students' bullying experiences, as reported in these surveys, ranged from 10% to 77%. Such variance may be a product of how bullying was defined and categorised, also because of differences in the period of reference (which ranged from in 'the past month', 'the last 3 months', '4 months' or '6 months', to in the 'past year') and the frequency criterion. It is also a matter how the incidents or experiences were counted and calculated.

Societal attitudes towards school bullying

Can teachers and schools be part of the problem?

The growing concern about school bullying in the last decade, among the media, social workers and parents, has led NGOs to conduct prevalence surveys as described. Scholars involved in these surveys are mostly from social work departments. Schools and teachers seem unenthusiastic about the topic – there has been a lack of voices and studies from teachers and unions. It is common for teachers to deny the existence of bullying in their schools. In Hong Kong, success in examinations is of utmost importance. Thus school teachers are overwhelmed by teaching and administrative loads and are usually too busy to attend to pupils' psycho-social needs.

Lam and Liu (2007) conducted a qualitative retrospective study of eight boys aged 12–17 years in Secondary 1 to 4 in a school considered of low educational quality. Six of the boys reported that they were members of a triad (gang) society. They conducted in-depth interviews individually with semi-structured questions about self-reported history of bullying experiences, and reflections on their own bullying experiences. From their accounts, some started to bully others as early as in the Primary years, and most of them started in Secondary One. Their bullying behaviours included physical, verbal, extortion and coercion. These students were asked how they became bullies and the mechanisms as well as the processes of development of bullying behaviours. Some reinforcers of bullying were identified from their accounts: getting a sense of security, a struggle for power, material gains, fun seeking and stress release.

Academically unsuccessful children who have little or no sense of achievement from school may choose to pursue non-academic goals. It is commonly held that the stress caused by exam-oriented curricula can promote destructive behaviours such as bullying. Parental requirements and reproaches which are taken as rejection and being looked down upon, can also indirectly lead to bullying behaviours when the students cannot cope with their negative emotions and project them onto others (Leung and To, 2009; Lam and Liu, 2007). When schools and parents target success, competition becomes an issue. Students in Hong Kong are trained to compete, even from early childhood when they compete with other children to get into well-known kindergartens.

Although endless competition is stressful and unwelcome, children in Hong Kong tend to hide their aversion to it. This extends to school bullying – children are taught not to express their feelings directly or assertively to things they do not welcome. As victims, children tend not to report it, because they do not know their rights. Moreover, victims are usually pressured into not reporting bullying to authorities. As bystanders, Hong Kong children struggle between trouble-avoidance, maintaining harmony (with bullies) or risking reporting. They may also be angry with the school for not stopping the bullying.

Legislative effort and responsibilities of the Education Bureau

In February 2004 the Legislative Council, in response to a series of bullying events, proposed research into the issue. The EDB summarised mostly Western studies on characteristics of bullies and victims, aggressive behaviours and parenting style and teachers' perceptions and attitudes towards bullying (Legislative Council, March 2004). The EDB claimed that it had adopted the suggestions of overseas scholars (Smith and Brain, 2000, Smith et al., 1999) and produced a set of resources for schools. The EDB took the stance that school bullying is not to be tolerated, and 'reminded' schools to adopt a 'whole school approach' in combating and preventing bullying.

School bullying has become a general school problem in Hong Kong schools. It is widespread, and common amongst school children in most, if not all, schools. Judging from pupil-based surveys, the school bullying incidents reported in the media were perhaps only the tip of an iceberg. School bullying amongst school children in Hong Kong is serious and under-reported, and it could happen in any kind of school; schools with a good reputation are no exception to this. However, it was not until the last decade that some programs or guidelines dealing with the problem of school bullying were developed by the governmental authorities, non-government organizations, and local practitioners (Fung and Wong, 2007; Wong et al., 2002; Education and Manpower Bureau, 2003;

Education and Manpower Bureau, 2004; Wong, 2003; Caritas Hong Kong Website, 2012; and Chapter 19).

The emergence of cyberbullying

As advances in Information Communications Technology ushered in a new digital era, bullying has changed its form. Cyberbullying made its global debut and Hong Kong was not immune. By mid-2012 there were 5,329,372 Internet users in Hong Kong, representing 74.5% of the population; and Internet access has become near-ubiquitous, as 87% of consumers have used the Internet in the past year, outpacing neighbouring markets like Singapore, Malaysia, Philippines, Thailand and Indonesia (Internet World Stats, December 2012) Internet usage in Hong Kong is particularly high among 12- to 44-year-olds, with over 9 out of 10 accessing the Internet on a monthly basis (Nielsenwire, December 2011). Teens and young adults spend approximately 10 hours per week on online games (Commission on Youth, 2008).

Like traditional bullying at school, cyberbullying can lead to severe outcomes. For example, a teenage girl attempted suicide after having sex with her boyfriend and it being disclosed online to the whole school by her best friend (Mingpao, 26 March, 2012). But different from bullying at school, cyberbullying arouses fears in the victim because much may be unknown to him/her, including the bully, the source, what will happen next and how long it will last. As another example, in 2005, Ah Chung, as a school student, experienced cyberbullying and 5 years later, at the age of 17 he stated, 'I was so scared because I didn't know who wrote about me and who hated me, as they were anonymous. I started to feel that anyone would attack me. I carried some iron bars and scissors with me to school', and 'I felt it was so unfair that I couldn't fight back, as I was afraid this would provoke them to attack me more in the Internet' (*China Daily*, Hong Kong Edition, 6 February, 2010).

Similarly, in 2013, Herbert, a school student, totally collapsed after his ex-girlfriend's boyfriend set up an online forum teasing his outlook, intelligence and even his sexual preference (*China Daily*, Hong Kong Edition, 5 April, 2013). A 15-year-old boy attracted more than 200 negative comments and got a name 'attention whore' after posting comments about unscrupulous vendors in the Ladies Market, and his personal details were also posted on a popular local forum by his friends (*China Daily*, Hong Kong Edition, 5 April, 2013).

The Administration of the Hong Kong government has declared that there is no statute law defining or governing 'cyberbullying'. The Privacy Commissioner for Personal Data stated that they had only received four cases since 2009 (up to 2012). It is believed that the true number of cases was likely to be much higher (*China Daily*, Hong Kong Edition, 4 March, 2013). The police have not kept any related statistics of 'cyberbullying' acts (Legislative Council, 2012).

Research studies on cyberbullying started to emerge in late 2009 in Hong Kong, as in mainland China, but so far are few in number. However, Hong Kong may be ahead of its neighbouring city, Macau, where have been no reports of it until 2013. Chan Kin Hong, Head of IT Crimes Division of Macau's Judiciary Police, is reported as saying that 'We cannot neglect that the problem exists in the territory' (*Macau Daily Times*, 15 August, 2011). Given the high use of ICT by young people (see above), there is a high chance that they will come across some forms of cyberbullying.

Three surveys on cyberbullying were carried out in Hong Kong in 2009–10. The Hong Kong Christian Service (Christian Service News, 2009) Fun Teen recruited 908 Secondary 4–6 students, the Hong Kong Federation of Youth (2010) conducted a survey with 559, 10- to 24-year-olds, and the Church of the United Brethren in Christ (Hong Kong News Net, 11 June, 2010) recruited 2,629 primary pupils and secondary students. All these surveys reported some 11–22% of school children having experienced cyberbullying. Surveys done by the Chinese University of Hong Kong, the Hong Kong Federation of Youth and the City University of Hong Kong (2010) reported higher figures, with 22–30% of participants reporting having ever experienced cyberbullying. Although cyberbullying does not necessarily happen in schools and among class-mates, the Hong Kong Federation of Youth (2010) survey found that 34–47% of cyberbullying happened among schoolmates; only 19–24% involved strangers. That means, the school plays an important role in the prevention and intervention of cyberbullying as well as for traditional school bullying.

Compared to traditional bullying, it may be difficult for parents, teachers and educators to uncover the problem of cyberbullying, let alone to work on the issue. This may be partly due to a lack of technological knowledge and experience on the adults' side (Beran and Li, 2005). In this regard, both teachers and parents need to be educated with some technological knowledge and information for the detection, prevention and intervention (see also Chapter 19).

A recent cross-cities survey on cyberbullying

In August–September 2013, a survey was conducted in Macau, Guangzhou and Hong Kong (穗港澳網絡欺凌調查報告, November

2013). A total of 2,460 questionnaires (Hong Kong: 1,134; Macau: 409; Guangzhou: 917) were collected jointly by the Hong Kong Playground Association, the Macau Federation of Neighborhoods and the Guangzhou Youth Cultural Palace. The average age of the respondents was 16 years; most were 12–24 years, but 19% were below 12 years old. Given the popularity of smart phones and social networking sites, it may not be surprising that overall 74% of participants had witnessed cyber-bullying; this was highest in Macau (70%), followed by Guangzhou (50%) and Hong Kong (44%). Overall, 64% of all participants had been cyberbullied in the preceding year; again highest in Macau (83%), followed by Guangzhou (65%) and Hong Kong (56%). Overall, 17% reported they had cyberbullied others; Macau highest (34%), followed by Guangzhou (15%) and Hong Kong (13%). These high percentages are in part because the survey asked if respondents had 'ever' been involved in these roles.

Percentages in Macau were the highest in all three roles (bully, victim and bystander), followed by Guangzhou, with Hong Kong consistently the lowest. Perhaps adolescents in Hong Kong are kept busy by heavy school work (much heavier than for those in both other cities. Attitudes may also differ: when asked if they considered cyberbullying behaviour to be a crime, overall 84% said 'yes'; but this was higher in Hong Kong (86%) than Guangzhou (83%) and Macau (79%).

The roles of cyber victims and bullies overlapped, as 65% of bullies considered themselves to be victims as well as bullies. The percentages involved as cyberbullies or victims increased with age. Across the three cities, of 453 participants aged below 12 years, 36% reported being victims and 9% bullies; of 478 aged 12–14 years, 66% reported being victims and 21% bullies; while of 596 aged 15–17 years, 75% reported being victims and 21% bullies. After a peak at this last age point, the risk of being a cyber-victim decreased to 69% at 18–24 years. Males were more likely than females to be both victims and bullies of cyberbullying, but there was no significant gender difference in bystand-ers. The more time spent on the Internet, the greater the risk of being involved in cyberbullying, as bystanders, victims and/or bullies.

In both Hong Kong and Macau, cyberbullying occurred primarily at home (16% and 22% respectively), followed by in school (15% and 20%), friends' home (12% and 20%) and game centres (11% and 16%), while in Guangzhou it occurred mainly in game centres (17%), then at school (12%), then at home (11%).

The three most common cyberbullying behaviours overall were 'harassment' followed by 'denigration' and 'masquerade' (out of the eight common types, namely 騷擾 harassment; 詆毀 denigration; 改圖

masquerade; 罵戰 flaming; 假冒 impersonation; 起底 outing, 纏擾 cyber stalking; and 杯葛 exclusion).

The 21-item Depression Anxiety Stress Scales (DASS21) indicated that youths involved in cyberbullying, both as bullies and victims, had significantly higher levels of both depression and anxiety than those who were not involved. Regarding coping strategies, 27% of participants reported that they would get help from a friend in the case of cyberbullying, 24% would call the police and 21% would seek help from social workers; only 13% would consider asking for help from a teacher.

Overall, if we put the prevalence of victims and bullies together, there is a prevalence of around 60–70% of being cyberbullied in some way at least once. If we compare this with studies done by the same organisation in previous years, 30% of participants reported being cyberbullied in 2010 and 2011, and 10% in 2009. This suggests a very rapid increase over a 4-year period.

Thus far, surveys done in Hong Kong are still at a preliminary stage and have mainly asked simple questions regarding occurrence. Only a couple of studies have made an attempt to investigate gender differences, feelings and psychological impacts of these acts. It can be said that more cyberbullying happens in boys, and that it peaks in Secondary Two (around 14 years old). The most commonly used platforms are social networks (50%) and SMS (40%), while over one quarter have uploaded indecent photos (Hong Kong Federation of Youth, 2010). Indecent photos posted and circulated can do a lot more harm to victims in the long run and this deserves serious attention. The negative impact is clear; in the Christian Service Fun Teen study (Christian Service News, 2009), 18% of Primary 4 to 6 participants reported being victims, and of these, 60% indicating being affected emotionally, 46% that this affected their everyday social life, 36% that their school life was affected and 15% that their family life was affected. Emotional impacts included 27% getting angry, 17% feeling hatred and 35% feeling helpless (they indicated they 'had no choice').

Nevertheless in Secondary grades, some half of the victims report that they have no intention of seeking help from teachers, as they considered that as useless. A worrying 1% expressed thoughts of ending their lives as their strongest reactions towards cyberbullying acts (Hong Kong Federation of Youth, 2010; Christian Service News, 2009). All these impacts were obvious in Ah Chung's case; he hid himself in the chapel during recess in order to avoid people. His social life came to a halt after being cyberbullied.

In response to the new and seemingly fast growing phenomenon of cyberbullying (see *China Daily*, Hong Kong Edition, 2 June, 2010), the Hong Kong Government started to sponsor NGOs and to fund universities to launch campaigns and intervention programs in schools in 2009. This is discussed further in Chapter 19.

Overall comments

School bullying is a general problem in Hong Kong, with schools of good repute being no exception. The media have uncovered the seriousness of bullying and thus led researchers to look into the prevalence and characteristics of bullying amongst school children. However, it was not until the last decade that programs and guidelines for dealing with the problem were developed by the governmental authorities, NGOs, and local practitioners (see Fung and Wong, 2007; Wong et al., 2002; Education and Manpower Bureau, 2003, 2004; Education Bureau of Hong Kong, 2008, 2012; Caritas Hong Kong Website). Details of these guidelines and programs are described in Chapter 19. Most cases that have caught the attention of the public or authorities are physical, or property-related; verbal and isolation bullying still lack attention, though they cause significant harm to victims. Because the consequences are less visible, much relational bullying remains hidden, awaiting schools to be more open to the issue and teachers to be able or trained to identify it.

Cyberbullying among school children and youth has become a problem which is more out of control than much traditional school bullying, both in terms of the drastic increase in experiences among young people and in terms of the forms of the acts, the broad range of platforms, namely, mobile, smart phone, social network, tablets, Apps, Whatsapp, Youtube and emails, their permeability, contexts and their consequences. All these had made identification, prevention and intervention more difficult than for traditional forms of school bullying.

From the latest study conducted and reported on cyberbullying in Hong Kong (穗港澳網絡欺凌調查報告, November 2013), Hong Kong seems to have a rather high cyberbullying rate, with 56% reporting ever being a cyber-victim compared to figures such as 35% in the US recently and also six years ago (Holfeld and Grabe, 2013; Kowalski and Limber, 2007; Williams and Guerra, 2007). However, another Hong Kong study in 2010 reported the cyber-victim rate as only 30% (Hong Kong Federation of Youth, 2010). Both Hong Kong studies asked participants if they were 'ever' bullied, and in addition they did not consider the 'imbalance of power' criterion. It does appear that the cyber victimisation rate has increased a lot in Hong Kong in the last 4 years. However, the varying definitional criteria, frequency cut-off, time reference period, samples, and how the questions were asked and collected, all vary between studies in Hong Kong and in other countries. This makes it very difficult to compare accurately across time and with studies done in other countries.

Overall conclusion

Research on both traditional school bullying and cyberbullying in Hong Kong remains scarce. Thus far, limited research has been done in Hong Kong on the psychological impact of bullying. First, the long term effects of bullying are not usually seen by teachers or schools. Second, bullying is still considered a taboo topic in Hong Kong society and few schools are willing to allow research to be done on it in their premises. With regard to the research that has been undertaken, varying types of studies, definitions and measurement criteria have made comparisons difficult if not impossible.

We can learn from studies done in the West, and we have adopted concepts, ideology and categorisations that have been used there for decades. This has helped in establishing a groundwork for initial investigation of this important issue. However, the phenomena of bullying and cyberbullying among young people in Hong Kong could be different or more complicated than those in the west. For example, there is the possible involvement of gangsters (Triad Society) and politicization of issues. Translation of terms is another important issue; the adaptation of questions from western instruments might lead to ambiguity and cause misunderstanding on the part of the participants. The situation has been worsened by disciplinary splits and some unawareness of theories available in other parts of the world.

Hong Kong could have benefited from studying the earlier experiences of neighbouring East Asian countries and cities (Lin, Kanetsuna and Lee, 2012). However, it was forced to react only when brutal cases happened or appalling news was reported by the media (Morrison, 2005). Both South Korea and Japan were alarmed by pupils committing suicide after being bullied, whereas Hong Kong was alerted by serious physical assaults that were videotaped and circulated via the Internet. In all these advanced Asian cities, including Hong Kong, the media played an important part in developing public awareness of the issue. It would be advantageous to conduct multi-disciplinary research, making full use of the knowledge and strengths of disciplines such as media and communications, information and electronic technology, and teacher education, in addition to the tradition of developmental psychology, sociology and (especially for cyberbullying) the legal profession. Also, we need to seriously consider in-depth qualitative and even longitudinal kind of studies to fill the current gaps in research.

REFERENCES

Apple Daily (10th December 2013). 疑遭欺凌10歲女生校園墮斃 (10-year old girl jumped to death after being bullied).

Beane, A. L. (1999). *The bully free classroom*. Minneapolis, MN: Free Spirit Publishing Co.

Beran, T. and Li, Q. (2005). Cyber-harassment: A new method for an old behavior. *Journal of Educational Computing Research*, 32, 137–153.

Breakthrough Youth Research Archives, (2003). 青少年網絡危機研究 (A study of internet crisis among Hong Kong youth.). Breakthrough Ltd.

Caritas Hong Kong (2012). Cyberbullying among the youth. Judge Tom, 7th October. www.ghs.edu.hk/sec/panel/ict/Project/12-13/F2_Web/2E_23/web/aricle_d.html Retrieved 12 Jan 2016

China Daily, Hong Kong Edition (2010). Cyberbullying a growing problem in city. S. Lee, 6th February.

China Daily, Hong Kong Edition (2009). School bullies get detention, probation. (11th September,

Hong Kong Edition. (2013). Bully for you!, 5th April.

Christian Service News (2009). Close to 2% youths experienced cyberbullying: We must join hands to stop the abusive trend, Issue 64, July 2009.

Commission on Youth (2008). Executive Summary. Retrieved 26 June, 2010, from www.coy.gov.hk/eng/report/it.htm

Department for Education and Skills (DFES) (2nd edn. 2000; rev.2002). *Bullying: Don't suffer in Silence. An anti-bullying pack for schools*. London: HMSO.

(2004). *Every child matters: Change for children*. Norwich: The Stationery Office.

Education and Manpower Bureau (2003). Implementation of comprehensive student Guidance Service. Education Bureau circular. EDBC019/2003. Hong Kong Government.

(2004). Co-creating a harmonious school–stop bullying web-based resource package. Hong Kong Government. http://peace2.edb.hkedcity.net/index.htm.

Education Bureau of Hong Kong (2008). Creating harmonious school. Hong Kong Education Bureau circular EDBC018/2008. Hong Kong Government.

(2012). IS Department, Hong Kong SAR Government (English) 2012-12-19 LCQ12:cyberbullying. Hong Kong Government.

Fung, A. L. C. and Wong, J. L. P. (2007). *Project C.A.R.E.: Children and adolescents at risk education*. Hong Kong: Hong Kong Christian Service.

Hong Kong Christian Service (2009). Press release on cyberbullying. www.hkcs.org/enews/e064/e06402.html Retrieved 12 Jan 2016

Hong Kong Federation of Youth (2010). A study on cyberbullying among Hong Kong Secondary students. HK Federation of Youth.

Hong Kong News Net (11 June, 2010). One in every ten Hong Kong students' victims of Internet bullying. www.hongkongnews.net/index.php/sid/646234 Retrieved 12 Jan 2016

Hong Kong Playground Association (2008). Press releases of the study on investigating the prevalence of bullying among adolescents in Hong Kong and Macao. Retrieved April 20, 2012 from www.hkpa.hk/new/doc/bullying_press_200408.pdf.

Holfeld, B. and Grabe, M. (2013). An examination of the history, prevalence, characteristics, and reporting of cyberbullying in the United States. In Li, Q., Cross, D. and Smith, P, K. (Eds.), *Cyberbullying in the global playground: Research from international perspectives* (pp. 117–142), Chichester: Wiley-Blackwell.

Kowalski, R. M. and Limber, S. P. (2007). Electronic bullying among middle school studies. *Journal of Adolescent Health*, 41, S22–S30.

Internet World Stats (December 2012). Internet usage in Asia. www.internetworldstats.com/stats3.htm Retrieved 12 Jan 2016

Lam, O. B. and Liu, W. H. (2007). The path through bullying - a process model from the inside story of bullies in Hong Kong Secondary schools. *Child and Adolescent Social Work Journal*, 24, 53–75.

Legislative Council (2012). Cyberbullying, 19 December, Hong Kong Government. Retrieved June 20th 2014 from www.info.gov.hk/gia/general/201212/19/P201212190360.htm

(2004). Referring to the Administration's response to his questions on bullying in schools. CB(2)1770/03–04 (01).Hong Kong Government.

Leung, C. H. and To, H. K. (2009). The relationship between stress and bullying among secondary school students. *New Horizons in Education*, 57, No.1, May.

Lin, S. F., Kanetsuna, T. and Lee, S. H. (2012). Bullying in eastern cultures. In A. O. Bernal, S. Y. Jimenez and P. K Smith (Eds.), *El acoso escolar y su prevención* [School violence and it's prevention] (pp. 145–171). Madrid: Biblioteca Nueva.

Macau Daily Times. (2011). Cyberbullying, a worrying trend: A new playground for teenagers, Tiago Azevedo, 25th August.

Menesini, E., Sanchez, V., Fonzi, A., Ortega, R., Costabile, A. and Feudo, G. L. (2003). Moral emotions and bullying: A cross-national comparison of differences between bullies, victims and outsiders. *Aggressive Behavior*, 29, 515–530.

Ming Pao (2004). 'Bullies in our Schools', a survey conducted by Legislative Council Member Chan Kam Lam, in affiliation with Ngau Tau Kok Kai Fong Welfare Association. 16th February, Democratic Alliance for the Betterment.

(2012). 'ESF's students kicked people instead of ball' (26th March).

Morrison, K. (2005). Bullying in schools. *Journal of the Education and Youth Affairs Department (DSEJ)*, *Macau*, May, 34–45.

Ng, J. W. Y. and Tsang, S. K. M. (2008). School bullying and the mental health of junior secondary school students in Hong Kong. *Journal of School Violence*, 7, 3–20.

NielsenWire (2011). New mobile obsession: U.S. teens triple data usage. 15 December, 2011. www.nielsen.com/us/en/insights/news/2011/new-mobile-obsession-u-s-teens-triple-data-usage/ Retrieved 12 Jan 2016

Olweus, D. (1991). Bully/victim problems among schoolchildren: Basic facts and effects of a school based intervention program. In D. Pepler and K. Rubin (Eds.), *The development and treatment of childhood aggression* (pp. 411–448). Hillsdale, N.J.: Erlbaum.

Sing Tao Daily (2003). 師生總動員減校園欺凌 (Whole school involved in reducing School Bullying), 23rd December.

Smith P. K. and Brain, P. (2000). Bullying in schools: lessons from two decades of research. *Aggressive Behavior*, 26, 1–9.

Smith, P. K., Morita, Y., Junger-Tas, J., Olweus, D., Catalano, R. and Slee, P. (Eds.) (1999). *The nature of school bullying: A cross-national perspective.* London and New York: Routledge.

South China Morning Post. (2010). Home truths about cyberbullying, 1st June.

TaKung Pao(2008). 港初中生欺凌行為明顯上升(Bullying behaviours obviously increased among secondary students). 12th December.

Wong, D. S. W. (2003). *School bullying and responding tactics: A life education approach.* Hong Kong: Arcadia Press.

  (2004). School bullying and tackling strategies in Hong Kong. *International Journal of Offender Therapy and Comparative Criminology*, 48, 537–553.

Wong, D. S. W, Chiu, S. K. S., Fung, A. Y. T. and Li, Y. Y. P. (2002). *Helping pupils away from bullying.* Hong Kong: Centre for Restoration of Human Relationships.

Wong, D. S. W., Lok, D. P. P., Lo, T. W. and Ma, S. K. (2008). School bullying among Hong Kong Chinese primary school children. *Youth and Society*, 40, 35–54.

Williams, K. R. and Guerra, N. G. (2007). Prevalence and predictors of internet bullying. *Journal of Adolescent Health*, 41, S14–S21.

香港教育專業人員協會 (2001年4月) 解決訓導工作困難計劃之問卷調查結果 香港教育專業人員協會[Professional Teachers Union, Survey on Difficulties of Disciplinary Teachers. Professional Teachers Union].

香港遊樂場協會、廣州市青年文化宮、澳門街坊會聯合總會 (Nov, 2013) 穗港澳網絡欺凌調查報告 (Nov, 2013) 香港遊樂場協會 [Cyberbullying in the three cities: Hong Kong, Macau and Guanzhou: A Survey Report. Hong Kong Playground Association.].

8   Comparisons between English *bullying* and Japanese *ijime*

Tomoyuki Kanetsuna

The concept of *bullying* is generally defined in western cultures as an aggressive behaviour characterised by repetition of actions and asymmetric power relationships (Olweus, 1999), or a systematic abuse of power (P. K. Smith and Sharp, 1994). However, the definition and understanding of bullying-like phenomena varies by culture (P. K. Smith et al., 2002; P. K. Smith, Kanetsuna and Koo, 2007). While some researchers emphasise or even assume the essential commonality of *bullying* across different cultures, others strongly assert that some bullying-like phenomena are fundamentally different. An interesting case is the comparison between *bullying* in western countries, and *ijime* in Japan. *Ijime* is the Japanese term considered the most similar concept to *bullying*, and has a research tradition spanning thirty years (Morita et al., 1999).

The comparison between *bullying* in England and *ijime* in Japan is important in terms of the differences of social and cultural context. Most affluent urban western countries, including England, are thought to be individualistic in nature, where people are expected to be self-reliant, independent and autonomously separated from their parents in their development (Hofstede, 1980; P. B. Smith, Bond and Kagitçibasi, 2005). Many non-western societies, including Japan, are on the other hand, thought to be collectivistic, with closely knit human and family relations. The rapid growth of economy and modernisation of Japanese society after the Second World War means that Japan today too is an affluent urban society where people have led more westernised ways of life. However, connectedness appears to continue in the realm of emotional interdependencies (Kagitçibasi, 1990; 1996). In modernising eastern cultures, children are expected to become autonomous, but at the same time, family relatedness is highly valued which leads to strong parental control, rather than the permissiveness often seen in individualistic societies (P. B. Smith et al., 2005). Japan also continues to be influenced by aspects of Confucian ideology, such that respect for elders, and fear of losing face in front of others, are stronger phenomena of interpersonal relationships than in the west.

These social and cultural differences can have strong relevance for psychological aspects of *bullying/ijime* phenomenon including how people in each country perceive and understand the nature of *bullying/ijime*, and what attitudes they might have towards bullies and victims, and towards actions against it. These psychological aspects could in turn affect the actual conditions of *bullying/ijime* in each country including its prevalence, major types, preferred coping strategies and actions of bystanders. However, until mid-1990s, there was little interchange between the Western and Japanese researchers in the issues of *bullying/ijime*, despite rather extensive research traditions in both countries. The first systematic comparison between *bullying* in England and *ijime* in Japan was conducted in 1998 as part of a large-scale cross-national study, together with the Netherlands and Norway, using a modified version of the Olweus self-report questionnaire (Morita, 2001). This was followed by a series of direct comparisons between pupils in England and Japan. Kanetsuna and Smith (2002) gave a self-report questionnaire to 207 pupils aged 13–14 years; Kanetsuna, Smith and Morita (2006) conducted in-depth structured one-to-one interview to 121 pupils aged 12–15 years; Kanetsuna and Smith (submitted) gave a self-report questionnaire to 1,967 pupils aged 12–15 years. In addition, Kanetsuna (2004) reported other findings not covered in the above studies.

These direct comparative studies between England and Japan aimed to examine children's general perceptions and understanding of *bullying/ijime* and its related themes. This was for two reasons. First, the 'adult' or standard definition often given in a self-report questionnaire survey has been found not always to be consistent with how children understand the phenomenon; young children typically conceive of *bullying* in broader terms without necessarily invoking 'intention', 'repetition of actions', and 'power imbalance between aggressors and victims' (Monks and Smith, 2006). Second, it is children themselves who actually conduct the behaviour or receive nasty treatment, and it is they who are most likely to notice that an incident is happening and decide whether or not to intervene and help victims or to support and reinforce aggressors.

In this chapter, I review the major findings of these direct comparative studies between *bullying* and *ijime*, focusing on common features as well as important differences in their perception. I then discuss the possible explanation of the differences that emerged and some practical implications for future studies.

Prevalence and basic nature of *bullying/ijime*

Direct physical and verbal forms of aggression were commonly well recognised as *bullying/ijime* among pupils in both countries. This was found both in an open-ended question (where pupils were asked what kind of behaviour they regarded as *bullying* [England] or *ijime* [Japan]) and closed-choice questions (where pupils were given different hypothetical scenarios and asked whether they regard each given scenario to be *bullying/ijime*). However, 'indirect' forms such as ignoring, social exclusion, and nasty rumour spreading and note sending were often more recognised as *ijime* among Japanese pupils than as *bullying* among English pupils (Kanetsuna, 2004).

In terms of perceived prevalence of these forms of *bullying/ijime*, direct verbal forms were perceived to be the most frequent in both countries, and this was consistent with children's understanding of what *bullying/ijime* is. However, indirect 'rumour spreading' and 'note-sending', which was often better recognised as *ijime* than as *bullying*, were also perceived to be as frequent as those verbal forms in both countries (Kanetsuna, 2004). This suggests that even though both direct and indirect forms of *bullying/ijime* are perceived to be happening equally in both countries, what children in each country regard as *bullying/ijime* seems different.

These differences in perceptions between English and Japanese pupils may partly stem from the history of interest in and research on the topic in each country. In England, research on *bullying* started in the mid-1980s, influenced by studies in Scandinavia, with the main focus on overt and direct forms of aggression (e.g., Olweus, 1978; 1993). In Japan, research on *ijime* started in the early 1980s, following the containment of school violence in the late 1970s. The issue of *ijime* was treated rather independently as a new social phenomenon by society, and the focus was put mainly on its indirect and covert nature in contrast to the more overt and direct nature of school violence. As a result, the term *ijime* is often recognised and used for aggressive behaviour which causes a victim more psychological than physical suffering, and even if the action itself is physical and direct, the focus is often placed not so much on its physically violent connotation but more on the psychologically negative effects on the victim (Morita et al., 1999). This means that pupils in England, because they often consider *bullying* as being by direct physical or verbal means, could be very sensitive to such direct forms of aggression, taking it more seriously than indirect forms, whereas the converse might be true in Japan.

Such basic understanding of *bullying/ijime* seems consistent with pupil's perceptions of the general nature of the phenomena

Table 8.1 *Pupils' general perceptions of the nature of* bullying/ijime *in each country*

	England	**Japan**
Perceived major forms	More direct (e.g., physical, verbal)	More indirect (e.g., ignoring, social exclusion)
Perceived prevalence	1. Verbal 2. Rumour spreading	1. Verbal 2. Rumour spreading
Common places	1. Playground 2. Elsewhere in school/ Outside school	1. Classroom 2. Elsewhere in school
Typical aggressors	1. Different class but the same year groups 2. Higher year groups	1. Same class 2. Different class but the same year groups
Relationships between aggressors and victims	Not know very well or at all	Know very well or friends

(see Table 8.1). B*ullying* in England was perceived as most likely to be conducted in the 'playground', either by pupils 'in different classes in the same year group' or 'in higher year groups'. They are by no means 'friends' of the victim; instead, it is more likely that bullies and victims 'may know each other but are not friends to each other' or 'they don't know each other very well or at all'. *Ijime* in Japan, on the other hand, was perceived most likely to be conducted in the 'classroom', by the victim's 'classmates' or at least pupils who are 'in different classes but the same year group'. Bullies and victims were perceived most likely to 'know each other very well' or to be 'friends' to each other. These perceptions and understanding of *bullying/ijime* in each country were found to be consistent throughout different forms of *bullying/ijime* behaviours (Kanetsuna and Smith, 2002; Kanetsuna, 2004; Kanetsuna and Smith, submitted). These findings support the argument by Morita et al. (1999) that indirect forms such as ignoring and social exclusion, which are better recognised as *ijime* by Japanese pupils, may not be effective unless the victim and the aggressors belong to the same social group, and unless it is conducted in a rather closed place like a classroom in Japanese schools where the victim finds it difficult to seek external help from either in or outside the classroom. In contrast, direct physical and verbal forms, better recognised as *bullying* by English pupils, are still effective even if bullies and victims are not sharing the same social group and have no prior relationships to each other.

Typical characteristics of bullies and victims

Regarding typical characteristics of bullies and victims, pupils in both countries seem to share common perceptions. As for the characteristics of bullies, pupils commonly perceived them to have internal personality problems and/or external environmental problems. The former included meanness, aggressiveness, impulsiveness, selfishness, insecurity, low self-esteem, loneliness and less sympathetic and empathetic feelings to others, while the latter included insecure and abusive family background, unpopularity among peers and lack of friends (Kanetsuna, 2004).

These appear, to a large extent, consistent with findings from previous studies, mainly in western countries. Cook, Williams and Guerra (2010) meta-analysed 153 studies to examine the predictors of bullying and victimisation. They concluded that the typical bully is the one who showed both externalising behaviours and internalising symptoms, and has both social competence and academic challenges. They also reported that the typical bully had both negative attitudes and beliefs about others as well as themselves. As for family background, the bully typically comes from a family with conflict and poor parental monitoring, and for the relationships with peers, they are more likely to perceive their school atmosphere negatively and tend to be negatively influenced by their peers (Cook et al., 2010). Similarly, Lereya, Samara and Wolke (2013), based on their meta-analysis of seventy studies of parenting and peer victimisation, reported that those who are both the bully and the victim (generally the so-called bully/victim) were more likely to be exposed to negative parenting behaviour including abuse, neglect and maladaptive parenting.

An interesting difference was, however, found in terms of 'popularity' and 'physical appearance'. A considerable number (about 25%) of Japanese pupils claimed that bullies were generally popular among peers, while very few (only 6%) of pupils in England thought the same way (Kanetsuna, 2004). This can be understood given that one of the most common forms of *ijime* is indirect means, so bullies must have some popularity or high status among peers to control others to manage what they want to get. In contrast, more pupils in England than Japan reported that bullies generally look strong (27% and 13% respectively). This again suggests that *bullying* in England seems to be perceived as more directly physical in nature, and the bullies should, therefore, be perceived as physically big, strong and threatening, but not necessarily popular.

In terms of typical characteristics of victims, pupils in both countries again showed similar perceptions. The majority of pupils in both countries (62% in England and 77% in Japan) perceived the typical victim as 'inactive /unassertive'. This included 'quiet', 'shy', 'inability to speak up, stand up, or fight back for themselves', 'vulnerable', 'too sensitive' and 'have low self-esteem' (Kanetsuna, 2004). These characteristics seem almost identical to what Olweus (1993) called 'the passive /submissive victim'. Olweus also claimed that this type of victim often does not have good friends in their class. Indeed, both about 30% of English and 20% of Japanese pupils claimed that the typical victim has very few or no friends, and that because they lack social skills, typical victims are neither popular among peers nor able to get along with other children (Kanetsuna, 2004). Similar findings have been reported in several different studies (e.g., Boulton and Smith, 1994; Boulton, 1995; Fox and Boulton, 2006).

Victim-blaming tendency and negativity of victims

Another important issue related to the typical characteristics of bullies and victims is the tendency to attribute the responsibility of such negative behaviour as *bullying/ijime* not to aggressors but to the victim's personality and behaviour. Asking children why they think bullies act in the way they do, nearly half of pupils in Japan suggested negative feelings of bullies towards victims (i.e., *because they don't like the victim*; *because the victim gets on the bullies' nerves*) (Kanetsuna, 2004). One of the reasons why pupils have such negative attitudes to victims could be related to their general understanding of typical characteristics of victims. A considerable number of pupils in both countries (43% in England and 38% in Japan) reported victims as 'somewhat different from others'. This included 'race', 'religion', 'cultural background', 'dialect and accent', 'socio-economic backgrounds', 'academic achievement', 'hobbies and interests' and 'general attitudes and values' (Kanetsuna, 2004). One explanation is that children could attempt to self-justify by using these 'differences' as a reason to pick on others, and this could in turn lead to victim-blaming tendency. In fact, nearly half of English pupils suggested such differences as one of the reasons to bully others. Kanetsuna and Smith (submitted) reported that although both English and Japanese pupils in their study considered 'aggressors' to be the most blamed for *bullying/ijime*, English pupils considered 'both aggressors and victims' to be blamed the next, and Japanese pupils blamed 'the victim' as much or more than 'both aggressors and victims'. It seems that quite a number of pupils in both countries do think the victims of *bullying/ijime* might get what they deserved to get, and this tendency seem to be more salient among pupils in Japan than in England.

These findings were again supported by previous studies. Morita and Kiyonaga (1994) reported that 66% of aggressors and 37% of reinforcers in their study blamed the victim for their *ijime* behaviour. Emphasising the group nature of *ijime,* they described this tendency as the result of 'the interaction process of homogeneity' among children, by which a child labelled as 'heterogeneous', who does not share the same values, attitudes, interests or social background with other children in the group, will either be excluded or forced in a threatening manner to become homogeneous (similar) to others. As a similar phenomenon of victim blaming has been described in South Korean pupils (Lee, Smith and Monks, 2011), it does seem one of the characteristics of collectivistic countries. However, this tendency is not exclusive to Asian countries. Gini (2008) examined the victim-blaming tendency of *bullying* among Italian pupils, and found that boys blamed the victim more than girls, and that the victim was considered more responsible in the case of direct forms of aggression. He argued that bystanders tend to blame victims when a serious event takes place, and in the case of *bullying,* children may have considered direct means such as hitting and kicking to be more serious, perhaps because of the more visible and immediate consequences, and even motivated by more serious causes than indirect bullying. In this sense, if pupils in Japan take indirect forms more seriously, but pupils in western countries such as Italy and England take direct forms more seriously, then we would expect that in Japan, victim blaming will be stronger for indirect forms, while in England it will be stronger for direct forms; but this needs further examination.

These negative attitudes to victims among pupils can not only make pupils inactive to help and support victims, but it can also make victims inactive to seek help from others. Indeed, although the majority of pupils in both England and Japan reported that they would tell others if they were victimised, nearly 20% of English pupils and almost 40% of Japanese pupils reported they would not (Kanetsuna, 2004). The most common response in both countries for the reason not telling others was 'the fear of the *bullying/ijime* getting worse'. This fear of future attacks can be fuelled by such negative attitudes to victims among pupils but also by a lack of trust and confidence towards adults as a helper.

Coping strategies

How individual victims cope with victimisation is another important issue of *bullying/ijime* problem. Whether a child becomes a persistent or long-term victim may depend greatly on how they cope with attempts at peer victimisation and harassment. Those who cope less well or get less

Table 8.2 *Pupils perceptions of recommended coping strategies for different forms of* bullying/ijime *(%) (adapted from Kanetsuna et al., 2006)*

	Physical		Verbal		Ignoring/ Social exclusion		Note sending/ rumour spreading	
	Engl.	Japan	Engl.	Japan	Engl.	Japan	Engl.	Japan
Seek help	81	53	72	26	16	29	74	14
Take direct action.	16	49	12	72	26	43	8	16
Avoidance	38	5	–	–	–	–	–	–
Passive behaviour	–	–	–	–	0	21	38	24
Ignoring	–	–	45	11	–	–	–	–
Reflect on yourself	–	–	–	–	0	16	–	–
Make new friends	–	–	–	–	77	11	–	–
Deny it	–	–	–	–	–	–	12	43

Engl. = English; Japan = Japanese; '–' = No response recorded. Some of the above strategies are categorised only for a particular type of *bullying/ijime* (e.g., 'Ignoring' is a category only for 'Verbal').

support will be easier targets for continued victimisation, with less risk to bullies (Perry, Kusel and Perry, 1988; P. K. Smith, Shu and Madsen, 2001). Kanetsuna et al. (2006) examined children's preferred coping strategies for different forms of *bullying/ijime* (see Table 8.2), and found that for direct physical *bullying/ijime*, more than 80% of pupils in England suggested the victim should 'seek help from others' including teachers, parents and friends. Although about half of Japanese pupils agreed this view, the other half thought that the victim should 'take direct action against bullies by themselves' including fighting back, arguing back, telling bullies to stop or asking bullies why they do it. Many fewer pupils in England suggested this, instead, more than one-third recommended some form of 'avoidance' behaviour including run away, walk away, move away or stay away from bullies, ignore them or transfer to another school.

A very similar pattern was found for direct verbal *bullying/ijime*. Most English pupils recommended the victim 'seek help from others' while most pupils in Japan recommended the victim 'take direct action against bullies'. Nearly half of pupils in England also recommended 'ignore the bullies'. However, this pattern was slightly changed for indirect forms such as ignoring and social exclusion. The majority of English pupils recommended the victim to 'make new friends'. In contrast, although nearly half of Japanese pupils still think the victim should 'take direct action against bullies', about one-third recommended 'seeking help from others'. Furthermore, about 20% recommended that they 'just put up with it', and some 15% blamed the victim and recommended the victim to 'reflect themselves on any fault and to try to improve themselves'. However, for indirect note sending and rumour spreading, the results were rather similar to those for direct physical and verbal *bullying/ijime*. The majority of pupils in England recommended 'seeking help from others', whereas nearly half of pupils in Japan recommended 'making clear for everyone that the rumour is not true /denying the rumour'. Interestingly, two-fifths of pupils in England reported that the victim should 'keep quiet about it /put up with it'.

From these results, pupils in both countries seem to have some idea of what they should do to cope with different kinds of *bullying/ijime* effectively. Japanese pupils seem clearly reluctant to seek help from others; instead, they appear to think taking direct actions against bullies are more useful coping strategies, especially for direct physical and verbal forms of *ijime*. In contrast, English pupils think that seeking help from others is very helpful. An important issue here is that although pupils do have some thoughts about how to cope with *bullying/ijime*, this does not mean they can always try what they believe to be the best coping strategies.

It seems likely that most of the time, victims of *bullying/ijime* cannot or do not do anything about it, but just put up with it as discussed above. Morita (2001) reported that 61% of victims in Japanese and 67% of victims in English samples in their cross-national study reported that they either did not do anything about it and put up with it or tried to behave as if they were not bothered about being bullied. Only 17% of victims in England and 16% of victims in Japan reported that they told teachers or friends about it and asked for help.

This issue of what they should and what they can actually do for *bullying/ijime* should be considered in relation to the effectiveness of each strategy. Given that there is always an imbalance of power between bullies and victims, where victims find it difficult to defend themselves effectively (Olweus, 1993), strategies such as telling bullies to stop, or fighting back, may not be as successful as seeking help from others. One explanation for the tendency for Japanese pupils to recommend such direct action may be the lack of trust towards teachers and peers as a defender or as an intervener to the situation.

Regarding the marked differences found in recommended coping strategies for indirect ignoring and social exclusion, English pupils appear to think that even when a group of pupils tried to ignore or exclude the victim, there should be others whom the victim can approach to and hang around with. In contrast, given that Japanese pupils are generally very reluctant to seek help from others, and that it should be very difficult to take any kind of direct action against bullies especially when the victim is ignored or excluded, there seems no way to cope with the situation but, as pupils suggested, just put up with it, unless the victim somehow makes a positive change about themselves so as to be accepted by peers again. This is probably one of the characteristic differences between *bullying* in England and *ijime* in Japan.

In contrast, about two-fifths of pupils in England reported that the victim should keep quiet about it/put up with it for note sending and rumour spreading. This appears not to be because there is no way to cope with the situation, but because they believe that this is not as serious as other forms of bullying, and therefore, the victim should just leave it as it is until everyone forgets about it. Japanese pupils, on the other hand, take this type of *ijime* more seriously, recommending that the victim should tell everyone that the rumour is not true. If the victim just ignored the rumour and left it as it is, the *ijime* could escalate to ignoring and social exclusion which Japanese pupils may find the most difficult to cope with.

Friendship formation and relevance to *bullying/ijime* behaviour

Morita and Kiyonaga (1994) argued that *ijime* in Japan is often regarded as a group phenomenon characterised by its covert and indirect nature. This can be because in Japanese schools, the social group is more likely to be formed within a class and pupils have fewer interactions with pupils in different classes or year groups compared to pupils in England. If this is the case, the difference in friendship formation, together with differences in the school system between England and Japan can be considered to play a significant role in characterising some of the differences between *bullying* in England and *ijime* in Japan.

Kanetsuna (2004) and Kanetsuna and Smith (submitted) found that although both English and Japanese pupils reported having a considerable number of friends in the same year group, Japanese pupils reported significantly more friends in the same year group, both in the same class (on average 6.5 friends for English pupils and 8.2 for Japanese) and in different classes in the same year group (on average 8.1 and 9.5 respectively), whereas English pupils had significantly more friends in different year groups than did Japanese pupils (on average 5.2 and 3.0 respectively). Furthermore, Japanese pupils were found to spend most time with friends in either their own classroom or outside school, whereas English pupils, besides the classroom, spend a lot of time with friends in the playground. In summary, English pupils spend considerable time with friends in the same and different year groups in the playground, whereas Japanese pupils have few friends (if at all) in different year groups and spend most time with friends in the classroom. This makes it understandable that *bullying* in England is often found to take place in the playground conducted by pupils in both the same years and higher years, while *ijime* in Japan is found to take place most often in the classroom conducted by the pupils in the same year groups. An important question to ask is where such differences in friendships and places of friendship come from, and how it might affect the differences between *bullying* and *ijime*. One explanation can be the school systems of each country.

In Japan, almost all state lower-secondary schools use a 'class system' in which all pupils are allocated to one of the classes at the beginning of the year (this usually lasts at least one academic year), and they take most lessons on this class basis in their own classrooms. Class-teachers are allocated to each class to organise the class and to supervise children who belong to their class. This class system provides cohesiveness of the class and fosters close relationships between pupils who belong to the same class, and possibly between pupils and the class-teacher. However, it could also make the classroom a much more closed system, where pupils have less opportunity to form friendships with pupils in other classes or in other year groups.

This class system appears to play a significant role in characterising the *ijime* problem in Japan as covert and indirect in nature. In such an environment, pupils as well as teachers tend to create unique characteristics or climate in their class, and if a pupil finds it difficult to fit in with such unique climate, she/he could easily be at great risk of isolation in the classroom and of becoming a target of *ijime*. As discussed earlier, *ijime* can be seen as 'the interaction process of homogeneity within a class' (Morita and Kiyonaga, 1994) where pupils who do not share the same values, attitudes, interests or social background or whatever with other children in the class, will be labelled as 'heterogeneous' and targeted by *ijime* behaviour. In other words, *ijime* in Japan could be seen as one of the strategies for pupils to maintain group cohesiveness of the class.

The term 'heterogeneous' can have a wide range of meanings depending on the climate of a class. For example, if the majority of the class is academically low achievers, then the high achiever could have a risk of becoming a victim of *ijime*; or vice versa. In such an environment, the reluctance of the victim to seek external help would be strengthened due to the difficulty in finding external help and the fear of on-going *ijime* getting worse. Furthermore, the reluctance of other members of the class to intervene in the situation or to inform the class-teacher would also be strengthened since such *ijime* behaviour often quickly spreads to the whole classroom, and *ijime* itself becomes one of the climates of the class. At this stage, other non-involved members of the class find themselves under pressure to choose which side they stand on. The answer is most likely to be the aggressors. Indeed, Morita and Kiyonaga (1994) reported that a classmate of the victim may take part in *ijime* so as to defend himself/herself and avoid being on the wrong side of the aggressors.

From this point of view, the different forms of *ijime* such as direct physical or verbal, or indirect social or relational aggression can be regarded as merely a means of exclusion of 'the heterogeneous' so as to keep the class a more desirable place for the majority. This could also explain why the perceived prevalence of different forms of *bullying/ijime* was quite similar between two countries, yet the general understanding of the nature of *bullying* and *ijime* was rather different. If *ijime* is used as a strategy to target the odd one out and to maintain or gain cohesiveness of the class, indirect ignoring and social exclusion could be more effective than any direct means. Thus, it is the background intentions to *bullying* or doing *ijime* that is more important rather than how it is carried out.

In contrast to the situation in Japan, most secondary schools in England adopt the subject-teacher-system in which pupils have specialist subject teachers and different classrooms for different lessons, and many schools also have a system of 'streaming' (class allocation based on pupils' overall ability) or of 'setting' (class allocation for individual subject based on pupils' ability). Most state schools also have a wide range of optional subjects that pupils can choose to take depending on their interests and future plan. Therefore, in state secondary schools in England, the class is not such a stable peer environment for children; instead, pupils often move from one class to another class according to their interests as well as ability for a particular subject. In addition, English pupils, compared to Japanese, spend more time in the playground where pupils from all age groups are playing. Therefore, pupils in England have more opportunity to mix with pupils in different classes as well as in different year groups and to form friendships with wider populations. In such an environment, direct physical and verbal bullying (rather than indirect social or relational) may be more likely to happen.

While the differences between *bullying* in England and *ijime* in Japan may not be fully explained by such differences of school systems and of pupils' friendship formations, they seem to be key elements. It suggests that the *ijime* problem in Japan may not be preventable with some of the strategies commonly used in England (Samara and Smith, 2008), such as whole school policies, playground upgrading or training of lunchtime supervisors. Instead, in addition to these whole-school and individual-based methodologies, class-based interventions may be more critical for successful interventions in Japanese schools (see also Chapters 4 and 16).

How individuals perceive their friendships within such a group seems also important and needs to be examined further. Assuming the collectivistic nature of *ijime* such that it is more often conducted within a group by one of its members (i.e., by the classmates in the classroom), pupils form much more intimate relationships within the group where children shift their identity as an individual to a member of the group. In other words, once individuals form some kind of group, each individual is more likely to lose their individual identity and form a new identity as a group member.

If this is the case in school classes in Japan, once an individual was excluded from the group, the person would lose or would feel they lost his/her identity as a whole, and that is probably what Japanese pupils find most difficult to cope with. In England, a more individualistic society, pupils form peer groups that may be characterised by more open relationships; they may form several different social groups with different people in their class or year group. Therefore, even if an individual was ignored or socially excluded from one group, he or she would still be able to join in another group. This may explain why pupils in England consider some forms of indirect aggression such as ignoring and social exclusion to be less severe or serious forms of *bullying* compared to more direct physical or verbal forms (Kanetsuna and Smith, submitted).

Conclusion: some limitations and implications

This chapter has reviewed some findings of the direct cross-national studies between *bullying* in England and *ijime* in Japan focusing on children's general perceptions and understanding of the nature of the phenomenon. This has included major types, prevalence, places, aggressors, relationships between aggressors and victims, typical characteristics of bullies and victims, preferred coping strategies and friendships and time spent in different places with those friendships. There are some commonalities as well as differences in their perceptions and understanding of the phenomenon of *bullying/ijime*.

English pupils perceived bullying as more direct physical or verbal than indirect forms, often conducted in the playground, either by pupils in different classes in the same year group or in higher year groups, whom the victims may know but not in a friendly way or do not know very well or at all. By contrast, pupils in Japan perceived *ijime* as more indirect form, often conducted in the classroom, by the victim's classmates or at least pupils who are in different classes but the same year group, whom the victims know very well. Pupils in both countries had similar perceptions of typical characteristics of bullies and victims, and both pupils seemed to have certain negative attitudes to victims, though victim-blaming tendency appeared to be more salient among pupils in Japan. In terms of preferred coping strategies, while pupils in England recommended seeking help from others, Japanese pupils seemed to prefer taking direct actions against bullies.

These differences may partly stem from the history of interest in and research on the topic in each country discussed earlier, yet could partly be explained by the school systems and pupils' friendships within the system in each country. As Morita et al. (1999) argued, indirect forms of *bullying/ijime* such as ignoring and social exclusion should be more effective if the aggressors and the victim belong to the same social group. Therefore, these types of *bullying/ijime* could be more likely to occur between pupils who know each other very well, and could be more likely to happen in closed places like the classroom, rather than in the playground. Direct physical or verbal forms of *bullying/ijime*, on the other hand, should be more likely from someone physically stronger than the victim, and unlike indirect forms, such direct physical or verbal forms of *bullying/ijime* can still be very effective if the victim has no knowledge about the aggressors. Also, these direct forms of *bullying/ijime* are more visible and easy for teachers and other pupils to intervene, and therefore, the playground could be a more likely place for this to happen.

Indeed, compared to English pupils who formed their friendships among broader populations and spent a lot of time with them in the playground, Japanese pupils formed their friendships on the basis of the class they belonged to, and spent most time with them in the classroom. It can be hypothesised that the different organisation of classrooms in the two countries, together with issues around group identity in Japanese pupils, lie behind much of the differences found between *bullying* and *ijime*, and to clarify these hypothesis would be an issue to be addressed in future research.

I should note some methodological limitations to the studies reviewed and discussed in this chapter. First, these studies examined how pupils perceive and understand the nature of *bullying/ijime*, but it is not certain from the data whether these perceptions and understandings were based on pupils' own experiences of involving *bullying/ijime* situation, or were based on what they had been taught at school, or possibly on what was considered socially desirable as a response. Secondly, the studies presented here were conducted about ten years ago, and thus *cyberbullying/ net-ijime*, which is one of the major forms of *bullying/ijime* today, were not included. Finally, the numbers of schools sampled in each study were different, and even though several schools were sampled in each country (e.g., Kanetsuna and Smith, submitted), generalisation to country differences must remain tentative. Nevertheless, this chapter provides important information about the issues of *bullying/ijime* problems that can be used as useful pointers for developing successful prevention and intervention activities.

REFERENCES

Boulton, M. J. (1995). Patterns of bully/victim problems in mixed race groups of children. *Social Development*, 4, 227–293.

Boulton, M. J. and Smith, P. K. (1994). Bully/victim problems in middle-school children: Stability, self-perceived competence, peer perceptions and peer acceptance. *British Journal of Developmental Psychology*, 12, 315–329.

Cook, C. R., Williams, K. R. and Guerra, N. G. (2010). Predictors of bullying and victimization in childhood and adolescence: A meta-analytic investigation. *School Psychology Quarterly*, 25, 65–83.

Fox, C. L. and Boulton, M. (2006). Friendship as a moderator of the relationship between social skills problems and peer victimisation, *Aggressive Behavior*, 32, 110–121.

Gini, G. (2008). Italian elementary and middle school students' blaming the victim of bullying and perception of school moral atmosphere. *Elementary School Journal*, 108, 335–354.

Hofstede, G. (1980). *Culture's consequences: International differences in work-related values*. Newbury Park, CA: Sage.

Kanetsuna, T. (2004). *Pupil insights into school bullying: A cross-national perspective between England and Japan*. Unpublished PhD thesis, Goldsmiths College, University of London.

Kanetsuna, T. and Smith, P. K. (2002). Pupil insights into bullying, and coping with bullying: A bi-national study in Japan and England. *Journal of School Violence*, 1, 5–29.

   (submitted). A comparison of children's perceptions and understandings of *bullying* in England and *ijime* in Japan; the role of friendships and of the school class.

Kanetsuna, T., Smith, P. K. and Morita, Y. (2006). Coping with bullying at school: children's recommended strategies and attitudes to school-based interventions in Japan and England. *Aggressive Behavior*, 32, 570–580.

Kagitçibasi, C. (1990). Family and socialization in cross-cultural perspective: A model of change. In: Berman, J. (ed.), *Cross-cultural perspectives: Nebraska*

Symposium on Motivation, pp. 135–200. Lincoln, NE: Nebraska University Press.

(1996). *Family and human development across cultures: A view from the other side.* Hillsdale, NJ: Lawrence Erlbaum.

Lee, S., Smith, P. K. and Monks, C. P. (2011). Perceptions of bullying-like phenomena in South Korea: A qualitative approach from a lifespan perspective. *Journal of Aggression, Conflict and Peace Research*, 3, 210–221.

Lereya, S. T., Samara, M. and Wolke, D. (2013). Parenting behaviour and the risk of becoming a victim and a bully/victim: A meta-analysis study. *Child Abuse and Neglect*, 37, 1091–1108.

Monks, C. P. and Smith, P. K. (2006). Definitions of bullying: Age differences in understanding of the term, and the role of experience. *British Journal of Developmental Psychology*, 24, 801–821.

Morita, Y. (2001). *Ijime no kokusai hikaku kenkyu (Cross-national comparative study of bullying)*, Japan: Kaneko Shobo.

Morita, Y. and Kiyonaga, K. (1994). *Ijime: Kyoushitsu no yamai (Bullying: The ailing classroom)*. Tokyo: Kaneko Syobo.

Morita, Y., Soeda, H., Soeda, K. and Taki, M. (1999). Japan. In Smith, P. K., Morita, Y., Junger-Tas, J., Olweus, D., Catalano, R. and Slee, P. (eds.), *The nature of school bullying: A cross-national perspective*, pp. 309–323. London and New York: Routledge.

Olweus, D. (1978). *Aggression in the schools: Bullies and whipping boys.* Washington, D.C.: Hemisphere.

(1993). *Bullying at school: What we know and what we can do.* Oxford: Blackwell.

(1999). Norway. In P. K. Smith, Y. Morita, J. Junger-Tas, D. Olweus, R. Catalano and P. Slee (eds.), *The nature of school bullying: A cross-national perspective*, pp. 28–48. London and New York: Routledge.

Perry, D. G., Kusel, S. J. and Perry, L. C. (1988). Victims of peer aggression. *Developmental Psychology*, 24, 807–814.

Samara, M. and Smith, P. K. (2008). How schools tackle bullying, and the use of whole school policies: Changes over recent years. *Educational Psychology*, 28, 663–676.

Smith, P. B., Bond, M. H. and Kagitçibasi, C. (2005) *Social behavior across cultures: Living and working with others in a changing world.* London: Sage.

Smith, P. K. and Sharp, S. (eds.) (1994). *School bullying: Insights and perspectives.* London: Routledge.

Smith, P. K., Cowie, H., Olafsson, R. and Liefooghe, A. P. D. in collaboration with 17 additional authors (2002). Definitions of bullying: a comparison of terms used, and age and sex differences, in a 14-country international comparison. *Child Development*, 73, 1119–1133.

Smith, P. K., Kanetsuna, T. and Koo, H. (2007). Cross-national comparison of 'bullying' and related terms: Western and Eastern perspectives. In Österman, K. and Bjökqvist, K. (eds.), *Proceedings of the XVI world meeting of the International Society for Research on Aggression, Santorini, Greece,* pp. 3–9. Åbo, Finland: Åbo Academy University Press.

Smith, P. K., Shu, S. and Madsen, K. (2001). Characteristics of victims of school bullying: Developmental changes in coping strategies and skills. In J. Juvonen and S. Graham (eds.), *Peer Harassment in School*, pp. 332–351. New York: Guilford.

9   Children's experience of and attitudes
towards bullying and victimization
A cross-cultural comparison between China
and England

Linqin Ji, Wenxin Zhang and Kevin Jones

The past decade has witnessed an increase of research interest in exploring the cross-national similarities and differences of bullying and victimization. Eslea et al. (2004) examined the friendship and loneliness among bullies and victims using data from seven countries (including China), and reported there were cultural variations in the way that bullying is related to sex, age, and social support. Other cross-national studies (Craig et al., 2009; Due et al., 2009; Due and Holstein, 2008; Molcho et al., 2009) have mainly explored the prevalence rates of bullying and victimization in different cultures. For example, Craig et al. (2009) made a cross-national profile of bullying and victimization among adolescents in forty countries, and revealed there were cross-cultural differences in the prevalence of bullying/victimization. Molcho et al. (2009) examined the time trends of bullying since 1994 to 2006 in more than twenty countries from Europe and North America. Employing a sample 162,305 students recruited from thirty-five countries, Due et al. (2009) revealed that family socioeconomic inequality was associated with adolescents' exposure to bullying, and adolescents lived in countries where socioeconomic differences are larger were at higher risk of being bullied.

These cross-national studies demonstrated that some characteristics of bullying/victimization vary across nations and cultures, and the nature of bullying/victimization shows cultural variations. However, these studies were mostly conducted among countries in Europe and North America, and little is known directly about differences as well as similarities in school bullying between western and eastern cultures.

Chinese cultures and bullying/victimization among Chinese children

China is a culture that is distinct from those of European or American countries. As found by Bond and colleagues (Chinese Cultural

Connection, 1987), Chinese culture possessed four sets of values, including integration, human-heartedness, moral discipline, and Confucian work dynamism. A comprehensive review on individualism and collectivism by Oyserman, Coon, and Kemmelmeier (2002) supported Bond and colleagues' findings, and reported that Chinese showed both less individualistic and more collectivistic characteristics compared to many other cultures. Furthermore, China was found to score higher on the tightness-looseness scale compared to most of the European countries and the United States (Gelfand et al., 2011), indicating higher strength of social norms and less tolerance of deviance in China. In sum, Chinese culture is characterized by such features as collectivism and tightness of social norms. Within a collectivistic culture with tight social norms as that of China, maintaining social harmony and positive interpersonal relationships is emphasized. As a result, behaviors that threaten the well-being of others and the group, such as aggression, are strictly forbidden, and during socialization children are taught to control their frustration, anger, and impulsive and defiant behaviors from the early years (X. Chen, 2010; Hofstede, 2001). These cultural features could have important implications for children's social behaviors such as aggression and bullying, such that compared to children in western countries, Chinese children are less likely to take part in behaviors such as aggression and bullying, and possess relatively more positive attitudes towards children who are bullied, etc.

The scientific research on school bullying in China began at the end of the 1990s, marked by Zhang, Wu, and Cheng (1999) publishing a review on school bullying. Researchers examined the prevalence of general bullying/victimization and different forms of victimization, children's attitudes towards and the correlates of bullying/victimization, and even carried out a small-scale intervention (e.g., S. P. Chen and Yue, 2002; Gu and Zhang, 2003; Lei and Chang, 2002; Lei et al., 2004; Qu, 2005; Wang et al., 2012; Zhang, 2002; and see Chapter 6).

It has been reported that the percentage of Chinese students who were involved in regular interactions as either bullies or victims were about 25% in primary schools and 15% in middle schools (S. P. Chen and Yue, 2002; Qu, 2005; Wang et al., 2012; Zhang, 2002), which was lower than that of many western countries, such as Italy (bullies, 29%; victims, 8%) (Genta et al., 1996) and England (primary school: bullies, 12%; victims, 27%; middle school: bullies, 6%; victims, 10%) (Whitney and Smith, 1993). As found in western cultures, the most prevalent form of victimization among Chinese children was verbal form, and followed by physical and relational forms in order (Zhang, 2002; Zhang et al., 2001). However, inconsistent with the theoretical hypotheses (Björkqvist,

Lagerspetz, and Kaukiainen, 1992) and findings in western cultures (Smith and Sharp, 1994; Rivers and Smith, 1994), Chinese boys were more likely than girls to suffer all the three forms of victimization (Zhang, 2002; Zhang et al., 2001).

English culture and bullying/victimization among English children

Similar to most affluent western countries, England is thought to be an individualistic culture, in which confrontations are seen as normal, and speaking one's mind and defending one's own interest are considered as characteristics of an honest person (Hofstede, Hofstede, and Minkov, 2010). These cultural values would have an effect of promoting aggression and bullying. Using data from TIMSS, Bergmuller (2013) demonstrated such an effect by finding that scores of individualism was a powerful predictor of principal-reported aggressive behavior (but not self-reported aggressive behavior) even after controlling for school and country characteristics such as school size and GDP. These cultural features definitely had important relevance to the problem of bullying/victimization among English children.

England is among the countries in which school bullying/victimization has been extensively explored. Smith and colleagues carried out large-scale surveys in England, and reported that 27 percent of junior/middle school pupils and 10 percent of secondary school students being bullied sometimes or more frequently and the corresponding percentages of bullying others were 12% and 6% in junior/middle schools and secondary schools respectively (Smith and Sharp, 1994), which was higher than those among Chinese children (Zhang, 2002). In England, the most prevalent form of bullying was name-calling (verbal bullying), and being physically hit was the next most frequent forms of bullying in both junior/middle and secondary schools. Significant gender differences existed in the prevalence of various forms of bullying/victimization, with boys being more likely to be physically hit and threatened, and girls more likely to be verbally and relational bullied (Smith and Sharp, 1994; Rivers and Smith, 1994). Other studies had also revealed the occurring characteristics of English children, including the prevalence of general bullying/victimization and their different forms, and the correlates (e.g., Jolliffe and Farrington, 2006; Karatzias, Power, and Swanson, 2002; Smith et al., 2004; and see Mellor, 1999; Smith, 1999 for reviews).

Researchers have made comparisons of bullying/victimization between England and other cultures, including Asian cultures such as Japan, and reported there were similarities and differences among English school children compared to those among children in other cultures in terms of the prevalence of, correlates of and attitudes towards bullying/victimization, etc. (Craig et al., 2009; Due et al., 2009; Eslea et al., 2004; Kanetsuna, Smith, and Morita, 2006; Menesini et al., 1997; Morita, 2001; Molcho et al., 2009).

Summary and aims of the current study

China and England possess different cultural values, with China characterized by collectivism and strong social norms, and England typically thought as individualistic. These cultural features could have important implications for children's experience of school bullying in each country, and we expected cross-cultural differences in school bullying/victimization among Chinese children compared to English children. Revealing these cross-cultural differences as well as similarities would contribute to an in-depth and insightful understanding of school bullying/victimization in eastern and western cultures.

While there had been studies examining bullying/victimization among Chinese and English school children conducted separately in each country, which shed some light on the cross-cultural similarities and differences of school bullying/victimization in China and England, a direct comparison was needed to systematically examine the similarities and differences of school bullying/victimization between China and England. The current study aimed to explore these issues employing a large scale Chinese sample and an English sample of primary and secondary school children and following the same methodology in each country. Specifically, we were interested to reveal the similarities and differences in the prevalence of general bullying/victimization and different types of victimization, and children's attitudes towards bullying/victimization in China and England.

Methods

In both Chinese and England samples, the data were collected near the end of the winter terms in 1998 and 1999. Before data collection, we first obtained the consent of school administration and the children's parents. The children were allowed to decline to take part if they wanted. All questionnaires were administered by the researchers to the classes of children. In China, 3,626 children (1,934 boys and 1,692 girls) were recruited from 10 primary schools and 4,573 children (2,319 boys and 2,254 girls) from 9 secondary schools. Schools were randomly sampled from Shandong Province and Hebei Province. In England, 573 children

(285 boys and 288 girls) were recruited from 10 primary schools and 413 children (213 boys and 200 girls) from 3 secondary schools. Schools were randomly sampled from the city of Worcester in England.

The Chinese sample completed the Chinese version of the Olweus Bully/Victimization Questionnaire (Zhang, Wu, and Jones, 1999) and the English sample completed the English version of the Olweus Bully/Victimization Questionnaire (Olweus, 1993). This questionnaire has two versions, the primary school version and the secondary school version. In both versions, three subscales were used in the current study to access children's experience of bullying and victimization: (1) about victimization, (2) about bullying others, and (3) attitudes towards bullying.

Specifically, the frequency of bullying others and being bullied were investigated by two items included in the questionnaire, *How often have you taken part in bullying other children at school this term?* and *How often have you been bullied at school this term?* A higher score on these items indicated more frequently bullying others or being bullied. According to previous research and the suggestions by Solberg and Olweus (2003), a bully or a victim was identified when a student reported having taken part in bullying or being bullied '2 to 3 times a month' or more. If a student reported having taken part in bullying and at the same time being bullied '2 to 3 times a month' or more, he or she would be allocated as a bully/victim.

The children also reported their experience of different types of victimization. In the primary school version, two items were used to assess children's experience of different types of victimization: *How often does it happen that other children don't want to spend playtime/breaktime with you, and you end up being alone?'* and *'In which way(s) are you bullied by other students?* The first item was to assess relational victimization, and the students were identified as being relationally victimized when they reported such experience had happened at least 'often' (equal to '2 or 3 times a month'). The second item was to assess physical victimization and verbal victimization. The students were identified as being physically victimized when they reported having been hit or kicked, and being verbally victimized when they reported having been called names.

In the secondary school version, students were identified as having been physically, verbally, or relationally victimized if they reported having experienced six kinds of victimization at least '2 to 3 times a month.' For each form of victimization, there were two items: being bullied physically, having money and other things taken away or damaged (physical); being bullied verbally, and being called names because of my accent (verbal); and being excluded from a group or completely ignored, and having a false rumors spread (relational).

The attitude subscale was used to investigate the children's attitudes towards bullying others and being bullied. In the primary school version, there were five items: three to investigate the emotional component (e.g., *how do you feel when you see a child is bullied in school?*) and two to investigate the behavioral inclination component (e.g., *what will you do when you see a child of your age bullied in school?*). In the secondary school version, there were nine items, four to investigate the emotional component (e.g., *how do you feel when you see a friend of yours is bullied in school?*) and five to investigate the behavioral inclination component (e.g., *what will you do when you see a child of your age bullied in school?*). Scores of emotional and behavioral components were calculated as the means of children's scores on the corresponding items, and score of attitudes was calculated by averaging children's scores on all items in this subscale. The items were all scored 0, 1, and 2, with a higher score indicated a more positive attitude, that is, a more sympathetic feeling to victims, and being more willing to help the victims and stop bullying behaviors.

Results

Prevalence of bullying/victimization roles among Chinese and English students in primary and secondary schools

The numbers of children allocated to each role (bullies, victims, or bully/victims), by gender and country, is shown in Table 9.1. To facilitate comparison by country and gender, these are shown as percentages in Table 9.2. In both countries, primary school children were more likely to be involved in all three bullying roles than secondary school children. Also, in both countries, boys were more likely to be involved as bullies or bully/victims than girls; they were also more likely to be victims except in Chinese primary schools.

In China, the difference in the percentage of children involved in bullying/victimization roles between primary schools and secondary schools was significant ($\chi^2 = 171.91$, df = 3, p<0.01). In England, the difference in the percentage of children involved in bullying/victimization roles between primary schools and secondary schools was also significant ($\chi^2 = 9.65$, df = 3, p<0.05).

To examine the cross-cultural difference in the prevalence rate of bullying/victimization, a series of Chi-square tests were conducted. The percentage of bullies was significantly higher among English children than among Chinese children (China: 2.5%, England: 4.3%; $\chi^2 = 9.66$, df = 1, p<0.01), while the percentage of victims was significantly higher among Chinese children than among English children (China: 14.8%,

Table 9.1 *Numbers of children in different bullying roles, by gender, in Chinese and English primary and secondary schools*

	Boys				Girls			
	Bully	Victim	Bully/victim	Uninvolved	Bully	Victim	Bully/victim	Uninvolved
China								
Primary school	101	344	72	1,417	20	333	26	1,313
Secondary school	72	304	21	1,922	11	230	7	2,006
England								
Primary school	20	41	10	214	8	40	2	238
Secondary school	10	21	4	178	4	17	0	179

Table 9.2 *Percentages of children in different roles in Chinese and English primary and secondary schools*

	Boys				Girls			
	Bully	Victim	Bully/victim	Uninvolved	Bully	Victim	Bully/victim	Uninvolved
China								
Primary school	5.2	17.8	3.7	73.3	1.2	19.7	1.5	77.6
Secondary school	3.1	13.1	0.9	82.9	0.5	10.2	0.3	89.0
England								
Primary school	7.0	14.4	3.5	75.1	2.8	13.9	0.7	82.6
Secondary school	4.7	9.9	1.9	83.5	2.0	8.5	0	89.5

England: 12.1%; χ^2 = 4.21, df = 1, p<0.05). No significant cross-national difference was found in the percentage of bully/victims (China: 1.5%, England: 1.6%; χ^2 = 0.03, df = 1, ps>0.05).

Comparison of children's experiences of different forms of victimization in China and England

Summing over countries, the percentages of children in primary schools who reported physical victimization, verbal victimization, and relational victimization were 18.3%, 43.8%, and 17.8% respectively, and the corresponding percentages among secondary school children were 8.0%, 23.1%, and 8.6%. Chi-square tests indicated that compared to secondary school children, more primary school children experienced physical victimization (χ^2 = 236.30, df = 1, p<0. 001), verbal victimization (χ^2 = 478.48, df = 1, p<0. 001), and relational victimization (χ^2 = 188.05, df = 1, p<0. 001).

Comparing Chinese and English pupils, the percentages of Chinese children who reported the three types of victimization were 12.8%, 31.0%, and 11.8% respectively, and the corresponding percentages among English children were 11.6%, 43.2%, and 20.5%. Chi-square tests indicated that English children were more likely to experience verbal victimization and relational victimization than Chinese children (verbal: χ^2 = 63.76, relational: χ^2 = 65.89, dfs = 1, ps<0.001).

To examine gender differences in the prevalence of various forms of victimization, a series of Chi-square tests were conducted separately on Chinese and English primary and secondary school children (see Table 9.3 for the relevant percentages). In the Chinese sample, more boys in both primary and secondary schools experienced physical victimization and relational victimization than girls, and verbal victimization was more prevalent among boys than girls in secondary schools. In the English sample, boys were more likely than girls to experience physical victimization and girls more likely to experience verbal victimization and relational victimization in primary schools. No gender difference was found in the experience of three types of victimization in English secondary schools.

Chinese and English children's attitudes towards bullying/ victimization

Table 9.4 presents the mean scores of children's attitudes towards bullying/victimization in Chinese and English primary and secondary schools, by role and by gender. In both countries, primary school

Table 9.3 *Percentages of children's experience of various forms of victimization in Chinese and English primary and secondary schools*

	Boys			Girls		
	Physical victimization	Verbal victimization	Relational victimization	Physical victimization	Verbal victimization	Relational victimization
China						
Primary school	20.9	43.9	20.1	16.0	41.2	11.8
Secondary school	10.9	28.5	10.2	5.6	18.4	6.4
England						
Primary school	22.3	46.3	21.6	11.1	55.7	33.2
Secondary school	6.7	33.3	9.6	3.2	32.1	13.5

Table 9.4 *Mean attitude scores of Chinese and English children to bullying/victimization*

	Emotional				Behavioral				Attitude			
	Bully	Victim	Bully/ victim	Uninvolved	Bully	Victim	Bully/ victim	Uninvolved	Bully	Victim	Bully/ victim	Uninvolved
China primary school												
boy	1.31	1.54	1.39	1.57	1.15	1.42	1.25	1.48	1.25	1.49	1.33	1.53
girl	1.29	1.59	1.74	1.59	1.36	1.44	1.54	1.53	1.31	1.53	1.61	1.56
secondary school												
boy	1.13	1.52	1.16	1.52	1.05	1.18	1.20	1.30	1.08	1.33	1.18	1.40
girl	0.75	1.53	1.38	1.60	0.78	1.15	1.00	1.31	0.77	1.32	1.17	1.44
England primary school												
boy	0.75	1.64	1.00	1.50	0.53	1.33	0.85	1.27	0.66	1.52	0.94	1.41
girl	1.00	1.72	1.50	1.77	0.69	1.55	1.25	1.58	0.88	1.65	1.40	1.69
secondary school												
boy	0.60	1.48	1.19	1.26	0.32	1.65	1.10	1.24	0.44	1.57	1.14	1.25
girl	0.94	1.81	–	1.58	0.60	1.84	–	1.47	0.75	1.82	–	1.52

children held more positive attitudes against bullying than secondary school children, and so did girls than boys. A two-way (country and school type) Analysis of Variance (ANOVA) was conducted to explore the differences in attitudes towards bullying/victimization between Chinese children and English children. Chinese children were found to score higher on the attitudes subscale than English children ($M_{Chinese}$ = 1.46, $M_{English}$ = 1.38, F(1, 9184) = 54.27, p<0.001), indicating that Chinese children were more sympathetic to victims, and more willing to help victims and stop bullying behaviors. Compared to children in secondary schools, children in primary schools held more positive attitudes ($M_{primary}$ = 1.52, $M_{secondary}$ = 1.39, F(1, 9181) = 220.12, p<0.001). A significant country × school interaction was found (F(1, 9181) = 36.99, p<0.001), with Chinese children holding more positive attitudes towards bullying than English children in secondary schools.

A repeated-measure ANOVA with the emotional component and behavioral component as repeated measures and country and school type as between-subject variables indicated a significant effect of interaction between country and the two components (F(1, 9181) = 44.73, p<0.01). While no cross-national difference was found on the emotional component of attitudes to bullying/victimization ($M_{Chinese}$ = 1.55, $M_{English}$ = 1.51), Chinese children reported a higher level of behavioral inclination to act against bullying than English children ($M_{Chinese}$ = 1.37, $M_{English}$ = 1.24).

Children's attitudes varied as a function of their statuses involved in bullying/victimization. Bullies were found to hold the least positive attitudes, and victims and uninvolved children held the more positive attitudes towards bullying/victimization (Chinese sample: M_{bully} = 1.17, M_{victim} = 1.43, $M_{bully/victim}$ = 1.35, $M_{uninvolved}$ = 1.47; English sample: M_{bully} = 0.66, M_{victim} = 1.62, $M_{bully/victim}$ = 1.05, $M_{uninvolved}$ = 1.48). There was a significant culture × role interaction in children's attitudes against bullying/victimization. Specifically, compared to bullies in English schools, bullies in Chinese schools showed relatively more positive attitudes. As can be seen in Table 9.4, among English children, compared to boys of the same status, girls always held more positive attitudes against bullying. However, the patterns of gender differences in attitudes towards bullying among Chinese children varied as a function of children's status in bullying. Especially in Chinese secondary schools, no significant difference in attitudes to bullying was found between victimized boys and victimized girls, and bullies among girls even showed less positive attitudes towards bullying compared to bullies among boys.

Discussion

Similarities of bullying/victimization among Chinese and English children

This study found some similarities in bullying/victimization among Chinese and English school children. Generally, primary school children and boys are more likely to take part in school bullying in both cultures. The most prevalent form of victimization was verbal victimization, which was followed by physical and relational forms in order. Moreover, primary school children held more positive attitudes towards bullying/victimization than did secondary school children, so did girls than boys, and victims and uninvolved children than bullies and bully/victims. These indicated that there was some commonality of school bullying/victimization across the two different cultures.

The age differences in bullying/victimization can be attributed to the development in such areas as social cognition, social skills to resolve peer conflict (Thompson, 2006), behavioral and emotional regulation (Rothbart and Bates, 2006; Saarni et al., 2006), and physical strength as well. Meanwhile, young children have a tendency to report social interactions which is actually not a bullying behavior as bullying, which also contributes to the high prevalence of bullying/victimization among primary school children (Arora, 1996; Koo, Kwak, and Smith, 2008).

The gender differences in the prevalence of general bullying/victimization and children's attitudes are consistent with findings in previous research (Menesini et al., 1997; Zhang, 2002; Zhang et al., 2002). The gender differences in bullying could be understood in terms of the differences of boys and girls in physical strength, behavioral and emotional regulation, and social cognition and empathy. Boys are stronger than girls physically, and less able to control inappropriate behaviors and emotions (W. Chen and Sang, 2002; C. Li et al., 2006), while girls are better than boys in taking others' perspectives and show higher levels of empathy (Selman et al., 1986). Furthermore, boys have been found to hold a higher level of justification of aggression (Fujihara et al., 1999), normative beliefs on aggression (Bellmore et al., 2005), and instrumental representations of aggression (Archer and Parker, 1994; Tapper and Boulton, 2000). Hence, essentially boys are more aggressive than girls, which could be applied to this subset of aggression, which is bullying.

Cross-cultural differences in bullying/victimization among Chinese and English children

Nevertheless some remarkable differences in children's experience of and attitudes towards bullying/victimization were found between China and England. Compared to Chinese children, English children were more likely to get involved in the problems of bullying/victimization, especially as bullies. Chinese children held more sympathetic attitudes to victims and were more willing to help victims and stop bullying than English children.

These cross-cultural differences could be explained by the different cultural values regarding aggression and bullying. As we have pointed out, Chinese culture is characterized by collectivism and a high level of social norms. Some research has examined the association between these cultural features and children's aggression. As reported by Bergeron and Schneider (2005), cultures characterized by collectivistic values, high moral discipline, a high level of egalitarian commitment, low uncertainty avoidance, and which emphasize values that are heavily Confucian showed lower levels of aggression. In a sample of Chinese adolescents, Y. Li and his colleagues (2010) reported that endorsement of collectivism was negatively, and endorsement of individualism positively, related to overt and relational aggression. Therefore, within a collectivistic culture as China, aggression and bullying goes strongly against cultural values which may explain the finding that Chinese children are less involved in aggression and bullying, and show a high level of anti-bullying attitudes.

Regarding the association between collectivism and bullying/victimization, Koo et al., (2008) suggested that a high bully-to-victim ratio could be a useful criterion in defining whether the bullying phenomenon in a nation is based on collectivism, as previous studies on samples from Japan and South Korea have reported a high ratio of the number of bullies to the number of victims. However, our comparison between Chinese and English children did not find such a result. One possible reason may be related to the operational definitions or measures of bullying in different cultures. As Koo et al., (2008) have pointed out, previous studies actually examined *ijime* in Japan and *wang-ta* in South Korea. Both *ijime* and *wang-ta* are more often verbal and social exclusion than physical kinds of bullying (Kanetsuna and Smith, 2002; Kanetsuna et al., 2006), and include mainly forms of social exclusion (Yokoyu, 2003), which occurs customarily when a group of children socially exclude a single pupil. Therefore, research on Japanese or South Korean children could find a relatively high bully-to-victim ratio. However, bullying in China includes not only social exclusion (relational bullying), but physical and verbal forms which may occur just when one child bullies another child or children. Hence, we did not find a high bully-to-victim ratio in the Chinese sample. Moreover, as mentioned previously, Chinese culture imposes strict rules on children's aggression and bullying, which may lead to Chinese children tending not to report their bullying behavior, hence the percentage of bully among Chinese school children is possibly underestimated.

Another interesting finding was related to the pattern of gender differences in children's experience of various forms of victimization in China and England. As reported by studies in England and other western countries (Felix and Green, 2010; Björkqvist et al., 1992; Smith and Sharp, 1994), boys tended to bully others or be victimized physically, while girls were more likely to get involved in relational form of bullying and victimization. We replicated the gender differences in prevalence of physical victimization among Chinese and English children. However, in terms of the prevalence of relational victimization, we found that Chinese boys were also more likely to be relationally victimized than girls, which differs from the usual finding among British (or western) children.

Relational bullying has been considered as an easy way to harm girls because girls usually establish close and tight friendship networks (Rubin, Bukowski, and Parker, 2006), and think highly of interpersonal relationships (Ruble, Martin, and Berenbaum, 2006). Consequently, it has been argued that relational bullying should be more prevalent among girls (Björkqvist et al., 1992). However, while commonly found, not all of the empirical findings support this statement (Ruble et al., 2006).

On the other hand, Fujihara and his colleagues (1999) examined the justification of various forms of aggression among Japanese, Spanish, and American students, and found that Japanese students showed a lower level of justification of indirect verbal aggression than American and Spanish students, indicating that oriental cultures showed less tolerance for indirect aggression compared to western cultures. This finding may provide some clues to explain the cross-cultural variations in the pattern of gender difference in relational aggression we found in the current study.

In brief, the current study found different gender patterns in children's experience of relational victimization between China and England, which could be understood to some extent by considering the children's different attitudes towards relational aggression in western and eastern cultures. Meanwhile, this result further demonstrated that it is not always the case that girls are more relationally aggressive than boys. Rather, there appears to be a cross-cultural variation or reversal in gender differences in relational forms of aggression and bullying.

Conclusions

This study made a cross-cultural comparison of the prevalence of and attitudes towards school bullying between China and England. The same instruments were administered on samples of children from primary and secondary schools in both cultures; hence, the results from both cultures could be compared directly. However, a weakness is that both the Chinese and English samples were mainly recruited in certain areas, and especially the English sample is relatively small and from just one particular city, which would limit the generalizability of the research findings to the whole nation.

This study revealed both similarities and differences in bullying/victimization among Chinese and English school children. Regarding similarities, in both cultures, primary school children and boys were more likely to take part in school bullying than secondary school children, verbal victimization was the most prevalent form of victimization, and primary school children and girls held more positive attitudes towards bullying/victimization than secondary school children. Regarding differences, these were found in the prevalence of general bullying/victimization and its various forms, in gender differences in relational bullying, and in children's attitudes. Thus, there are commonalities as well as cross-cultural variations in school bullying/victimization. Examining these cross-cultural similarities and differences will contribute to an in-depth understanding of school bullying/victimization, and the design of effective intervention program on school bullying should take these commonalities and cultural variations into consideration.

The differences in bullying/victimization between China and England could be attributed to the different positions of two countries in the cultural dimensions of collectivism vs. individualism and tightness vs. looseness. However, further research should examine empirically the associations between bullying/victimization roles and these macro-cultural values, and with the subtle attitudes and beliefs possessed by children in different cultures regarding bullying/victimization, including attitudes to and justifications of different forms of bullying/victimization, and their social representations concerning these.

REFERENCES

Archer, J. and Parker, S. (1994). Social representations of aggression in children. *Aggressive Behavior*, 20, 101–114.

Arora, C. M. J. (1996). Defining bullying: Towards a clearer general understanding and more effective intervention strategies. *School Psychology International*, 17, 317–329.

Bellmore, A. D., Witkow, M. R., Graham, S., and Juvonen, J. (2005). From beliefs to behavior: The mediating role of hostile response selection in predicting aggression. *Aggressive Behavior*, 31, 453–472.

Bergeron, N. and Schneider, B. H. (2005). Explaining cross-national differences in peer-directed aggression: A quantitative synthesis. *Aggressive Behavior*, 31, 116–137.

Bergmuller, S. (2013). The relationship between cultural individualism-collectivism and student aggression across 62 countries. *Aggressive Behavior*, 39, 182–200.

Björkqvist, K., Lagerspetz, K., and Kaukiainen, A. (1992). Do girls manipulate and boys fight? Developmental trends in regard to direct and indirect aggression. *Aggressive Behavior*, 18, 117–127.

Chen X. (2010). Socioemotional development in Chinese children. In M. H. Bond (Ed.), *Handbook of Chinese psychology* (pp. 37–52). Oxford, UK: Oxford University Press.

Chen, S. P. and Yue, G. A. (2002). A survey of bullying in primary and junior middle schools (in Chinese). *Psychological Science*, 25, 355–356.

Chen, W. and Sang, B. (2002). An overview of research on self-control in children. *Advances in Psychological Science*, 10, 65–70.

Chinese Culture Connection. (1987). Chinese values and the search for culture-free dimensions of culture. *Journal of Cross-Cultural Psychology*, 18, 143–164.

Craig, W., Harel-Fisch, Y., Fogel-Grinvald, H., et al. (2009). A cross-national profile of bullying and victimization among adolescents in 40 countries. *International Journal of Public Health*, 54, 216–224.

Due, P. and Holstein, B. E. (2008). Bullying victimization among 13 to 15 year old school children: Results from two comparative studies in 66 countries and regions. *International Journal of Adolescent Medical Health*, 20, 209–221.

Due, P., Merlo, J., Harel-Fisch, Y., et al. (2009). Socioeconomic inequality in exposure to bullying during adolescence: A comparative, cross-sectional, multilevel study in 35 countries. *American Journal of Public Health*, 99, 907–914.

Eslea, M., Menesini, E., Morita, Y., O'Moore, M., Mora-Merchan, J. A., Pereira, B., Smith, P. K. and Zhang, W. (2004). Friendship and loneliness among bullies and victims: Data from seven countries. *Aggressive Behavior*, 30, 71–83.

Felix, E. D. and Green, J. G. (2010). Popular girls and brawny boys: The role of gender in bullying and victimization experiences. In S. R. Jimerson, S. M. Swearer and D. L. Espelage (Eds.), *Handbook of bullying in schools: An international perspective* (pp. 173–186). London: Routledge.

Fujihara, T., Kohyama, T., Andreu, J. M., and Ramirez, J. M. (1999). Justification of interpersonal aggression in Japanese, American, and Spanish students. *Aggressive Behavior*, 25, 185–195.

Gelfand, M. J., Raver, J. L., Nishii, L., Leslie, L. M., Lun, J., Lim, B. C., et al. (2011). Differences between tight and loose cultures: A 33-nation study. *Science*, 332, 1100–1104.

Genta, M. L., Menesini, E., Fonz, A., Costablile, A., and Smith, P. K. (1996). Bullies and victims in schools in central and southern Italy. *European Journal of Psychology of Education*, 11, 97–110.

Gu, C. H. and Zhang, W. X. (2003). A survey on the relations of the bullying problem among primary school children to their personality (in Chinese). *Acta Psychologica Sinica*, 35, 101–105.

Hofstede, G. (2001). *Culture's consequences: Comparing values, behaviors, institutions and organizations across nations*. Thousand Oaks, CA: Sage.

Hofstede, G. H, Hofstede, G. J., and Minkov, M. (2010). *Cultures and organizations: Sofware of the mind* (3rd edn.). New York, NY: McGraw-Hill.

Jolliffe, D. and Farrington, D. P. (2006). Examining the relationship between low empathy and bullying. *Aggressive Behavior*, 32, 540–550.

Kanetsuna, T. and Smith, P. K. (2002). Pupil insights into bullying, and coping with bullying: A bi-national study in Japan and England. *Journal of School Violence*, 1, 5–29.

Kanetsuna, T., Smith, P. K., and Morita, Y. (2006). Coping with bullying at school: Children's recommended strategies and attitudes to school-based interventions in England and Japan. *Aggressive Behavior*, 32, 570–580.

Karatzias, A., Power, K. G., and Swanson, V. (2002). Bullying and victimization in Scottish secondary schools: Same or separate entities? *Aggressive Behavior*, 28, 45–61.

Koo, H., Kwak, K., and Smith, P. K. (2008). Victimization in Korean schools: The nature, incidence, and distinctive features of Korean bullying or wang-ta. *Journal of School Violence*, 7, 119–139.

Lei, L. and Chang, L. (2002). Adolescent victims in school bullying: Some predictors (in Chinese). *Exploration of Psychology*, 22, 38–43.

Lei, L., Wang, Y., Guo, B. L., and Chang, L. (2004). The influence of classroom norms on the relations between social behaviors and peer victimization (in Chinese). *Acta Psychologica Sinica*, 36, 563–567.

Li, C.-S. R., Huang, C., Constable, R. T., and Sinha., R. (2006). Gender differences in the neural correlates of response inhibition during a stroop sinal task. *NeuroImage*, 32, 1918–1929.

Li, Y., Wang, M., Wang, C., and Shi, J. (2010). Individualism, collectivism, and Chinese adolescents' aggression: Intracultural variations. *Aggressive Behavior*, 36, 187–194.

Mellor, A., (1999). Scotland. In Smith, P. K., Y. Morita, J. Junger-Tas, D. Olweus, R. Catalano and P. Slee (Eds.), *The nature of school bullying: A cross-national perspective* (pp. 97-111). London: Routledge.

Menesini, E., Eslea, M., Smith, P. K., Genta, M. L., Giannetti, E., Fonzi, A., and Costabile A. (1997). Cross-national comparison of children's attitudes towards bully/victim problems in school. *Aggressive Behavior*, 23, 245–257.

Molcho, M., Craig, W., Due, P., Pickett, W., Harel-Fisch, Y., Overspeck, M., and the HBSC Bullying Writing Group. (2009). Cross-national time trends in bullying behavior 1994–2006: Findings from Europe and North America. *International Journal of Public Health*, 54, S225–S234.

Morita, Y. (2001). *Ijime no kokusai hikaku kenkyu (Cross-national comparative study of bullying)*. Japan: Kaneko Shobo.

Olweus, D. (1993). *Bullying at school: What we know and what we can do.* Oxford: Blackwell.

Oyserman, D., Coon, H. M., and Kemmelmeier, M. (2002). Rethinking individualism and collectivism: Evaluation of theoretical assumptions and meta-analyses. *Psychological Bulletin,* 128, 3–72.

Qu, W. (2005). Investigation and remedy of young children's bullying behavior (in Chinese). *Studies in Preschool Education,* 29, 1–3.

Rivers, I. and Smith P. K. (1994). Types of bullying behavior and their correlates. *Aggressive Behavior,* 20, 359–368.

Rothbart, M. K. and Bates, J. E. (2006). Temperament. In W. Damon, R. Lerner, and N. Eisenberg (Eds.), *Handbook of child psychology: Vol. 3. Social, emotional, and personality development* (6th edn., pp. 99–166). New York: Wiley.

Rubin, K. H., Bukowski, W. M., and Parker, J. G. (2006). Peer interactions, relationships, and groups. In W. Damon, R. M. Lerner, (Series Ed.), N. Eisenberg, (Vol. Ed.), *Handbook of child psychology: Vol. 3. Social, emotional, and personality development* (6th edn., pp. 573–646). New York: Wiley.

Ruble, D. N., Martin, C. L., and Berenbaum, S. A. (2006). Gender development. In W. Damon, R. M. Lerner, (Series Ed.), N. Eisenberg, (Vol. Ed.), *Handbook of child psychology: Vol. 3. Social, emotional, and personality development* (6th edn., pp. 858–932). New York: Wiley.

Saarni, C., Campos, J. J., Camras, L. A., and Witherington, D. (2006). Emotional development: Action, communication, and understanding. In W. Damon, R. Lerner, and N. Eisenberg (Eds.), *Handbook of child psychology: Vol. 3. Social, emotional, and personality development* (6th edn., pp. 227–299). New York: Wiley.

Selman, R. L., Beardslee, W., Schultz, L. H., Krupa, M., and Podorefsky, D. (1986). Assessing adolescent interpersonal negotiation strategies: Toward the integration of structural and functional models. *Developmental Psychology,* 22, 450–459.

Smith, P. K. and Sharp, S. (1994). *School bullying: Insights and perspectives.* London: Routledge.

Smith, P. K., Talamelli, L., Cowie, H., Naylor, P., and Chauhan, P. (2004). Profiles of non-victims, escaped victims, continuing victims and new victims of school bullying. *British Journal of Educational Psychology,* 74, 565–581.

Smith, P. K. (1999). England and Wales. In P. K. Smith, Y. Morita, J. Junger-Tas, D. Olweus, R. Catalano, and P. Slee (Eds.), *The nature of school bullying: A cross-national perspective* (pp. 68–90). London: Routledge.

Solberg, M. E., and Olweus, D. (2003). Prevalence estimation of school bullying with the Olweus bully/victim questionnaire. *Aggressive Behavior,* 29, 239–268.

Tapper, K. and Boulton, M. (2000). Social representations of physical, verbal, and indirect aggression in children: Sex and age differences. *Aggressive Behavior,* 26, 442–454.

Thompson, R. (2006). The development of the person: Social understanding, relationships, conscience, self. In W. Damon, R. Lerner, and N. Eisenberg

(Eds.), *Handbook of child psychology: Vol. 3. Social, emotional, and personality development* (6th edn., pp. 26–98). Hoboken, NJ: Wiley.

Wang, H., Zhou, X., Lu, C., Wu, J., Deng, X., Hong, L., Gao, X., and He, Y. (2012). Adolescent bullying involvement and psychosocial aspects of family and school life: A cross-sectional study from Guangdong province in China. *PLoS One*, 7: e38619.

Whitney, I. and Smith, P. K. (1993). A survey of the nature and extent of bullying in junior/middle and secondary schools. *Educational Research*, 35, 3–25.

Yokoyu, S. (2003). Bullying and developmental psychology clinics: focusing around how to work on trauma and recovery from bullying. In M. Tsuchiya, K. Soeda, and K. Oride (Eds.), *Nakuso gakko no ijime – Nippon to sekai [Eliminating bullying in schools – Japan and the world]*. Kyoto: Minerva Press.

Zhang, W. X. (2002). Prevalence and major characteristics of bullying/victimization among primary and junior middle school children (in Chinese). *Acta Psychologica Sinica*, 34, 387–394.

Zhang, W. X., Wang, L. P., Gong, X. L., Wu, J. F., and Zhang, K. (2002). Children's attitude toward bullying in school (in Chinese). *Psychological Science*, 25, 226–227.

Zhang, W. X., Wang, Y. W., Ju, Y. C., and Lin, C. D. (2001). Types of bullying behavior and its correlates (in Chinese). *Psychological Development and Education*, 17, 12–17.

Zhang, W. X., Wu, J. F., and Cheng, X. (1999). The review of child bullying research in foreign countries (in Chinese). *Journal of Developments in Psychology*, 7, 37–42.

Zhang, W. X., Wu, J. F., and Jones, K. (1999). The modification of a Chinese version of the Olweus Bully/Victim Questionnaire (in Chinese). *Psychological Development and Education*, 15, 7–11.

10 Peer support in England, Japan and South Korea

Helen Cowie and Alana James

This chapter overviews the nature of peer support as it is currently practised in English, Japanese and South Korean schools. We outline the extent and varieties of peer support use in the three countries individually using the available research evidence. How peer support methods may be adapted to tackle the different forms of bullying which are present in the three nations is then explored. Finally, we consider the importance of readiness within schools and educational systems for peer support systems to take root and flourish.

The nature of peer support

The practice of peer support appears to give direction to young people's desire to be an active citizen in their school. Peer support systems are generally defined as flexible frameworks within which children and young people are trained to offer emotional and social support to fellow pupils (Cowie, 2011; Cowie and Smith, 2010) through appropriate training in such skills as mentoring, active listening, conflict resolution, befriending and representation of young people's issues in school councils.

Whilst widespread use of peer support originated in western countries, it is currently used in many countries around the world (Cowie and Smith, 2010). The development of peer support initiatives appears linked to the increasing importance of tackling social issues within schools. Its history runs in parallel with that of pastoral care, with peer support emerging around the same time that formal pastoral care approaches began to be seen in schools. One reason that peer support may be popular in so many countries is that it offers an approach for the achievement of pastoral care, rather than a prescriptive 'one size fits all' method. It can take a variety of different forms, be modified to target different aims and be developed over time within a school environment.

More recently, peer support systems have become internationally popular as anti-bullying interventions, in line with the UN Convention on the Rights of the Child (Cowie and Smith, 2010; UN, 1989). Peer support may act as both a bullying prevention method, and as an intervention. The adoption of peer support within a whole-school policy has been shown to create opportunities for young people to be proactive in challenging bullying when they encounter it and to support its victims, as well as contribute to a school ethos in which bullying is less acceptable. The use of peer support in England, Japan and South Korea is outlined below, summarising what is known from the research evidence available for each country. This is followed by a consideration of cultural differences in the use of peer support as an anti-bullying initiative.

Peer support in England

Peer support programs have become increasingly popular in UK schools. The Department for Children, Schools and Families (DCSF) funded piloting of new types of peer mentoring by three organisations in 2007, and contracted a long-term peer mentoring pilot scheme in 180 English schools, run by the *Mentoring and Befriending Foundation* (MBF, a national strategic body which focuses on influencing policy and supporting mentoring and befriending at all ages) over 2006 and 2007 (DCSF, 2008a; DCSF, Press notice 2007/0212). A survey of 240 schools in England (130 primary and 110 secondary) found that around 62% had developed some form of peer support system (Houlston, Smith and Jessel, 2009). These systems were perceived as being beneficial in promoting emotional health and well-being in the schools (Houlston, Smith and Jessel, 2011). Cowie et al. (2008) demonstrated that peer support systems have the capacity to improve pupils' sense of safety from aggression and bullying at school. Their research (a survey of 931 pupils) was carried out in four secondary schools, each with a well-organised pastoral care system and an active anti-bullying policy. Two schools that had already developed a peer support system were matched with two schools that had yet to commence their peer support training. Those students who were aware of their school's peer support system reported feeling significantly safer at school and were more likely to feel able to talk about negative things that had happened to them than similar students in the control schools. In other words, for those students, the observation or experience of the helpfulness of peer support had led them to view sharing of worries and anxieties as a positive coping strategy.

In Western countries, elementary school schemes generally adopt a buddying/befriending approach or a conflict resolution approach. Within England, it has been found that primary schools report using befriending most commonly, followed by mediation, whilst secondary schools report using mentoring followed by befriending. Schools, which have been running peer support over a long time, also report using mixed methods simultaneously (Houlston et al., 2009). In addition, some primary schools incorporate other activities for peer supporters such as leading games, supporting reading and carrying out one-to-one work with vulnerable pupils who find it hard to make friends (Cowie et al., 2004; Cowie and Jennifer, 2008; Thompson and Smith, 2011). Secondary school schemes typically train peer mentors to build on the methods adapted for younger age-groups, for example by running a lunchtime club, being available in a 'drop in' room, facilitating workshops in tutor groups, or mentoring younger pupils in need, and make use of a more sophisticated range of active listening and problem-solving skills (Thompson and Smith, 2011). An initiative by the charity *Beat Bullying* (now dissolved) trained CyberMentors to mentor other young people both offline in their schools and communities, and online (Kaenel-Platt and Douglas, 2012).

Research studies consistently find that peer supporters benefit from their training and practice, reporting enhanced feelings of confidence in their capacity to communicate and to offer effective help (Cowie et al., 2002; Naylor and Cowie, 1999; Smith and Watson, 2004). They also report a sense of doing something useful for their school community and pride in the value of their peer supporting role. Houlston et al. (2011) documented measurable gains in self-esteem for peer supporters.

Those who make use of the peer support systems mainly report that it is helpful to them and that they would recommend it to fellow students who are experiencing interpersonal difficulties, such as being bullied, although a minority report that they did not find it helpful (Cowie and Olafsson, 2000; Smith and Watson, 2004). The reasons given by satisfied users typically refer to the helpfulness of having someone who listens and of being able to explore a range of coping strategies with an understanding peer (Cowie et al., 2002).

With regard to the school ethos, most of the research is qualitative and largely indicates satisfaction with the systems and a perception that the school climate improves following the introduction of a peer support system (Mental Health Foundation, 2002; Thompson and Smith, 2011). However, the evidence also indicates that a proportion of pupils remain sceptical about the impact of peer support on the ethos of the school and about its power to reduce rates of bullying and increase pupil perceptions of safety. By secondary school stage, positive perceptions of improvements in school ethos tend to decline with the age of the students (Houlston and Smith, 2009). In situations where the system is not well advertised throughout the school, Cowie et al. (2008) found that pupils in their control group (schools with no system of peer support) reported feeling safer than did pupils in the schools with peer support. The positive effects were only felt by those who were aware that their school had a peer support system in place. In their international review of peer support research, Cowie and Smith (2010) concluded that peer support systems that are widely promoted in the school, are generally viewed in a positive way. The head teacher and the staff who run the schemes play a substantial part in integrating peer support systems into the wider school policies on children's emotional health and well-being

Peer support in Japan

Peer support has become increasingly popular in Japan since the 1990s (Toda, 2005). The Japanese Peer Support Association (JPSA) provides training and support for practitioners. There is a continuing desire to learn from international best practice; early approaches were influenced by the success of peer support in other countries (Toda, 2005; Toda and Ito, 2005) and JPSA regularly organises study trips abroad to countries such as the UK.

In Japan, peer support systems have however adapted to national culture and values. Japanese teachers place a strong emphasis on building close relationships with their students and encourage them from an early age to work together in small, supportive groups in which they learn, eat, clean the classroom and carry out projects together. These groups become closely bonded and, as a result, individual members are likely to offer spontaneous social and emotional support to others (Toyama-Bialke, 2003). Observations in Japanese pre-school classrooms indicate that teachers encourage other children to deal with 'deviant' behaviour within the peer group. So children who misbehave are encouraged to correct their misdeeds by modelling themselves on the well-behaved majority group. This approach can also be observed in elementary and junior high schools where disruptive students are not excluded from school life but rather are encouraged to reintegrate with their peers by, for example, participating in school clubs. This was confirmed in a cross-cultural comparison of the sources of social and emotional support amongst adolescents in United States and Japan (Crystal et al., 2008) which found that US students were more likely to perceive *family*, rather than peers, as sources of support, whereas Japanese students were more likely to perceive *peers* as the major source of support.

At the same time, Japanese society is more likely than other countries to engage in 'moral panic' about the minority of children who do not maintain the desired interpersonal harmony (Gill, 2007). In response to such concerns, the Japanese government made the decision in 2001 to place part-time counsellors in all state junior high schools in order to deal with the perceived rise in emotional and behavioural difficulties, including bullying. There has also been a shift towards a more flexible curriculum with more emphasis on social and emotional learning. Curriculum reforms, most recently instituted in 2011, have aimed to ease the pressure on children to perform academically by measures such as reducing the number of subject hours in the national curriculum. There is also a greater emphasis now on nurturing *ikiru chikara,* which refers to the balanced development of physical power, social skill, morality and academic attainment.

The media have also played an important part in heightening awareness of the damaging effects that bullying can have on young people's self-esteem, social relationships and academic achievement. In addition, the media have publicised case study material on the emotional impact on students who were subjected to extreme pressure to succeed in examinations in order to get to high-status universities. Changes have emerged out of media focus upon problems in schools, including school violence and bullying, which were considered linked to the pressures of university entrance examinations (Tsuneyoshi, 2004).

It is against this background that we explore the development of peer support in Japan, which, as a method formally implemented within the educational system, has evolved into a range of different but overlapping approaches. Japanese researchers and practitioners have shown great willingness to learn from Western countries about peer support and have been active in inviting academics and trainers, including the authors of this chapter, to share knowledge and expertise. Three strands of peer support are apparent. Each one of these strands has influenced the research and practice of JPSA. However, there remain some tensions among practitioners eager to promote their own particular brand of peer support (Cowie and Kurihara, 2009).

One strand has adopted peer support to nurture a positive climate in the whole school by training every pupil, often in methods close to the existing moral education curriculum. This approach also includes peer tutoring. A second strand uses peer support to allay group fears and anxieties by helping groups of students who have been identified as being potentially vulnerable or at risk, for example, elementary students who may be extremely anxious about making the transition to junior high school. This type of peer support often takes the form of campaigns or group newsletters. A third strand uses one-to-one peer support to allay individual fears and anxieties.

Peer support to nurture a positive climate in the whole school

One very influential approach to peer support (Nakano, 2003) focuses on the whole-school community by training all students to develop self-awareness, empathy and interpersonal skills. Activities which aim to encourage such qualities include field trips, cleaning the neighbourhood, gardening projects and peer tutoring. Nakano and Kokubu (2000) propose that teachers and counsellors should collaborate in partnership in order to strengthen children's resilience and that, rather than concentrating solely on psychopathology, counsellors should be actively involved with teachers in creating a caring school community.

Much of the evaluation of this 'whole-school' approach to peer support has in practice been carried out within classroom groups. For example, Ochi (2008) found that self-esteem improved in her classroom after she introduced social skills training into her class. One key outcome was that children in the class became friendlier in their everyday interactions with others and rates of bullying decreased. Similarly, Shiomi and Nagano (2008) found that students' self-efficacy scores in one junior high school class improved after they experienced nine sessions of peer support training.

Peer support to allay group fears and anxieties

Some practitioners have gone beyond such a global approach to target potentially vulnerable groups of students. For example, Taki (2000, 2001, 2005) proposes that peer support training should occur in two phases. The first phase involves basic social skills training for all students in order to facilitate better social interaction with others; the second phase involves the training of older students to help younger students who may be experiencing difficulties. From this perspective, the second phase builds on the skills learned in the first phase in order to address common peer group fears and anxieties.

Japanese practitioners have been especially active in developing schemes to induct elementary school students into junior high school through newsletters, greetings campaigns and other forms of mentoring (Toda, 2005; Toda, Nishiumi and Yoshida, 2003; Toda and Ito, 2005). An early example is described by Kawata (1996) who piloted the Q&A (Question and Answer) Method at a junior high school in Kanazawa City. Here the students wrote about their worries anonymously to a team of volunteer peer supporters who then circulated their answers in a newsletter for the whole school. Since many of the problems were common ones, such as fear of being bullied, the letters were read with great interest by all students and were used to foster a more caring supportive ethos in the schools involved, while still protecting the identity of those who had voiced their concerns.

Peer support to allay individual fears and anxieties

The above global approaches to whole groups of students have evolved in some instances into peer support for individuals with particular difficulties. For example, Takeuchi (2008) developed a method involving peer support between a junior high school and an elementary school through the medium of an anonymous newsletter. The elementary school students wrote letters describing social and emotional issues that concerned them and the junior high school students responded to them in confidence. Similarly, Mihara (2008) describes how peer supporters circulated a newsletter designed to offer confidential help to children with interpersonal difficulties. Mihara integrated the new initiative with other supportive activities such as training students to offer peer tutoring in reading and to support younger students in swimming lessons. One significant outcome was that the number of school absentees decreased dramatically. Additionally, the ethos of the whole school improved as the peer supporters gained in confidence that their method was having a positive influence.

Still other peer support methods have evolved with a counselling focus by training students in active listening. Here pupil helpers are trained (usually by a qualified counsellor or psychologist) to use active listening skills to support peers in distress. Regular supervision (whether by a qualified counsellor or by the teacher who managed the peer support scheme) is an essential feature. Yokozawa and Inoue (2006) trained specially selected volunteers to provide a confidential e-mail service for peers in distress. The evaluations by users of this service were extremely positive indicating that this form of support was helpful for adolescent mental health. Additionally, peer supporters appreciated clinical supervision of their practice.

Themes within Japanese peer support practice

Japanese practice has developed within a context of active influence from international peer support practice, but has its own distinct features. As seen, unique forms have emerged within Japan such as the Q&A Handout method and others using anonymous newsletters. In a qualitative study with key informants, including senior members of JPSA, teachers and researchers, across several Japanese regions, James (2012) identified three key themes within peer support practice, including several relating to distinct features of Japanese practice:

Conflicts: Tensions existed amongst the different forms of peer support in Japan, as noted by Cowie and Kurihara (2009), including the conflict between the approaches favoured by JPSA and the official conception of peer support supported by the government;

Support for practitioners: Peer support practitioners could receive support in numerous and increasing ways. Despite conflicts between different approaches, the existence of a national association provides cohesive support and fosters a community of practitioners. This is quite different from the picture seen in England, where numerous different charities and organisations have championed various forms of peer support. Membership of JPSA has rapidly expanded, and there is additionally increasing support from local education boards/government. For example, members of JPSA reported being asked to provide training to teachers across whole cities. A particular feature of Japanese practice was also the supportive relationships between university academics and practitioners, with individual teachers often receiving support from professors/researchers with expertise in peer support.

Barriers to practice: The amount of time staff in schools devoted to running peer support could be considerable, meaning that support from either other staff, university academics or through JPSA was essential. Fitting peer support into school life was challenging, as it competed with school sports and other extracurricular clubs. Despite the recent reforms, it was perceived that there was a lack of emphasis upon social and emotional learning within the curriculum, and thus incorporating peer support into classroom time was also difficult.

There is, however, a lack of empirical research evidencing these perceptions of peer support practitioners, and in general for the practice of peer support in Japan. Despite the extensive Japanese practice of peer support, there is a need for greater rigorous research on the benefits and impact of the systems being run.

Peer support in South Korea

Peer support appears not to be as established in South Korean schools or at least not conceptualised in the same way as in England or Japan. There is little English-language literature available relating to use of peer support systems in South Korea, but this is likely to be due in part at least to lack of formal research rather than lack of use. Although the term 'peer support' does not seem to be widely used, formal peer counselling has been used in the South Korean school system since the 1990s (Rho and

Kim, 2004, 2007). Peer counselling involves counselling activities run by pupils for other pupils of a similar age. It has been described as developing from university practice, where peers who experienced group counselling were encouraged to become involved in peer counselling as a leader or co-leader (Rho and Kim, 2004, 2007). The Korean Youth Counselling Institute (KYCI, part of the Ministry of Culture) then developed a national project in 1994, with peer counselling programs for primary and secondary school pupils. This project was on a very large-scale; between 1995 and 2004 over 48,500 children were trained as peer counsellors and over 5,700 teachers and counsellors trained to be supervisors for peer counselling (as cited in Rho and Kim, 2007).

Reasons reported for using peer counselling in South Korea are similar to those reported for the popularity of peer support in other countries. Peer counselling has been considered important because peers are more likely to share their problems with peers and friends than with adults, and to have shared understanding of problems (Rho and Kim, 2007). It can also prevent problems becoming more serious, and provide an extra source of support where school counsellors are limited. Rho and Kim (2007) identified seven criteria for the establishment of a formal peer counselling system in South Korean high schools. These were that: there are trained teachers; supervision or training is carried out once or twice every month; a peer counselling group is formed in the school; there are peer counselling groups in each grade; training or activities occur over thirty hours per year; pupils can access peer counsellors when they have a problem; and the peer counselling group has been operating for over four years.

A meta-analysis of the efficacy of peer counselling looked at thirty-six studies of school pupils, university students and other adults, from 1990 to 2003 (Rho and Kim, 2004). It is not possible to derive a clear picture of how many peer counselling schemes were covered by the studies reviewed, as the article reports only numbers of effect sizes; the majority of effect sizes were however from high school pupils (n = 72, 45.9%), followed by middle school pupils (n = 48, 30.6%) and elementary school pupils (n = 22, 14%). Peer counselling was found to have positive effects upon school-related attitudes, communication skills, interpersonal relationships and particularly on antisocial behaviour. A large mean effect size was found overall, indicating that the observed impacts of the peer counselling in the studies were strong. The effect size was largest for university peer counsellors, then middle school pupils, adults, high school pupils and much lower for elementary school peer counsellors. The authors also made a cautious suggestion that peer counselling could have a positive impact upon school violence or *wang-ta*, the Korean equivalent of bullying which largely involves social exclusion (see Chapter 5), though reduction of bullying did not appear to be an outcome specifically targeted by the approach.

Group counselling has been reported specifically within a bullying prevention program derived from reality therapy and choice theory, with some influence from the Olweus Bullying Prevention Program (Kim, 2006). Sixteen children in grade 5 or 6, who had been bullied in elementary school, were randomly assigned to either a treatment group, which met for two group counselling sessions per week over five weeks, or a no treatment control group. However, whilst some elements of victims of bullying supporting each other are described, there was an adult group leader and there appears to have been greater focus upon increasing victims' responsibility for their behaviour rather than upon social relationships per se. The main outcome measure was participants' levels of self-responsibility, which increased in the treatment group.

Use of peer support as an anti-bullying approach has also been reported in a qualitative study of peer support and other anti-bullying work in South Korea. James (2012) interviewed key informants in two regions of South Korea, including teachers, researchers and representatives for a youth violence charity, the Foundation for Prevention of Youth Violence. Participants generally did not recognise peer support systems as a concept, but a range of practices were reported which clearly invoked the principles of children supporting other children. An informal approach to tackling bullying was 'pupil pairing', where a teacher asked other pupils to support a victim of bullying. The other pupil was usually a child not involved in the bullying but considered especially helpful, who would befriend the victim and encourage others to become friends with them too.

Participants in the study by James (2012) also reported a cross-age system where university students mentored school pupils, as well as a peer listening pilot. Peer counselling classes were also reported – most likely linked to the formal widespread use of peer counselling classes. Additionally, the Foundation for Prevention of Youth Violence had begun development of a scheme where mothers were trained to provide peer support training to pupils. This charity also provided a website where professionals supported children but had found that children spontaneously supported each other.

James (2012) found that the informants were supportive of the practice of peer support in general but identified barriers to its widespread use in South Korean schools. Some were concerned about children dealing with serious matters, emphasising the need for supervision of peer supporters. The strongest barrier was a perceived lack of time for staff to run peer support and for pupils to participate, due to the great pressure on staff and students to achieve academic success. South Korean pupils have been shown to spend longer hours studying inside and outside of school compared to those in most other countries, which prevents them from spending time socialising and in extracurricular activities (Paik, 2001). Peer tutoring systems have been reported however (e.g., Park, Sim and Roh, 2008), suggesting that peer support that is aimed at academic improvement may be well suited for South Korean schools.

Overall, it has been seen that systems are in use where children support their peers and peer counselling has been practised on a national scale. In this way, one method of peer support has been incorporated into the education system to a degree not seen in the other countries. However, the broad umbrella concept of peer support as a way to empower children does not seem to have taken hold in the same way as in England and Japan. Whilst there may be some barriers to individual teachers and schools developing and running their own system, when peer support is instigated within the South Korean education system it has been successful. As in other countries, peer support has been used to tackle bullying, but the emphasis appears to be on supporting victims rather than dealing with bullies. This could potentially be related to the nature of *wang-ta*, involving social exclusion and a need for victims to be re-integrated, but greater research is needed into the use of peer support as an anti-bullying method in South Korea before any conclusions may be made.

A cross-cultural perspective on peer support as an anti-bullying approach

One reason peer support has become popular internationally is as a means to tackle school bullying, and this is reflected in all three countries examined here. For example, schools in England have cited dealing with bullying amongst whole-school aimed reasons for peer support (Houlston et al., 2009), bullying is one of the concerns that can be met in Japanese Q&A Handout systems, and in South Korea peer counselling has been used to support pupils with bullying-related difficulties. Peer support is not prescriptive and indeed the ways in which schemes are used as anti-bullying approaches are not uniform across, or within, the three countries.

The nature of bullying itself also differs, particularly between Western and Eastern countries. In the United Kingdom, bullying typically involves older children victimising younger children, in small groups, using physical and verbal means (Craig et al., 2009; Smith, 2004; Smith et al., 1999). *Ijime* in Japan and *wang-ta* in South Korea predominantly involve social exclusion by peers in the same class, grade or whole school (Kanetsuna and Smith, 2002; Koo, Kwak and Smith, 2008; Morita et al., 1999). For peer support to be effective as an anti-bullying intervention, it seems likely that practice would generally be adapted to meet the challenges inherent within the type of bullying present within a country. Therefore some differences could be expected.

In England, peer support is likely to provide support to victims through less formal befriending systems or via more formal face to face peer counselling. The focus here is on the individual victim rather than the bully or the wider school community, although some practitioners claim that peer support will create a more positive school climate, which will in turn lead to a bullying reduction.

Both bullying and peer support in England typically involve older children focusing on younger children. This means that pupils experiencing bullying may well be expected to request support from pupils, who are in the same school years as the children bullying them. A disadvantage to involving peer supporters in the same school year as the bullies may be that victims are more hesitant to approach them for fear they will also act in this way, or will tell the bullies. This has been seen in two longitudinal studies of systems in English secondary schools, with lack of trust being a barrier to pupils in younger years accessing support from older peer counsellors (James, 2012). Involving older pupils in the provision of peer support does present an opportunity for the perpetrators of bullying to be influenced. Interestingly, English peer support systems in general do not appear to be set up to effectively deal with the nature of the bullying experienced in schools.

Within Japan, the social exclusion inherent within *ijime* places a child outside the social group and, given the importance of group belonging in Japan, thus may involve shame and humiliation. Anonymous forms of advice giving are seen as more suited to the Japanese culture, overcoming the barrier of an individual's sense of shame and loss of face when admitting a problem (Toda, 2005). Therefore Q&A Handout approaches are well-adapted to the nature of Japanese bullying.

Approaches that train all pupils in a class, grade or school in peer support skills to foster a harmonious climate and positive interpersonal relationships are also well suited to tackling social exclusion. Peer mediation training in Japan particularly increases the likelihood that conflicts will be resolved before they escalate to long-term bullying. Involving the whole peer group is well suited to prevent or tackle bullying which may be perpetrated by large numbers of classmates. Unlike in usual approaches in England, both potential bullies and victims are necessarily involved.

Peer counselling classes in South Korean schools are very similar to the face-to-face listening approach that may be used in England. The emphasis in South Korea, as in the United Kingdom, is on supporting victims and enhancing school climate rather than on directly challenging perpetrators. The idea of 'classes' implies more of a community feel to the peer support, situating it within a group of peers. Therefore it could potentially reduce *wang-ta*, typically perpetrated by a large portion of the victim's peer group, by fostering a positive interpersonal climate. The pupil pairing approach reported is also designed to reduce social exclusion, with a helpful child being asked to befriend the victim and reintegrate them into the class community.

Looking at the bigger picture, although peer support is used for many reasons other than school bullying, it seems likely that the extent of peer support would be related to the overall extent of anti-bullying work in a country. The increasing use of peer support in the United Kingdom and Japan reflects the growing concern about bullying and the need to address it. Limited early work in the United Kingdom began in the 1970s, but research in both the United Kingdom and Japan really began in the 1980s. Generally, there is a longer history of government anti-bullying work and legislation in the United Kingdom, especially if general pastoral care work is taken into consideration (see Chapter 1).

In South Korea, anti-bullying work was particularly initiated following the work on *ijime* in Japan; the government has run national anti-bullying campaigns, and put into places a lot of measures and legislation (see Chapters 3 and 4). However, James (2012) identified a gap between policy and practice; key informants perceived that anti-bullying campaigns were short-term and that policies were not effectively implemented. Similarly, Yoon et al. (2011) cite evidence that there has been no systematic anti-bullying work and that incidents are likely to be hushed up, and found that South Korean teachers' responses to a hypothetical bullying situation were split into taking action or ignoring. Whether action would be taken was influenced by teachers' gender and length of experience but not by whether they had received anti-bullying training or the existence of a school anti-bullying policy or program. It seems likely that peer support methods could take root more extensively in South Korea only once anti-bullying work in general is on firmer ground.

The concept of readiness: integrating peer support into whole-school policies

Differences that appear between peer support methods, their focus and effectiveness, may simply reflect the fact that some schools are at a later stage of readiness for more sophisticated forms of peer support than others. It would appear that more advanced systems, involving multiple approaches, could evolve once schools have prepared the ground for peer support, for example, by providing social skills training for all pupils (Cremin, 2007).

It has been seen within England that schools running peer support over a longer period of time have typically expanded to incorporate more than one approach (Houlston et al., 2009). The emotional climate of a school is also important. Baginsky (2004), writing about peer mediation for UK schools, argued that schools with didactic teaching styles and authoritarian discipline will be less affected than schools that already focus on the process and values of peer mediation. Smith and Watson (2004), in a study of peer support schemes in England, also noted that there could be a clash of values in schools where the cooperative values of peer support and the importance of a pupil voice do not already exist.

Cowie and Jennifer (2008) proposed that, before schools introduce an intervention such as peer support, they should conduct a needs assessment that involves all members of the school community. In this way, all members of the school community – adults and students alike – benefit from this process of consultation by discovering what common fears and anxieties are and how their needs might be met.

As we have seen, some educators in Japan have emphasised the need to establish an enhanced culture of cooperation and concern for others in the whole school (the educational model) before training individual volunteers in more advanced skills (the counselling model). This kind of approach is in complete harmony with the principles of peer support since the experiential process of learning about social and interpersonal skills provides the fertile soil in which more sophisticated forms of peer support will flourish. Once all students have received some form of training in social and life skills, the next step typically involves more intensive practice of peer support within the classroom to resolve everyday disputes and to address the problem of bullying. Out of this experience there evolves the wish on the part of students (often at this stage volunteers, rather than the whole class) to offer peer support to younger students in some way, whether through peer tutoring or through activities that facilitate an easy transition from one school to another. Finally, the most advanced forms of peer support involve specially trained volunteers, supported through clinical supervision, who are skilled enough to help individual students in distress within the limits of their expertise. At each stage, teachers and counsellors have the potential to share their knowledge and to collaborate, in school (where possible) and also in training workshops.

Reports of peer support in South Korea are too few for any observations to be drawn about links between school readiness and effectiveness. However, the barriers perceived by the key informants in James' (2012) qualitative study indicate that a lack of readiness within the education system in general may be limiting wider use of peer support outside of the national program of peer counselling classes. Until there is space for peer support to fit alongside the emphasis upon academic success, it is unlikely that many individual schools will develop schemes. Further development of anti-bullying work in general might also be needed for peer support to become a widespread anti-bullying approach. In contrast, the wider use in England and Japan of a variety of peer support methods appears to reflect educational systems more conducive to the principles of peer support. In the United Kingdom, generally the international recognition of the rights of the child has translated into space within the curriculum, for example, in a citizenship curriculum (DfES, 2003), and there is great emphasis upon children's social and emotional well-being within government initiatives. For example, in England there has been: Every Child Matters (DfES, 2003), Safe to Learn (DCSF, 2008b) and Healthy Schools (an initiative running since 1999, initiated by the then Department for Children, Schools and Family and the Department of Health). As we have seen, in Japan, there is a tradition of schools nurturing positive relationships amongst pupils, and recent educational reforms have aimed to increase the focus upon children's emotional well-being.

At a time when there are international calls for indicators of children's emotional health and well-being (UNICEF, 2007), it is appropriate that Japan and South Korea should be developing peer support services in schools, because there is sufficient evidence to indicate its role as part of a whole-school policy in creating schools where children feel safe and respected, and where they learn effectively.

In conclusion, we argue that there is some evidence that peer support can be an effective means to enhance children and young people's social relationships and the emotional climate of schools in both western and eastern countries. However, further research needs to be done to evaluate in particular the distinctive methods that have evolved in both Japan and South Korea. The trend towards increasing international use looks set to continue, particularly as more countries recognise the need for anti-bullying measures within education systems. We advocate that practitioners across and within countries should learn from each other, with a focus upon developing peer support systems which are embedded into whole-school policies and well-designed to meet the nature of bullying and other problems faced by pupils. It is also important that schools adopt effective methods such as peer support that provide a structure within which children and young people can develop strategies for addressing real-life issues in their school communities.

REFERENCES

Baginsky, W. (2004). Peer mediation in the UK: A guide for schools. *NSPCC Inform*. Retrieved 10 February, 2014, from www.nspcc.org.uk/inform/resourcesforteachers/classroomresources/peermediationintheuk_/wda48928.html

Cowie, H. (2011). Peer support as an intervention to counteract school bullying: listen to the children. *Children & Society*, 25, 287–292.

Cowie, H., Boardman, C., Dawkins, J. and Jennifer, D. (2004). *Emotional health and well-being*. London: Sage.

Cowie, H., Hutson, N., Oztug, O. and Myers, C. (2008). The impact of peer support schemes on pupils' perceptions of bullying, aggression and safety at school. *Emotional and Behavioural Difficulties*, 13, 63–71.

Cowie, H. and Jennifer, D. (2008). *Managing violence in schools: A whole-school approach to best practice*. London: Sage.

Cowie, H. and Kurihara, S. (2009) Peer support in Japan: inside and outside perspectives. *Gendai Esprit*, 502, 61–72.

Cowie, H., Naylor, P., Talamelli, L., Chauhan, P. and Smith, P. K. (2002). Knowledge, use of and attitudes towards peer support. *Journal of Adolescence*, 25, 453–467.

Cowie, H. and Olafsson, R. (2000). The role of peer support in helping the victims of bullying in a school with high levels of aggression. *School Psychology International*, 21, 79–95.

Cowie, H. and Smith, P. K. (2010). Peer support as a means of improving school safety and reducing bullying and violence. In B. Doll, W. Pfohl and J. Yoon (Eds.) *Handbook of youth prevention science*, pp. 199–193. New York: Routledge.

Craig, W., Harel-Fisch, Y., Fogel-Grinvald, H., Dostaler, S., Hetland, J., Simons-Morton, B., Molcho, M., Gaspar de Mato, M., Overpeck, M., Due, P., Pickett, W., the HBSC Violence and Injuries Prevention Focus Group and the HBSC Bullying Writing Group. (2009). A cross-national profile of bullying and victimization among adolescents in 40 countries. *International Journal of Public Health*, 54, S216–S224.

Cremin, H. (2007). *Peer mediation*. London: Open University Press.

Crystal, D. S., Kakinuma, M., DeBell, M., Azuma, H. and Miyashita, T. (2008). Who helps you? Self and other sources of support among youth in Japan and the USA. *International Journal of Behavioral Development*, 32, 496–508.

Department for Children, Schools and Families (Press notice 2007/0212). *Ed Balls Announces £3m for Anti-Bullying Pilots*. Retrieved 10 February, 2014, from http://webarchive.nationalarchives.gov.uk/+/www.direct.gov.uk/en/Nl1/Newsroom/DG_071489

(2008a). *Formalised peer mentoring pilot evaluation*. DCSF-RR033. London: HMSO.

(2008b). *Safe to learn: Embedding antibullying work in schools*. London: HMSO.
Department for Education and Skills (2003). *Every child matters*. London: HMSO. 345.
(2003). *National curriculum for citizenship*. London: HMSO.
Gill, T. (2007). Review of juvenile delinquency in Japan: Reconsidering the 'crisis', edited by Gesine Foljanty-Jost. *Journal of Japanese Studies*, 33, 447–451.
Houlston, C. and Smith, P. K. (2009). The impact of a peer counselling scheme in an all girl secondary school. *British Journal of Educational Psychology*, 79, 69–86.
Houlston, C., Smith, P. K. and Jessel, J. (2009). Investigating the extent and use of peer support initiatives in English schools. *Educational Psychology*, 29, 325–344.
(2011). The relationship between use of school-based peer support initiatives and the social and emotional well-being of bullied and non-bullied students. *Children and Society*, 25, 293–305.
James, A. I. (2012). *The use and impact of peer support schemes in schools in the UK, and a comparison with use in Japan and South Korea*. Unpublished PhD thesis, Goldsmiths, University of London.
Kaenel-Platt, J van and Douglas, T. (2012). Cybermentoring. In A. Costabile and B.A. Spears (Eds.), *The impact of technology on relationships in educational settings* (pp. 151–157). London: Routledge.
Kanetsuna, T. and Smith, P. K. (2002). Pupil insights into bullying, and coping with bullying: A bi-national study in Japan and England. *Journal of School Violence*, 1, 5–29.
Kawata, H. (1996). To enable children to collaborate to keep them healthy. *Journal of the Junior High School of the Faculty of Education, Kanazawa University*, 39, 137–155.
Kim, J. (2006). The effect of a bullying prevention program on responsibility and victimization of bullied children in Korea. *International Journal of Reality Therapy*, XXVI, 4–8.
Koo, H., Kwak, K. and Smith, P. K. (2008). Victimization in Korean schools: the nature, incidence, and distinctive features of Korean bullying or wang-ta. *Journal of School Violence*, 7, 119–139.
Mental Health Foundation (2002). *Peer Support: Someone to turn to. An evaluation report of the MHF peer support program*. London and Glasgow: Mental Health Foundation.
Mihara, M. (2008). Introduction and development of programs that improve interpersonal relationship formation ability. *Japanese Annals of Peer Support*, 5, 11–22.
Morita, Y., Soeda, H., Soeda, K. and Taki, M. (1999). Japan. In P. K. Smith, Y. Morita, J. Junger-Tas, D. Olweus, R. Catalano and P. Slee (Eds.). *The nature of school bullying: A cross-national perspective* (p. 309–323). London and New York: Routledge.
Nakano, Y. (2003). Counseling systems as a means for preventing delinquency. In G. Foljanty-Jost (Ed.), *Juvenile delinquency in Japan: Reconsidering the 'crisis'* (pp.199–210). Leiden: Brill.

Nakano, Y. and Kokubu, Y. (2000). *Kore nara dekiru kyoshi no sodateru kaunsering (School counselling: Effective implementation)*. Tokyo: Tokyo Shoseki.

Naylor, P. and Cowie, H. (1999). The effectiveness of peer support systems in challenging school bullying: the perspectives and experiences of teachers and pupils. *Journal of Adolescence*, 22, 467–479.

Ochi, Y. (2008). *One and only me, and one and only you: Self-esteem improved in the classroom*. Sapporo: Paper presented at the JPSA Annual Conference, Sapporo, August 2008.

Paik, S. J. (2001). Educational productivity in South Korea and the United States. *International Journal of Educational Research*, 35, 535–607.

Park, S., Sim, H. and Roh, H. (2008). A study of the strategies of peer tutoring in computer literacy education. *British Journal of Educational Technology*, 39, 933–934.

Rho, S. and Kim, K. (2004). A meta-analysis on the effectiveness of peer counseling conducted in Korea. *The Korean Journal of Youth Counseling*, 12, 3–10 (abstract only in English).

(2007). A delphi study on the establishment standards of peer counselling in high school. *The Korean Journal of Youth Counseling*, 15, 29–38 (abstract only in English).

Shiomi, K. and Nagano, K. (2008). *Peer support program's effect on participants' self-efficacy*. Sapporo: Paper presented at the JPSA Annual Conference, Sapporo, August 2008.

Smith, P. K. (2004). Bullying: Recent developments. *Child and Adolescent Mental Health*, 9, 98–103.

Smith, P. K., Morita, Y., Junger-Tas, J., Olweus, D., Catalano, R. and Slee, P. (Eds.) (1999). *The nature of school bullying: A cross-national perspective*. London and New York: Routledge.

Smith, P. K. and Watson, D. (2004). *Evaluation of the CHIPS (ChildLine in Partnership with Schools) Program*. Research Report RR570. DfES Publications, PO Box 5050, Sherwood Park, Annesley, Nottingham NG15 0DJ.

Takeuchi, K. (2008). A study of the peer support activities from junior high school students to elementary school students. *Japanese Annals of Peer Support*, 5, 37–42.

Taki, M. (Ed.) (2000). *Peer support de hajimeru gakkou dukuri: tyuugakkou-hen (Change school by Japanese peer support program for junior high schools)*. Tokyo: Kaneko Shobo.

(Ed.) (2001). *Peer support de hajimeru gakkou dukuri: syogakkou-hen (Change school by Japanese peer support program for elementary schools)*. Tokyo: Kaneko Shobo.

(2005). Peer Support systems in Japan. In M. Tsuchiya, P. K. Smith, K. Soeda and K. Oride (Eds.), *Ijime/bullying: Responses and measures to the issues on ijime/bullying in schools in Japan and the world*. Kyoto: Minerva Publishing Company (available only in Japanese).

Thompson, F. and Smith, P.K. (2011). *The use and effectiveness of anti-bullying strategies in schools*. Research Brief DFE-RB098 (2011). London: DfE.

Toda, Y. (2005). International comparison of peer support in Japan. In M. Tsuchiya, P. K. Smith, K. Soeda and K. Oride (Eds.), *Ijime ni torikunda kuniguni [Responses to the issue of ijime/bullying]*. Kyoto: Minerva Publishing Company (available only in Japanese).

Toda, Y. and Ito, M. (2005). Some variations of peer support in Japan. *Peer Support Networker*. Retrieved 10 February, 2014, from http://peersupport.ukobservatory.com/

Toda, Y., Nishiumi, M. and Yoshida, H. (2003). *The evaluation of 'on paper method' peer support practice in an elementary school. Annual Report of Center for Educational Research and Practice*, Niigata: Faculty of Education and Human Sciences, Niigata University.

Toyama-Bialke, C. (2003). The 'Japanese triangle' for preventing adolescent delinquency – strengths and weaknesses of the family-school relationship from a comparative perspective. In G. Foljanty-Jost (Ed.), *Juvenile delinquency in Japan: Reconsidering the 'crisis'* (pp. 19–50). Leiden: Brill.

Tsuneyoshi, R. (2004). The new Japanese educational reforms and the achievement 'crisis' debate. *Educational Policy*, 18, 364–394.

UNICEF (2007). *A world fit for us: The children's statement from the United Nations*. New York: UNICEF.

United Nations (1989). *Convention on the Rights of the Child*. London: UNICEF. Retrieved Dec 3rd 2015 from www.unicef.org.uk/Documents/Publication-pdfs/UNCRC_PRESS200910web.pdf Retrieved April 6, 2011, from www2.ohchr.org/english/law/crc.htm.

Yokozawa, N. and Inoue, T. (2006). Evaluation of peer support for adolescents via e-mail. *Adolescentology*, 24, 392–399.

Yoon, J., Bauman, S., Choi, T. and Hutchinson, A. S. (2011). How South Korean teachers handle an incident of school bullying. *School Psychology International*, 32, 312–329.

Part III

Issues in cross-national comparisons

11 Theoretical and methodological issues in making cross-national and cross-cultural comparisons

Esther Guillaume and David Funder

As the study of psychological phenomena across cultures continues to grow, the troubles of such efforts are being illuminated. Common problems arise when a single "universal" measure is translated into many languages and used across cultures without considering that (a) the items underlying a construct may not be the same across all cultures, thus validity is lacking, (b) the utilization of scales and forthrightness of responses may vary from culture to culture, (c) when reporting frequencies of behaviors, participants compare themselves to members within their own cultures, yet researchers compare participants to members outside their own cultures, and (d) linguistic equivalence may not be achieved through translations. Current publications are teeming with theories about the universality of latent constructs, indigenous vs. imported dimensions, and cultural specifics. Therefore, when making cross-cultural comparisons it is essential to note that a phenomenon (such as bullying) may have similar and different meanings, related behaviors, and consequences – both at the individual and societal level – across cultures.

What are cross-cultural differences?

In order to compare psychological phenomena across cultures, a host of issues needs to be considered before any firm conclusions about cultural differences in people may be drawn. Method biases are often present, but also the very existence of any psychological phenomena itself – and resulting behavioral manifestations across nations – is often in question. As a rather new endeavor, exploratory cross-cultural studies are necessary and welcome in cross-cultural research. Thoughts, emotions, and/or behaviors differ across groups of people, and to determine how these differences come about, the goal is to:

...define similarities and differences in individual psychological functioning in various cultural and ethnocultural groups; the relationships between psychological variables and socio-cultural, ecological and biological variables; and of ongoing changes in these variables (Berry, Poortinga, and Segall, 2002, pp. 3).

Strong opinions regarding just how deeply culture resides within human behavior are often found in the literature. Some evidence suggests that humans genetically share universal traits, meaning that behaviors associated with such attributes are biologically based tendencies independent of culture, thus comparable (Jang et al., 1998; McCrae and Costa, 1996; McCrae and Allik, 2002; Yamagata et al., 2006). Still, other evidence suggests that genetic differences exist across populations of people, and that certain cultures create social environments tailored to suit those differences, possibly to mediate the genetic expressions of undesirable traits and behaviors (Way and Lieberman, 2010). If genetic differences do indeed exist among populations or cultures of people, then making cross-cultural comparisons would prove difficult – if not impossible – because certain psychological constructs would not replicate across cultures. Therefore, the distinction between differences among people and differences among practices presents a key concern because the origin of known differences may be ignored, or even worse, assumed.

In fact, without cultural assignment it is nearly impossible to determine which psychological and behavioral differences are genetically based rather than ecological or situation-specific, thus making it difficult to prescribe universal therapies and interventions, for example. Or, more likely, even if a concept is shared across cultures, the underlying attributes or behaviors that go along with the phenomenon may differ in several ways: the attributes associated with the construct may be added or lessened; they may be stronger or weaker; or they may have different factors associated with the overall dimension. In fact, the basic role of culture in psychological functioning is often misunderstood or misconstrued, or displayed in such abstract terms that it may become meaningless. For example, there are many ways to define and conceptualize "individualism" and "collectivism." Some evidence even suggests that European Americans are not more individualistic than African Americans or Latinos, and not less collectivistic than Japanese or Koreans (Oyserman, Coon, and Kemmelmeier, 2002). Addressing this chicken-or-egg conundrum often forces researchers to argue on theoretical rather than empirical grounds, and maybe it is appropriate to favor description rather than interpretation of cultural differences.

General approaches in studying psychological phenomena within and across cultures

Many frameworks have been used for studying cultures, and the most common include the following: personality, individualism-collectivism, values, attitudes, and evolutionary standpoints (Lonner and

Adamopoulos, 1997). Within these frameworks, researchers will tend to absorb one of three approaches: *absolutist, relativist,* or *universalist.*

The *absolutist* approach defines characteristics that bring people together as a human race, reducing as much "noise" as possible in order to tap into true human nature. According to this theory, all humans are born with similar biological structures and psychological characteristics (Berry et al., 2002). The goal then, is to get around any moderating behavioral expression due to culture, and pinpoint underlying shared human experience. Because the absolutist approach focuses on psychological constructs that result from the universal genetic structures (Yamagata et al., 2006), differences in constructs or psychological phenomena that appear among people may be considered genetic (Way and Lieberman, 2010). Happiness, depression, aggression, and certain personality traits are just a few psychological dimensions that are often assumed universal and comparative across cultures. In terms of bullying, absolutists would be most interested in the behaviors that are reported most frequently, despite culture. By focusing on broad psychological behaviors widely shared across nations, there is little concern for biases in constructs or instruments.

This also means that measures can be developed in one culture and imported in to another with little effort. These are often referred to as etic studies, which is the examination of behavior from outside a particular culture or system (Pike, 1967). Again, the assumption here is that the culture should not moderate the most important psychological behaviors because psychological phenomena are shared across cultures. The majority of etic studies compare the universality of a construct and instrument (usually Western). For example, most well-known personality inventories have been translated and administered in many cultures. In fact, there exists good evidence for the universality of broad personality traits across multiple nations, with some confirming that the Big Five domains are generalizable across cultures (Allik and McCrae, 2004; De Fruyt et al., 2009; Hendricks et al., 2003; McCrae, 2001). By examining dictionaries in many nations, lexical approaches attempt to find and confirm the words most often used in person description in many cultures, and have done so (Ashton, Lee, de Vries, et al., 2006; Ashton, Lee, Perugini et al., 2004).

In terms of bullying, the Olweus Bully/Victim Questionnaire scale is frequently used to compare bullying behaviors across cultures. The scale can also determine the most common bullying/victim behaviors or factors across cultures, in a broad manner. Because of the general nature of the questions (e.g., "I was left out from a group"), there exists good reliability and validity of the scale, and there is good evidence to suggest that the scale is a useful tool for international comparisons in bully/victim behaviors (Kyriakides, Kaloyirou, and Lindsay, 2007). In other words, the general concept of bullying exists across cultures, and when viewed in a broad manner, there is universality to many of the behaviors associated with being a bully and a victim.

However, general descriptions of psychological phenomena leave a lot out of the picture, and may lead to very expansive – but empty and uninformative – conclusions about psychological cultural features. In contrast to the absolutist position, *relativists* believe that person characteristics and behaviors are necessarily moderated by culture (Berry et al., 2002). As such, culture produces qualitatively different constructs within cultures that are thus incomparable across cultures. Therefore, ethnocentrism is not a concern in the development of theories and measures; instead, a relativist approach really requires that measures be constructed within a culture, and not shared across cultures.

These are often referred to as emic studies, which examine behavior from within a system or culture (Pike, 1967). Behavioral differences do not result from genetic differences among groups of people, but from social or ecological variations in an environment. When disparities across cultures are noted, relativists stop at the level of description, taking great caution in comparing cultural groups to one another. Because the western dominance of psychological constructs and instruments overwhelmed the field of cross-cultural research, a movement toward indigenous psychology began in response. Many felt that the use of Western instruments introduced biases and ignored variations of behavior expression, thereby enhancing negative stereotypes or views of "other" cultures. In order to find suitable methods for examining cultures, cultural/ indigenous psychologists set aside any type of comparative approach.

Therefore, emic studies adopt the local language, and examine the unique aspects of any given culture. Naturally, psychological phenomena examined are culture-bound, resulting in a bottom-up approach to the development of psychological theories and measures. The lexical approach may be used for these types of studies as well, but they purposely focus on the unique constructs encoded in the language. A few attempts have been made to come up with emic taxonomies of situations. For example, Yang, Read, and Miller (2006) used Chinese *idioms* to construct a Chinese taxonomy of situations. Idioms provide powerful descriptive supremacy; only the most prevalent cultural experiences can be captured in idioms, and they may be best for describing the truest psychological aspects of situations (Yang et al., 2006). A method like this is most popular among anthropologists and cultural psychologists, but is generally incompatible with cross-cultural research.

A third approach, *universalism*, attempts to understand the interactions of shared human characteristics, along with unique environmental effects equally. A universalist will look for both similarities and differences among cultures, and attempt to understand which behaviors are shared and which are independent among cultures. Usually, latent constructs are defined in a host nation, and then measures to test those constructs will vary by culture, as necessary (Berry et al., 2002). When the same set of descriptive items apply across cultures, quantitative comparisons can be made. However, this is not always the case. In terms of the construct of bullying, the frequencies of some bullying behaviors vary across cultures (Konishi et al., 2009), as do their relationships to age and sex (Eslea et al., 2004). Certain aspects of the measures being used to compare bullying rates across cultures would need to be revised, or additional measures should be applied. If not, qualitative comparisons should be used to illustrate the aspects that vary across cultures (Konishi et al., 2009). If differences in the structure or number of factors appear for any given construct, then theoretical analyses need to be done.

Emic-etic studies from both cultural and cross-cultural perspectives avoid solely applying constructs from one culture to another, or indigenously extracting adjectives from dictionaries (Cheung, van de Vijver, and Leung, 2011). The goal is to employ certain universal items or constructs with cross-cultural validity, while developing culture-specific measures using qualitatively focused methods. One way to do this is to employ survey methods and conduct focus groups within a given culture, along with the use of instruments with universal constructs and items. In an effort to design a combined emic-etic measure of personality, Cheung, Cheung, and Zhang (2010) compared the Minnesota Multiphasic Personality Inventory, an instrument that has been widely utilized in cross-cultural research, to a similarly constructed inventory of local Chinese items, the Chinese Personality Assessment Inventory. Making comparisons of both measures revealed universal items suitable for cross-cultural research not only in China and in the United States, but also many other cultures as well (Cheung et al., 2010). Di Blas, Forzi, and Peabody (2000) replicated the structure of the etic Big Five personality in Italian, but they also took care to uncover a three-factor personality structure that was a better fit in the Italian culture. Likewise, Katigbak, Church, and Akamine (1996) and Benet-Martinez and Waller (1997) found that etic-emic approaches to uncovering personality revealed a universal Big Five structure, as well as unique factor structures in Filipino and Spanish cultures, respectively. Perhaps these types of combined emic/etic studies will be the future of cross-cultural research. However, if costs to develop such measures are high, it will certainly be an undertaking few will achieve.

Equivalence and bias issues in cross-cultural research

Beyond the general approaches a researcher may adopt in cross-cultural work, deeper methodological issues need to be considered as well. There exists a fair amount of literature about the difficulty in making cross-cultural comparisons, and most of it circles back to specific methodological approaches (van de Vijver and Leung, 2011). First, concerns result from an inability to experimentally assign persons to cultures; quasi-experimental designs do not allow matching on background variables. Because true experimental conditions cannot be achieved in cross-cultural research, the choice, construction, and application of items and constructs need to be considered with great care. Next, biases in the construction and application of measures likely occur because it cannot be assumed that what exists in one culture, applies to another. Biases will lead to measurement errors, and result in pseudo differences or similarities in comparisons. Only when measurement equivalence is established can cross-cultural results be compared.

Equivalence

One focal issue in cross-cultural research is equivalence (or invariance) of measures. Equivalence occurs when an instrument mimics the same constructs across cultures, and proper translations are achieved. Haphazard methods may easily distort differences; either they are diminished, or (more commonly) enlarged. Van de Vijver and Leung (2011) provide a thorough explanation of equivalences, including a proposed sequence: Construct, Structural, Measurement, through to Scalar.

Construct nonequivalence/inequivalence: Inequivalence happens when a construct from one culture does not exist in another. For example, *hikikomori*, in which Japanese youths experience severe social withdrawal and become recluses in their parents' homes, is a unique psychological phenomenon that seems limited to Japanese culture (Teo and Gaw, 2010). To avoid inequivalence, a stark relativist approach is taken. Phenomena within a culture are viewed in a detailed fashion, keeping constructs unique and culture-specific. Cross-cultural comparisons are not made.

Structural equivalence: When an item or construct exists across cultures, and the instrument captures it, then structural/functional/conceptual/configural equivalence is achieved. In terms of constructs, this type of equivalence is concerned with the *pattern* of factor leadings, and demands the underlying dimensions are the same. In general, personality traits such as extraversion, conscientiousness, agreeableness, neuroticism, and openness to experience have this type of equivalence across cultures (McCrae and Costa, 1997). Problems are noted if the predictor loads more factors in the culture where the instrument was created over the culture into which it was imported. One way of examining this equivalence is to compare factor loadings in each culture, and this is typically done using exploratory factor analyses (Berry, Poortinga, and Segall, 2002).

Measurement unit/metric equivalence: If the units of measurement remain the same, then measurement unit equivalence is achieved. Measurement unit equivalence implies that factor loadings of each item are not only the same, but are also of equal *strength* across cultures. A common example of this equivalence, in terms of physical measurement, is the Kelvin and Celsius temperature scales. The units for each scale are equal distances apart, even though the starting point is different. Subtracting 273 from the Celsius scale converts to Kelvin, and once done, it is possible to compare both scales because they have the same units of measurement (van de Vijver and Leung, 1997).

Oftentimes, it is the culture in which the construct was developed that has heavier loadings, and this may lead researchers to incorrectly conclude that real differences exist in the latent construct across cultures. In a series of simulation studies, Chen (2008) demonstrated how invariance in the strength of factor loadings leads to pseudo cultural differences in self-esteem between Americans and East Asians. Chen (2008) suggests that the differences often reported in self-esteem between the two cultures are likely inflated due to lower factor loadings and reliability of the self-esteem scale for East Asians. One way to test for measurement invariance is through the use of confirmatory factor analysis (Stein, Lee, and Jones, 2006).

Scalar equivalence: When the scales have identical strengths and factor loading patterns, scalar equivalence is achieved. This is the highest level, and only at this level can mean values of a construct be truly compared cross-culturally. It is possible for a scale to demonstrate structural equivalence without demonstrating scalar equivalence (Nye et al., 2008). Either lower level (i.e., metric or structural) may be achieved, but both are necessary for scalar equivalence. One way to detect scalar equivalence is through confirmatory factor analysis (Byrne and Stewart, 2006).

Bias

Biases refer to the introduction of systematic sources of variation that lead to equivalence issues. Biases occur because of differences in the ways in which an instrument or item is perceived or functions across cultures, or when a construct does not replicate across cultures. Commonly, bias is introduced through poor measures, administration techniques, and item development. Van de Vijver and Leung (2011) identified three types of biases: Construct, Method, and Item.

Construct bias: Construct bias occurs when the characteristics that make up a psychological phenomenon are not matched across cultures. This happens when the definition and/or behaviors associated with the construct differ in some form. Construct bias leads to construct nonequivalence, thereby affecting all other levels of equivalence, and will make cross-cultural differences appear larger than they actually are. Intelligence tests often lack construct validity because they are limited to reasoning, memory, and knowledge. Other aspects, such as social intelligence (the ability to effectively navigate the social environment) either are deemphasized or absent in intelligence tests, but some cultures consider superior social skills an important form of intelligence (Goleman, 2006). Not only has intelligence been defined differently across cultures, but within cultures as well. IQ test scores in the United States systematically varied based on the socio-economic status of the taker, making those from disadvantaged backgrounds appear less intelligent. However, literacy skills and cultural backgrounds of the developers shaped the questions, giving test-takers of a similar class an advantage (Marks, 2011). Although significant improvements in IQ testing have been made, some still believe that "intelligence" is a culturally bound construct, not a human universal.

Likewise, the notion of *amae* in Japanese culture encourages its youth to form tight, interdependent relationships with family. Westerners may see this as being overly dependent, which is associated with more negative than positive connotations. Western youth are encouraged to develop a sense of independence as they age, whereas dependency does not have the same negative connotations in Japanese culture (Marsella et al., 2000). Therefore, because western social structures do not support tight interdependent family units, the construct of *amae* would not be comparable across cultures.

One-way construct bias can occur is if the construct itself tends to be very broad in nature, and "short" versions of an instrument with too few items are unable to capture all those that may be relevant within different cultures. Another more typical way a construct bias can occur is when constructs themselves are culture-bound and leave out additional items that may be relevant to other cultures. For example, Snyder (1987) hypothesized that some individuals would be more likely to guide their behaviors by situational cues rather than internal dispositions. He developed a scale that typed people as either "high self-monitors" or "low self-monitors." Although this scale worked with a US sample, hypotheses about other cultures were not supported. For example, members of collectivist cultures are thought to adjust their behaviors to situations more so than members of individualistic cultures, so more high self-monitors were expected in collectivist cultures. However, this was not the case. In fact, just the opposite was found. Lower self-monitoring was found in collectivist cultures. After examination of the self-monitoring scale, it was apparent that many of the items were similar to extraversion, and extraversion tends to be lower in collectivist cultures. It was necessary to reconceptualize self-monitoring in Chinese samples, and develop a new scale to include items referencing the self to ingroups, social contexts, and social status (Gudykunst, 1989). Once the items were adjusted, hypotheses were then supported in that it was more typical to find low self-monitors in individualist cultures, and high self-monitors in collectivist cultures (Gudykunst, 1989).

Finally, when a construct has not been supported, multimethod studies and local surveys are a couple of ways to address the unique aspects within a culture (van de Vijver and Tanzer, 2004).

Method bias: If the psychological construct is represented in an instrument, but the application introduces pseudo group differences, method bias occurs. In other words, the manner in which the study is conducted introduces variables that affect the results and lead to pseudo results. Even if a construct exists in multiple cultures, the way it is presented and perceived in a measure may affect responses. Method bias can occur in many ways: differences in samples, administration and procedures, and/or the way the items in the instrument prompt differential response styles.

Sample bias

When differences in the characteristics of samples influence results, sample bias occurs. Varying the population by comparing university students to community members, for example, is one way to confound results. Another way is to vary motivations among samples by pay, course credit, or volunteerism. One way to deal with sample bias is to match samples on all background variables (i.e., education, age, sex, socio-economic status). However, this may limit the representativeness of a particular population.

Administration bias

Administration and procedural biases may occur because of two things: physical environments and test administrators. If the physical environments are drastically different, such as a formal lab compared to an informal outside environment, or an online vs. an in-person test, participants may feel more or less comfortable answering personal questions. Problems with test administrators could create experimenter effects when untrained personnel administer tests. Communication problems, cultural insensitivity, and unfamiliarity with the population are a few examples brought on by inadequately informed personnel. One way to deal with administration biases is to develop rigorous procedural manuals, especially if the interview and interviewee are from different cultures.

Instrument bias

A more common and much-discussed form of method bias is instrument bias, and this occurs when an instrument elicits certain responses unrelated to its purpose. Different groups of respondents may approach items in a consistently different manner, inflating differences. This may result from unfamiliarity with items or differences in response styles or use of scales.

One type of instrument bias is *response bias*, which can happen in at least two ways. One form is *socially desirable responding*. This occurs when individuals systematically endorse items that are socially desirable, such as those relating to friendliness, work ethic, or intelligence/cognitive abilities. This may be an individual differences problem, but it can also be a cultural phenomenon. Ross and Mirowsky (1984) compared Anglos, Mexicans, and Mexican-Americans and found that responding in a way to put one's best face forward is more common among those of Mexican origin. Ross and Mirowsky also suggested that lower socioeconomic status or less power might be correlated with socially desirable responding. Another form of response bias is *extreme responding*, where individuals tend to use the far ends of Likert scales, making few middle endorsements on a scale. Familiarity of an item on a scale may lead to assuredness about one's standing with the item, resulting in extreme checking. For example, a person may feel more certain about his or her stance on "talkativeness" than on a more abstract and unfamiliar item like "self-possessiveness"; additionally, respondent fatigue may lower motivation to make fine distinctions among items. It may be easier to "agree" or "disagree" than to "somewhat agree" or "somewhat disagree" about an item (Hui and Triandis, 1985). Possible remedies for dealing with extreme responding would be to use forced-choice measures, or change the points on a Likert scale. For example, some evidence suggests that extreme responding disappears among Hispanics when a ten-point scale is used instead of a five-point scale (Hui and Triandis, 1989). Cheung and Rensvold (2000) suggest test-retest or structural equation modeling as possible methods of detecting extreme response sets.

Item bias: This type of bias occurs when the members of different cultures have the same underlying construct (e.g., bullying), but the items do not have the same familiarity or usage across cultures. When item bias is present, issues with scalar equivalence occurs. This can happen because of poor translations or the use of idioms. Unclear items can result in middle category endorsements (Kulas and Stachowski, 2009). One way to remedy poor translation is to do back-translations, but to then allow for linguistic variation in items instead of exact translations. Controlling for idioms is more in depth, and clarity of all items must be discussed before translations are attempted.

Differential item function (DIF) is one way to examine item bias (Kulas and Stachowski, 2009), and item response theory can be used to assess the items (Huang, Church and Katigbak, 1997). If members of one culture are more likely to endorse a particular item than individuals from another culture, yet both groups actually have the same level of an item, then that item would be said to have DIF. For example, Singaporeans and Australians have been known to approach items on a scale in different manners, possibly due to differing levels of modesty (Tanzer, 1995). Other explorations at the item level of analysis suggest that there is substantial evidence of DIF in studies using the NEO personality inventory, and that mean-level comparisons across cultures cannot be done (Church et al., 2011). Sometimes participants' differing approaches to items get elaborated into cultural differences when in fact, those "differences" are essentially meaningless (Huang et al., 1997).

Reference group effects

A final methodological issue that may affect results from cross-cultural comparisons is the reference group effect, which is brought on by the use of Likert scales. For example, if one asks respondents to rate their talkativeness, they will judge themselves based on the nature of those in their own culture, family, ingroup, or peer group. In other words, those who live in very social cultures may not see themselves as being very talkative; but they are when compared to those in less socially oriented cultures. Unlike the other methodological issues previously discussed, the reference group effect will actually diminish cultural differences that exist.

Consequently, the mean of an item on a Likert scale represents the average level of the reference group of the participant (Heine et al., 2002). Credé, Bashshur and Niehorster et al. (2010) demonstrated the effect of reference groups by telling participants to rate themselves on personality measures using Likert scales, and then rate themselves again on those same measures, but in comparison to a reference group (family, peers, or people in general). Substantial within-person differences in ratings resulted, depending on the group that was referenced.

Utilizing forced-choice measures for cross-cultural comparisons

Forced choice measures (e.g., q-sorts) may be one of the simplest ways to reduce some of the methodological issues previously discussed. Q-sort items are arranged in a nine-step, quasi-normal distribution, with only the most relevant items being placed in the "highly characteristic" and "highly uncharacteristic" piles, and the majority of items placed in the middle, neutral piles. The 100-item California Adult Q-sort (CAQ) is a measure of personality (Block, 1978), and the 68-item Riverside Behavioral Q-sort (RBQ) functions as a parallel means to assess behavior (Furr, Wagerman, and Funder, 2010). Recently, the 89-item Riverside Situational Q-sort (RSQ) was revised for cross-cultural assessment of situations (Funder and Guillaume, 2013). All three of these q-sorts are available in numerous languages for cross-cultural assessment.

The main advantages of using q-sorts for cross-cultural assessment are that they correct entirely, or in part, for several issues with response sets, and reference group effects. Social desirable responding (tendency to rate "good" items high and "bad" items low) is reduced because participants can only place a few items in the most extreme categories. Extreme responding (rating items as very high or low regardless of content) and acquiescing (tendency to say "yes" to any item) is impossible with q-sorts because each item is not rated on its own scale, but instead compared to all the other items, thus the quasi-normal distribution assures that items will vary. Additionally, the halo effect, which is the tendency to rate groups of items similarly to each other (e.g., if one "goodness" item is rated high then all other "good" items also get rated high) is partially corrected by q-sorts because there is generally no room to put all items of a type (e.g., all socially desirable items) into a single category. Finally, q-sorts may lessen the reference group effect because respondents are asked to make comparisons among the items (not to others), which would then make the same items the "reference group" for all cultures utilizing the measure.

Although few studies have used forced choice measures for cross-cultural comparisons (Funder et al., 2012), this method shows great promise for future work in cross-cultural research.

Conclusions

Globalization has brought people and ideas together from all corners of the world, so it should be expected that at least some cultural differences dissipate. However, careful work of researchers may also attenuate cultural differences due to better methods of research, translations, measures, and constructs. One overarching theoretical consideration that goes beyond construct development, instrument development, application, and assessment, is the question of, "*What* is psychological?" For some who take a cultural approach, values, beliefs, and observed psychological phenomena resulting from cultural experiences are internalized, and integrated into the stable characteristics of a person (Markus and Kitayama, 1998). For example, Kim and Markus (1999) reasoned that westerners have an internalized preference for things that express their uniqueness, whereas East Asians have an internalized preference for things that express their conformity. They demonstrated this in a study in which they gave Americans and Japanese a choice between a unique pen and a majority pen. Indeed, when given the option to choose a pen, westerners choose the unique pen and East Asians choose the majority pen.

However, these observed differences might simply be outward strategies, adapted for proper functioning within a society. The choice of majority pen over a unique pen may have been situation-specific, and nothing to do with a preference to be similar to others. By simply changing the situation in which the pen was presented (from monitored to anonymous), Yamagishi, Hashimoto and Schug (2008) found that pen preferences between cultures evened out, and East Asians choose the unique pen as often as westerners. Yamagishi and colleagues reasoned that although East Asians preferred the unique pen, they often choose the majority pen because they did not want to be seen as taking a resource others may have desired. The preference was not to be similar to others, but to avoid appearing selfish. The stereotype that the Japanese are conformists may result from war propaganda during World War II (Takano, 2008; Takano and Sogon, 2013), and not provide much ground in the way of truth. Differences in societal structures may not reflect innate differences within cultural groups, but ecological or sociopolitical and sociocultural disparities beyond a people's control. In turn, each culture adapts specific behaviors to function, but these behaviors are not internalized (Yamagishi et al., 2008).

These are just a couple of conflicting theoretical arguments that demonstrate how difficult it is to compare persons and behaviors across cultures. Through increased efforts of researchers in the past few decades, many are attempting to resolve the conflicting cross-cultural assumptions that appear to be grounded more in stereotypes than in actual evidence. Yet scholars are far from consensus. If and when differences are found, it is important to view them with caution, and to consider all possible explanations, especially large differences, as they likely result from cultural biases in assumptions, theories, models, and measures. Methodological issues in cross-cultural research are extremely difficult – or maybe, impossible – to eradicate from the literature, but gradually more and more studies are attempting to address the methodological issues in making cross-cultural comparisons, many of which are the first of their kind (Konishi et al., 2009).

Finally, reporting similarities or null findings is as important as reporting differences because that uproots long-held negative stereotypes about "other" cultures. No matter what approach or method is used, ultimately, results are inextricably linked to researchers' theories and methods, which may introduce many forms of biases. Collaborative research may be one way to attenuate stereotypes and biases in cross-cultural research. Still, correct interpretations of cross-cultural differences may remain the most difficult task of all. The role of culture in psychological phenomena is a shifting, mutable thing, difficult to measure, and even more difficult to understand.

REFERENCES

Allik, J. and McCrae, R. R. (2004). Toward a geography of personality traits: Patterns of profiles across 36 cultures. *Journal of Cross-Cultural Psychology*, 35, 13–28.

Ashton, M. C., Lee, K., de Vries, R. E., Perugini, M., Gnisci, A., and Sergi, I. (2006). The HEXACO model of personality structure and indigenous lexical personality dimensions in Italian, Dutch, and English. *Journal of Research in Personality*, 40, 851–875.

Ashton, M. C., Lee, K., Perugini, M., Szarota, P., de Vries, R. E., Di Blas, L., Boies, K., and De Raad, B. (2004). Factor structure of personality-descriptive adjectives: Solutions from psycholexical studies in seven languages. *Journal of Personality and Social Psychology*, 86, 356–366.

Benet-Martinez, V. and Waller, N. G. (1997). The Big Seven factor model of personality description: Evidence for its cross-cultural generality in a Spanish sample. *Journal of Personality and Social Psychology*, 69, 701–718.

  (1997). Further evidence for the cross-cultural generality of the big seven factor model: Indigenous and imported Spanish personality constructs. *Journal of Personality*, 65, 567–598.

Berry, J. W., Poortinga, Y. H., and Segall M. H. (2002). *Cross-cultural psychology*. New York: Cambridge University Press.

Block, J. (1978). *The Q-sort method in personality assessment and psychiatric research*. Palo Alto, CA: Consulting Psychologists Press. (Original work published 1961).

Byrne, B. M. and Stewart, S. M. (2006). The MACS approach to testing for multigroup invariance of a second-order structure: A walk through the process. *Structural Equation Modeling*, 13, 287–321.

Cheung, F. M., Cheung, S., and Zhang, J. (2010). Convergent validity of the Chinese personality assessment inventory and the Minnesota multiphasic personality inventory-2: Preliminary findings with a normative sample. *Journal of Personality Assessment*, 82, 92–103.

Cheung, F. M., van de Vijver, F. J. R., and Leong, F. T. L. (2011). Toward a new approach to the study of personality in culture. *American Psychologist*, 66, 593–603.

Cheung, G. W. and Rensvold, R. B. (2000). Assessing extreme and acquiescence response sets in cross-cultural research using structural equations modeling. *Journal of Cross-cultural Psychology*, 31, 187-212.

Chen, F. (2008). What happens if we compare chopsticks with forks? The impact of making inappropriate comparisons in cross-cultural research. *Journal of Personality and Social Psychology*, 95, 1005–1018.

Church, A. T., Alvarez, J. M., Mai, N. T. Q., French, B. F., Katigbak, M. S., and Ortiz, F. A. (2011). Are cross-cultural comparisons of personality profiles meaningful? Differential item and facet functioning in the revised NEO personality inventory. *Journal of Personality and Social Psychology*, 101, 1068–1089.

Credé, M., Bashshur, M.R., and Niehorster, S. (2010). Reference group effects in the measurement of personality and attitudes. *Journal of Personality Assessment*, 92, 390–399.

De Fruyt, F., De Bolle, M., McCrae, R. R., Terracciano, A., and Costa, P. T. (2009). Assessing the universal structure of personality in early adolescence: The NEO-PI-R and NEO-PI-3 in 24 cultures. *Assessment*, 16, 301–311.

Di Blas, L., Forzi M., and Peabody D. (2000). Evaluative and descriptive dimensions from Italian personality factors. *European Journal of Personality*, 14, 279–290.

Eslea, M., Menesini, E., Morita, Y., O'Moore, M., Mora-Merchan, J. A., Pereira, B., Smith, P. K., and Zhang, W. (2004). Friendship and loneliness among bullies and victims: Data from seven countries. *Aggressive Behavior*, 30, 71–83.

Funder, D. C. and Guillaume E. (2013). Revised RSQ for international research (version 3.15). Unpublished manuscript, Riverside: University of California.

Funder, D.C., Guillaume, E., Kumagi, S., Kawamoto, S., and Sato, T. (2012). The person-situation debate and the assessment of situations. *Japanese Journal of Personality*, 21, 1–11.

Furr, R. M., Wagerman, S. A., and Funder, D. C. (2010). Personality as a manifest in behavior: Direct behavioral observation using the revised Riverside Behavioral Q-sort (RBQ-3.0). In C. R. Agnew, D. E. Carlston, W. G. Graziano, and J. R. Kelly (Eds.), *Then a miracle occurs: Focusing on behavior in social psychological theory and research* (pp. 186–204). New York: Oxford University Press.

Goleman, D. (2006). *Social intelligence*. New York: Bantam.

Gudykunst, W. B., Gao, G., Nishida, T., Bond, M. H., Leung, K., Wang, G., and Barraclough, R. A. (1989). A cross-cultural comparison of self-monitoring. *Communications Research Reports*, 6, 7–12.

Heine, S. J., Lehman, D. R., Peng, K., and Greenholtz, J. (2002). What's wrong with cross-cultural comparisons of subjective Likert scales? The reference-group effect. *Journal of Personality and Social Psychology*, 82, 903–918.

Hendricks, A. A. J., Perugini, M. Angleitner, A. Ostendorf, F., Johnson, J. A., De Fruyt, F., Hřebíčková, M., Kreitler, S., Murakami, T., Bratko, D., Conner,

M., Nagy, J., Rodríguez-Fornells, A., and Ruisel, I. (2003). The Five-Factor Personality Inventory: Cross-cultural generalizability across 13 countries. *European Journal of Personality*, 17, 347–373.

Huang, C. D., Church, A. T., and Katigbak, M. S. (1997). Identifying cultural differences in items and traits: Differential item functioning in the NEO personality inventory. *Journal of Cross-Cultural Psychology*, 28, 192–218.

Hui, C. H. and Triandis, H. C. (1985). The instability of response sets. *Public Opinion Quarterly*, 49, 253–260.

  (1989). Effects of culture and response format on extreme response style. *Journal of Cross-Cultural Psychology*, 20, 296–309.

Jang, K. L., McCrae, R. R., Angleitner A., Rieman R., and Livesley, W. J. (1998). Heritability of facet level traits in a cross-cultural twin sample: support for a hierarchical model of personality. *Journal of Personality and Social Psychology*, 74, 1556–65.

Katigbak, M. S., Church, T. A., and Akamine, T. X. (1996). Cross-cultural generalizability of personality dimensions: Relating indigenous and imported dimensions in two cultures. *Journal of Personality and Social Psychology*, 70, 99–114.

Kim, H. and Markus, H. R. (1999). Deviance or uniqueness, harmony or conformity? A cultural analysis. *Journal of Personality and Social Psychology*, 77, 785–800.

Konishi, C., Hymel, S., Zumbo, B. D., Li, Z., Taki, M., Slee, P., Pepler, D., Sim, H., Craig, W., Swearer, S. M., and Kwak, K (2009). Investigating the comparability of a self-report measure of childhood bullying across countries. *Canadian Journal of School Psychology*, 24, 82–93.

Kulas, J. T. and Stachowski, A. A. (2009). Middle category endorsement in odd-numbered Likert response scales: Associated item characteristics, cognitive demands, and preferred meanings. *Journal of Research in Personality*, 43, 489–493.

Kyriakides, L., Kaloyirou, C. and Lindsay, G. (2007). An analysis of the Revised Olweus Bully/Victim Questionnaire using the Rasch measurement model. *British Journal of Educational Psychology*, 76, 781–801.

Lonner, W. J. and Adamapoulos, J. (1997). Culture as antecedent to behavior. In J. W. Berry, Y. H. Poortinga and J. Pandey (Eds.), *Handbook of cross-cultural psychology* (pp. 43–83). Needham Heights, MA: Allyn and Bacon.

Marks, D. F. (2011). IQ variations across time, race, and nationality: An artifact of differences in literacy skills. *Counselor Education and Supervision*, 50, 643–664.

Markus, H. R. and Kitayama, S. (1998). The cultural psychology of personality. *Journal of Cross-Cultural Psychology*, 29, 63–87.

Marsella, A. J., Dubanoski, J., Hamada, W. C., and Morse, H. (2000). The measurement of personality across cultures: Historical, conceptual, and methodological issues and considerations. *American Behavioral Scientist*, 44, 41–62.

McCrae, R. R. (2001). Trait psychology and culture: Exploring intercultural comparisons. *Journal of Personality*, 69, 819–846.

McCrae, R. R. and Allik, J. (2002). *The five-factor model of personality across cultures*. New York: Kluwer Academic.

McCrae, R. R. and Costa, P. T. (1997). Personality trait structure as a human universal. *American Psychologist*, 52, 509–516.

(1996). Toward a new generation of personality theories: Theoretical contexts for the five-factor model. In J. S. Wiggins (Ed.), *The five-factor model of personality: Theoretical perspectives* (pp. 51–87). New York: Guilford.

Nye, C. D., Roberts, B. W., Saucier, G., and Zhou, X. (2008).Testing the measurement equivalence of personality adjective items across cultures. *Journal of Research in Personality*, 42, 1524–1536.

Oyserman, D., Coon, H. M., and Kemmelmeier, M. (2002). Rethinking individualism and collectivism: Evaluation of theoretical assumptions and meta-analyses. *Psychological Bulletin*, 128, 3–72.

Pike, K. L. (1967). *Language in relation to a unified theory of the structure of human behavior*. The Hague: Mouton.

Ross, C. E. and Mirowsky, J. (1984). Socially-desirable response and acquiescence in a cross-cultural survey of mental health. *Journal of Health and Social Behavior*, 25, 189–197.

Snyder, M. (1987). *Public appearances, private realities: The psychology of self-monitoring*. New York: Freeman.

Stein, J. A., Lee, J. W., and Jones, P. S. (2006). Assessing cross-cultural differences through use of multiple-group invariance analyses. *Journal of Personality Assessment*, 87, 249–258.

Takano, Y. (2013). Japanese culture explored through experimental design. In A. Kurlyo (Ed.), *Intercultural communication.* (pp. 405–412). Thousand Oaks, CA, US: Sage Publications.

Takano, Y. and Sogon, S. (2008). Are Japanese more collectivistic than Americans? Examining conformity in in-groups and the reference-group effect. *Journal of Cross-Cultural Psychology*, 39, 237–250.

Tanzer, N. K. (1995). Cross-cultural bias in Likert-type inventories: Perfect matching factor structures and still biased? *European Journal of Psychological Assessment*, 11, 194–201.

Teo, A. R. and Gaw, A. C. (2010). Hikikomori, a Japanese culture-bound syndrome of social withdrawal? A proposal for DSM-5. *Journal of Nervous and Mental Disease*, 198, 444–449.

van de Vijver, F. J. R. and Leung, K. (1997). *Methods and data analysis for cross-cultural research*. Thousand Oaks, CA, US: Sage Publications.

(2011). Equivalence and bias: A review of concepts, models, and data-analytic procedures. In F. J. R. van de Vijver and D. Matsumoto (Eds.), *Cross-cultural research methods in psychology* (pp. 15–45). New York, NY: Cambridge University Press.

van de Vijver, F. and Tanzer, N. K. (2004). Bias and equivalence in cross-cultural assessment: An overview. *European Review of Applied Psychology*, 54, 119-135.

Way, B. M. and Lieberman, M. D. (2010). Is there a genetic contribution to cultural differences? Collectivism, individualism, and genetic markers of social sensitivity. *Social and Affective Neuroscience*, 5, 203–211.

Yamagata, S., Suzuki, A., Ando J., Ono Y., Kijima, N., Yoshimura, K., Ostendorf, F., Angleitner, A., Riemann, R., Spinath, F. M., Livesley, W. J., and Jang K. L. (2006). Is the genetic structure of human personality universal? A cross-cultural twin study from North America, Europe, and Asia. *Journal of Personality and Social Psychology*, 90, 987–998.

Yamagishi, T., Hashimoto, H., and Schug, J. (2008). Preferences versus strategies as explanations for culture-specific behavior. *Psychological Science*, 19, 579–584.

Yang, Y., Read, S. J., and Miller, L. C. (2006). A taxonomy of situations from Chinese idioms. *Journal of Research in Personality*, 40, 750–778.

12 Educational systems
A basis for some comparative perspectives

John Jessel

In view of the diversity of settings that may exist both within and across countries on a worldwide scale, providing a broad perspective on the Eastern and Western educational systems within which the notion of bullying in schools can be considered is not straightforward. For those attempting to make cross-national comparisons, some basic parameters linked to the structure of different educational systems that provide a context within which some aspects of bullying can be examined are outlined in this chapter.

With regard to the Scandinavian, Central/Southern European, North American, Australasian and Eastern regions that feature in this book, the countries that are focused on include Norway, Finland, England (sometimes United Kingdom where statistics are provided on that basis), the Netherlands, Germany, France, Italy, Spain, the United States of America (US), Canada, Australia, New Zealand, Japan, South Korea, mainland China and Hong Kong.

Where data are available and where it may be helpful, these countries are considered individually. However, as the education provision within any one country is not assumed to be homogenous, rather than trying to uniquely characterise the school systems within each country, some of the data are used only to illustrate how particular aspects of a school system can vary. Through this, the intention is to suggest vocabulary that can be used to describe some of the basic organisational qualities of different schools so that any comparisons might be made more easily.

Economic and international context

Although representing a wide variety of cultures, all of the countries named above, apart from mainland China and Hong Kong, currently belong to the Organisation for Economic Co-operation and Development (OECD). Additionally, most of the countries, including China and Hong Kong as a region of China, also belong to the Group of 20 (G20) countries by virtue of their economic and financial status. In view of this, they can be considered to be able to play an active part in searching for and promoting effective policies aimed at enhancing social and economic prospects, including providing incentives for greater efficiency in schooling (OECD 2013a). For example, through the Programme for International Student Assessment (PISA) the OECD has examined educational performance across countries, and the OECD Directorate for Education and Skills has drawn together a huge body of data to allow international comparisons on a range of indicators that it updates annually (OECD, 2013b). Sources such as this will be referred to in the sections that follow.

Responsibility for schooling and types of schooling available in each country

All of the countries focused upon have a public- or state-run system that is responsible for the provision of education over the school years. At national level, this is often through a ministry (sometimes referred to as a department) of education, which is usually concerned with the quality of overall school provision including the curriculum. Having said that, some responsibilities may be devolved down to a more local or municipal level with varying levels of autonomy. In some countries, the education system may be relatively centralised and uniform while in others it may be subject to variation, such as through region. In the case of the US, Canada and Australia, for example, a federated system operates where a central (federal) government oversees a number of regions, each which may have some level of autonomy.

Other systems that are not administered by government may also operate within many countries. These may be private (sometimes referred to as 'independent' or 'non-state') and include education provided through religious affiliations. Institutions with a religious affiliation may teach the range of subjects found elsewhere but may also teach religious education and uphold the beliefs, principles and practices belonging to their particular faith, while in other institutions the latter may be less evident.

Private institutions may select students and are usually funded through tuition charges. More specifically, an institution may be classified as private if it is controlled and managed by a non-governmental organisation and its Governing Board may not be publicly selected (EACEA, 2012). Alternatives exist, such as private grant-aided institutions, which may have their own funding arrangements with government agencies. In some countries (e.g., United Kingdom) the idea of a private school, or institution, usually applies where younger students (e.g., prior to university) are taught, while in other countries (e.g., the United States) a private school or institution can refer to any age-group or level including university.

Levels of education: an international standard classification of education

Education systems can vary widely from one country to another, both in terms of the way they are organised and in terms of what is included in the curriculum. The terminology used to describe different aspects of education systems can also vary both within and across countries. In view of this, the United Nations Educational, Scientific and Cultural Organization (UNESCO) has developed and regularly updates an International Standard Classification of Education (ISCED) so that statistics and indicators for different countries can be more easily compared in terms of uniform and internationally agreed definitions (UNESCO, 2012). There are currently 195 Members and 9 Associate Members of UNESCO, and all of the countries (including Hong Kong insofar that it is linked with China) featured in this chapter have been long-standing members.

The classification is in part based on the notion of 'levels' of education. This assumes that educational experience can be grouped into categories, which can be ordered and represent 'broad steps of educational progression in terms of the complexity of educational content' (UNESCO, 2012, p. 13). The classification system as a whole applies to a range of formal and non-formal education programmes available for those at any age. These may be planned and run by public organisations or recognised private bodies, with non-formal education providing an alternative or complementing formal education as part of lifelong learning (e.g., literacy programmes, adult education, apprenticeships, technical or vocational education, or special needs education) (ibid.). If the range of possible levels applicable from early childhood to adulthood is taken as a whole, then the classification system is complex: as programmes for older students become more specialised or 'advanced' then a number of different education pathways may be provided. However, the years represented by the lower levels, usually referred to as 'schooling', in all countries can be represented in the main by a linear sequence of levels through which all students would be expected to pass. The 'Level Descriptions' for the most recent available version of the Classification System (ISCED 2011) that apply to the school years in all member countries are summarised in Table 12.1.

Table 12.1 *Level descriptions based on the International Standard Classification of Education (ISCED 2011) (Adapted from UNESCO, 2012).*

Level	ISCED (2011)	Description	Other terms used for the programmes
0 (01)	**Early childhood education (01 early childhood educational development)**	Education designed to support early development in preparation for participation in school and society. Programmes designed for children below the age of 3.	Early childhood education and development, play school, reception, pre-school or *educación inicial*. For programmes provided in crèches, daycare centres, nurseries or *guarderías*.
0 (02)	**Early childhood education (02 pre-primary education)**	Education designed to support early development in preparation for participation in school and society. Programmes designed for children from age 3 to the start of primary education.	
1	**Primary education**	Programmes typically designed to provide students with fundamental skills in reading, writing and mathematics and to establish a solid foundation for learning.	Primary education, elementary education, basic education
2	**Lower secondary education**	First stage of secondary education building on primary education, typically with a more subject-oriented curriculum.	Secondary school (stage one/lower grades if one programme levels 2 and 3), junior secondary school, middle school or junior high school. If programme spans levels 1 and 2, the terms elementary education or basic school (stage two/ upper grades).
3	**Upper secondary education**	Second/final stage of secondary education preparing for tertiary education and/or providing skills relevant to employment. Usually with an increased range of subject options and streams.	Secondary school (stage two/upper grades), senior secondary school or (senior) high school.

In the ISCED 2011, Level 0 covers early childhood education for all ages, including very young children. There are two categories of ISCED Level 0 programmes: early childhood educational development, and pre-primary education. The former (code 01) has educational content designed for children below three years of age, whilst the latter (code 02) is designed for children from age three years to the start of primary education. This sub-division has been introduced in ISCED 2011 and does not exist in earlier versions. Table 12.1 indicates different ways that programmes at ISCED level 0 may be classified but for international comparability purposes, the term 'early childhood education' is used (UNESCO, 2012).

Table 12.1 also shows the ways that programmes classified as ISCED Level 1 may be referred to and, again, for international comparability purposes the term 'primary education' is used for this level. Similarly, the term 'lower secondary education' is used to label ISCED Level 2 and the term 'upper secondary education' is used to label ISCED Level 3 (UNESCO, 2012).

Levels of education and student age

There is a rough correspondence between the ISCED levels and student age across all the countries discussed; however, this will be considered in more detail below. It should be noted that whilst many countries use words equivalent to 'child' or 'children' for those at nursery or beginning primary school, the word 'pupil' is also used in many English-speaking countries to refer to those at primary and secondary level. 'Student' has often been used to denote the recipients of education beyond the primary and secondary years (such as at university) although it is increasingly being used in relation to the schools years. With the exception of the younger age groups, the terminology used in this chapter reflects this latter trend apart from those country-specific instances where it may be more appropriate to use an alternative.

Although there are some exceptions, primary education (ISCED 1) typically begins when children are between five and seven years of age and continues for a period of between four and six years. In England, for example, compulsory education begins at the start of the school term (beginning in either September, January or April) following the fifth birthday. If they turn five between September to March, they will start in a 'reception' class (ISCED 0) prior to the school academic year in the following September. However, since many children begin primary school in the September following their fourth birthday they will be placed in reception for an entire academic year. In the

Netherlands, many children begin school at the age of four, with compulsory schooling from the age of five, and ISCED 1 beginning at the age of six (Eurydice, 2013a).

In most cases, from the ages of 10, 11 or 12 primary education is followed by lower secondary education. Upper secondary education (ISCED 3) usually begins when students are around 15 or 16 years of age and may continue for 2 to 5 years (Eurydice, 2013b). It is for students in the secondary age-range that the structure of different educational systems can become more complex owing to different types of provision. As a rule, if education is of a more general nature and carried out in what is deemed to be a school setting then it can be regarded as secondary education, while technical and vocational provision in other types of institution may be referred to as further education (UNESCO, 2012). In some countries, there may also be middle schools that provide for students who would otherwise be in the later primary and early secondary years. Again, this provision and the age-range it applies to can vary both within and between countries.

Figure 12.1 outlines the educational provision commonly available for children in each country up to secondary level and uses English terminology that is frequently adopted and which can, as a rule, be aligned with that given in Table 12.1. In view of the potential complexity and for the purposes of this chapter, the secondary levels of education shown in Figure 12.1 include any provision that may be made for technical or vocational, as well as general education.

The school years and compulsory education

In all of the countries considered, education is compulsory for all children at some point in their lives. Compulsory education invariably means compulsory full-time education where schooling takes place for the greater part of the working day, week and year. Figure 12.2 shows the ages where schooling is compulsory for each country.

Overall, Figure 12.2 suggests that there is relatively little variation in the age at which children should begin compulsory education in all the countries concerned. This is typically from around five or six years of age, although Finland is notable in that it has a relatively late starting age of seven. Compulsory education can continue up to between 16 and 18 years of age and internationally the trend has been to make upward adjustments (Spielhofer et al., 2007). In England, for example, compulsory education will continue to 18 years of age in 2015 (DfE, 2012a). In many countries, the end of compulsory education may occur at the beginning of upper secondary (ISCED 3) schooling (Eurydice, 2013b).

Age of students in years

Country	0	1	2	3	4	5	6	7	8	9	10	11	12	13	14	15	16	17	18
Norway	Kindergarten						Primary			Primary and secondary are single structure				Lower secondary			Upper secondary		
Finland	Early childhood/pre-primary education						Pre-sch.	Comprehensive school (primary and secondary single structure)									Upper secondary		
England			Nursery			Primary						Secondary							
Netherlands	Childcare centers		Playgroups	Primary									Secondary						
Germany	Creche			Kindergarten			Primary				Secondary Stage I						Secondary Stage II		
France	Creche			Nursery			Primary					Collège/Secondary				Lycée/Upper secondary			
Italy	Creche			Infant school			Primary					Secondary I/Middle			Secondary II				
Spain	Kindergarten			Infant school			Primary						Compulsory secondary				Optional secondary		
USA		Pre-school			Pre-kind.	Kindergarten						Middle school			High school				
Canada	Pre-elementary/kindergarten						Elementary school						Middle school*		Secondary/high school				
Australia			Early years		Kind/g.	Primary							Secondary						
New Zealand	Early childhood education					Primary								Secondary					
Japan				Kindergarten			Elementary						Lower secondary/middle			Upper secondary			
South Korea	Nursery			Kindergarten			Primary						Middle school			High school			
Mainland China				Pre-school			Elementary school						Middle school			High school			
Hong Kong				Kindergarten			Primary						Junior secondary			Senior secondary			

Figure 12.1 Educational provision for students up to eighteen years of age for each country
(*Sources*: Eurydice, 2013c; OECD, 2013c; CIC, 2013; CMEC, 2013; NIER, 2013; GOV.cn, 2005; EDB, 2014)
*For some Canadian jurisdictions only, otherwise termed as 'secondary' or 'high school'.

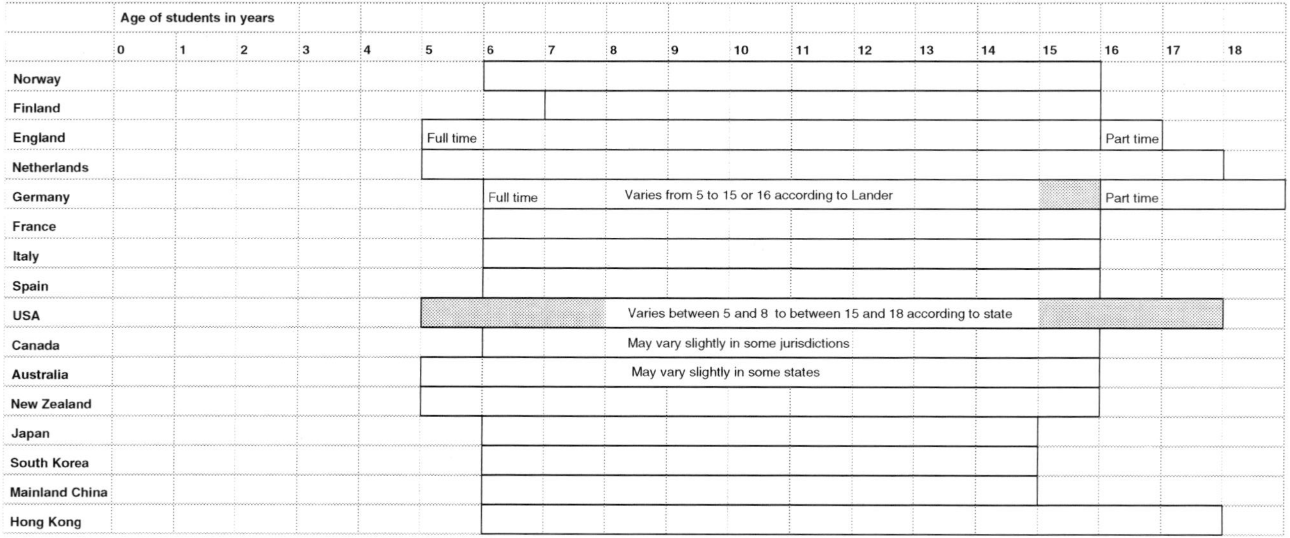

Figure 12.2 Compulsory schooling according to age for each country
(*Sources*: Eurydice, 2013c; OECD, 2013c; CMEC, 2013; GOV.cn, 2005; EDB, 2014).

School enrolment rates

In practice for all of the countries considered and where data are available, it appears that nearly all students attend school during the compulsory years. This is suggested from the enrolment rates for the 5–14 age group in 2011 (OECD, 2013c) which are shown in Figure 12.3. Moreover, it is also apparent from the OECD figures that many students attend school in the years prior to the compulsory period as well as in the years following it. This may be because of the aspirations of students or their families and because this is a right to which the educational systems in some countries are committed or because private provision is available. Figure 12.3 shows the enrolment rates for children in the 3–4 age range as well as for those between 15 and 19 years old. Apart from Finland, Canada and Australia, enrolment rates are well in excess of 60 per cent for 3- to 4-year-olds, and for all of the countries are very nearly 80 per cent or above for 15- to 19-year-olds. Although no directly comparable data are available for China and Hong Kong, as far as the other Eastern countries are concerned, enrolment rates are in excess of 80 per cent for the age groups either side of the compulsory period. Data from the above OECD source also show that 32 per cent of children in Korea who are 2 years old or less also participate in some form of schooling. For the other countries

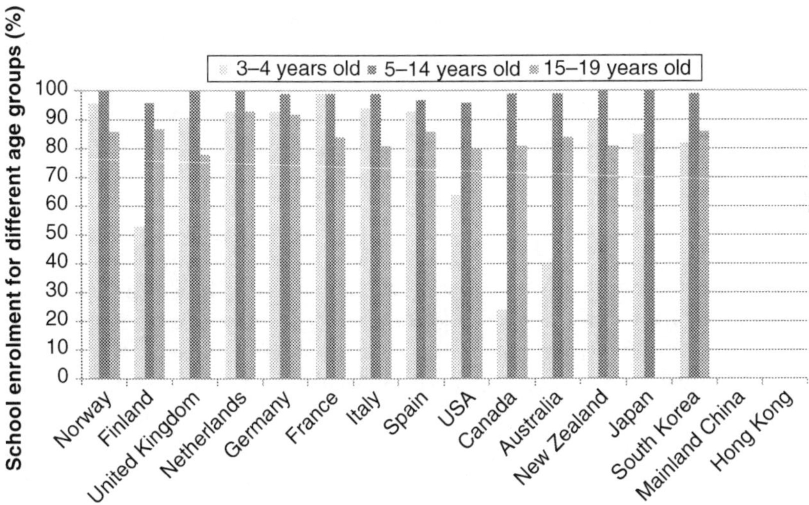

Figure 12.3 School enrolment rates by age (2011) for each country (*Source*: OECD, 2013c).

where data are available for 2 years and under (UK, Germany, France and Italy), the enrolment varies between only 3 and 8 per cent.

Student cohorting and year groupings

In most schools in the countries considered, for the majority of teaching purposes, students are grouped into year cohorts based on their age. For example, in England, those born between the beginning of September and the end of the following August are grouped together as a common school 'year'. In other countries, the terms 'grade' or 'form' may be used to signify a given year group. Although widespread, the use of the term 'grade' is potentially confusing in that it is also used in the context of assessment to signify level of achievement. In view of this, as far as possible the term 'school year' will be used in this chapter to signify cohorting. For example, School Year 1 for most countries begins with the year in which schooling becomes compulsory, with students moving on to their second year as School Year 2 students, and so on, for many countries until the end of their schooling.

There are exceptions, however, in how this chronology is represented and, allowing for translation, Figure 12.4 shows the terminology commonly adopted in relation to each country. Since the age at which primary education becomes compulsory varies from one country to another and, depending on the region, within a country, the school year or grade corresponding to a given age will differ. For example, Figure 12.4 shows that a child turning 9 years of age would normally be placed in Year 5 in England, Grade 4 in Canada, and Year 3 in Finland. Countries such as France and Italy have their own terminology, which is also abbreviated in Figure 12.4.

School year, or grade, retention/repetition

While the matching of an age-group to a given school year is widely applicable within any one country, there is nevertheless the possibility that some students, usually in connection with academic ability, are moved forward into a cohort where the majority of their classmates may be predominantly older or, conversely, may be subject to 'grade retention' or 'grade repetition' whereby they are required to repeat a period of schooling or held back and placed with students who are predominantly younger (Ikeda and Garcia, 2013). Here 'grade' rather than 'school year' is used, partly because the term is widespread internationally and partly because the context of its use gives rise to less ambiguity.

	Age of students in years																				Terminology
	0	1	2	3	4	5	6	7	8	9	10	11	12	13	14	15	16	17	18	19	
Norway							1	2	3	4	5	6	7	8	9	10	VG1	VG2	VG3	VG4	Grade
Finland							1	2	3	4	5	6	7	8	9	10	11				Year
England						1	2	3	4	5	6	7	8	9	10	11	12	13			Year
Netherlands					1	2	3	4	5	6	7	8	9	10	11	12					Group
Germany							1	2	3	4	5	6	7	8	9	10	11	12			Grade
France				PS	MS	GS	CP	CE1	CE2	CM1	CM2	S/6e	C/5e	Q/4e	T/3e	S/2de	P/1ère	T/Tle			see Key
Italy							E1	E2	E3	E4	E5	M1	M2	M3	S1	S2	S3	S4	S5		see Key
Spain							PdP	SdP	TdP	CdP	QdP	SdP	PdESO	SdESO	TdESO	CdESO	PdB	SdB			see Key
USA							1	2	3	4	5	6	7	8	9	10	11	12			Grade
Canada							1	2	3	4	5	6	7	8	9	10	11	12			Grade
Australia							1	2	3	4	5	6	7	8	9	10	11	12	13		Year
New Zealand						1	2	3	4	5	6	7 / F1	8 / F2	9 / F3	10 / F4	11 / F5	12 / F6	12 / F7			Year*
Japan							E1	E2	E3	E4	E5	E6	M1	M2	M3	H1	H2	H3			see Key
South Korea							1	2	3	4	5	6	7	8	9	10	11	12			Grade
Mainland China							E1	E2	E3	E4	E5	E6	Ls1	Ls2	Ls3	Hs1	Hs2	Hs3			Year
Hong Kong							P1	P2	P3	P4	P5	P6	F1	F2	F3	F4	F5	F6			see Key

KEY:
Norway: videregående skole (ongoing school) (VG)
France: Petite section (PS), Moyenne section (MS), Grande section (GS), Cours préparatoire (CP), Cours élémentaire première année (CE1), Cours élémentaire deuxième année (CE2), Cours moyen première année (CM1), Cours moyen deuxième année (CM2), Sixième (6e), Cinquième (5e), Quatrième (4e), Troisième (3e), Seconde (2de), Première (1ère), Terminale (Tle).
Italy: Elementaire (E), Media (M), Superiore (S)
Spain: Primero (PdP), Segundo (SdP), Tercero (TdP), Cuarto (CdP), Quinto (QdP), Sexton (SdP) (de primaria); Primero (PdESO), Segundo (SdESO), Tercero (TdESO) Cuarto (CdESO), Enseñanza Secundaria Obligatoria (ESO'); Primero (PdB), Segundo (SdB) (de Bachillerato).
New Zealand: Form (F)
Japan: Elementary (E), Middle (M), Higher (H)
Mainland China: Elementary (E), Lower secondary (Ls), Higher secondary (Hs)
Hong Kong: Primary (P), Form (F)

Figure 12.4 Student age and school year groupings
(*Sources*: Eurydice, 2013c; OECD, 2013c; CIC, 2013; CMEC, 2013; NIER, 2013; GOV.cn, 2005; EDB, 2014).

In a large-scale PISA survey carried out in 2012 (OECD, 2013d), 15-year-old students were asked whether they had repeated a school year in primary, lower secondary or upper secondary school. For all the OECD countries that took part in the survey, an average of 7 per cent of students had repeated a year while attending primary school, 6 per cent a lower secondary year and 2 per cent an upper secondary year (ibid.). The details for the countries considered in this chapter are shown in Figure 12.5. In Norway and Japan, no grade repetition was reported. Countries such as the Netherlands, Germany, France and Spain have relatively high rates of grade repetition, which vary from around 20 to 33 per cent.

School year grouping and level of education

Based on the same 2012 PISA survey (OECD, 2013d), Figure 12.5 shows the average age, and also the proportion of children who are of 5 years of

	Age of entry into primary school		Year/Grade repetition	15-year-olds in different school years and education levels			
	Average age (years)	Percentage of students who started at: 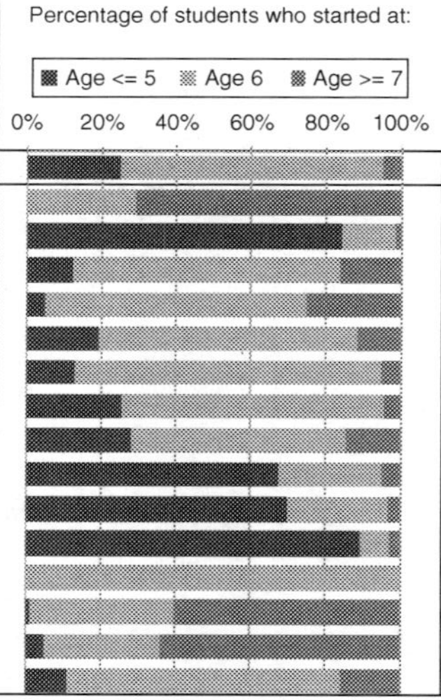 (Age <= 5, Age 6, Age >= 7)	Percentage of students who repeated one or more years/grades	Percentage of students in: 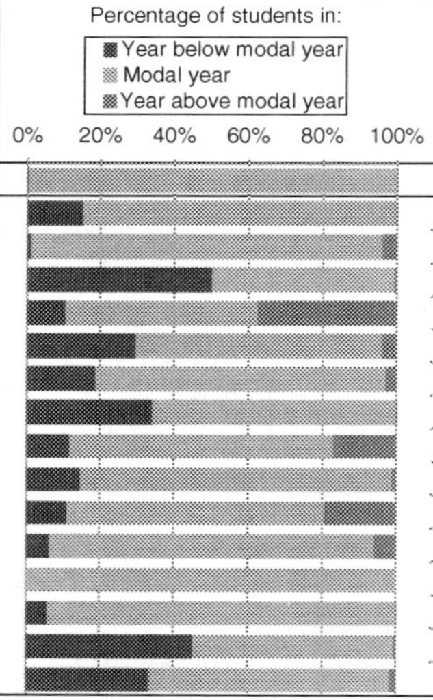 (Year below modal year, Modal year, Year above modal year)	Lower secondary (ISCED 2) %	Upper secondary (ISCED 3) %	Variation in student year level SD
Norway	5.8		0.0		100	0	0.08
Finland	6.7		3.8		100	0	0.39
United Kingdom	5.0		2.7		0	100	0.22
Netherlands	6.1		27.6		70	30	0.57
Germany	6.2		20.3		98	2	0.67
France	5.9		28.4		30	70	0.57
Italy	5.9		17.1		2	98	0.51
Spain	5.8		32.9		100	0	0.67
United States	5.9		13.3		12	88	0.55
Canada	5.2		8.0		14	86	0.42
Australia	5.2		7.5		81	19	0.55
New Zealand	5.1		5.4		6	94	0.35
Japan	6.0		0.0		0	100	0.00
Korea	6.6		3.6		6	94	0.24
Shanghai-China	6.7		9.1		44	56	0.65
Hong Kong-China	6.1		15.9		33	67	0.68

Figure 12.5 Age at which students start school for each country (Adapted from OECD, 2013c)

age or below, 6 years of age or 7 and above on entry into primary school. From Figure 12.5, it is apparent that the United Kingdom, Canada, Australia and New Zealand have a higher proportion of children beginning this stage at a younger age whilst children in Finland, South Korea and China (Shanghai) begin when they are older. It is also apparent that all children in Japan begin primary school in the same year of age.

The combined effect of grade repetition and variation in the starting age for primary education can lead to students from a given age group being placed in different school years and different levels of education. Figure 12.5 shows that 15-year-old students are generally placed in similar school years in Norway, the United Kingdom, Japan and South Korea. In contrast, greater variations exist in the school years in which 15-year-olds in the Netherlands, Spain, China (Shanghai) and Hong Kong are placed.

The majority of 15-year-old students are likely to be in School Years 9, 10 or 11 and this is consistent with the modal school year for 15-year-olds in countries participating in the PISA survey where for OECD countries as a whole, 74 per cent of students are reported to be at the modal year, 9 per cent in school years above and 17 per cent in the years below (OECD, 2013d). From Figure 12.5, it can be seen that all 15-year-olds in Japan and over 95 per cent in Norway and the United Kingdom are placed in the modal school year, while only around 50 per cent of students in the Netherlands are in the modal year.

School groupings for secondary education

In many countries, students may enrol or be placed in different types of secondary school. This may be for the purpose of dividing students according to education provision such as more general academic or vocational pathways. In some countries, such as England, this can take place on the start of secondary school at around the age of 11, while in others this may occur later on from around the age of 15. Selection may be based on assessed aptitude or ability and in the Netherlands, for example, not only school placement but also school year grouping and type of educational programme may be subject to a high degree of student selectivity (OECD, 2013d).

Class groupings

Methods of grouping students into 'classes' for teaching purposes can vary according to country or region, and whether schools are situated in urban or less densely populated rural areas. For schools that have a sufficient number of students within each year group, class groupings are most usually based upon ability, and judged by examinations, school entrance tests or information provided from earlier schooling.

The terminology used for different types of ability grouping or stratification may not always be used consistently, but some of the logical possibilities that have become established in England and other countries are summarised by Sukhnandan (1998). For example, within larger schools, a given year group may be divided into 'bands', each consisting of a number of classes of students judged to be of broadly similar general ability. Grouping according to an overall assessment of general ability also includes 'streaming' (or 'tracking' in the US) where students remain in the same classes for most taught subjects. Some schools may also adopt a 'setting' policy ('regrouping' in the US) so that a student may be placed in one class according to assessed ability for a particular subject and then placed in another class for another subject, and so on. Setting may apply to a whole year group, a specific band, or for one or more subjects taught and students regrouped accordingly throughout the school day.

A further 'within-class grouping' possibility may be adopted when a class is subdivided into smaller groups that are taught separately. With 'mixed ability' grouping ('heterogeneous grouping' in the US) class groups may consist of students considered to be of as wide a range of ability that is provided for within the school. In general, for reasons of practicality, mixed-ability grouping, including within-class grouping typically for maths and reading, has dominated small primary schools in England, while larger primary and secondary schools have adopted ability groupings such as streaming and setting (ibid.).

Apart from occurring naturally within single-sex schools, a further organisational possibility that can be adopted in mixed schools is same-gender grouping. This can apply to all, or a subset of subjects taught (such as physical education) and could also be further subject to various forms of ability grouping.

The merits of the above grouping systems have been the subject of extensive debate, not only in terms of achievement and academic performance but also regarding impact upon behaviour in school associated with social effects such as labelling, self-image, well-being and the formation of subcultures (Hargreaves, 1967; Ireson and Hallam, 2001; Ireson, Hallam and Plewis, 2001; Belfi et al., 2012).

Organisational structures for education

With regard to the more detailed provision of education, different organisational structures are identifiable that may take account of the age-range an institution spans and the kind of curriculum it offers. Three broad organisational models for compulsory education have been distinguished across Europe (EACEA, 2012) and reference to these may also be helpful when describing educational systems elsewhere. These classifications refer to the UNESCO ISCED terminology (Eurydice, 2013b, p. 3), namely:

Single structure education. Education is provided in a continuous way from the beginning to the end of compulsory schooling, with no transition between primary (ISCED 1) and lower secondary education (ISCED 2), and with general education provided in common for all pupils.

Common core curriculum provision. After completion of primary education (ISCED 1), all students follow the same common core curriculum at lower secondary level (ISCED 2).

Differentiated lower secondary education. After completion of primary education (ISCED 1), either at the beginning or some time during lower secondary education (ISCED 2), students are enrolled in distinct educational pathways or specific types of schooling.

Single structure education is evident in Norway and Finland and lasts up to the end of compulsory education (EACEA, 2012). This structure is also evident in some eastern European countries where the different levels of education (including upper secondary education in some cases) are provided in the same school (OECD, 2011).

A common core provision is found in around half of all European countries including England, France, Spain and Italy. Here, following their primary education, the same curriculum is followed by all students over the duration of their lower secondary education up to the end of compulsory education at age of 15 or 16 (EACEA, 2012).

Primary education followed by differentiated secondary education available through different educational pathways is evident in the Netherlands and in Germany. In preparation for this, a choice must be made usually from the age of 10 in Germany and from the age of 12 in the Netherlands (EACEA, 2012).

Prior to education that is differentiated, much of the main provision can be characterised in terms of a 'general education' which has been defined as 'education programmes that are designed to develop learners' general knowledge, skills and competencies, as well as literacy and numeracy skills, often to prepare participants for more advanced education programmes at the same or a higher ISCED level' (UNESCO, 2012, p. 14). As students move through the education system from the primary towards the upper secondary years, there is often the possibility of taking different subject options. 'General education', typically provided within schools, has been distinguished from 'vocational education' which may include work-based components, such as apprenticeships; the latter having been defined as 'education programmes that are designed for learners to acquire the knowledge, skills and competencies specific to a particular occupation, trade, or class of occupations or trades' (UNESCO, 2012: 14).

School transfer

The concept of school transfer often relates to the move by students from a school in one location to another. For example, children may attend primary schools, which are smaller and nearer to where they live, and then move to secondary schools, which are larger and will serve a correspondingly larger area. A number of different primary schools could typically feed into a secondary school, and from the pupils' perspective this stage of transition is marked by different groupings. In some cases where a secondary school takes students from a large number of feeder schools, a student from a given primary school may be placed amongst a group of peers, all of whom could be unfamiliar. If choice of primary and secondary school is allowed then not only will many pupils be meeting other pupils for the first time but they may also find themselves in a situation where class groupings change significantly. In such cases, the transition from primary to secondary schools can also be marked by a change from a student being well-known and taught most subjects by one class teacher, to being taught by many subject teachers who each see them for a limited time each week.

In England, although primary and secondary schools can be on the same site, this is the exception rather than the rule and transition in most state schools occurs at around eleven years of age (Riggall and Sharp, 2008). The possible effects on factors such as on performance and well-being, has led to 'all-through schools' offering provision from primary to secondary on the same site (hitherto more frequent in the independent sector) recently becoming more popular in England (Vaughan, 2011). Reasons behind this may relate to management, continuity and progression of the curriculum, cost effectiveness through sharing resources, a common ethos which can allow a shared set values and a strong framework for social, moral and spiritual development of students which in turn could have an impact upon expectations in terms of behaviour (DfES, 2004). Inspection reports also claim that the strengths of all-through schools relate to climate and ethos, quality of relationships, partnerships with parents and the local community (HMIE, 2010). In particular, if strong links between schools and parents and carers develop from connections established when children are in their early or primary years, then all-through schools could build on this and reduce the likelihood of parental or carer presence becoming diminished and disappearing at secondary school level as children get older.

Transfer, of course, can occur at stages other than from primary to secondary. The age at which school transfer occurs can vary within any one country and, as is evident from Figure 12.1, from one country to another. The move from nursery or kindergarten may involve some form of transition as may lower to upper secondary. Although groupings may change, these transitions can be seen as less marked in terms of institution size, pedagogy and teacher continuity. In view of this, there may be certain advantages in the models adopted by some schools in countries such as France, Norway, Japan and the United States, which have a 'three-tiered' compulsory schooling system, which can include a middle school. Single comprehensive systems that include primary and secondary students are prevalent in Norway and Finland, although in the latter case the comprehensive stage consists of a lower school (7–12 years of age) and an upper school (13–15 years of age), after which students move to either an academic or vocational school (Sutherland et al., 2010). In New Zealand, although standard primary schools are for children between five and around twelve or thirteen years of age, some all-through schools for children from five through to around seventeen or eighteen also exist (Riggall and Sharp, 2008).

School size

School size, measured as the number of students enrolled in a given school, can vary considerably within any given country and also varies across countries. Sources of data relating to this are available from comparative surveys such as the Program for International Student Assessment (PISA, 2009), the Progress in International Reading Literacy Study (PIRLS, 2011) and the Trends in International Maths and Science (TIMSS 2011) surveys. Based on an analysis of these data carried out by Scheerens, Hendriks and Luyten (2014), Figures 12.6 and 12.7 show the average primary and secondary school size for those countries where data are available. The median for each country is also shown because, in many cases, the distribution is positively skewed. A further measure of caution is needed when interpreting the figures because what is reported as 'school size' within the surveys relates to a specific location and if a school spans a number of different locations (such as with age or gender groupings) then the entire school as an administrative entity may be larger than apparent from the reported data. With regard to bullying,

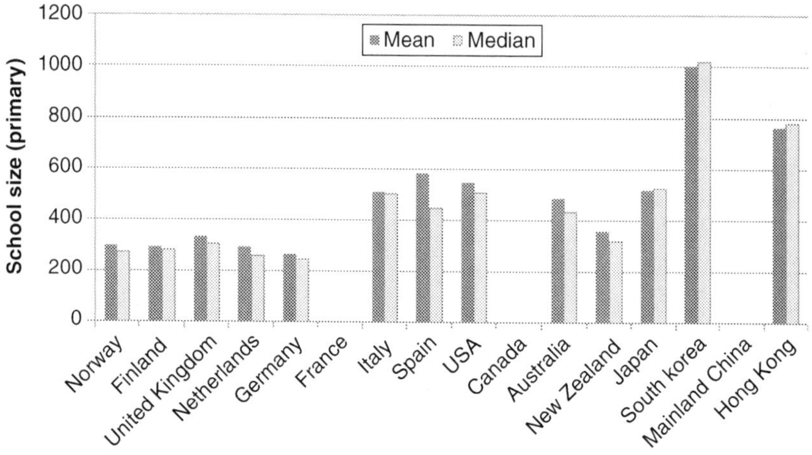

Figure 12.6 School size – primary TIMSS (adapted from Scheerens et al., 2014).

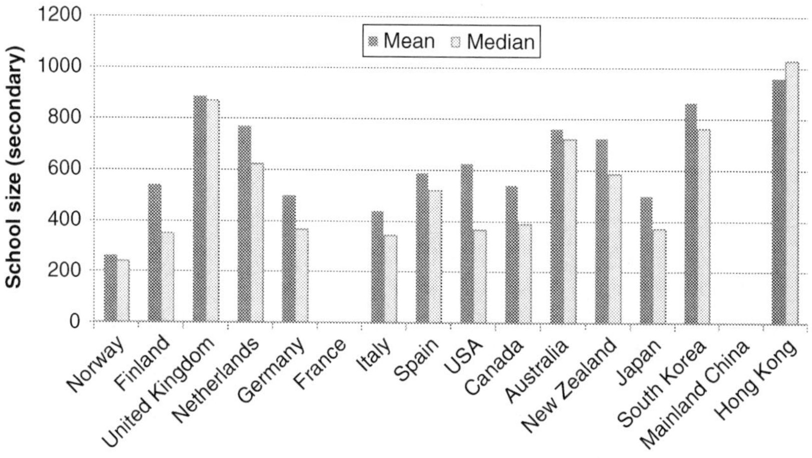

Figure 12.7 School size – secondary PISA (adapted from Scheerens et al., 2014).

while smaller numbers of pupils at one location may be a factor to be considered, at another level the resources available across a larger multi-location school may be another important factor.

With the above provisos in mind, the lowest reported average primary school size is 264.1 for Germany, while South Korea has an average size of 1,002.0. More generally, the countries in Scandinavia and Central Europe including the UK have smaller school sizes than the countries in the other regions. This latter trend, however, is not so apparent for secondary schools, which range from 258.7 in Norway to 960.7 in Hong Kong. The reported size for secondary schools is generally larger than primary schools for most countries, although from comparing Figures 12.6 and 12.7 exceptions include Italy, Japan and South Korea.

From further analysis of the PISA data, major differences in school size are apparent in Germany, Italy and the Netherlands. In these countries, secondary school enrolments range from around 100 to over 1,000 (EACEA, 2012). This has been accounted for in terms of geographical factors and differences between urban and rural areas, the latter said to account for the greatest differences in school sizes in Europe. Differences in school size recorded in Finland and Norway are relatively low. Norway, moreover, has a scattered population and many of the primary and lower secondary schools are small and only 26 per cent of all schools have more than 300 pupils (NMER, 2007).

The relatively large secondary school size for the UK shown in Figure 12.7 is consistent with the general trend towards a reduction in the number of smaller secondary schools with corresponding increases in size. For example, over the period between 1970–71 and 2012–13 the number of secondary schools fell by 32 per cent with average number of students increasing from around 300 to over 900 (Parliament UK, 2013). According to the available statistics for January 2012, out of 3,268 state-funded mainstream secondary schools in England, 317 had up to 500 students, 1,405 had between 501–1,000 students, 1,226 had 1,001–1,500 students and 320 schools had over 1,500 students (DfE, 2014).

A similar trend in the average size of mainstream secondary schools in the US has also been found, namely, from 684 in 1990–91 to 795 in 2000–1 (NCES, 2003). As with England, there are wide variations in school size with 13 per cent of the student population in secondary schools with fewer than 500 students and 39 per cent enrolled in secondary schools with over 1,500 students being reported in 2000–01 (NCES, 2002). It has also been reported that in 1998 the largest secondary school in the US enrolled over 5,000 students, with 274 secondaries having more than 2,750 students (Muir, 2000).

Class size

The average number of students attending classes in primary and lower secondary schools for each country is shown in Figure 12.8. The averages are based on the OECD 2009 Indicators (OECD, 2013c) and are limited

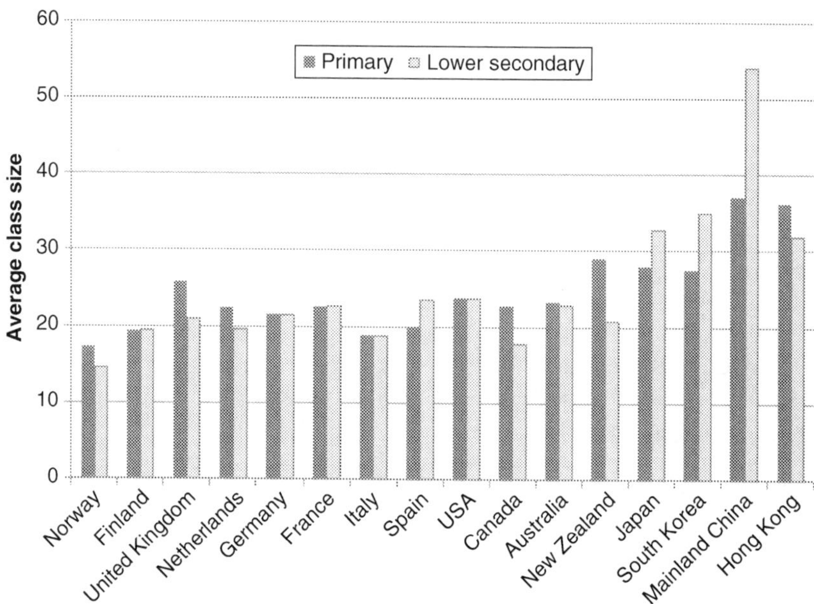

Figure 12.8 Average class size primary and lower secondary
(*Source*: OECD, 2013c).

to primary and lower secondary education because class size is difficult to define and compare at higher levels, where students often attend several different classes according to the different subject options in which they specialise. The OECD figures used for the number of students per class for lower secondary are based on the number of students attending the highest number of common (usually compulsory) courses of study rather than those being taught in subgroups. From inspecting Figure 12.8 a larger class size is readily apparent for Eastern countries with notably large secondary classes in China.

Duration and structure of the school day

In view of a measure of autonomy given to many schools, the duration and exact structure of the school day, including start and end times as well as breaks, can vary from school to school both within, across countries and may also be subject to variation over a number years in response to political or economic factors. Across the school year, some countries (e.g., France, Germany and Spain) require a minimum number of hours which usually increase as pupils get older while other countries (e.g., Finland and the Netherlands) recommend a total number of hours for a level of education, with schools deciding how this time is allocated for each school year. For other countries (e.g., England) there is no mandatory minimum (NFER, 2013).

Although widely reported in non-governmental, non-academic sources and the news media, the availability of more systematic data that can be authenticated for the duration and structure of the school day appears limited. In view of this, only an indication of what may be typical in a subset of countries and some of the factors that could be relevant to situations involving are presented. The details given in this section, therefore, are not intended to provide a de facto statement for each country but more as a means of illustrating ways in which these variables might present themselves in different locations.

Duration of school day: With regard to the duration of the school day, Kamette (2011) gives a very broad outline of how school time is organised in some European countries, based on their legal requirements. For example in Germany, lessons are traditionally confined to the morning, starting between 7:30 and 8:30 a.m. and ending between 11:30 a.m. and 1:30 p.m. However, this may vary according to whether the school week lasts five or six days, and the number of lessons, typically lasting 45 minutes, per week which increases as students get older. More recently, however, in response to criticisms related to social inequalities and working women, some schools have operated on an all-day basis, that is, until 4 or 5 p.m. at least three times per week. Although in Italy teaching at primary level may take place only in the mornings, over the last one or two decades the norm has been for teaching to take place in the afternoon as well.

Kamette (2011) also reports that in Spain lessons traditionally are held in the morning and in the afternoon. These usually start between 9 and 10 a.m. with the morning session lasting between three and three and a half hours. This is followed by a break of two and a half hours with lessons in the afternoon continuing until 4 or 5 p.m. However, there have been more recent moves towards a non-stop day with lessons often starting at 9 a.m. and continuing to 2 p.m., and followed by extracurricular activities later in the afternoon. A similar trend towards a non-stop day is also noted with primary schools in the Netherlands: while schools have usually started at 8:30 a.m. and continued to 3 or 4 p.m. (secondary longer than primary) with a one-hour midday lunch break, lessons in primary schools can end at around 2 p.m. with the children eating in the classroom rather than a separate eating area.

In keeping with government guidelines (UKSI, 1999; DfE, 2012b), many schools in England start from around 8:30 or 9 a.m. for a morning session followed by a break at lunchtime for approximately an hour before an afternoon session that may continue to between 3 and 4 p.m. However, this could change following more recent legislation (DfE, 2013) giving all schools in England more freedom to decide the day length and the start and end times.

From figures across the US reported by Colasanti (2007), the length of an average teaching day across the elementary, middle and high school years is just over 5 hours, but this can vary from around 3 to 6 hours. A more detailed illustration of this is given in the guidelines for schools in Chicago which, for the elementary and middle school years 6–8, suggest that over an average 7-hour teaching day, 6 hours of instruction are given which includes 45 minutes for a lunch break and 15 minutes for other non-instructional activities such as movement between lessons and use of the toilet (Chicago Public Schools, 2012).

In Japan, primary school often begins around 8:30 a.m. and continues to around 3:00 p.m. (NIER, 2013), with secondary school ending around 5 p.m. (Maruyama, 2011).

Reports of the duration of the school day in China vary considerably. At one extreme according to a press report, this can be as long as 12 hours and followed by two to four hours of homework (SCMP, 2014), while Xinhua (2009) cites a survey carried out by the China Youth and Children Research Centre that Chinese secondary students have study hours that are longer than in other countries such as Japan, the US and South Korea. According to the report, over three quarters of Chinese students say they spend more than eight hours at school with over half saying they study at least an additional two hours a day at home.

Lesson lengths: Lesson periods can vary widely in duration for different schools and sometimes the periods can be doubled for subjects where practical work may be undertaken. In a survey carried out by Roth et al. (2006) on students in their eighth school year, data for the mean, standard deviation (SD), median and range in length for science lessons were obtained. Among the countries surveyed, lessons ranged from 38 to 90 minutes ($SD = 8$) in the Netherlands with a mean of 47 minutes and a median of 46 minutes. Lessons in the US ranged between 33 and 119 minutes ($M = 51$, median 46, $SD = 16$). In Australia lessons lasted between 21 and 92 minutes ($M = 49$, median 45, $SD = 14$), and for Japan lessons fell in a narrower range of 40 to 65 minutes with a mean of 50 and a median of 51 minutes ($SD = 4$).

Homeroom/specialist teachers: In primary schools, students usually stay in one classroom or 'homeroom', with the same teacher for most or all subjects. However, in secondary schools in many countries students are taught by subject specialists. Students may also move to different rooms, for example laboratories for science lessons. Not only will a given group of students meet a succession of different teachers over the course of a day but if they are placed in sets for some subjects then the class groupings may also change from one lesson to another. This can introduce uncertainty and anxiety and can have an effect on attainment and social and emotional well-being (Sutherland et al., 2010). However in some countries, notably Japan, students at secondary level stay in their own homeroom for most lessons while the subject specialist teachers move from one homeroom to another (NIER, 2013).

Assemblies: Apart from lessons and other curriculum-related activities that are taught, the daily school routine may be comprised of assemblies or gatherings for a whole school, or for subdivisions that involve larger numbers of students than normally comprise a taught class. Assemblies may involve national or faith-related content or content around issues, sometimes of a topical nature, as well as to communicate information. There may also be relatively brief occasions each day when students may gather on a daily basis in separate rooms for administrative purposes such as registration of attendance and for notices or the dissemination of general information. On these occasions, the students may not be in their normal class groupings and may be with students from different year groups.

Two illustrative case studies of a school day: For most students in their primary or secondary years in Finland, based upon PISA data (CEA, 2006), a typical school day can start between 8 and 10 a.m. and end between 1 and 4 p.m. Lessons are typically 45 minutes long and breaks (requiring primary students to use a playground) last 15 minutes. A 30-minute lunch break is usual with food available at a school cafeteria. Other refreshments may also be available in the afternoon in those cases where the school day is longer. This account also refers to school clubs and other interest groups which meet after school and are often run by teaching staff. The journey between home and school is also referred to; students may walk or use a bicycle where shorter (less than 5 km) distances are involved. Over this distance, transport organised by the school might include payment for bus fares or other kinds of transport such as school taxis in rural areas.

An illustration of a typical school day in Japan is made available through the Ministry of Education, Culture, Sports, Science and Technology (NIER, 2013) and is based on a composite of multiple sources of data adapted below. In this, the primary school day is described as beginning at around 8:30 in the morning. Children initially gather in their 'homeroom' classroom with their teacher. Children who are on 'day duty' lead the morning greetings and the other children follow by saying the greetings. The morning assembly then takes place where a teacher relays messages or cautions. Assembly is followed by the first teaching period in the same classroom and then by a second period. A break between the second and third period allows enough time for children to play outside if the weather permits. This is followed by the third and fourth period and then school lunch. Children on 'serving duty' bring lunch to the classroom and those on day duty call the *Itadaki-masu* (let's eat) greetings before eating. After lunch, children are required to clean their classrooms and this is followed by a lunch break where they can play in the school playground, in the gym or other designated areas. In view of the small space available, year groups are rotated in terms of where and when they play. A fifth period follows the lunch break and lessons such as science may last for two consecutive periods with a specialised teacher. After a total of six periods, the children return to their homeroom where the homeroom teacher tells them what to bring for the next day or confirms homework. The duty children lead a *Sayonara* (good-bye) greeting for the end of the school day around 3 p.m.

Break times and their supervision

In some countries the notion of a break can relate to time spent away from taught periods so that time is allowed for students to move between lessons, play or socialise inside or outside the main school buildings in designated spaces such as common rooms and playgrounds, eat or drink and also leave school to return home for a given period. In some cases, they may be allowed to use their break time to go to a library or finish homework. The terminology varies but a 'break' can also be referred to, for example, as 'recess', 'playtime' or 'lunchtime'.

Following a survey in England and Wales, Blatchford and Baines (2006) reported the majority of primary and secondary schools having either a 15 or 20-minute morning break with lunchtimes of around an hour for the majority of primary schools, and it tending to be shorter for many secondary schools. However, afternoon break provision varied considerably: for younger primary students, roughly two thirds of schools had either a 10 or 15-minute break and most of the remaining schools had no break at all. For older primary students, only around a quarter had an afternoon break and most of the remaining primary schools together with nearly all secondary schools had no break at all. Thus, younger students generally have longer break times. Blatchford and Baines (2006) found that in comparison to a similar survey conducted some fifteen years previously, the duration of lunch breaks had become less for schools generally, but particularly for secondary schools.

Blatchford and Baines' (2006) study also found differences in supervision arrangements and areas that students were permitted during their breaks. In general, primary school students were required to use outside playground areas while secondary school students also had some access to other areas including inside school buildings. Nearly two thirds of secondary students were also allowed off site during lunchtimes, although in around half of these cases parental permission was required. Supervision of break times was carried out by teachers and support workers, the latter often taking this role at primary level at lunchtimes. For secondary schools, closed circuit television (CCTV) was also evident in roughly two thirds of cases in both the school and school grounds, while for primary schools and their grounds this was only found in about one quarter of cases.

Across countries, more generally, other possibilities for the timing of schools breaks and lunchtimes include having them staggered, often for different year groups for logistical reasons. During such times drinks and other refreshments may be available, either in a canteen or other area temporarily designated for that purpose. In some instances, lunch may be consumed in the classroom. Students may bring their own lunch, purchase food or in some cases this may be provided without direct cost, or they may go home to lunch. In larger schools meals may be provided in more than one 'sitting' (UNESCO IBE, 2011).

Summary and concluding comments

Over the course of this chapter some of the basic variables relating to what might be termed 'the school years' have been outlined for a number of countries representing parts of the world that are often thought of as 'East' and 'West'. Although historic and cultural traditions can give rise to differences in the way that educational systems including schools are organised and some country-specific trends are discernible, there are also many broad similarities across all of the countries considered.

Almost all of the countries have compulsory schooling that starts either at the age of five or six (Finland being the only exception). While all of the Eastern countries currently require children to begin by the age of six, some Western countries have set the age at five. Apart from Hong Kong, the period over which schooling is compulsory is nine years in the Eastern countries and at least ten years in the remaining countries. However, the period over which students spend in some form of schooling extends significantly beyond this minimum. It was noted that educational provision is available in all the countries for children from the age of three and that a high proportion of children participate in this. For the majority of countries provision is available at an even earlier age and South Korea is notable in terms of enrolment at this level. Similarly, a variety of educational options extend beyond the compulsory period for older students and, where data are available, the take-up reported for these is predominantly over 80 per cent in both East and West.

With regard to school size, it was apparent that this was larger for primary schools in South Korea and Hong Kong (with no reliable data available for China as a whole) than in other countries. This pattern is similar for secondary schools, although the UK, the Netherlands, Australia and New Zealand also have relatively large school sizes. An East-West pattern was more noticeable for class size, especially for secondary schooling, which from the data reported is greater in the East in comparison to the West.

Comparisons between East and West of the length of school day are not easily made in that reports from different sources are not always consistent and, furthermore, it is not always clear whether the figures relate only to teaching time or whether they also include break periods. Although longer school days for some Eastern countries have been reported, no clearly verifiable statistics appear to be available.

When attempting to make comparisons between schools in different countries with regard to such notions as academic performance and achievement, there is a vast array of data that has been collected and some of the sources have been drawn upon in this account. However, with regard to some aspects of schooling that could relate to the circumstances of bullying, such as the structure of the school day and how any breaks are supervised, there appears to be less verifiable data from which systematic comparisons can be made.

From examining the sources that do exist, a range of terminology is evident and the process of translation into English may have contributed to inconsistencies in use that have been found. Although the intention has been to present a set of basic descriptive terms that are commonly used, it should be borne in mind that because of the complexity and variety of different educational systems it is possible that some of these terms will be understood and used differently.

Although country-specific trends can be identified for some variables, for others the differences that occur within any one country may be just as wide ranging as the differences that may occur between countries. Therefore, when investigating even the most basic organisational and physical characteristics of educational systems and institutions within which bullying may occur, what should be evident from this account is that in all cases the specific qualities of any school setting or settings referred to will need careful description.

REFERENCES

Belfi, B., Goos, M., De Fraine, B. and Van Damme, J. (2012). The effect of class composition by gender and ability on secondary school students' school well-being and academic self-concept: A literature review. *Educational Research Review*, 7, 62–74.

Blatchford, P. and Baines, E. (2006). A follow up national survey of breaktimes in primary and secondary schools. *Final Report to Nuffield Foundation*. London: Institute of Education.

CEA (2006). *The Finnish PISA 2006 pages*. Centre for Educational Assessment, University of Helsinki (Online). Available from www.pisa2006.helsinki.fi/ education_in_Finland/school_day/structure_of_the_school_day.htm (Accessed: 20 December, 2013).

Chicago Public Schools (2012). *Full school day*. Principal Guide 1: Parameters. Chicago IL: Chief Instruction Office.

CIC (2013). *Structure of schools*. Government of Canada, Citizenship and Immigration Canada Offices (Online). Available from www.cic.gc.ca/ english/newcomers/before-education-schools.asp (Accessed: 19 January, 2014).

CMEC (2013). *Education in Canada: An overview*. Council of Ministers of Education, Canada (Online). Available from www.cmec.ca/299/Education-in-Canada-An-Overview/ (Accessed: 19 January, 2014).

Colasanti, M. (2007). Minimum number of instructional minutes/hours in a High School day. *State Notes: Scheduling/School Calendar*. Denver, CO: Education Commission of the States.

DfE (2012a). *Raising the Participation Age (RPA) Regulations: Government response to consultation and plans for implementation* (Online). Available from www.education.gov.uk/ (Accessed: 19 January, 2014).

  (2012b). *Advice on school attendance*. Department for Education (Online). Available from: www.education.gov.uk (Accessed: 12 February, 2014).

  (2013). *School day and school year*. Department for Education and Schools. Updated: 22 February 2013 (Online). Available from: http://webarchive .nationalarchives.gov.uk/20131216163513/, www.education.gov.uk/schools/ pupilsupport/behaviour/attendance/a00221847/school-day-school-year (Accessed: 12 February, 2014).

  (2014). *Number of secondary schools and their size in student numbers*. Department for Education (Online). Published 9 January 2014. Available from www.gov.uk/government/publications/number-of-secondary-schools-and-their-size-in-student-numbers (Accessed: 5 March, 2014).

DfES (2004). *All-age schooling: A resource*. HMSO: Department for Education and Skills (Online). Available from www.innovationunit.org/ (Accessed: 5 December, 2013).

EACEA (2012). *Key data on education in Europe 2012*. Brussels: Education, Audiovisual and Culture Executive Agency.

EDB (2014). *Hong Kong: The facts*. Information Services Department, Education Bureau, The Government of the Hong Kong Special Administrative Region of the People's Republic of China (Online). April 2014. Available from www.edb.gov.hk (Accessed: 4 May, 2014).

Eurydice (2013a). *Compulsory age of starting school in European countries, 2013*. NFER (Online) January 2013. Available from www.nfer.ac.uk/shadomx/ apps/fms/fmsdownload.cfm?file_uuid=3B48895C-E497-6F68-A237- BCD7AB934443andsiteName=nfer (Accessed: 19 January, 2014).

(2013b). *The structure of the European education systems 2013/14: Schematic diagrams* (Online). Available from http://eacea.ec.europa.eu/education/ eurydice/facts_ (Accessed: 5 December, 2013).

(2013c). *Facts and figures: compulsory education in Europe 2013/14*. European Commission Education, Audiovisual and Culture Executive Agency (EACEA) (Online). Available from http://eacea.ec.europa.eu/education/ eurydice/index_en.php. (Accessed: 19 January, 2014).

GOV.cn (2005). *China's education system* (Online) Available from http://english .gov.cn/2005-08/27/content_26661.htm (Accessed: 4 January, 2014).

Hargreaves, D. H. (1967). *Social relations in a secondary school*. London: Routledge and Kegan Paul.

HMIE (2010). *Opening up learning in all-through schools*. Livingston: HM Inspectorate of Education. Online Available: www.hmie.gov.uk. Retrieved 12 Jan 2016

Ikeda, M. and Garcia, E. (2013). Grade repetition: A comparative study of academic and non-academic consequences. OECD Journal: Economic Studies 8, 269–315.

Ireson, J. and Hallam, S. (2001). *Ability grouping in education*. London: Paul Chapman.

Ireson, J., Hallam, S. and Plewis, I. (2001). Ability grouping in secondary schools: Effects on pupils' self-concepts. *British Journal of Educational Psychology*, 71, 315–326.

Kamette, F. (2011). Organisation of School Time in the European Union. Policy Paper, *European issues* No. 212. Paris: Fondation Robert Schuman. (Online) Available from www.robert-schuman.eu (Accessed: 1 March, 2014).

Maruyama, H. (2011). *Education in Japan*. Ministry of Education, Culture, Sports, Science and Technology (MEXT), National Institute for Educational Policy Research (NIER) (Online). Available from www.nier.go.jp/English/EducationInJapan/Education_in_Japan/ Education_in_Japan.html (Accessed: 1 March, 2014).

Muir, E. (2000). Smaller schools: how much more than a fad? *American Educator*, 23, 40–46.

NCES (2002). *Digest of education statistics 2002*. National Centre for Educational Statistics. Washington DC: Institute of Education Sciences, US Department of Education. (Online) Available from: http://nces.ed.gov/programs/digest/ d02/tables/dt094.asp (Accessed: 3 February, 2013).

(2003). *Digest of education statistics 2003*. National Centre for Educational Statistics (2003). Washington DC: Institute of Education Sciences, US Department of Education. (Online) Available from: http://nces.ed.gov/programs/digest/d02/ch_2.asp#3 (Accessed: 3 February, 2013).

NFER (2013). *Lesson time and school starting ages: The picture across Europe*. National Foundation for Educational Research in England and Wales. (Online) 26 April, 2013. Available from www.nfer.ac.uk/about-nfer/news/lesson-time-and-school-starting-ages-the-picture-across-europe.cfm (Accessed: 19 January, 2014).

NIER (2013). *Education in Japan* (online). Ministry of Education, Culture, Sports, Science and Technology (MEXT), National Institute for Educational Policy Research (NIER). (Online) Available from www.nier.go.jp/English/EducationInJapan/Education_in_Japan/Education_in_Japan.html (Accessed: 1 March, 2014).

NMER (2007). *Education – from kindergarten to adult education.* Norwegian Ministry of Education and Research, Publication Number: F-4133E (Online). Available from www.kunnskapsdepartementet.no (Accessed: 7 September, 2013).

OECD (2011). *Improving lower secondary schools in Norway 2011*, Reviews of National Policies for Education, OECD Publishing(Online). Available from http://dx.doi.org/10.1787/9789264114579-en (Accessed: 21 November, 2013).

(2013a). *About the OECD* (Online). Available from www.oecd.org/about/ (Accessed: 21 November, 2013).

(2013b). *OECD Programme for International Student Assessment (PISA)* (Online). Available from www.oecd.org/pisa/ (Accessed: 21 November, 2013).

(2013c). *Education at a glance 2013: OECD indicators*, OECD Publishing (Online). Available from http://dx.doi.org/10.1787/eag-2013-en (Accessed: 4 January, 2014).

(2013d). *PISA 2012 results: What makes a school successful? – Resources, policies and practices* (Volume IV) (Online). Available from http://dx.doi.org/10.1787/9789264201156-en (Accessed: 21 January, 2014].

Parliament UK (2013). *Schools and class sizes.* Parliament of the United Kingdom Briefing Paper SN/SG/2625 (Online). Available from www.parliament.uk/briefing-papers/sn02625.pdf (Accessed: 23 February, 2014).

PISA (2009) see www.oecd.org/pisa

PIRLS (2011) see timssandpirls.bc.edu/

Riggall, A. and Sharp, C. (2008) *The structure of primary education. England and other countries (Primary Review Research Survey 9/1)*, Cambridge: University of Cambridge Faculty of Education.

Roth, K. J., Druker, S. L., Garnier, H. E., Lemmens, M., Chen, C., Kawanaka, T., Rasmussen, D., Trubacova, S., Warvi, D., Okamoto, Y., Gonzales, P., Stigler, J. and Gallimore, R. (2006). *Teaching science in five countries: Results from the TIMSS 1999 video study* (NCES 2006-011). U.S. Department of Education, National Center for Education Statistics. Washington, D.C.: U.S. Government Printing Office.

Scheerens, J., Hendriks, M. and Luyten, H. (2014). School size effects: review and conceptual analysis. In H. Luyten (Ed.), *School size effects revisited: A qualitative and quantitative review of the research evidence in primary and secondary education*. (Online) Available from www.nwo.nl/...school-size.../ Programmaraad+voor+onderwijsonderzoek+ %7C+School+size+effects +revisited+%7C+Hans+Luyten,+Maria+He... (Accessed: 3 March, 2014).

SCMP (2014). South China Morning Post 14 May, 2014 *School pressure to blame for Chinese youth suicides, official study finds* (Online). Available from www.scmp.com/news/china/article/1512032/school-pressure-blame-chinese-youth-suicides-official-study-finds (Accessed: 20 May, 2014).

Spielhofer, T., Walker, M., Gagg, K., Schagen, S. and O'Donnell, S. (2007). *Raising the participation age in education and training to 18: Review of existing evidence of the benefits and challenges*. Research Report No DCSF-RR012. Slough: National Foundation for Educational Research

Sukhnandan, L. (1998) *Streaming, setting and grouping by ability: A review of the literature*. Slough: National Foundation for Educational Research.

Sutherland, R., Ching Yee, W., McNess, E. and Harris, R. (2010). *Supporting learning in the transition from primary to secondary schools*. Bristol: University of Bristol.

TIMSS (2011) see timssandpirls.bc.edu/

UKSI (1999). The Education (School Day and School Year) (England) Regulations 1999, *Statutory instruments* 1999, No. 3181. Her Majesty's Stationery Office (Online). Available from www.legislation.gov.uk/uksi/ 1999/3181/resources (Accessed: 12 February, 2014).

UNESCO (2012). *International Standard Classification of Education ISCED 2011*. Montreal: UNESCO Institute for Statistics.

UNESCO IBE (2011). *World data on education*, Seventh edition. International Bureau of Education UNESCO (Online). Available from www.ibe.unesco.org/ en/services/online-materials/world-data-on-education/seventh-edition-2010-11.html (Accessed: 3 April, 2014).

Vaughan, R. (2011) Schools commissioner signals new age of all-through academies. *Times educational supplement*, 2 September (Online) Available from www.tes.co.uk/article.as, R.px?storycode=6110529 (Accessed: 22 January, 2014).

Xinhua (2009). Survey: Chinese high school students study more. *China view* Xinhua News Agency, Beijing, March 24 (Online). Available from http:// news.xinhuanet.com/english/2009-03-24/content_11062935.htm (Accessed: 3 April, 2014).

13 Individualism/collectivism as predictors of relational and physical victimization in Japan and Austria

*Dagmar Strohmeier, Takuya Yanagida
and Yuichi Toda*

Individualism and collectivism (I/C) are widely used constructs to explain cross-national differences in victimization in Eastern and Western countries. Most often I/C on the national level is used as explaining variable and cross national differences or similarities are post-hoc attributed to I/C, without measuring these constructs on the individual level (e.g., Bergmüller, 2013; Forbes et al., 2009). Neglecting individual variations regarding I/C is highly problematic, because people living in the same country might differ regarding their levels of individualism and collectivism (Li et al., 2010; Triandis, 1995).

Instead of exclusively relying on descriptive research regarding a wide range of cultural characteristics of nations (e.g., Hofstede, 2001), the present study proposes a rather focused definition of I/C and applies an innovative measure specifically designed for adolescents. The main goal of this research is to investigate whether individual variations of I/C are able to predict level differences of relational and physical victimization among Japanese and Austrian youth. Furthermore, the present study explores differences regarding the group nature of relational and physical victimization by comparing the number of perpetrators in Japan and Austria.

Measuring individualism and collectivism in adolescents

Usually, individualism and collectivism (I/C) have been broadly defined referring to several content domains. For instance, Kim et al. (1994, p. 43) proposed four main defining attributes, namely *the meaning of*

Acknowledgments We thank all schools and students who participated in this study. We thank Anja Lampert and Eva-Maria Schiller for their help with data collection and data entry. Yuichi Toda was awarded with the Excellence Grant of the Upper Austrian Government (Innovatives OÖ 2010plus) to visit Linz as a guest researcher in August 2012 to work on this paper.

the self, the structure of goals, the behaviour as function of norms and attitudes, and *the focus of the needs of the in-group or social exchanges.* In addition, sixty further potentially relevant attributes in individualistic and collectivistic cultures were identified. The richness of content domains led to the development of numerous instruments measuring I/C among adults. Some instruments captured I/C as unidimensional, bipolar construct (e.g., Hui, 1988), while others distinguished several independent I/C constructs (e.g., Fischer et al., 2009; Singelis et al., 1995; Triandis and Gelfand, 1998). Oyserman, Coon, and Kemmelmeier (2002, p. 9) categorized each item out of twenty-seven available scales to clarify what I/C exactly referred to and identified six content domains capturing individualism, for example, *Independent, Goals, Compete, Unique, Private Self-know, Direct Communicate* and eight content domains capturing collectivism, for example, *Related, Belong, Duty, Harmony, Advice, Context, Hierarchy,* and *Group.* To date, I/C has most often been measured with a selection of these content domains while no agreement on a narrow core definition of I/C has been achieved.

Studies comparing Japanese adults with adults stemming from individualistic countries in several content domains produced inconclusive results (see Oyserman et al., 2002). Therefore, there is an ongoing debate whether Japanese people should be considered collectivistic or not (Markus and Kitayama, 1991; Takano and Sogon, 2008). We assume that these inconsistencies partly stem from the heterogeneity of content domains investigated in the different studies and from individual variations among Japanese people regarding their level of I/C.

Therefore, we propose a rather focused definition and a new measure of I/C. We define the I/C construct as *group orientation characterized by the degree of convergence of an individual's opinion with an anchor group opinion.* Following this definition, 'individualism' can be described as a cognitive process in which the distinction between self and group opinion is existent and obvious. In contrast, 'collectivism' can be described as a cognitive process in which the distinction between self and group opinion is not existent or negligible. Hui (1988) suggested several relational contexts that could serve as anchor groups for adults. So far, for adolescents no relational contexts to measure I/C have been proposed. Because youth are enrolled in schools, we decided to take the class as the anchor group for the purpose of the present study. To capture the essence of the proposed definition of I/C, we applied a measurement strategy which did not rely on a selection of content domains but on difference scores based on items covering self and group opinion.

Cross-cultural research on victimization

In the literature, two broad forms of victimization are distinguished: (1) direct victimization that includes overt physical as well as verbal attacks and (2) relational victimization that comprises all kinds of (covered) behaviours that damage or manipulate social relations to hurt someone else (Card et al., 2008). Although these two concepts of victimization were developed in Western countries, they have also been validated by cross cultural research (e.g., Forbes et al., 2009; Kawabata, Crick, and Hamaguchi, 2010, Li et al., 2010).

Moreover, there has been a discussion regarding the cross-cultural nature of bullying – a subcategory of aggressive behaviour characterized not only by intent to hurt but also by power imbalance and repetition (e.g., Smith et al., 2002; Smorti, Menesini and Smith, 2003; Ucanok, Smith, and Sertkaya Karasoy, 2011). It was shown that Western bullying differs from the Eastern phenomena (e.g., *ijime* in Japan or *wang-ta* in South Korea) both on a conceptual level and regarding terms used (Koo, Kwak, and Smith, 2008; Smith et al., 2002; Strohmeier et al., 2013; Taki, 2003).

In Japan, *ijime* is considered to be 'a type of aggressive behaviour by (which) someone who holds a dominant position in *a group-interaction process*, by intentional or collective acts, causes mental and/or physical suffering to another person *inside a group*' (Morita and Kiyonaga, 1986; our italics). Similarly, Taki et al. (2008, p. 8) defined *ijime* as 'mean behaviour or a negative attitude that has clear intentions to embarrass or humiliate others who occupy weaker positions *in a same group*' (our italics). *Ijime* was found to be a 'within-group' phenomenon which happens between 'friends' (Kanetsuna and Smith, 2002; Nesdale and Naito, 2005). In Japan, a group of perpetrators or even the whole class harasses a single victim (Akiba, 2004; Kanetsuna and Smith, 2002; Toda, Strohmeier, and Spiel, 2008). The group nature of *ijime* has also been post-hoc explained by I/C on the national level (Treml, 2001) and it was argued that collectivistic values like conformity pressure could underlie this kind of group-based harassment (Akiba, 2004).

To the best of our knowledge, no study ever explored whether the numbers of perpetrators for relational and physical victimization differ between individualistic and collectivistic countries.

Individualism/collectivism as predictors of victimization

Bergeron and Schneider (2005) conducted a meta-analysis to explain cross-national variability in aggressive behaviour applying three broad measures of cultural values. Based on 36 studies conducted in 28 different countries and comprising 42,517 participants it was shown (1) that countries high on individualism had higher levels of aggression than countries high on collectivism and (2) that different dimensions of I/C on the national level significantly predicted the observed variations in aggressive behaviour. These findings suggest that a collectivistic attitude shared on a national level operates as a protective factor against aggression and victimization. Collectivistic countries in which individuals perceive themselves as embedded in a collectivity placing a high value on the needs of the group show lower levels of aggression than individualistic countries in which individuals perceive themselves as more independent from others promoting their own interests.

Similarly, Forbes et al. (2009) investigated levels of direct and indirect aggression among young adults aged nineteen years living in China, Poland, and the United States. According to Hofstede's classification system (2001), these three countries differ regarding I/C on the national level. In line with the results of Bergeron and Schneider (2005), levels of both direct and indirect aggression were higher in individualistic countries (United States and Poland) compared with the collectivistic country (China). Thus, in China both direct and indirect aggressive acts might be perceived as a threat to collectivistic values and are thus much more avoided compared with individualistic countries. However, not all studies report such plausible associations between I/C on the national level and relational and physical aggression. Landsford et al. (2012) investigated level differences of relational and physical aggression among children aged seven to ten years living in nine different countries. While in China, Italy, and Thailand – countries high on collectivism – children reported higher levels of relational aggression compared with physical aggression; in Colombia and Philippines, no such differences were observed; and in Kenya and Jordan even higher levels of physical compared with relational aggression were reported. Moreover, in the two countries high on individualism – Sweden and the United States – no level differences of relational and physical aggression were found.

These inconsistencies lead us to question whether it is wise to explain in a post-hoc way any national differences observed in direct and indirect aggression and victimization with I/C only on the national level. Extending previous studies, Li et al. (2010) measured the individual levels of I/C among Chinese 7th and 8th graders. Although there was substantial intracultural variation of I/C among Chinese youth, no direct association between I/C and relational and overt aggression was found. Because collectivism is normative in collectivistic countries like China, individual variations in I/C may not be directly associated with relational and overt aggression. However, these associations might change in individualistic countries in which a high level of individual collectivism might operate as a protective factor against indirect and direct victimization. To date, no cross-national study ever investigated this issue.

Therefore, the following four hypotheses were investigated in the present study:

Hypothesis 1: levels of the self-group distinction (I/C)

The mean differences between self and group distinction are expected to be smaller for Japanese compared to Austrian adolescents, because Japanese adolescents are considered to be more collectivistic compared with Austrian adolescents who are considered to be more individualistic (Hofstede, 2001). Moreover, substantial intracultural variability in the two samples is expected. However, because the in-group homogeneity is known to be high in collectivistic countries compared with individualistic countries (Triandis, 1995), the variances of the self and group distinction items are expected to be smaller for Japanese compared to Austrian adolescents.

Hypothesis 2: perceived number of perpetrators of relational and physical victimization

Both Japanese and Austrian adolescents will perceive relational victimization as more group-based compared with physical victimization, because the indirectness of relational victimization makes it much more difficult for the victim to identify possible perpetrators compared with direct victimization. Because the interpretation of relational victimization is much more ambiguous than physical victimization, it is likely that in Japan relational victims who are supposed to have a smaller self-group distinction (more collectivistic), suspect more peers to be involved in the harassment compared with relational victims in Austria who are supposed to have a greater cognitive self-group distinction (more individualistic).

Hypothesis 3: levels of relational and physical victimization

Controlling for individual levels of self-group distinction (I/C), Japanese adolescents are expected to report lower levels of physical and relational victimization than Austrian adolescents. This result would indicate that a collectivistic orientation on the national level might operate as a protective factor against both indirect and direct aggression reported in previous studies (Bergeron and Schneider, 2005; Forbes et al., 2009).

Hypothesis 4: individual levels of the self-group distinction (I/C) as predictors of victimization

In addition to national level differences in I/C, it is also expected that individual levels of the self-group distinction (I/C) are a protective factor against relational and physical victimization (Li et al, 2010). However, the strength of these associations is expected to differ between Japan and Austria. The individual collectivistic orientation might be less protective in a context where most of the people are group oriented like in Japan compared with a context where most of the people are rather self-centered like in Austria. Thus, the associations between individual variations in I/C and victimization might be weaker among Japanese adolescents compared with Austrian adolescents.

Method

Study design and procedure

Japanese and Austrian adolescents participated in this research. These two countries were chosen, because Austria represents a individualistic culture, while Japan represents a collectivistic culture (Singelis et al., 1995; Triandis, 1995).

Japanese adolescents were recruited from sixteen classes of one elementary and one junior high school situated in a city in Japan. In Japan, compulsory schooling starts at a child's sixth birthday and lasts nine school years; elementary school comprises grades 1 to 6 and junior high school comprises grades 7 to 9. To be allowed to collect data in these two schools, the study had to be accepted by the school principals and teachers. Data were collected in November 2006.

Austrian adolescents were recruited in eleven classes of one elementary and one academic secondary school situated in a city in Austria. In Austria, compulsory schooling starts at a child's sixth birthday and lasts nine school years; elementary school comprises grades 1 to 4. After primary school, pupils can either attend a general secondary school (grade 5 to 8) or an academic secondary school (grade 5 to 12). To be allowed to collect data in these two schools, the study had to be accepted by the local school council, the school principals and the parents. Data were collected in December 2006.

In both countries, questionnaires were administered in classes and it took about 50 minutes to complete. About 90% of eligible pupils participated in the study.

Participants

Altogether, 532 Japanese students (53% boys) aged 12.3 years (SD = 1.8) and 277 Austrian students (54% boys) aged 12.0 years (SD = 1.8) participated. The first language of all participating students in Japan was Japanese and in Austria it was German. In both countries, students were enrolled in schools serving middle class families.

Instruments

Self-Group Distinction (I/C) Scale. This newly developed scale comprised two question blocks containing seven items. Three main content domains of individualism and collectivism, *advice seeking, group activity*, and *independence* taken from Oyserman et al. (2002) were used for these items.

Perceived Group Opinion: The first question block measured the perceived group opinion and was given with the following introduction:

> *In this section, we want to know what your class thinks about various topics. Please think about the general opinion in your class.*

What does your class think . . .

(1) . . . of classmates asking for advice when they have a problem? (Advice seeking)
(2) . . . of solving tasks in groups? (Group activity)
(3) . . . of classmates holding a different opinion than the teacher does? (Independence)
(4) . . . of classmates, who do not want to participate in group activity? (Group activity, reversed)
(5) . . . of other classmates, who want to push through their own opinion? (Independence)
(6) . . . of classmates solving a difficult task completely on their own? (Independence)
(7) . . . of a classmate refusing to change his or her opinion, even though all the others think differently than he or she does? (Independence)

Personal Opinion: The second question block measured the personal opinion and was given with the following introduction:

> *In this section, we want to know what you think about various topics.*
> *Please think about your own opinion.*

What do you think . . .

(1) . . . of classmates asking for advice when they have a problem? (Advice seeking)
(2) . . . of solving tasks in groups? (Group activity)
(3) . . . of classmates holding a different opinion than the teacher does? (Independence)
(4) . . . of classmates, who do not want to participate in group activity? (Group activity, reversed)
(5) . . . of other classmates, who want to push through their own opinion? (Independence)
(6) . . . of classmates solving a difficult task completely on their own? (Independence)
(7) . . . of a classmate refusing to change his or her opinion, even though all the others think differently than he or she does? (Independence)

For all items, the following answer options were presented on a five-point Likert-Scale: My class thinks/I think this is *very good (scored 5), rather good (4), neither good nor bad (3), rather bad (2)*, and *very bad (1)*.

To measure the levels of the *Self-Group Distinction (I/C)*, the difference of each pair of items (perceived class opinion – personal opinion) was computed. The absolute values of the differences represent the degree of the *Self-Group Distinction (I/C)*. The higher the deviation from zero (meaning class and personal opinion are identical); the more individualistic is the person. For this measurement approach, the content of the *Self-Group Distinction* scale is not of primary interest but rather the degree of convergence between an adolescent's personal opinions with the class opinions. Scale scores are derived by averaging the items (absolute values of the differences). The reliability of this scale was $\alpha = 0.73$ for the whole sample, $\alpha = 0.60$ for the Austrian sample, and $\alpha = 0.73$ for the Japanese sample.

Frequency of Victimization. The peer nomination measure developed by Crick and Grotpeter (1995) was changed into a self-assessment measure and slightly modified. In Japan, it is difficult to conduct peer nominations in schools because of ethical considerations. Therefore, in studies conducted in Japan peer nomination measures are often changed into self-assessments (e.g., Isobe and Hishinuma, 2007). Before presenting the behavioural descriptions, a standard explanation was given in the questionnaire.

In this section we ask you some questions about negative experiences at school. We will ask you how often several negative things happened to you and how many classmates were involved in it. Please think about the last six months and tell us your experiences honestly. Please answer each question carefully.

Five items comprised the relational victimization scale:

During the last 6 months, *how often* has a young person or a group of young persons...

(1) left you out on purpose when it was time to play or do an activity?
(2) who was mad at you got back at you by not letting you in their group anymore?
(3) told lies about you to make other kids not like you anymore?
(4) told you they won't like you unless you do what they say?
(5) tried to keep others from liking you by saying mean things about you?

Three items comprised the physical victimization scale:

During the last 6 months, *how often* has a young person or a group of young persons...

(1) hit you?
(2) pushed or shoved you?
(3) kicked or pulled you by the hair?

Alternative answer options were *never (scored 1), once or twice (2), sometimes (3), once a week (4),* and *nearly every day (5).* Scale scores are derived by averaging the items. The reliability of the relational victimization scale was $\alpha = 0.78$ for the whole sample, $\alpha = 0.74$ for the Austrian sample, and $\alpha = 0.80$ for the Japanese sample. The reliability of the physical victimization scale was $\alpha = 0.80$ for the whole sample, $\alpha = 0.76$ for the Austrian sample, and $\alpha = 0.82$ for the Japanese sample.

Group Nature of Victimization. Based on Crick and Grotpeter (1995) eight new items were developed. Five items comprised relational victimization:

During the last 6 months, *who* has

(1) left you out on purpose when it was time to play or do an activity?
(2) got back at you by not letting you in their group anymore because they were mad at you?
(3) told lies about you to make other kids not like you anymore?
(4) told you they won't like you unless you do what they say?
(5) tried to keep others from liking you by saying mean things about you?

Three items comprised physical victimization:
  During the last 6 months, *by whom* have you been…

(1) hit?
(2) pushed or shoved?
(3) kicked or pulled by the hair?

Alternative answer options were *this never happened to me, this was most often done by a single kid, this was most often done by two kids,* and *this was most often done by a group of kids.*

Results

Levels of self-group distinction (I/C)

To check for differences between Austrian and Japanese adolescents on the *Self-Group Distinction* items, we conducted a 2 x 7 MANOVA. Multivariate tests using Pillai's Criterion showed a significant main effect for *country, F* (7, 737) = 24.27, $p < 0.01$, $\eta^2 = 0.19$. Follow-up univariate tests revealed a significant effect for *country* for all seven Items. As shown in Table 13.1, the means of the seven *Self-Group Distinction* scores (difference scores between perceived class opinion and personal opinion) were smaller in the Japanese sample than the Austrian sample. Moreover, the variances were not homogenous between the Japanese and Austrian sample (Levene tests for all items p < 0.01). The inspection of standard deviations indicates that the variances are smaller in Japan than in Austria.

Table 13.1 *Levels of self-group distinction (I/C)*

	Japan *M (SD)* *N* = 484	Austria *M (SD)* *N* = 261	*F* (1, 775)
to ask for advice	0.29 (0.59)	0.75 (0.85)	74.53**
to solve tasks in groups	0.29 (0.62)	0.62 (0.80)	41.34**
to hold a different opinion than the teacher	0.28 (0.58)	0.67 (0.94)	49.51**
do not want to participate in group activities	0.35 (0.66)	0.75 (0.94)	46.86**
to push through one's own opinion	0.34 (0.62)	0.77 (0.84)	64.58**
to solve a difficult task completely on one's own	0.36 (0.70)	0.64 (0.78)	23.70**
to refuse to change one's opinion	0.30 (0.62)	0.78 (0.91)	71.39**

Note: **$p < 0.01$. *$p < 0.05$.

Perceived number of perpetrators of relational and physical victimization

Relational victimization was more often group-based than physical victimization in both countries. While 75–77% of the victims of the three forms of physical harassment indicated that a single child was the perpetrator, these numbers ranged between 32% and 63% for the five forms of relational harassment. As shown in Table 13.2, in three out of five forms of relational harassment an interaction effect with country was observed. While in Japan 42–63% of victims of these three kinds of relational harassment indicated that two children were the perpetrators, 43–68% of victims in Austria perceived a single child as perpetrator. For physical victimization, no such differences were found.

Levels of relational and physical victimization

To check for level differences, a multiple analysis of covariance (MANCOVA) was calculated with country (Japan vs. Austria) as an independent factor, the self-group distinction scale (I/C) as covariate and the eight victimization items as dependent variables (see Table 13.3). Multivariate tests using Pillai's Criterion indicated that the variable country, F (8, 769) = 16.99, $p < 0.01$, $\eta^2 = 0.15$, and the covariate I/C, F (8,769) = 4.49, $p < 0.01$, $\eta^2 = 0.05$, were significant. Follow-up univariate analyses revealed that Austrian youth reported higher levels in three out of five forms of relational harassment compared with Japanese youth. However, Japanese youth reported higher levels in one out of three forms of physical harassment compared with Austria.

Self-Group Distinction (I/C) as predictor of relational and physical victimization

The data was first inspected descriptively (see Table 13.4). Scale means of manifest variables indicated that the self-group distinction was larger in Austrian compared with Japanese youth, indicating that they are more individualistic. Moreover, Austrian youth reported higher levels of relational victimization compared with Japanese youth. No differences regarding physical victimization were found. Bivariate correlations revealed differences regarding the associations between the three constructs in the two samples (see Table 13.4).

Next, a series of structural equation models were calculated using Mplus 7.0 (Muthen and Muthen, 2012). In the first step, measurement models were conducted. In the second step, a multiple

Table 13.2 *Percentages and numbers of perpetrators of relational and physical victimization.*

	a single kid		two kids		a group of kids		χ^2
	Japan	Austria	Japan	Austria	Japan	Austria	
left him/her out on purpose	21%	43%	63%	33%	16%	23%	21.48**
	(N = 27)	(N = 48)	(N = 80)	(N = 37)	(N = 20)	(N = 26)	
got back by not letting him/her in the group	29%	68%	42%	24%	29%	8%	19.59**
	(N = 12)	(N = 66)	(N = 17)	(N = 23)	(N = 12)	(N = 8)	
told lies to make him/her not liked	37%	61%	42%	24%	21%	15%	11.07**
	(N = 33)	(N = 54)	(N = 38)	(N = 21)	(N = 19)	(N = 13)	
told others don't like him/her	63%	64%	25%	18%	13%	18%	0.93[ns]
	(N = 30)	(N = 25)	(N = 12)	(N = 7)	(N = 6)	(N = 7)	
kept others from liking him/her	42%	59%	34%	26%	25%	15%	4.51[ns]
	(N = 39)	(N = 32)	(N = 32)	(N = 14)	(N = 23)	(N = 8)	
hit	75%	74%	18%	17%	7%	9%	0.27[ns]
	(N = 153)	(N = 66)	(N = 37)	(N = 15)	(N = 15)	(N = 8)	
push or shove	78%	73%	19%	23%	3%	4%	0.99[ns]
	(N = 117)	(N = 74)	(N = 28)	(N = 24)	(N = 5)	(N = 4)	
kick or pull hair	77%	78%	19%	19%	4%	3%	0.41[ns]
	(N = 95)	(N = 45)	(N = 23)	(N = 11)	(N = 5)	(N = 2)	

Note: **$p < 0.01$. *$p < 0.05$.

Table 13.3 *Levels of relational and physical victimization.*

	Japan M (SD) N = 507	Austria M (SD) N = 272	covariate I/C F (1, 775)	country F (1, 775)
left him/her out on purpose	1.37 (0.72)	1.72 (0.98)	9.38**	16.52**
got back by not letting him/her in the group	1.13 (0.52)	1.55 (0.81)	9.29**	47.01**
told lies to make him/her not liked	1.30 (0.73)	1.58 (0.98)	26.56**	4.60**
told others don't like him/her	1.17 (0.61)	1.25 (0.70)	4.76*	0.36^{ns}
kept others from liking him/her	1.33 (0.76)	1.32 (0.73)	19.10**	3.49^{ns}
hit	1.91 (1.30)	1.55 (1.02)	6.76**	21.11**
push or shove	1.56 (1.01)	1.66 (1.03)	9.26**	0.02^{ns}
kick or pull hair	1.45 (0.90)	1.37 (0.82)	1.57^{ns}	2.70^{ns}

Note: **$p < 0.01$. *$p < 0.05$.

Table 13.4 *Scale means and bivariate correlations.*

Variables	Japan M (SD) N = 520	Austria M (SD) N = 274	country F (3, 790)	1	2	3
1. Self-Group Distinction (I/C)	0.33 (0.42)	0.71 (0.46)	131.61**	–	0.07	0.03
2. Relational victimization	1.26 (0.50)	1.48 (0.60)	31.86**	0.31**	–	0.35**
3. Physical victimization	1.64 (0.93)	1.52 (0.79)	2.99^{ns}	0.20**	0.35**	–

Note: **$p < 0.01$. *$p < 0.05$. Correlations above the diagonal are for Japan, below the diagonal for Austria.

group structural equation model was estimated (see Figure 13.1). Maximum likelihood estimation using the MLR estimator of Mplus was implemented providing standard errors and test statistics that are robust to non-normality of the data and to non-independence of observations. In addition, we controlled for the nested data structure at the class level. The ICCs were higher in Austria ($0.08 >$ ICCs < 0.12) than in Japan ($0.00 >$ ICCs < 0.05). Three criteria were used in evaluating the model fit: the chi-square test, the Comparative Fit

Index (*CFI*; Bentler, 1990), and the root mean squared error of approximation (*RMSEA*; Steiger, 1990).

Measurement models

Multiple group measurement models (Japan vs. Austria) were calculated separately for relational victimization (5 items), physical victimization (3 items), and self-group distinction (7 items). Intercept invariance models (for more details see Chen, 2008) were calculated in which the latent means in the Japanese sample were constrained to 0, the latent means in the Austrian sample were freely estimated, the factor loadings and intercepts were freely estimated but constrained to be equal between the two groups, while the residuals were allowed to differ between Japan and Austria.

Relational Victimization. The intercept invariance model showed an acceptable fit, χ^2 (18) = 116.51, p < 0.01, CFI = 0.91, RMSEA = 0.12.

Physical Victimization. The intercept invariance model showed an acceptable fit, χ^2 (4) = 22.52, p < 0.01, CFI = 0.94, RMSEA = 0.11.

Individualism/Collectivism (I/C). The intercept invariance model showed an acceptable fit, χ^2 (40) = 65.20, p < 0.01, CFI = 0.93, RMSEA = 0.04.

Multiple group structural model

The multiple group SEM model imposing strict measurement invariance had an excellent fit, χ^2 (198) = 388.83, *p* < 0.01, *CFI* = 0.90, *RMSEA* = 0.049. The inspection of the associations between self-group distinction (I/C) and victimization revealed striking differences between Japanese and Austrian adolescents (see Figure 13.1).

In Austrian youth, self-group distinction (I/C) was moderately associated with relational victimization (β = 0.46, p < 0.01) and physical victimization (β = 0.32, p < 0.01), while in Japanese youth, these associations were not significant. In both groups, relational and physical victimization were related with each other (r = 0.39 for Austrian and r = 0.44 for Japanese youth). In line with the results of the MANOVAs, the latent means of the self-group distinction were different between Japanese and Austrian (p < 0.01) indicating higher levels among Austrian youth.

Discussion

Instead of attributing observed cross country differences regarding victimization in a post-hoc way to stereotypical cultural characteristics of

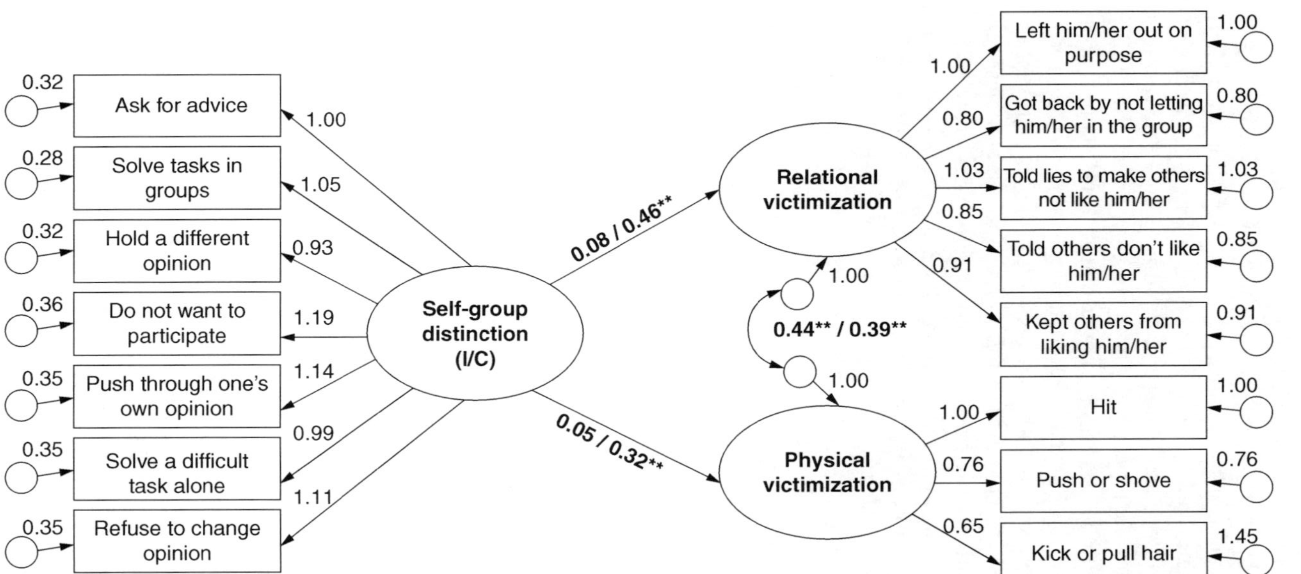

Figure 13.1 Individual levels of the Self-Group Distinction (I/C) as predictors of victimization. For factor loadings and intercepts (freely estimated but constrained to be equal between groups) the unstandardized regression weights are displayed. For the associations between self-group distinction (I/C), relational and physical victimization the standardized regression weights are displayed. Associations for Japanese youth are before the slash, for Austrian youth after the slash.

countries like collectivism and individualism (I/C), the goals of the present study were (1) to innovatively measure I/C in Japanese and Austrian adolescents and (2) to examine whether individual variations of I/C predict level differences of relational and physical victimization similarly among Japanese and Austrian youth. Thus, the present approach acknowledges that people living in the same country differ regarding their individual level of individualism and collectivism (Li et al., 2010; Triandis, 1995) and demonstrates that individual levels of I/C are differently associated with victimization in Japan and Austria.

Despite a substantial individual variation in I/C, Japanese adolescents were more collectivistic than Austrian adolescents who were more individualistic. Japanese youth reported lower levels of relational victimization than Austrian youth, but no differences were found for physical victimization. Both Japanese and Austrian adolescents perceived relational victimization as more group based compared with physical victimization. No associations between individual variations of I/C and victimization were found among Japanese adolescents, but higher levels of collectivism were associated with lower levels of both physical and relational victimization in Austria.

Before discussing the findings, we should note some important limitations of the study. Data were collected via self-assessments which can be considered as a limitation of the present research, although self-assessments are considered to be a reliable source of information by many researchers (Little et al., 2003; Pellegrini and Bartini, 2000). This strategy was chosen, because it is very difficult to conduct peer nominations in Japanese schools because of ethical considerations. Therefore, peer nomination measures are often changed into self-assessments in Japan (e.g., Isobe and Hishinuma, 2007). Also, the present study solely relied on cross sectional data which is a limitation of the present approach. Although we modeled directions of associations based on good theoretical reasons, longitudinal data would have provided more rigorous evidence to infer causal directions implied in the models.

Self-Group Distinction as a measure for I/C

In the present study, the I/C construct was characterized by the degree of the convergence of an individual's opinion with an anchor group opinion. Consequently, we applied a measurement strategy that did not rely solely on a selection of content domains but on difference scores based on items covering self and group opinion. Difference scores are an ideal measurement approach in the present study, because individualism was defined as a cognitive process characterized by rather a large distinction between self and group opinion, while collectivism was defined as a cognitive process characterized by rather a small distinction between self and group opinion. In line with this definition, the analyses revealed that the mean differences of all seven-item pairs of the new measure were smaller for Japanese compared to Austrian adolescents. Moreover, the intracultural variability in the Japanese sample was smaller than in the Austrian sample. This was exactly what we expected, because the in-group homogeneity is known to be higher in collectivistic countries compared with individualistic countries (Triandis, 1995). We regard these results as important evidence for the validity of the newly developed measure. Our results also indicate that despite substantial individual variation, Japanese adolescents are more collectivistic than Austrian adolescents. This is an important result given the many inconsistent findings discussed in the literature (e.g., Markus and Kitayama, 1991; Oyserman et al., 2002; Takano and Sogon, 2008).

Group nature of relational and physical victimization

Japanese and Korean bullying – *ijime* and *wang-ta* – have been found to be a special kind of in-group harassment characterized by mean behaviour from a group of perpetrators or even the whole class against a single victim (e.g., Kanetsuna and Smith, 2002; Koo et al., 2008; Morita and Kiyonaga, 1986; Nesdale and Naito, 2005). This group nature of the Eastern forms of bullying has often been explained post-hoc by I/C on the national level (Treml, 2001) and it has been argued that collectivistic values underlie this kind of harassment (Akiba, 2004). Thus, although the group nature of *ijime* has already been investigated, cross-cultural research on relational and physical victimization in Eastern and Western countries has been lacking.

In line with our hypothesis, relational victimization was perceived as more group based compared with physical victimization in both Japan and Austria. While around 75% of victims in Japan and Austria were able to identify a single peer as perpetrator of physical victimization, these numbers were remarkably lower for relational victimization. Importantly, country moderated these associations for three forms of relational victimization but not for physical victimization. In Japan, relational victims suspected either two peers or a group of peers to be the perpetrators, while in Austria the majority of relational victims identified a single peer as perpetrator.

The perception of the group nature of the relational harassment might be related with the indirectness of the behaviour. Because the number of perpetrators of indirect aggressive acts is not easily observable, it is likely that relational victims in Japan that are supposed to have an interdependent view of the self suspect more peers to be involved than relational victims in Austria that are supposed to have an independent view of the self (Markus and Kitayama, 1991). The present findings highlight that it is important to also distinguish physical and relational forms of *ijime* in future cross-national studies to better understand its group nature.

Cross-national level differences in relational and physical victimization

Because the collectivistic orientation on the national level was found to operate as a protective factor against both indirect and direct aggression in a meta-analysis (Bergeron and Schneider, 2005), we hypothesized that controlling for individual levels of self-group distinction (I/C), Japanese adolescents would report lower levels of both physical and relational victimization than Austrian adolescents. However, our results yielded inconsistent results. When looking at relational victimization on item basis, Japanese youth scored lower on three out of five items compared with Austrian youth. However, when looking at physical victimization, Japanese adolescents scored higher on one out of three items in comparison with Austrians. Such inconsistencies were also reported by Lansford et al. (2012) comparing level differences of relational and physical aggression between nine countries.

These inconsistent results raise the question of whether it is wise to post-hoc attribute level differences of aggression, bullying, or victimization between countries on their 'cultural' characteristics. Such 'culture' based interpretations might be highly misleading, because countries differ on very many characteristics, for example educational systems (see Chapter 12) and policies. The most recent HBSC study demonstrated quite a large variability regarding the levels of being bullied and bullying others among mainly 'individualistic' countries (Currie et al., 2012), For many years, Austria has consistently been identified as one of the countries with comparatively high prevalence rates of bullying and physical fighting. Thus, to attribute the higher levels of relational victimization in Austria to its 'individualistic' culture is probably not warranted.

Self-Group Distinction (I/C) as a predictor of victimization in Japan and Austria

We expected that individual levels of self-group distinction (I/C) would operate as a protective factor against relational and physical victimization (Li et al., 2010) in both Japan and Austria. This was because we hypothesized that in both Japan and Austria a smaller self-group distinction is an indicator for a group orientation or collectivism, while a larger self-group distinction is an indicator for self-centeredness or individualism. We also expected that the strength of these associations would differ between Japan and Austria. Contrary to our expectations, in Japan, the individual variability of I/C which was generally much lower compared to Austria was not associated with victimization, while in Austria higher levels of collectivism were associated with lower levels of both physical and relational victimization. Li et al. (2010) who investigated the associations between collectivism and individualism and aggression among Chinese adolescents reported similar findings.

Given the present evidence, it is difficult to fully explain these results. However, the present data indicates that whether I/C measured on the individual level is a protective factor for victimization or not depends on contextual factors. In a context in which most of the individuals are collectivistic, no associations were observed, while in a context in which most of the individuals are rather individualistic, being group oriented turned out to be a protective factor against peer victimization. Thus, in future studies we recommend measuring I/C on the individual level instead of assuming I/C on the national level, in order to better understand the complex interplay between I/C and aggression, bullying, and victimization.

REFERENCES

Akiba, M. (2004). Nature and correlates of ijime [bullying] in Japanese middle schools. *International Journal of Educational Research*, 41, 216–236.

Bentler, P. (1990). Comparative fit indexes in structural models. *Psychological Bulletin*, 107, 238–246.

Bergeron, N. and Schneider, B. H. (2005). Explaining cross national differences in peer-directed aggression: A quantitative synthesis. *Aggressive Behavior*, 31, 116–137.

Bergmüller, S. (2013). The relationship between cultural individualism-collectivism and student aggression across 62 countries. *Aggressive Behavior*, 39, 182–200.

Card, N. A., Stucky, B. D., Sawalani, G. M, and Little, T. D. (2008). Direct and indirect aggression during childhood and adolescence: A meta-analytic review of gender differences, intercorrelations, and relations to maladjustment. *Child Development*, 79, 1185–1229.

Chen, F. F. (2008). What happens if we compare chopsticks with forks? The impact of making inappropriate comparisons in cross-cultural research. *Journal of Personality and Social Psychology*, 95, 1005–1018.

Crick, N. R. and Grotpeter, J. K. (1995). Relational aggression, gender, and social-psychological adjustment. *Child Development*, 66, 710–722.

Currie, C., Zanotti, C., Morgan, A., Currie, D., de Looze, M., Roberts, C., et al. (Eds.). (2012). *Social determinants of health and well-being among young people: Health behaviour in school-aged children (HBSC) study: International report from the 2009/2010 survey.* Copenhagen: WHO Regional Office for Europe.

Fischer, R., Ferreira, M. C., Assmar, E., Redford, P., Harb, C., Glazer, S., et al. (2009). Individualism-collectivism as descriptive norms: Development of a subjective norm approach to culture measurement. *Journal of Cross-Cultural Psychology, 40,* 187–213.

Forbes, G., Zhang, X., Doroszewicz, K., and Haas, K. (2009). Relationships between individualism-collectivism, gender, and direct or indirect aggression: A study in China, Poland, and the US. *Aggressive Behavior, 35,* 24–30.

Hofstede, G. (2001). *Culture's consequences: Comparing values, behaviors, institutions, and organizations across nations.* Thousand Oaks: Sage.

Hui, C. H. (1988). Measurement of individualism – collectivism. *Journal of Research in Personality, 22,* 17–36.

Isobe, M. and Hishinuma, Y. (2007). Overt and relational aggression and impression formation in Japanese university students. *Japanese Journal of Personality, 15,* 290–300.

Kim, U., Triandis, H. C., Kagitcibasi, C., Choi, S. C., and Yoon, G. (1994). *Individualism and collectivism: Theory, method, and application.* Thousand Oaks, CA: Sage.

Kanetsuna, T. and Smith, P. K. (2002). Pupil insights into bullying, and coping with bullying: A bi-national study in Japan and England. *Journal of School Violence, 1,* 5–29.

Kawabata, Y., Crick, N. R. and Hamaguchi, Y. (2010). The role of culture in relational aggression: Associations with social-psychological adjustment problems in Japanese and US school-aged children. *International Journal of Behavioral Development, 34,* 354–362.

Koo, H., Kwak, K. and Smith, P. K. (2008). Victimization in Korean schools: The nature, incidence, and distinctive features of Korean bullying or wang-ta. *Journal of School Violence, 7,* 119–139.

Lansford, J. E., Skinner, A. T., Sorbring, E., Di Giunta, L., et al. (2012). Boys' and girls' relational and physical aggression in nine countries. *Aggressive Behavior, 38,* 298–308.

Li, Y., Wang, M., Wang, C., and Shi, J. (2010). Individualism, collectivism, and Chinese adolescents' aggression: Intracultural variations. *Aggressive Behavior, 36,* 187–194.

Little, T. D., Jones, S. M., Henrich, C. C., and Hawley, P. H. (2003). Disentangling the 'whys' from the 'whats' of aggressive behavior. *International Journal of Behavioral Development, 27,* 122–133.

Markus, H. R. and Kitayama, S. (1991). Culture and self: Implications for cognition, emotion, and motivation. *Psychological Review, 98,* 224–253.

Morita, Y. and Kiyonaga, K. (1986). *Ijime: Kyousitsu no Yamai [Ijime: the disease of the classroom].* Tokyo, Japan: Kanekoshobo.

Muthen, L. K. and Muthen, B. O. (2012). *Mplus User's guide.* Los Angeles, CA: Muthen and Muthen.

Nesdale, D. and Naito, M. (2005). Individualism-Collectivism and the attitudes to school bullying of Japanese and Australian students. *Journal of Cross-Cultural-Psychology*, 36, 537–556.

Oyserman, D., Coon, H. M., and Kemmelmeier, M. (2002). Rethinking individualism and collectivism: Evaluation of theoretical assumptions and meta-analyses. *Psychological Bulletin*, 128, 3–72.

Pellegrini, A. and Bartini, M. (2000). An empirical comparison of methods of sampling aggression and victimization in school settings. *Journal of Educational Psychology*, 92, 360–366.

Singelis, T. M., Triandis, H. C., Bhawuk, D. P., and Gelfand, M. J. (1995). Horizontal and vertical dimensions of individualism and collectivism: A theoretical and measurement refinement. *Cross-Cultural Research*, 29, 240–275.

Smith, P. K., Cowie, H., Olafsson, R. F., and Liefooghe, A. P. D. (2002). Definitions of bullying: A comparison of terms used, and age and gender differences, in a fourteen-country international comparison. *Child Development*, 73, 1119–1133.

Smorti, A., Menesini, E., and Smith, P. K. (2003). Parents' definitions of children's bullying in a five country comparison. *Journal of Cross Cultural Psychology*, 34, 417–432.

Steiger, J. (1990). Structural model evaluation and modification: An interval estimation approach. *Multivariate Behavioral Research*, 25, 173–180.

Strohmeier, D., Aoyama, I., Gradinger, P., and Toda, Y. (2013). Cyber-victimization and cyberaggression in eastern and western countries: Challenges of constructing a cross culturally appropriate scale. In S. Bauman, D. Cross and J. Walker (Eds.) *Principles of cyberbullying research: Definitions, measures, and methodology.* (pp. 202–221). New York: Routledge.

Takano, Y. and Sogon, S. (2008). Are Japanese more collectivistic than Americans? Examining conformity in in-groups and the reference-group effect. *Journal of Cross-Cultural Psychology*, 39, 237–250.

Taki, M. (2003). Ijime bullying: characteristic, causality and intervention. *Oxford Kobe seminar: Bullying in schools.* Kobe, Japan: Kobe Institut.

Taki, M., Slee, P., Hymel, S., Pepler, D., Sim, H., and Swearer, S. (2008). A new definition and scales for indirect aggression in schools: Results from the longitudinal comparative survey among five countries. *International Journal of Violence and School*, 7, 3–19.

Toda, Y., Strohmeier, D., and Spiel, C. (2008). Process model of bullying. In T. Katoh and H. Taniguchi (Eds.), *Dark side of interpersonal relationships.* (pp. 117–131). Kyoto: Kitaohji-Shobo.

Treml, J. (2001). Bullying as a social malady in contemporary Japan. *International Social Work*, 44, 107–117.

Triandis, H. C. (1995). *Individualism and collectivism.* Boulder: Westview Press.

Triandis, H. C. and Gelfand, M. J. (1998). Converging measurement of horizontal and vertical individualism and collectivism. *Journal of Personality and Social Psychology*, 74, 118–128.

Ucanok, Z., Smith, P.K., and Sertkaya Karasoy, D. (2011). Definitions of bullying: Age and sex differences in a Turkish sample. *Asian Journal of Social Psychology*, 14, 75–83.

14 Linguistic issues in studying bullying-related phenomena
Data from a revised cartoon task

*Peter K. Smith, Keumjoo Kwak, Rubina Hanif,
Tomoyuki Kanetsuna, Jess Mahdavi, Siu-Fung Lin,
Ragnar Olafsson and Zehra Ucanok*

Although standardised instruments, such as the Olweus questionnaire, are often used to compare bullying across different countries, often little attention is paid to the words used to translate the term *bullying*. But this Anglo-Saxon term, while well recognised in northern Europe, does not have a close cognate in the Latin languages; and terms with somewhat different meaning are used in eastern countries such as Japan and South Korea. In Japan, *ijime* is generally taken as the concept closest to *bullying*, but there appear to be some important differences. Similar phenomena in South Korea can be described by *wang-ta*. In this chapter we review this issue, and describe the cartoon task (P. K. Smith et al., 2002), which was developed to examine the meaning of bullying-related terms in different languages. We consider some limitations of the original cartoon task, especially in relation to bullying phenomena in non-western countries such as Japan and Korea. We then describe the development of an expanded version of the cartoon task, and some findings using this in nine western and eastern cultures.

Etic and emic approaches

Many researchers compare findings across cultures using standardised instruments – usually, self-report questionnaires. For example, the World Health Organisation surveys on Health Behaviour in School-aged Children (HBSC) provide data on bullying, based on a single victim item and a single bully item adapted from the Olweus questionnaire. This asks how often a child has been bullied, or bullied others, over the past couple of

Acknowledgements: The development of the cartoon task was supported in part by a grant from the Japan Foundation Endowment Committee. Thanks also to Pamela Burton for drawings, and Gary Kogan, Hyojin Koo, Annie Lee, Josephine Ng, Björg Nordfjord, Susan Reid and Erin Smith, for help in data gathering.

280

months. Craig et al. (2009) provided findings from the 2005–06 survey, with a data set from forty countries, mostly European, but also including the United States, Canada, Russian Federation and Ukraine. Currie et al. (2012) provided data from the 2009–10 survey, with a data set from 38 countries, again mostly European, but also including the United States, Canada, Russian Federation, Armenia and Ukraine. Such data has been used in a comparative way, for example to demonstrate an appreciable correlation, around 0.6, between countries with high-income inequality and rates of bullying others (Elgar et al., 2009).

Such approaches assume an essential commonality of 'bullying' across different cultures. However, other researchers assert that terms for *bullying* in different languages, may have different meanings. For example, *bullying* in England, *ijime* in Japan and *wang-ta* in South Korea are different in terms of how they are defined and their meaning to respondents in surveys (Morita et al., 1999; Lee, Smith and Monks, 2011). In a study in Vietnam, Horton (2012) pointed out how *bat nat*, the nearest equivalent term to bullying, had a distinct meaning, of being made to do something you would not otherwise do.

This tension reflects the difference between 'etic' and 'emic' research traditions in attempts to draw cross-cultural comparisons, as in anthropology generally. An 'etic' approach uses preconceived categories (such as 'bullying') to draw comparisons, using standard instruments. An 'emic' approach instead elicits meaningful categories for each particular culture, from analysis and informants within that culture. Some balance needs to be drawn between these perspectives, if we aim to analyse cultural differences. At extremes, an etic approach rides roughshod over genuine differences, while an emic approach fails to allow any meaningful comparisons or generalisations at all.

Structured questionnaire approaches in studying bullying

Many studies have used structured questionnaires of some kind, usually self-report inventories or nomination procedures. For example, an adapted version of the Olweus questionnaire was used in a cross-national study in Norway, England, the Netherlands and Japan (Morita, 2001). Four teams used an identical questionnaire with the same age groups (10–14 years) at the same time of year (June) and on a reasonably national basis; the data shown in Table 14.1 were based on a common question *How often have you been bullied at school in the last six months?* (with five response options: the data comprise the last three, sometimes, once a week, several times a week; excluding never, or only once or twice).

Table 14.1 *Rates of being victimised, from a similar self-report questionnaire given in four countries (details in text).*

Victim	Total	Girls	Boys	10 years	11 years	12 years	13 years	14 years
England	12.2	11.8	12.7	18.7	13.1	12.1	10.5	7.6
The Netherlands	13.9	13.1	14.8	14.7	16.6	14.2	10.3	7.1
Norway	10.0	9.1	11.1	12.4	11.9	9.5	10.0	–
Japan	9.6	9.0	9.9	13.4	9.9	9.5	8.2	6.5

This etic procedure, apparently so simple, followed intense and sometimes difficult negotiations among the four teams involved, in designing a common questionnaire (P. K. Smith, Kanetsuna and Koo, 2007). Some were issues around response alternatives, and some about actual questions asked. The four teams finally agreed a solution: a questionnaire embodying 'core questions' (in all versions) plus 'option questions' (only if that team wished to include them). The core questions included the one on 'how often have you been bullied at school, in the last six months?'; this common question allowed cross-national comparisons to be made (Table 1).

But is it the same question? The respective terms used would have been *mobbing* (Norwegian), *bullying* (English), *pesten* (Dutch) and *ijime* (Japanese). Do these mean the same to pupils? The standard definitions of *bullying*, and *ijime*, while similar, show some differences:

> *Bullying*: 'A student is being bullied or victimized when he or she is exposed, repeatedly and over time, to negative actions on the part of one or more other students' (Olweus, 1999, p.10).

> *Ijime*: 'A type of aggressive behaviour by which someone who holds a dominant position in a group interaction process, by intentional or collective acts, causes mental and/or physical suffering to another inside a group' (Morita et al., 1999, p.311).

These two definitions share the concept of repeated negative acts, but the definition of *ijime* puts more emphasis on its group or collective nature, and the possibility of mental suffering. It also puts emphasis on the dominant group position of the bully, although this imbalance of power is usually also considered as a criterion for bullying in western cultures (Hunter, Boyle and Warden, 2007).

To try to ensure consistency of response, questionnaires can give a 'standard' definition at the start; for example in the Olweus questionnaire this takes the form: 'We say a young person is being bullied, or picked on, when another young person, or a group of young people, say nasty and unpleasant things to him or her. It is also bullying when a young person is hit, kicked or threatened, locked inside a room, *sent nasty notes, when no-one ever talks to them* and things like that. These things can happen frequently and it is difficult for the young person being bullied to defend himself or herself. It is also bullying when a young person is teased repeatedly in a nasty way. But it is not bullying when two young people of about the same strength have the odd fight or quarrel'.

But this approach has two possible drawbacks. One is a practical one: do pupils filling in a questionnaire, actually remember this long definition and use it when they come later to answer *How often have you been bullied at school this term?* The second is a conceptual one, the etic/emic issue. Can such an approach be 'culture-neutral', or does it ignore important cultural differences in how bullying-like phenomena are understood by pupils? For example, could *ijime* be substituted for *bullying* in the above definition, without any problem?

Some interesting differences can nevertheless emerge, even from core questions as in the four-nation study. For example, this study (Morita, 2001), plus subsequent direct comparison between pupils in England and Japan using questionnaire surveys (Kanetsuna and Smith, 2002; Kanetsuna, 2004; Kanetsuna, Smith and Morita, 2006), identified several important differences between *bullying* in England and *ijime* in Japan. In Japan, pupils who do *ijime* to others are more often in the same year group, and often are (former) 'friends' of the victim. It happens more often in the classroom. It often involves ignoring and social exclusion. Pupils have rather pessimistic or negative attitudes to school-based interventions. In England, pupils who *bully* others are more often in higher years, and less often former 'friends'. It often happens in the playground. It is more often physical or verbal than involving social ignoring or exclusion. Pupils have relatively positive attitudes to school-based interventions (see Chapter 8 for more detail).

A large-scale survey by Koo, Kwak and Smith (2008) in South Korea (see also Chapter 5) found some similar phenomena. Across five main areas of the country, 2,926 pupils aged 11–16 years were given a questionnaire on *wang-ta*. The rates of being *wang-ta* (victim) more than just once or twice in a term, averaged out at 5.8% – quite low in international terms (as can be seen from Table 14.1). But the rates of doing *wang-ta* (bully) more than just once or twice in a term, averaged out at 10.2% – quite high in international terms. Victim rates were higher in boys

(7.3%) than girls (4.2%); bully rates were higher in girls (11.1%) than in boys (9.3%) – different from many other findings.

Similar to the findings for *ijime*, the reported grade of those doing *wang-ta* was mostly in the same class (77%), with only 3% in a higher grade. The number of pupils doing *wang-ta* reported by victims was also quite high; only 17% reported one bully, whereas 50% reported around 3 to 5 bullies, and 33% reported around 10 bullies or even more (by contrast in Europe some 30–50% of bullying is by 1 pupil).

What are the explanations for these differences between bullying-like phenomena, in eastern and western cultures? One set of explanations may simply lie in systemic differences in the educational systems (see Chapter 12); for example in the amount of time spent in home base classrooms by pupils; the extent and supervision of break times; and the amount and types of anti-bullying/anti-ijime interventions at school level and national level (for example, in England, there is a legal requirement for all schools to have an anti-bullying policy; and there are considerable government resources for anti-bullying work).

Another set of explanations lies in broader cultural differences amongst these societies. Hofstede (1980) and Hofstede, Hofstede and Minkov (2010) proposed five or six main dimensions differentiating cultures (see also Chapters 13 and 20). The most well -known is *Collectivism* vs. *Individualism*. Li et al. (2010) examined intracultural variation in Chinese adolescents, linking endorsement of collectivism with less use of overt and relational aggression. However, a more collectivistic culture may imply a greater possibility of concerted whole-group (e.g., whole-class) norms emerging, which could at times be aggressive – thus the possibility of severe whole-class aggression and shunning of a victim. Koo et al. (2008) argued that greater collectivism may explain an emphasis on class-based exclusion and a greater ratio of bullies to victims found in South Korea and Japan.

A second dimension is *Power distance*; perhaps related to Confucianism, aspects of this such as greater respect for elders is typically higher in eastern societies; this may include older pupils, such that (ab)use of power by older persons may be more likely to be seen as legitimate and not as bullying (Hofstede, 1980; P. B. Smith, Bond and Kagitçibasi, 2005). A third dimension is *Masculinity/femininity*, reflecting distinctive gender roles. In countries high on the masculine end of this dimension, males are expected to be more tough and aggressive. Thus higher bullying rates could be predicted especially for males; so a greater male-female difference in bullying rates.

A third aspect to consider in understanding the differences in reported bullying-like phenomena is that in these comparisons, pupils are asked about *ijime* or *wang-ta* or *bullying* (or other terms…). So, are the reported differences actual differences in behaviour, or just differences between the meanings of the terms, so how *ijime* and *bullying* are interpreted in that culture? It is conceivable (if unlikely) that the behaviours are very similar in all these countries, and that the differences are due to the verbal labels we use for description. Some kinds of *bully* behaviours might not be seen as *ijime*, and vice-versa, so the reporting of the same behaviours might be different. Or, the behaviours may be different, irrespective of the verbal labels used. International comparative work is clearly faced with difficulties in finding terms in different languages to correspond to the English word *bullying*. The issue of comparability of terms is central for the accurate interpretation of national and cross-national findings. Although a definition of *bullying* or *ijime* may be given in questionnaires, pupils may actually respond to the usual meaning of the term used for bullying in their language.

The word *bullying* has Anglo-Saxon roots, and appears well understood in northern European languages, even though different words may be used, such as *mobbing*. In southern European countries, generally with Latin roots for the languages, there is no simple corresponding word for *bullying*, although there are words for violence and aggression – such as *prepotenza* or *violenza* in Italian. This issue had come to light earlier in comparisons among European countries. Use of the Olweus questionnaire in England and in Italy had suggested that rates of 'being bullied' are much higher in Italy than in England (Genta et al., 1996) – maybe by a factor of two. But in Italy, the term *prepotenza* was commonly used for *bullying* in these surveys. *Prepotenza* was suspected of having a broader meaning than *bullying*. In fact, in recent years Italian researchers and the media have co-opted the new term *il bullismo*, to fill this conceptual gap for a term similar to bullying (Fonzi, 1997; Genta, 2002; Menesini, 2000).

The Cartoon Test

The Cartoon Test was designed to find out more about how these different terms are understood. As part of an EC-funded program of research on bullying, the cartoon test was developed to explore these linguistic issues on a cross-national basis (P. K. Smith et al., 2002). This test used 25 stick figure cartoons, showing different kinds of scenarios between pupils, many hostile or 'bullying'. Altogether 14 countries participated, with 13 main languages: Austria (south Germanic dialect), China (Mandarin), England (English), France (French), Germany (German), Greece (Greek), Iceland (Icelandic), Italy (Italian), Japan (Japanese), Norway (Norwegian), Portugal (Portuguese), Slovenia

Table 14.2 *Loadings of bullying-related terms from different countries, on five clusters from the cartoon test (details in text).*

Term	Non-aggressive	Physical aggression	Physical bullying	Verbal (direct + indirect)	Social exclusion
Bully	4	34	94	91	62
Prepotenze	10	71	92	86	90
Ijime	4	9	50	87	39
Wang-ta	3	12	58	82	47

(Slovenian), Spain (Spanish) and Thailand (Thai). This constituted 11 European and 3 eastern countries.

In each of the 14 countries, terms for bullying-like phenomena were found from dictionaries and researchers, and children's focus groups used to select 3 to 6 terms comprehensible to children aged 8 and 14 years. The cartoons were then shown to pupils in sequence, one term 'X' at a time, with pupils asked if each cartoon is an example of 'X'. This was designed to be a move towards a more emic approach – looking at terms used in each culture (such as *bullying*, *harassment*, *teasing* in English), and their individual profile of meaning – while retaining an etic component in relating these terms to a broad range of common pupil scenarios. Use of stick figures was intended to avoid particular cultural connotations (such as clothes, skin colour and appearance).

The research identified five main clusters of cartoons that got similar responses from the total sample: non-aggressive (4 cartoons), physical aggression (2 cartoons), physical bullying (with imbalance of power) (5 cartoons), verbal bullying (including rumour spreading as well as direct verbal attacks) (9 cartoons) and social exclusion (5 cartoons). As an example, Table 14.2 (top three rows) shows the weighting of *bullying*, *prepotenze* and *ijime* on these five clusters (from P. K. Smith et al., 2002).

All three terms score very low on the non-aggressive cartoons, as expected. *Bullying*, and *ijime*, is low on physical aggression. *Prepotenze* is confirmed as a broader term than *bullying*, with a much higher loading on physical aggression (fighting between equals) compared to either *bullying* or *ijime*. This probably explains the 'higher incidence' of 'bullying' in Italy when it was assessed by *prepotenze* in earlier studies.

Other studies using the cartoon task

Smorti, Menesini and Smith (2003) used the 25-cartoon set to compare parents' definition of children's bullying in a five-country comparison

(Italy, Spain, Portugal, England and Japan). Japanese parents saw the verbal and severe social exclusion cartoons as particularly high on bullying-related terms. Besides country comparisons, the cartoon test proved useful for other purposes. Menesini, Fonzi and Smith (2002) compared the attribution of meanings to terms related to bullying by teachers and pupils, in Italy. They found that there was agreement as regards cartoons showing physical aggression, but that cartoons showing social exclusion and gender exclusion were less often seen as, for example, *prepotenza* or *violenza*. Monks and Smith (2006) used a reduced set of cartoons to examine age-related differences and the role of individual experiences of peer victimization in the understanding of bullying in a UK sample. Age groups differed in how they characterised bullying; 4- to 6-year-olds and 8-year-olds used one dimension, a distinction between aggressive and nonaggressive acts, 14-year-olds and adults gave a two-dimensional solution, also distinguishing between physical and non-physical (social/relational or verbal) acts. There were no significant differences in how bullying was characterised between boys and girls, or between children involved or not involved in bullying roles.

Examining social exclusion further

Although both *ijime* and *bullying* are lower on physical aggression than physical bullying, and although both are high on verbal bullying, *ijime* surprisingly does not come out high on social exclusion (Table 14.2). This seemed in contradiction to both earlier conceptual work and empirical study, comparing Japan and England (Morita et al., 1999; Kanetsuna and Smith, 2002). But, did the 25-cartoon task capture the full reality of *ijime*? The kinds of social exclusion featured in this cartoon set were rather 'mild'. Three of the cartoons were to do with playing together: Matt won't let Lenny play today, Sebastian never lets Rob play, and Henry and his friends won't let Ray play with them (English male version); while two were gender-based: the girls won't let Mark skip with them because he's a boy, and the boys won't let Karen play football because she's a girl. These can be seen as more 'playground-based' than 'classroom-based', and they do not describe anything like whole-class 'shunning' as was described in case studies by Tanaka (2001) in Japanese classrooms.

Some more resolution of this apparent contradiction was found, when we pursued further research in South Korea. The original cartoon study (P. K. Smith et al., 2002) did not include Korean terms. Focus group work with South Korean pupils (Koo, 2005) established that three terms used most by them to describe bullying-type behaviours were (in order of frequency) *wang-ta, jun-ta* and *eun-ta* (*tta* or *ta* means isolation, being singled out). Using the cartoon test with South Korean pupils, Koo (2005) found a profile for *wang-ta* very similar to *ijime* (lower row of Table 14.2). Of the Korean terms studied, it has the closest profile to *bullying;* hence, this term was used in the Koo et al. (2008) survey. But *wang-ta* (like *ijime*) is surprisingly low on social exclusion, especially as the etymology of this Korean term embodies the idea of exclusion.

We therefore looked more closely at the five specific cartoons in the social exclusion cluster. Three showed straightforward social exclusion from games by same-sex classmate(s), but two showed exclusion on the basis of gender. These all seemed to join in one social exclusion cluster in western countries, but not in South Korea (nor in Japan, when we examined the original data set in more detail). We found that the two gender-based cartoons were seen as *bullying* in England (by 59% of pupils), but not as *ijime* in Japan (only 21% of pupils) or as *wang-ta* in South Korea (only 15% of pupils).

It seems that the previous method of cluster analysis used was culturally insensitive (the overall analysis being dominated by western data sets – 11 out of 14 countries; P. K. Smith et al., 2002). When these two gender-based items were removed, the loadings on the remaining three-item social exclusion cluster rose to 51% for *ijime* and 67% for *wang-ta*. But more fundamentally than just removing the gender-based items, what counts as or best represents social exclusion? The kinds of social exclusion featured in the cartoon set were not very severe. We decided that a cartoon set with wider cultural scope would be needed to encompass different and perhaps more severe kinds of social exclusion (e.g., whole class exclusion) seen in South Korea and Japan.

Another cultural issue was to explore the use of age/grade as a justification for making another pupil do something (for example, to see if this might be seen as *bullying* in England, but not as *ijime* in Japan). In addition, the cartoon set needed updating to new forms of bullying such as text message bullying (cyberbullying).

The expanded cartoon test

An expanded set of cartoons was assembled. The original 25 cartoons were retained (with a few minor wording changes), plus 7 new social exclusion cartoons; 4 new cartoons on abuse of age/grade position; 2 cartoons on new types of 'bullying'; 1 new ambiguous cartoon; and 1 new 'neutral' cartoon. Figure 14.1 shows two new, more classroom-based and arguably more severe, social exclusion cartoons. Figure 14.2 shows two of the new cartoons on abuse of age/grade. The full list of 40-cartoon captions is given in Table 14.3. The captions give female names

Table 14.3 *Captions for the modified version of the cartoon set (English set, female names; modifications in italics)*

1 Helen and Jo don't like each other and start to *hit each other.*
2 Tiffany starts to *hit* Wendy.
3 Mary starts to *hit* Linda, who is smaller.
4 Samantha starts to *hit* Fatima because she said Samantha was stupid.
5 Hilary starts to *hit* Rosalind every break time.
6 Serla tells Alison that, if she doesn't give her money, she will hit her.
7 Sally and her friends start to *hit* Kirsty.
8 *Natalie starts to hit Anne, who is in a lower-year-grade, because Anne disagreed with Natalie.*
9 *Pamela and Emily hit each other playfully and laugh.*
10 *Delia makes her classmate Samantha carry her school bags every day.*
11 *Amanda makes Vicky, who is in a lower class, carry her school bags every day.*
12 Lara borrows Helena's ruler and accidentally breaks it.
13 Sharon takes Carol's ruler and breaks it.
14 Mary forgot her pen so June lends her one of hers.
15 Danielle says nasty things to Janet.
16 Ann says nasty things to Debbie every week.
17 Julia says nasty things to Lisa about the colour of her skin OR Julia says nasty things to Lisa about her way of speaking (note: this is original sanctioned alternative).
18 *Kerry walks with a stick until her injured leg gets better. Kathy says nasty things to her about it.*
19 Kim says nasty things to Victoria because she is gay.
    (note: it is understood that this cartoon is sometimes omitted)
20 Rosie makes fun of Mandy's hair. They both laugh.
21 Elaine makes fun of Sue's hair. Sue is upset.
22 *Wendy sends nasty text messages to Linda every break time.*
23 Emma asks Heidi if she would like to play.
24 *Stephanie insists on Estelle joining in their game, even though Estelle does not want to.*
25 Chloe won't let Denise play today.
26 Natalie never lets Jean play.
27 Jenny and her friends won't let Claire play with them.
28 *The rest of the team won't let Millie take part in a competition, even though she is one of the best players, because she is from a lower year group.*
29 *No one wants to be with Julia for a paired activity.*
30 *Jess does not have any friend in her school.*
31 The girls won't let Mark skip with them because he is a boy.
32 The boys won't let Karen play football because she is a girl.
33 *Classmates never speak to Reena because she is a teacher's favourite.*
34 *Lalitha and her friends won't speak to Ann because she wants to be with lots of people, and not just part of their gang.*
35 *Tatiana and her friends suddenly stop talking and stay silent when Karina enters the classroom.*
36 *Everyone in the class treats Tiffany as if she were not there.*
37 Keely tells everyone not to talk to Patricia.
38 *Anna tells everyone not to talk to Ros because Ros is very popular among the boys.*
39 Fran spreads nasty stories about Melanie.
40 *Susie writes nasty things about Jodie on the walls of the school toilets.*

Figure 14.1 Two new social exclusion cartoons
(a) No one wants to be with Julia for a paired activity.
(b) Tatiana and her friends suddenly stop talking and stay silent when Karina enters the classroom.

Figure 14.2 Two new abuse of age/grade cartoons
(a) The rest of the team won't let Millie take part in a competition, even though she is one of the best players, because she is from a lower year group.
(b) Amanda makes Vicky, who is in a lower class, carry her school bags every day.

from the English set; however, appropriate local names were used in each language, and male names were used with male pupils, or randomly with mixed sex classes.

The countries involved and terms used are shown in Table 14.4. A protocol for using the new set was devised and shared amongst everyone participating. First, the English cartoon captions were translated into the other language, for example, Japanese. Second, another person back-translated the captions into English, not knowing the original, and this was checked for fidelity (and any discrepancies discussed). Then in each

Table 14.4 *Details of samples and feedback on use*

Country/ language	Number of pupils, and schools	Terms used	Feedback on task timing and attention	Feedback on suitability of cartoons
JAPAN Japanese	135; 3 schools in Chiba and Osaka	*ijime, ijiwaru*	too long for more than 1 term with 8-year-olds	text message and 'sexual orientation' cartoons not suitable for 8 years
SOUTH KOREA Korean	1,100; 10 schools in Seoul and provinces	*wang-ta, gipdan-gorophim, gipdan-ttadolim, pokryuk*	no problems, but a bit long for 8-year-olds	no issues
ENGLAND English	82; 2 schools in London	*bullying, harassment, teasing*	two terms enough for 8-year-olds	no major issues
CANADA English	86; 2 schools in New Brunswick and Nova Scotia	*bullying, teasing, being picked on*	two terms enough for 8-year-olds	'sexual orientation' cartoon not suitable for 8 years
ICELAND Icelandic	90; 2 schools in Reykjavik	*einelti, skilja ut undan, strida*	too long for 8-year-olds	no major issues
MAINLAND CHINA Mandarin	91; 3 schools in Shanghai	*qifu, qiya, wuru*	no problems	no major issues
HONG KONG Cantonese	142; 2 schools in Hong Kong	*ha yan*	tiring for 8-year-olds	captions long on 2 cartoons
PAKISTAN Urdu	120; 6 schools in Islamabad	*ghunda pan, tang karna, dhamkana*	no problems, they did not lose concentration	'sexual orientation' cartoon not suitable
TURKEY Turkish	124: 2 schools in Ankara	*zorbalik, dislamak, alay etmek, eziyet etmek, korkutmak, taciz etmek*	14-year-olds no problem, but 8-year-olds often said that some cartoons were very similar and it was long	'sexual orientation' cartoon omitted by researcher

country a small number of terms (usually 3 or 4) for bullying and social exclusion type behaviours were selected; this was done initially from dictionaries and thesauruses, questionnaires used and popular and academic writings, but followed up by focus groups with children (not taking part in the main study) to check on usage and broad understanding of terms. The cartoons were prepared on laminated cards, overhead transparencies or PowerPoint, and the set of 40 cartoons given to 8-year-olds and 14-year-olds from a 'normal' school (i.e. not a school for children with special needs; not a fee-paying school for financially well-off families). We aimed for a minimum of 40 pupils (20 boys and 20 girls) at each age. Investigators followed ethical guidelines appropriate for their own country/institution, but including informed consent from pupils and teachers/parents, rights to not answer or withdraw with no negative consequences, and an information sheet/help sheet and/or person available for help should the material bring up actual experiences of bullying/victimisation.

Each investigating team was asked to check how long it took to work through the forty cartoons for each term, and whether younger children especially lost concentration (and if so, when). They were also asked to debrief the pupils afterwards by explaining this is a new set of cartoon pictures, and ask pupils whether there were any cartoons or captions that were difficult to understand or that they had comments on. The data was gathered in the various countries between 2005 and 2007.

The feedback from the teams indicated that overall, the task took some 20–40 minutes with 8-year-olds, 10–20 minutes with 14-year-olds. The feedback on concentration is shown in Table 14.4. From this, it is clear that the task worked well with 14-year-olds, but not so well with 8-year-olds due to length, if several terms were used. As regards to feedback on the suitability of the cartoons (see Table 14.4), generally all seemed okay apart from cartoon 19 on sexual orientation cartoon ('Kim says nasty things to Victoria because she is gay'); in some countries this was not seen as appropriate, especially for 8-year-olds.

Here, we restrict the analysis to the data from 14-year-olds, given some difficulties in concentration with the 8 years olds. We present percentage 'yes' responses to selected cartoons, for the terms which appear closest to *bullying*: *Ijime* (Japan), *Wang-ta* (South Korea), *Bullying* (England, Canada), *Einelti* (Iceland), *Qifu* (China – mandarin), *Ha yan* (Hong Kong – cantonese), *Ghunda pan* (Pakistan – Urdu) and *Zorbalik* (Turkey). Data for nine cartoons of particular interest are shown in Table 14.5.

Table 14.5 *Some findings from use of an expanded version of the Cartoon Test in nine countries: cartoon caption, percentage 'yes' responses and comment, for eight cartoons.*

Ijime	Wang-ta	Bully Eng/Can	Einelti	Qifu	Ha yan	Ghunda pan	Zorbalik
Hilary starts to hit Rosalind every break time.							
93	28	100/98	87	77	93	95	82
Physical bullying: all terms score high, except wang-ta.							
Pamela and Emily hit each other playfully and laugh.							
0	9	2/0	6	9	9	5	6
Clearly not bullying: all terms score very low.							
The rest of the team won't let Millie take part in a competition, even though she is one of the best players because she is from a lower year group.							
29	49	81/69	64	46	62	77	46
Using age/grade as justification (1) lowest for ijime; highest for western terms.							
Amanda makes Vicky, who is in a lower class, carry her school bags every day.							
78	23	81/71	58	52	72	64	76
Using age/grade as justification (2) lowest for wang-ta.							
Jenny and her friends won't let Claire play with them.							
98	82	85/71	68	66	24	75	49
Social exclusion: all high except ha yan (and maybe zorbalik).							
The girls won't let Mark skip with them because he is a boy/the boys won't let Karen play football because she is a girl.							
25/27	33/35	88/90 51/53	28/28	11/27	14/16	31/19	40/41
Social exclusion by gender: low for eastern terms, only high for bullying.							
No one wants to be with Julia for a paired activity.							
76	85	56/36	56	32	14	56	31
Severe social exclusion (1): highest for wang-ta and ijime.							
Tatiana and her friends suddenly stop talking and stay silent when Karina enters the classroom.							
84	79	86/47	54	25	6	35	35
Severe social exclusion (2): high for ijime and wang-ta; also for bullying (England).							

Selected findings

The first row of Table 14.5 shows percentage responses for cartoon 5, Hilary starts to hit Rosalind every break time. So, for example, 93% of the 14-year-olds in the Japanese sample saw this as an appropriate example of *ijime*. Since this caption brings in the concept of repetition, it is also a good example of bullying (100% in England and 98% in Canada) and also of the terms in the other countries; with the interesting exception of South Korea, where only a minority of 25% saw this as an illustration of *wang-ta*. *Wang-ta* also scored relatively low in the physical aggression and physical bullying clusters in the earlier study (see Table 14.2), and it appears that it is weighted much more towards verbal and severe kinds of social exclusion.

The next row shows results for cartoon 9, Pamela and Emily hit each other playfully and laugh. This is an example of a control cartoon, to ensure that pupils do not just get in a set of saying 'yes' to every cartoon and to give a validity check. In fact, all scores are low on this ranging from 0% to a maximum of 9%.

The third and fourth rows show findings for cartoons 28 and 11; these are two new cartoons relating to abuse of age or grade level (Figure 14.2). For cartoon 28, The rest of the team won't let Millie take part in a competition, even though she is one of the best players, because she is from a lower year group, most pupils in England and Canada see this as *bullying*; so also do many pupils (around half or more) in the other countries, except Japan. Japanese pupils often do not see this as *ijime*, the score of 29% being noticeably the lowest (and less than the 49% for *wang-ta* in South Korea, and 46% for *qifu* in China). Interestingly, a different profile is seen for cartoon 11, Amanda makes Vicky, who is in a lower class, carry her school bags every day. This again is seen as bullying by most children in England and Canada, and a majority in all other countries, including Japan, with the exception here of South Korea, where only 23% see this was *wang-ta*. The example in cartoon 11 is more physical, and the example in cartoon 28 more exclusion based, which may explain the very different weightings for *wang-ta* here. In any event, it suggests that situations where age or grade is being used as a means of getting someone to do something they might not want to do (or not do something they would like to do), may not be seen so negatively in Japan or South Korea as in many other cultures, but depending very much on the kind of situations involved.

The final five cartoons in Table 14.5 show situations of social exclusion. Cartoon 27, Jenny and her friends won't let Claire play with them, was used in the original study. It scores quite highly for all countries, with the notable exception of *ha yan* in Hong Kong (Cantonese), which appears to have a more physical meaning. It is also somewhat lower for *zorbalık* in Turkey, which has been shown to loads more on physical aggression and bullying, than on social exclusion (Ucanok, Smith and Karasoy, 2011). Cartoons 31 and 32, the two gender-based exclusion cartoons, are seen as *bullying* by most pupils in England, and a majority in Canada; but only by a minority in the other countries. This was predicted for the eastern cultures, but was a surprise for Iceland.

Cartoons 29, No one wants to be with Julia for a paired activity, and 35, Tatiana and her friends suddenly stop talking and stay silent when Karina enters the classroom, are two new and more classroom-based exclusion cartoons (Figure 14.1). Here, as predicted, there are high responses for both *ijime* in Japan, and *wang-ta* in South Korea. Scores are moderate in England, Canada and Iceland and in Pakistan. Interestingly, scores are low for *qifu* in mainland China and especially in Hong Kong, where as noted before, *ha yan* appears to be a term more relating to physical actions, and to be low on social exclusion generally.

Summary

The expanded cartoon test was found to be suitable for use, for 14-year-olds. The captions were understood, and the task held pupils' attention for the time needed to run through 3 or 4 different terms in the language. In some cultures, however, the cartoon about sexual orientation was considered not appropriate and was omitted. The task may be less suitable for 8-year-olds, especially if more than 1 or 2 terms are used.

Looking at some of the findings presented in Table 14.5, it seems that the term *bullying* is similar in meaning in England and Canada, though generally more inclusive in England (generally scores on the cartoons being higher, Table 14.5). There are considerable variations in meaning of terms corresponding to *bullying*; for example, *bullying* includes gender-based exclusion, but other terms do not. Of the eastern terms, *wang-ta* is low on physical bullying, but both *wang-ta* and *ijime* are high on severe social exclusion; by contrast, *ha yan* (and to some extent *qifu* and *zorbalık*) are low on social exclusion cartoons; *ijime* and *wang-ta* are low on some age/grade-related cartoons, but depending very much on the kind of situation depicted.

The terms shown in Table 14.5 are those that will often be used in definition-based questionnaires or surveys. It is apparent that equivalence between these terms is far from exact. Different terms pick up different weightings of physical, verbal and social exclusion items. Furthermore, the kinds of social exclusion will be weighted differently in different societies. Also, situations where age or grade is used as justification, are viewed differently – sometimes seen as more acceptable in Japan or South Korea.

The historical dimension of this kind of research should be borne in mind; the meaning of words changes with time. This has been documented in South Korea by Lee, Smith and Monks (2012), where some new terms seem to be partly supplementing or replacing *wang-ta* as a term used by pupils. In Cantonese as spoken in Hong Kong, it appears that *ha yan* may be broadening in meaning to include social exclusion situations, quite possibly as a result of recent anti-bullying awareness raising in that city (see Chapter 7).

The study reported here can be regarded as pilot work, in the sense that the forty-cartoon set was being used for the first time, and (with the exception of South Korea) with relatively small samples. Nevertheless, it demonstrates that it can be a sensitive tool for examining cultural differences in meaning. Now put together several years ago, it might be even further expanded by some cartoons exemplifying different kinds of cyberbullying, which has diversified so much in the last few years (P. K. Smith, 2012). We clearly need to remain open to a combination of methodologies in studying bullying-like phenomena, and to be aware of the dangers of simplicity and ethnocentrism when making cross-cultural comparisons. Greater understanding in these areas will have implications for intervention strategies and help us understand how interventions in one country may need adaptation when tried in a different cultural context.

REFERENCES

Craig, W., Harel-Fisch,Y., Fogel-Grinvald, H., Dostaler, S., Hetland, J., Simons-Morton, B., Molcho, B., Gaspar de Mato, M., Overpeck, M., Due, P., Pickett, W., HBSC Violence & Injuries Prevention Focus Group, and HBSC Bullying Writing Group (2009). A cross-national profile of bullying and victimization among adolescents in 40 countries. *International Journal of Public Health*, 54 (Suppl 2), 216–224.

Currie, C. et al. (eds.). (2012). *Social determinants of health and well-being among young people. Health Behaviour in School-aged Children (HBSC) study: International report from the 2009/2010 survey.* Copenhagen: WHO Regional Office for Europe.

Elgar, F. J., Craig, W., Boyce, W., Morgan, A. and Vella-Zarb, R. (2009). Income inequality and school bullying: Multilevel study of adolescents in 37 countries. *Journal of Adolescent Health*, 45, 351–359.

Fonzi, A. (Ed.) (1997). *Il bullismo in Italia.* Florence: Giunti.

Genta, M. L. (Ed.) (2002). *Il bullismo: Bambini aggressivi a scuola.* Rome: Carocci.

Genta, M. L., Menesini, E., Fonzi, A., Costabile, A. and Smith, P. K. (1996). Bullies and victims in schools in central and southern Italy. *International Journal of Educational Research*, 11, 97–110.

Hofstede, G. (1980). *Culture's consequences: International differences in work-related values*. Newbury Park, CA: Sage.

Hofstede, G., Hofstede, G. J. and Minkov, M. (2010). *Cultures and organizations: Software of the mind*. New York: McGraw-Hill.

Horton, P. (2012). *Bullied into it: Bullying, power and the conduct of conduct*. Gloucestershire: E&E Publishing.

Hunter, S. C., Boyle, J. M. E. and Warden, D. (2007). Perceptions and correlates of peer-victimization and bullying. *British Journal of Educational Psychology*, 77, 797–810.

Kanetsuna, T. (2004). *Pupil insights into school bullying: A cross-national perspective between England and Japan*. Unpublished PhD thesis, Goldsmiths College, University of London.

Kanetsuna, T. and Smith, P. K. (2002). Pupil insights into bullying, and coping with bullying: A bi-national study in Japan and England. *Journal of School Violence*, 1, 5–29.

Kanetsuna, T., Smith, P. K. and Morita, Y. (2006). Coping with bullying at school: children's recommended strategies and attitudes to school-based interventions in England and Japan. *Aggressive Behavior*, 32, 570–580.

Koo, H. (2005). *The nature of bullying in South Korean schools*. Unpublished PhD thesis, Goldsmiths College, University of London.

Koo, H., Kwak, K. and Smith, P. K. (2008). Victimization in Korean schools: The nature, incidence and distinctive features of Korean bullying or wang-ta. *Journal of School Violence*, 7, 119–139.

Lee, S-H, Smith, P. K. and Monks, C. (2011). Perceptions of bullying-like phenomena in South Korea: a qualitative approach from a lifespan perspective. *Journal of Aggression, Conflict and Peace Research*, 3, 210–221.

(2012). Meaning and usage of a term for bullying-like phenomena in South Korea: A lifespan perspective. *Journal of Language and Social Psychology*, 31, 342–349.

Li, Y., Wang, M., Wang, C. and Shi, J. (2010). Individualism, collectivism, and Chinese adolescents' aggression: Intracultural variations. *Aggressive Behavior*, 36, 187–194.

Menesini, E. (Ed.) (2000). *Bullismo: Che fare?* Florence: Giunti.

Menesini, E., Fonzi, A. and Smith, P. K. (2002). Attribution of meanings to terms related to bullying: A comparison between teacher's and pupil's perspectives in Italy. *European Journal of Psychology of Education*, 17, 393–406.

Monks, C. and Smith, P.K. (2006). Definitions of 'bullying': Age differences in understanding of the term, and the role of experience. *British Journal of Developmental Psychology*, 24, 801-821.

Morita, Y. (2001). *Ijime no kokusai hikaku kenkyu [Cross-national comparative study of bullying]*. Japan: Kaneko Shobo.

Morita, Y., Soeda, H., Soeda, K. and Taki, M. (1999). Japan. In P. K. Smith, Y. Morita, J. Junger-Tas, D. Olweus, R. Catalano and P. Slee (Eds),

The nature of school bullying: A cross-national perspective (pp. 309–323). New York and London: Routledge.

Olweus, D. (1999). Sweden. In P. K. Smith, Y. Morita, J. Junger-Tas, D. Olweus, R. Catalano and P. Slee (Eds.), *The nature of school bullying: A cross-national perspective* (pp. 2–27). London and New York: Routledge.

Smith, P. B., Bond, M. H. and Kağitçibasi, C. (2005). *Social behavior across cultures: Living and working with others in a changing world.* London: Sage.

Smith, P. K. (2012). Cyberbullying and cyber aggression. In S. R. Jimerson, A. B. Nickerson, M. J. Mayer and M. J. Furlong (Eds.), *Handbook of school violence and school safety: International research and practice* (pp. 93–103). New York: Routledge.

Smith, P. K., Cowie, H., Olafsson, R. and Liefooghe, A. (2002). Definitions of bullying: a comparison of terms used, and age and sex differences, in a 14-country international comparison. *Child Development,* 73, 1119–1133.

Smith, P. K., Kanetsuna, T. and Koo, H. (2007). Cross-national comparison of 'bullying' and related Terms: Western and Eastern perspectives. In Österman, K. and Björkqvist, K. (Eds.), *Contemporary research on aggression: School violence.* Proceedings of the XVI World Meeting of the International Society for Research on Aggression, Santorini (pp. 3–9). Greece. Åbo, Finland: Åbo Academy University Press.

Smorti, A., Menesini, E. and Smith, P. K. (2003). Parents' definition of children's bullying in a five-country comparison. *Journal of Cross-Cultural Psychology,* 34, 417–432.

Tanaka, T. (2001). The identity formation of the victim of 'shunning'. *School Psychology International,* 22, 463-476.

Ucanok, Z., Smith, P. K. and Karasoy, D. S. (2011). Definitions of bullying: Age and gender differences in a Turkish sample. *Asian Journal of Social Psychology,* 14, 75–83.

Part IV

Practical measures to reduce bullying problems

15 Actions to prevent bullying in western countries

Peter K. Smith, Fran Thompson, Wendy Craig, Irene Hong, Phillip Slee, Keith Sullivan and Vanessa A. Green

In this chapter, we discuss what schools can do about bullying, and what the evidence base is for the effectiveness of such actions, in western countries. We draw on findings internationally but focus primarily on England, other countries in Europe, the United States and Canada, and Australia and New Zealand. We mention what legal provisions there are relevant to school bullying, what guidance and resources are available, and we consider the various proactive, peer support and reactive strategies that schools can and do use to reduce bullying. We also review the effectiveness of monitored program-based interventions.

Cyberbullying has posed new challenges for anti-bullying interventions in the last decade. The use of mobile phones and the internet has grown at a tremendous rate in this century, transforming the lives of young people. As the access to new technology increases, so does the opportunity for cyberbullying. The EU Kids Online project (Livingstone et al., 2011 p. 25) found that: *being bullied, … is the risk that upsets (children) most, more than sexual images, sexual messages, or meeting online contacts offline*. Research indicates that as traditional bullying decreases, levels of cyberbullying have remained unaltered or may be increasing (Rigby and Smith, 2011; Hasebrink, 2014). Although cyberbullying predominantly takes place outside of school, the 'fallout' is often brought into school.

School-based interventions are targeted at individuals, the class or the whole school; some at the behaviour of those doing the bullying; some at those who are victims; some at bystanders or likely defenders. Some further relevant areas of intervention or change, such as family-based interventions, or wider societal changes, while important, are outside the scope of this review.

Anti-bullying interventions in England

National guidance became available in England with the *Don't Suffer in Silence* pack (DfE, 1994; revised as DfES, 2000, 2002), developed as a result of the Sheffield project (see below). This was subsequently replaced by a suite of guidelines in *Safe to Learn* (DCSF, 2007). This has now been archived and following a change of government, the Department for Education issued a more concise set of advice for schools (DfE, 2013; www.education.gov.uk/publications). This guidance clearly extends the school responsibility for dealing with bullying outside the school premises and school day. In order to enforce this requirement, the Ofsted (Office for Standards in Education) framework has been extended to include an assessment of strategies used for dealing with bullying (including cyberbullying) in the schools inspection (Ofsted, 2012).

Bullying and the law

There is no one law in England for bullying but there are several laws that can be applied to bullying and cyberbullying. The DfE guidance (2013) foregrounds legislation as a way of responding to bullying, including cyberbullying. The amended Education Act (2011) extended the head teacher's remit to search and confiscate phones; to regulate pupil conduct outside the school and to permanently exclude pupils. It also introduced same-day detentions and increased protection for teachers. Other laws cited included The Equality Act (2010), which can be used for discrimination and prejudice-based bullying; The Children Act (1989) which can be used for safeguarding (e.g., sexting) and The Public Order Act (1986) which can be used for harassing or threatening behaviour. The Communications Act (2003, section 127); The Malicious Communications Act (1988) and The Protection from Harassment Act (1997) can be used in serious cases of cyberbullying. The guidance also advises that the police should be involved if schools feel a criminal offence has been committed.

Anti-bullying organisations

Besides government advice, there has been support and materials for schools, parents and young people from the Anti-Bullying Alliance (www.anti-bullyingalliance.org.uk/), Bullying Intervention Group (www.bullyinginterventiongroup.co.uk), ChildLine (www.childline.org .uk), DitchTheLabel (www.ditchthelabel.org), Kidscape (www.kids cape.org.uk), ChildNet International (www.childnet.com) and others. Organisations producing resources for schools for e-safety and cyberbullying include the Child Exploitation and Online Protection Centre (CEOP: www.thinkuknow.co.uk) and the Safer Schools Partnership

(SSP, a police initiative: (www.justice.gov.uk/youth-justice/prevention/safer-school-partnerships).

The Sheffield project

In England, the main evaluated intervention program was the Sheffield project, from 1991–93 (P. K. Smith and Sharp, 1994). This used 23 intervention schools and 4 control schools. It embodied developing a whole school policy, plus a choice from a range of other intervention components (curriculum work, quality circles, assertiveness training, playground work, peer support). There was a reduction in victimisation rates of around 17% in being bullied for primary schools, but only around 3–5% in secondary schools; there was however a high positive correlation between the amount of effort put in by schools, and the outcomes achieved. At that time and since, the main philosophy of anti-bullying work in England has been for schools to choose from a range of intervention strategies in order to implement their anti-bullying policy.

Range of interventions

Thompson and Smith (2011) carried out a study for the DfE, which examined what anti-bullying strategies were actually used by schools, and how effective they thought they were. The following sections draw on this report, discussing particular strategies that can be and are used in schools. We have divided these into broadly *proactive strategies* in the school and playground, designed to make bullying less likely to happen; *peer support* (which can be both proactive and reactive); and *reactive strategies*, as ways of dealing with bullying incidents once they have occurred. Although introduced here primarily in the English context, these categories are of course very widely applicable.

Proactive strategies

Whole school policy on bullying: By law, English schools are required to have a behaviour policy to include encouraging good behaviour and preventing all forms of bullying among pupils (Education and Inspections Act, 2006). Anti-bullying policies can either be contained in the behaviour policy or be separate. School policies vary in scope and quality; P. K. Smith et al. (2012) found many policies in English schools contained a definition of bullying; statements about the improvement of school climate; and how sanctions relate to the type and severity of the incident. However, fewer policies included cyberbullying, homophobic bullying and bullying based on disability or faith; or procedures to follow up on incidents. There is little evidence that having a good policy in itself helps reduce school bullying, but it does provides a framework for the school's response involving the whole school community: pupils, teachers, learning mentors, school support staff, governors and parents/carers.

Curricular materials/approaches: Classroom activities are often used to address bullying issues in an age, gender and culturally appropriate way. These can include both passive activities such as reading literature, or viewing audiovisual materials; and more active forms, such as designing and acting drama/role play, having debates or workshop activities. In computer-based games, children can act out roles and see the consequences in a virtual environment (Sapouna et al., 2009). Curricular approaches can raise awareness of bullying and the schools' anti-bullying policy, but the effects may only be temporary if curriculum work is not backed up by continuing anti-bullying work and policy (P. K. Smith and Sharp, 1994). OFSTED (2003) reported schools with the most successful approaches to bullying took full account of pupils' views, dedicating curriculum and tutorial time to discussing relationships and matters like bullying. Curriculum work was most effective when delivered through creative, interactive lessons with skilled staff.

Co-operative group work: This involves pupils working together to solve a common task (for example, designing a newspaper) in which each person can make their own contribution. It has the potential to involve and integrate vulnerable, bullied children in the class peer group, and has been shown to help in this respect; but the activities can be disrupted by bullying children (Cowie et al., 1994).

Quality circles: These are problem-solving groups of pupils formed for regular classroom sessions with a set of procedures to follow about group formation, data gathering and presentation of outcomes. They can be used for a range of subjects, including bullying. Paul, Smith and Blumberg (2012) reported on their use in an English secondary school in the context of understanding and reducing bullying. The process engaged pupils interest, and pupils suggested a range of solutions; the information gained was useful to staff in understanding how bullying was changing over time (e.g., new forms of cyberbullying) and gave some suggestions for intervention.

Personal, Social, Health and Economic education (PSHE): Most schools provide some form of PSHE, and it is often the main way of delivering anti-bullying work through the curriculum (Thompson and Smith, 2011). It can develop pupil awareness of different types of bullying, raise awareness of the consequences of bullying and promoting ways of challenging it and coping with its effects. One widely used resource has been SEAL (Social and Emotional Aspects of Learning), a whole-school approach to developing social and emotional skills. In primary schools, the SEAL program is based around seven themes, one of which is 'Say No to Bullying'; this focuses on: what bullying is; how it feels; why people bully; how schools can prevent and respond to it; and how children can use their social and emotional skills. An evaluation by Humphrey et al. (2008) found a significant impact for the small group work component of the program; the skill and experience of the facilitators appeared crucial, and recommendations included more standardised training and greater parental involvement. A similar program was launched in secondary schools in 2005 as SEBS (Developing Social, Emotional and Behavioural Skills). It included a Year 7 learning and teaching resource, with four themes: A place to learn (setting the context for learning); Learning to be together (social skills and empathy); Keep on learning (motivation); and Learning about me (understanding and managing feelings). An evaluation by Humphrey, Lendrum and Wigelsworth (2010) reported a lack of structure and consistency in the delivery of the secondary SEAL curriculum, recommending that schools needed greater guidance about maximising the impact of the resource.

Assertiveness training: Bullied or at-risk pupils can be taught specific strategies for dealing with difficult situations, including bullying, in assertive rather than passive or aggressive ways. Through regular in-class or after school sessions, pupils can talk about their experiences and learn and practice effective responses. Assertiveness training can be expensive and time-consuming and requires periodic refresher sessions to be most effective. It can help victims develop useful strategies, but it does not solve bullying on its own (P. K. Smith and Sharp, 1994).

Working in the playground: Especially in primary schools, children can spend a considerable period in the playground, and a relative lack of supervision can provide opportunities for bullying (see Chapter 1; Blatchford, 1998). An effective playground policy and well-designed play areas can help to reduce bullying (DCSF, 2007). Work on the physical environment of the playground includes structuring or redesigning it to provide more creative opportunities for pupils during break and lunch times, and reduce boredom and bullying. This can be a participatory process for pupils and include playground design exercises and mapping bullying hot spots (P. K. Smith and Sharp, 1994). OFSTED (2003) identified features of good practice including the efficient checking of the school site, setting up safe play areas or quiet rooms and close supervision at the start and finish of the school day. Training of lunch-time supervisors can provide them with additional skills in organising games, recognising bullying behaviours, interviewing pupils and dealing with bullying and conflict situations. One important aspect is distinguishing bullying from playful fighting; Boulton and Flemington (1996) found positive results from using a video illustrating the differences between play fights, real fights and bullying.

Peer support schemes

Based on a national survey, Houlston, Smith and Jessel (2009) estimated that 62% of schools in England used some kind of structured peer support scheme. Peer support uses pupils' experience, knowledge and skills in a planned and structured way both to prevent and reduce bullying. Peer supporters either volunteer or are selected by school staff and trained to deal with interpersonal conflicts, social exclusion and bullying in proactive and non-violent ways.

In primary schools, these are often befriender schemes for playtimes, to help pupils feeling sad or having no one to play with. Some schemes are based on playground buddies (clearly identifiable by special caps/clothing) helping lonely or bullied children during breaktimes or lunchtimes. Other schemes focus on organising playground games, or on running lunchtime clubs which are open to all but offer companionship to lonely pupils. In secondary schools, they are often peer mentoring or counselling schemes, usually in a confidential area or designated room, manned by peer supporters at certain times, where pupils can go to seek help or, alternatively contact can be made through a worry/bully box or the school intranet. Buddy schemes can be used at transition to help the youngest Year 7 pupils adjust to a new school.

Reviewing a number of evaluations of peer support in schools, Cowie and Smith (2010) concluded that as a means of reducing bullying, peer support schemes could operate in three ways. First, through a general improvement in the school environment; there was good evidence that schools using well-managed peer support schemes were seen as more caring and concerned about pupil well-being, and the schemes are known and supported by pupils and staff; also, peer supporters themselves generally benefit from the experience (Houlston and Smith, 2009). Second, through helping individual pupils who used the scheme to stop being victimised; for this there is anecdotal evidence from individual cases. Finally, through reducing general rates of bullying throughout the school; for this the evidence is very equivocal, as most of the relevant studies do not report significant changes in general levels of bullying behaviour as a result of implementing a peer support scheme.

Crucial issues in peer support include the selection and training of peer supporters; the gender balance in recruitment (there are often more girl than boy volunteers, particularly in the secondary sector); adequate and continuing supervision by an accessible member of staff; effective promotion of the scheme; and sufficient take-up that peer supporters feel positive in their role (Cowie and Smith, 2010).

Reactive strategies

Reactive strategies are a response to bullying incidents when they have happened. Reactive strategies range from sanction-based approaches, through restorative practices, to more indirect and non-punitive approaches. In England, the DfE recommends that schools should apply disciplinary measures or sanctions to pupils who bully in order to show clearly that their behaviour is wrong (DfE, 2013). However, many anti-bullying practitioners prefer less direct approaches, at least for less severe cases of bullying.

Direct sanctions: This is a collective term describing a range of punishments, which may vary in severity and be used on a graded scale if bullying persists. They can range through reprimands/serious talks from the head teacher; meetings involving parents or carers; temporary removal from class; withdrawal of privileges and rewards; disciplinary measures such as detentions; punishment such as litter-picking/school clean-ups; through to temporary or permanent exclusion. Direct sanctions are expected to impress on the perpetrator that what he/she has done is unacceptable and to promote understanding of the limits of acceptable behaviour; to give an opportunity for pupils who bully to face up to the harm they have caused and learn from it; to deter him/her from repeating that behaviour; to signal to other pupils that the behaviour is unacceptable and deter them from doing it; and to demonstrate publicly that school rules and policies are to be taken seriously. Thompson and Smith (2011) found that the majority of schools (92%) used sanctions of some kind, especially serious talks, with the more serious sanctions mainly being used in secondary schools.

Restorative approaches: This is a collective term for practices coming from ideas of restorative justice, in contrast to the retributive justice of a sanction-based approach (Sellman, Cremin and McCluskey, 2013). The underlying principle is to work to resolve conflict, repair harm and restore good relationships, offering the victim the opportunity to have their harm or loss acknowledged and reparation made. The perpetrator is made aware of the victim's feelings and encouraged to acknowledge the impact of what s/he has done and make amends. If a pupil refuses to do so or does not abide by the decisions reached, a school may then resort to sanctions. Thompson and Smith (2011) found that 69% of schools were using some form of restorative approaches to deal with bullying incidents by 2009–10, and 88% claimed to be developing a restorative ethos and culture.

Restorative approaches range from informal conversations through to formal facilitated meetings or conferences. In a short or mini-conference, an informal meeting is held between the pupils involved, led by a trained member of staff, in which incidents and harm caused are examined, and the offender(s) are asked to discuss possible means of reparation. In a full restorative conference, a formal, structured meeting takes place involving pupils, along with their parents/carers, friends and school representatives, who are brought together to discuss and resolve an incident. The staff member leading the conference is highly trained, and prior to this large meeting, holds individual interviews with the participants to ensure a full conference is appropriate, and that everyone is completely prepared for it.

Effective use of restorative approaches depends on pupils being able to talk about feelings and relationship issues. A good 'seedbed' for this is use of problem solving circles or circle time, in the normal curriculum. In circle time, under teacher supervision, pupils arrange their chairs in a circle, and discuss a problem which needs resolving. All pupils are given the opportunity to speak, but only one is able to talk at any given time. Pupils are largely positive to circle time, in terms of learning about and expressing feelings and solving problems, but it is important that teachers have sufficient training and experience of good practice.

A national evaluation by the Youth Justice Board (2004) found that 92% of conferences were resolved successfully, and three months later, 96% of agreements remained intact. Although no general improvements in pupil attitudes were found at a whole school level, most school staff reported that their school had benefited. Thompson and Smith (2011) found that schools that committed fully to a restorative ethos, with a whole school approach backed up by adequate training in restorative techniques for staff, had most success. Without this, tensions can arise between the prevailing practices of the school, often sanction-based, and restorative principles.

The Pikas method or method of shared concern: The method of shared concern or Pikas method is a non-punitive, counselling-based approach developed in Sweden by Pikas (1989, 2002) which deconstructs the group dynamic of bullying. It uses a combination of individual and group meetings, in a five-step sequence: individual talks with suspected bullies; individual talk with the victim; preparatory group meeting; summit meeting; and follow up of the results. This approach is expected to sensitise bullying children to the harm they are doing to the victim (enabled by a lack of hostile blaming attitude on the part of the interviewer), encourage positive behaviours to the victim, and also encourage provocative victims to change their behaviour in positive ways.

In an independent evaluation in English schools, P. K. Smith, Cowie and Sharp (1994) reported that teachers trained in the Pikas method felt that it was an appropriate and helpful response to bullying; and among pupils who experienced it, three quarters reported that bullying had decreased following the intervention. However in some cases the bullying child(ren) had switched their attention from the initial victim, to another child outside of the group. It appeared to be a useful short-term intervention for reducing bullying behaviours, but in the case of persistent bullying, further interventions would be required.

Support group method: The support group method (formerly called the No Blame approach) was developed in England by Robinson and Maines (2007). It is a non-punitive approach which aims to change problem behaviours through a mixture of peer pressure to elicit a prosocial response, and self-realisation of the harm and suffering caused to the victim. There are seven steps: the facilitator talks individually to the bullied pupil; a group meeting of 6 to 8 students is then set up, some suggested by the victim but without his/her presence; the facilitator explains to the group that the victim has a problem, but does not discuss the incidents that have taken place; the facilitator assures the group no punishment will be given, but instead all participants must take joint responsibility to make the victim feel happy and safe; each group member gives their own ideas on how the victim can be helped; the facilitator ends the meeting, with the group given responsibility for improving the victim's safety and well-being; follow-up individual meetings are held with group members one week after the meeting to establish how successful the intervention has been.

The support group method aims at lasting change rather than retribution, through developing emotional awareness, peer support and empathy amongst pupils involved. In a slight adaptation of the method, Young (1998) reported that 80% of support group sessions resulted in immediate success and 14% in delayed success; with the remaining 6% having only limited success. An evaluation by P. K. Smith, Howard and Thompson (2007) found that over half of schools using the method (53%) rated its effectiveness as very satisfactory, 30% said it was rather satisfactory and the remainder were neutral. The support group method was adapted considerably in use, and the seven steps were not always followed. Issues of parental involvement, and backup availability of sanctions, were commonly mentioned. No direct evidence was provided as to whether the support group method was able to support and improve the behaviour of pupils who bullied others.

Interventions for cyberbullying Although methods of dealing with traditional bullying may often be helpful for cyberbullying (particularly as the same children are often involved), it is also important to develop different interventions to prevent and respond specifically to cyberbullying. Some schools have responded by updating anti-bullying policies to include cyberbullying; introducing Acceptable Use Policies for internet use in school; providing ongoing e-safety training for staff, pupils, peer supporters and parents; and using the police to 'lay down the law' about the legality and illegality of online bullying (Thompson, Robinson and Smith, 2013).

The *Child Exploitation and Online Protection Centre (CEOP)* was founded in 2006; although primarily tasked with tackling online sex offenders, CEOP Education has produced resources and training in child protection and e-safety that have become very popular in schools. CEOP resources cannot be used until staff undergo a free, half-day training session. Resources, which include a range of films and lesson plans, can be used in PSHE or for whole-school assemblies. CEOP regularly evaluate their resources through their own online questionnaires completed by staff and students.

Davidson, Martellozzo and Lorenz (2009) evaluated the CEOP ThinkUKnow internet safety program (www.thinkuknow.co.uk), and recommended a series of changes including ongoing review and monitoring of training; regular evaluation of their resources to ensure quality control; improvement and updating of the website; increased engagement with parents/carers; the use of more realistic scenarios for films; targeting girls' risk-taking behaviours on social networking sites and providing ongoing support and training for trainers.

An evaluation of CEOP's short film, Exposed, about sexting for 14- to 16-year-olds found that girls, younger students and those involved in sexting incidents in the past gave the film its highest ratings. As sexting (the act of sending of sexually explicit images or texts using mobile phones) is becoming more common, it was recommended that this film needed to be shown to even younger year groups (Thompson et al., 2013)

The *BeatBullying cybermentors* scheme (*https://cybermentors.org.uk/*) provided virtual peer support originally designed to support young people involved in cyberbullying, although it came to have a more general remit. Students, usually recruited in schools, were trained by BeatBullying staff in 2-day training workshops. CyberMentors mentor online in and out of school; have an online identity and are protected from abuse by a software filter called netmod.

Banerjee, Robinson and Smalley (2010) found that the BeatBullying mentors reduced bullying in five intervention schools by raising awareness of bullying and supporting the youngest students at transition. However, schools varied in their promotion of the schemes and the supervision of mentors; not all school staff were engaged and the scheme needed ongoing monitoring. An online evaluation found that the vast majority of cybermentor and cybermentee respondents were young females (Thompson et al., 2013). Although this gender imbalance is evident in most peer support schemes (Cowie and Smith, 2010), this could put boys off accessing the scheme. However the scheme ended when BeatBullying went bankrupt in 2014.

The *Safer Schools Partnership (www.justice.gov.uk/youth-justice/preven tion/safer-school-partnerships)* was a scheme in which police officers were placed in secondary schools for an allotted time each week. Bowles, Reyes and Pradiptyo (2005) evaluated the SSP pilot scheme, finding that it had had a positive impact and delivered measurable improvements. In SSP pilot schools, truancy and absence rates had reduced; relationships with and attitudes to the police were distinctly more positive; levels of offending had reduced whilst examination performance had improved.

Another evaluation focussed on the SSP's effectiveness in both preventing and responding to cyberbullying. Schools responding to a cyberbullying interventions questionnaire reported the SSP was effective in both preventing and responding to cyberbullying, although the initiative was expensive (Thompson et al., 2013). In the recent economic climate of cuts, many SSPs have been removed from schools.

Program interventions in Western Europe

So far we have discussed individual components of anti-bullying interventions; but of course, most schools use some combination of these. For example, Samara and Smith (2008) found that in 2006 numerous English schools reported using not only a whole-school policy, but also 80% used circle time, 74% used drama/role play, 57% used trained playground supervisors and 28% used either the Support Group or Pikas (i.e., non-punitive) methods.

Individual components have also been evaluated in other European countries. For example, Menesini, Nocentini and Palladino (2012) reported on a web-based project called *Noncadiamointrappola* (Let's not fall into a trap). Students developed a website to promote peer-to-peer content against bullying and cyberbullying, and peer educators were trained, and monitored the website, answering questions and monitoring discussions. *Noncadiamointrappola* was later expanded to involve bystanders and teachers more, and with a Facebook page to integrate the web forum. An evaluation found significant reductions in traditional bully and victim rates, and cyber victim rates.

However, there are also programs available with a more structured set of components and sequence of activities. The most well-known are the Olweus Bullying Prevention Program and KiVa; but there are many others. There are now a considerable number of pre/post-test studies that have examined the effect of program-based interventions against bullying; see for example P. K. Smith, Pepler and Rigby (2004), Spiel, Salmivalli and Smith (2011), Strohmeier and Noam (2012), and Eisner and Malti (2012).

The Olweus Bullying Prevention Program (OBPP) The first program intervention was the Norwegian Nationwide campaign against bullying (see Chapter 1). This was developed by Olweus into the OBPP (Olweus, 1999). The fully evolved OBPP has school-level components (such as a Bullying Prevention Coordinating Committee, introducing school rules against bullying), classroom-level components (such as class meetings and meetings with parents), individual-level components (such as serious talks and intervention plans for involved students) and community-level components (such as supportive partnerships with community members); see Olweus and Limber (2010).

Several evaluations have been reported of the OBPP in Norway. The First Bergen Project (1983–85) involved 42 schools using an early version of the OBPP as an addition to the Norwegian Nationwide campaign. The effect on rates of bullying was dramatic with reported victim rates falling by around 50%, for both boys and girls. There were also reductions in anti-social behaviour and general improvements in school climate. A second Bergen Project (1997–98) involved 14 intervention schools and 16 comparison schools. Bullying decreased by between 21–38% in intervention schools, with no change or increase in comparison schools. A first Oslo project (2001–2) covered 37 schools, which showed reductions of some 30–45% in victimisation and bullying. Olweus and Limber (2010) reported findings associated with a New National initiative in Norway, with reductions in the range of 37%–49%. The success of the OBPP in Norway is thus substantial and well-replicated.

The program has been used outside Norway, but with less consistent success (see also Olweus and Limber, 2010). In Germany, the

Schleswig-Holstein project, 1994–96 (Hanewinkel, 2004) used the OBPP school, class and individual level interventions, in 37 primary and secondary schools. There were quite small decreases in victim and bully rates up to age 16, but some increase at ages 17–18. In the Netherlands, Fekkes, Pijpers and Verloove-Vanhorick (2006) worked with 15 intervention and 30 control schools, using a program modelled on the OBPP with an emphasis on written anti-bullying policy. Victim rates decreased by 25% in intervention compared to control schools in the first year, but with no significant effects at second year follow-up. In the light of these mixed findings, together with those from the United States (see below), it appears that the OBPP has proved highly effective in Norway, but so far has not translated so effectively into other cultural contexts.

The KiVa program In Finland, the KiVa Koulu program was developed over the period 2006–9 (Salmivalli, Kärnä and Poskiparta, 2010). KiVa includes universal interventions (e.g., via the classroom) and targeted interventions (individual discussions with victims and bullying children, and using prosocial, high-status peers to be defenders). The classroom work includes an anti-bullying virtual learning environment; the KiVa computer game uses simulated characters and episodes learn facts and try out strategies, which can then be applied to everyday life at school.

The academic year 2007–8 provided an opportunity for a randomised control trial of KiVa. Kärnä et al. (2011a) reported on data for grades 4–6 from 78 schools, randomly assigned to intervention or control, with about 4,000 pupils in each condition. By the end of the year, the control schools showed modest reductions in bully and victim rates from self-report, and not much change on peer report. However, the KiVa intervention schools showed significantly greater reductions on the self-report measures, and also significant reductions on peer reports of being a victim. Peer reports also showed reductions in bully assistant and reinforcer roles compared to controls. The KiVa schools, compared to control schools, showed a 30% reduction in self-reports of being a victim, and 17% reduction in self-reported bullying of others. Kärnä et al. (2012) reported corresponding analyses for grades 1–3 (38 intervention and 36 control schools), and grades 7–9 (38 intervention and 35 control schools). For grades 1–3, again there were significant reductions in victim and bully rates. The findings were more mixed for the oldest age group, grades 7–9, with no significant intervention effects for self-reports of victim or bully; there was a reduction in victim rates by peer report, but not for peer-reported bullying. Overall, Kärnä and colleagues calculated that for the entire age range, there was some 20% reduction in prevalence, this being considerably larger in the younger age groups but smaller and/or non-significant in older adolescents.

Kärnä et al. (2011b) reported on a further evaluation carried out during 2009–10 using a cohort-sequential design with 888 schools and some 150,000 students, across grades 1 to 9. Generally, the KiVa program reduced bully and victim rates significantly, but somewhat less than in the RCT trials.

KiVa is now being tried out in the Netherlands as KiVa+ with the addition of using social network analysis (Huitsing and Veenstra, 2012, and Chapter 1) to better identify targeted interventions. Randomised control trials are also under way in Estonia, Italy and Wales, in Europe, and in Delaware in the United States (Salmivalli, personal communication, 23/09/2013).

Interventions in North America

The main goal of this section is to review the bullying prevention evidence based programs developed in North America, that have demonstrated empirical evidence of successful outcomes. Three Canadian bullying prevention developed programs are described: WITS, the Quest for the Golden Rule (designed for students aged 5 through 11) and The Fourth R (designed for high school students aged 14 through 18). Three US programs are described: Second Step and Steps to Respect (designed for students aged 5 through 12) and the Safe Ambassador Program (designed for students aged 9 through 17).

Recent discussion of interventions focused in North America can be found in IOM/NRC (2014). This also includes a summary of the legal position in the United States. Out of 50 states, 49 now have enacted anti-bullying laws. The content of the laws across states is quite diverse, and little is known about how effective they are.

Canadian programs

WITS Programs: The WITS Primary Program is a community-based, school-wide bullying and peer victimisation prevention program, designed for children in Kindergarten to Grade 3, with the WITS LEADS Program intended for older children in Grades 4 to 6. Both WITS programs aim to bring children together with their schools, families and communities to create responsive and safe environments to prevent bullying and peer victimisation. Individuals from these social contexts and environments are recruited to help deliver a consistent message about conflict resolution and bullying and victimisation.

WITS specifically targets children's social behaviours and addresses risks for peer victimisation. The WITS acronym – Walk away, Ignore, Talk it out and Seek help – encourages children to use their 'wits' when resolving peer conflicts. Moreover, it provides both children and adults a common language in which to talk about peer victimisation.

This intervention is a literature-based curriculum that integrates WITS messages, storybook-based lesson plans and activities with existing classroom learning objectives to increase children's awareness of peer victimisation. The lesson plans, including pre- and post- questions and activities, are available online and are tailored to each province's regular curricular objectives. Teachers play a major role in the delivery of the WITS program, and also take part in one 90-minute online module that provides guidance on how to integrate WITS into the classroom. In addition to school staff, community leaders (e.g., police officers, firefighters, elders) play an important role in the program's success and provide yearlong support. Parents are also invited to participate by learning about the program and reading WITS books to students.

Results from short term and longitudinal program evaluations indicate that the WITS Primary program is effective in reducing victimisation in young elementary school children (Leadbeater and Sukhawathanakul, 2011). After receiving WITS training, students' reports of relational and physical victimisation decreased significantly (Leadbeater, Hoglund and Woods, 2003). Moreover, teachers in the intervention group rated their students as more socially competent and responsible than did teachers in the control group (Leadbeater and Sukhawathanakul, 2011). During a 6-year follow-up evaluation, researchers again confirmed that levels of physical victimisation and relational victimisation decreased significantly, while social competence increased; however, as students transitioned from elementary to middle school, program effects dropped (Hoglund, Hosan and Leadbeater, 2012). All training modules and resources for the WITS Program are available at no cost at www.witsprogram.ca. The WITS Programs have been implemented in over 300 schools across Canada. Canadian-French language adaptations of the WITS Primary and Intermediate program are also available. For more information, see the WITS website at www.witsprogram.ca/schools/primary-program.

Quest for the Golden Rule: This is a novel, electronic bullying prevention program designed for students in grades 2–5. It aims to teach children about bullying prevention messages, and train them on effective social skills and problem-solving skills. By using animated, interactive computer simulations, children are able to practice various social skills and bullying prevention strategies with virtual characters in a private, safe environment. The program consists of three modules: Bark Academy, which introduces children the different types of bullying, and teaches them about social justice, safety and fairness; Mission to Mars, which teaches children about social skills needed to make friends; and Ghoul School, which addresses how to respond to bullying incidences in a safe, respectful manner. Students must respond to social problems in prosocial ways in order to move onto the next 'level'; this ensures that children learn the intended skills.

A preliminary evaluation of the Quest for the Golden Rule indicate that there were significant improvements in students' knowledge and attitudes in all three domains: safety and fairness in schools, social skills and strategies to cope with bullying (Rubin-Vaughan et al., 2011). The majority of students reported enjoying playing the games, which supports the universal applicability of the program. Although there were some gender differences in the modules that showed greatest improvements, overall, the Quest for the Golden Rule is effective in teaching both boys and girls bullying prevention strategies and bullying-related issues. Further research should be conducted to validate these results. For more information, see the Practi-Quest Corp website at http://practiquest.com.

Fourth R: skills for youth relationships: This is a comprehensive, school-based curriculum designed to reduce risky adolescent behaviours related to violence (bullying, dating violence), sexuality and substance use. It encourages students to focus on relationship goals, teaches students skills to build healthy relationships and helps youth make safe, responsible choices with both peers and dating partners. It has been implemented in ten provinces and territories, as well as in eighteen states. The Fourth R is delivered in the classroom by teachers who undergo a six-hour training workshop. The program is composed of twenty-one 75-minute lessons that cover three units: personal safety and injury prevention, as well as healthy growth and sexuality and substance use and abuse. The lessons and activities differ slightly for males and females to emphasise gender-specific issues. However, both curricula use video resources, role-playing exercises and handouts to increase interpersonal and problem solving skills.

A program evaluation two and a half years after implementation indicated that levels of physical dating violence were significantly lower in the intervention group than in the control group (Wolfe et al., 2009). However, there were no significant differences in the levels of physical peer violence (including bullying) between intervention and control groups. Another study reported that students who had received Fourth R training were more likely to use negotiation skills and were less likely to succumb to negative peer pressure during role play activities, as compared to control students (Wolfe et al., 2012). The Fourth R program is effective in reducing adolescent dating violence, and in building interpersonal skills; however, it lacks empirical evidence to be used exclusively as a bullying prevention program. For more information about the Fourth R, visit https://youthrelationships.org.

Bullying prevention programs in the United States

Second Step: This is a universal violence prevention program that promotes social-emotional learning and the development of social competencies and self-regulation behaviours. It aims to decrease impulsive, high-risk and aggressive behaviours and increase students' socio-emotional competence as well as academic success. It was first developed in the United States and has since been adapted for use in Canada, Australia, New Zealand, Germany, Norway and the United Kingdom.

Second Step is comprised of three developmentally appropriate programs for children in preschool/kindergarten, elementary (grades 1–5) and middle school (grades 6–8). The program consists of approximately 15 lessons that take between seven and fifty minutes, delivered in classrooms by teachers and/or other youth service providers. A Family Guide is also available for parents to provide additional support and practice of strategies learned in school.

All three programs focus on providing Empathy Training, Emotion Management, and Impulse Control and Problem Solving skills. The preschool and elementary programs cultivate self-regulation skills and social-emotional competencies, while the middle school program also addresses strategies for bullying. Although the earlier programs do not directly focus on bullying, they lay the groundwork by teaching children how to manage emotions and problem-solve peer conflicts through group discussions, modelling, coaching, role-play and practice in the classroom. The middle school program builds upon these skills to target and reduce risk factors for problematic, inappropriate behaviours, while also promoting protective factors such as positive social interactions with peers and teachers.

Although Second Step is not explicitly a bullying prevention program, social-emotional learning can be a vital and effective component in bullying prevention efforts through teaching students the skills necessary to engage with others in a prosocial manner and providing students with strategies to cope with peer conflicts (B. H. Smith and Low, 2013). By developing youths' social competence, students may be better equipped to make friends, reducing the likelihood and impact of victimisation. Moreover, empathy training and emotion management can work to empower bystanders to respond to bullying. An evaluation of Second Step by Espelage et al. (2013) found that students enrolled in schools that implemented the Second Step program were less likely to report involvement in physical aggression compared to students in control schools; however, they found no intervention effect for verbal aggression/bullying, sexual harassment or peer victimisation. Other researchers found that students in the Second Step program reported less aggression, improved social competence and prosocial behaviour, and as well, required less adult intervention in cases of peer conflict (Frey et al., 2005; Edwards et al., 2005). However, the gains made in social competence during the first year did not hold up during the second year of the program; there was no longer a significant group difference between the intervention and control groups (Frey et al., 2005). Thus, although the Second Step program is linked with significant decreases in some subtypes of aggression, and increases in positive behaviours, it has minimal effects on decreasing bullying perpetration and victimisation. For more information on the Second Step program and the Bullying Prevention Unit, visit the Committee for Children website at www.cfchildren.org.

Steps to Respect: This is a comprehensive, school-wide bullying prevention program developed for children in Grades 3 to 6. It aims to: involve school staff and increase adult awareness (monitoring) and responsiveness (intervention) to bullying incidents; instil a sense of social responsibility and agency to enact change within students; and cultivate social-emotional skills that increase students' emotional competence. It promotes a safe school environment by emphasising the need for all members of the school community to work together to recognise, report and decrease bullying. It also helps students develop positive and supportive peer relationships. Steps to Respect's school-wide program guide is instrumental in modifying school climate and attitudes towards bullying by establishing school-wide policies and procedures designed to help decrease bullying incidents.

The program's curricula are divided into three distinct grade-based levels: Level 1 is designed for students in Grades 3– 4, Level 2 for those in Grades 4–5 and Level 3 for those in Grade 5–6. There are eleven, 50-minute skill and literature-based lessons that are delivered over a 12-week period. These lessons use cognitive-behavioural techniques to establish norms of social responsibility, and encourage social-emotional behaviours (Huesmann and Guerra, 1997). Specifically, students are taught various bullying prevention skills and strategies such as recognition of different forms of bullying, assertive responding and appropriate help-seeking behaviours. Students are also trained in social-emotional skills such as empathy, perspective taking, emotion regulation skills and safe conflict resolution strategies. In addition to classroom lessons, staff training is a crucial component: all adults in the school, including teachers, principals, bus drivers and cafeteria staff, are trained to recognise and respond appropriately to bullying incidents.

An initial evaluation reported greater declines in children's observed bullying and argumentative behaviour and increases in observed agreeable interactions in students who had participated in the Steps to Respect program compared to control-group students (Frey et al., 2005). Moreover, students reported feeling a greater sense of responsibility to stand up for those being victimised, less acceptance of bullying and increased adult responsiveness (Frey et al., 2005). However, there were no differences in self-reported levels of aggression between intervention and control groups. A follow up evaluation found that overall levels of observed bullying perpetration, victimisation, destructive bystander behaviour and non-bullying aggressive behaviours significantly decreased in the intervention group compared to the control group. However, similar to the initial study, no significant changes were found in self-reported levels of bullying or victimisation (Frey et al., 2009). Another evaluation study also found no group differences between intervention and control groups in student levels of self-reported levels of victimisation or bullying perpetration, although there were significant improvements in school climate, decreased levels of physical bullying perpetration as reported by teachers and fewer school bullying-related problems (Brown et al., 2011). For more information on the Steps to Respect program, visit the Committee for Children website at www.cfchildren.org.

Safe School Ambassadors (SSA) Program: This is a student-centred, skills-based, bystander education program that aims to improve schools' social-emotional climate and reduce bullying, cyberbullying and other forms of violence in schools. SSA has been implemented in thirty-two states in the United States and in two Canadian provinces. The program (similar to KiVa, see above) specifically recruits socially influential students to reduce bullying. The program recognises the influence of peer bystanders in reinforcing aggression in children who bully, and as well as the impact bystanders can have in resolving conflicts (Craig, Pepler and Atlas, 2000; Slaby, 2005). By training student leaders in age appropriate, non-violent communication and conflict resolution and intervention skills, these Ambassadors may be able to change social norms surrounding bullying. Selected student ambassadors and adult program mentors undergo a 2-day interactive training process.

Additional support, supervision and opportunities to practice are provided regularly to ensure sustainability of the program.

An evaluation conducted two years after implementation found that male Ambassadors reported intervening in bullying incidences more frequently than did students in the control school group (Pack et al., 2011). Ambassadors' friends also reported observing more helpful interventions and fewer incidences of mistreatment. Student suspension rates in SSA program schools declined significantly over time, as well as compared to control schools. However, there were no differences in school climate between SSA program schools and control schools, and no school-wide program effects; no clear trends emerged to distinguish program schools from controls schools (Pack et al., 2011). Overall, the SSA program shows some promise in empowering students and increasing rates of bystander intervention. For more information visit http://community-matters.org/programs-and-services/safe-school-ambassadors.

The OBPP in the United States An example of an imported program is the use of the OBPP in the United States. Limber et al. (2004) reported on the South Carolina project, 1994–95, with 11 intervention schools and 28 control schools, using the OBPP with added peer community involvement measures. No significant effects were found in victim rates, but bullying rates were reduced by some 25% in intervention schools compared to some increase in control schools. Bauer, Lozano and Rivara (2007) reported on the Seattle project, 2003–5, with 10 intervention schools, and 3 control schools, using the OBPP. There were no significant main effects on victim rates, attitudes to intervene or perceptions of safety, but there was a significant improvement in intervention schools in perceptions of other students as likely to intervene. However Olweus (personal communication, 03/10/2013) has stated that encouraging results are being found in an evaluation with 300 schools and 70,000 students, followed over 2–4 years in Pennsylvania.

North America: summary There are few programs developed in North America that have empirical evidence indicating decreases in bullying and/or victimisation. Many programs that are currently implemented are imported from other countries and consequently may be limited in their effectiveness due to the cultural differences. But North America has much to learn from other countries with respect to effectively preventing and intervening in bullying and victimisation.

Interventions in Australasia

Australia

In 1994, a Federal Government inquiry into bullying recommended the development, implementation and evaluation of programs to reduce school bullying (Commonwealth Government of Australia, 1994). However, nearly a decade passed before the government acted on these recommendations; in July 2003, the National Safe Schools Framework (NSSF) was endorsed by all Australian Ministers of Education; see http://education.qld.gov.au/studentservices/behaviour/resources/nssf.html. This is discussed below.

Bullying and the Law in Australia – has anything changed? In one of the first published papers of its kind, Slee and Ford (1999, p. 38) wrote that 'In Australia, there is an urgent need for some debate and consideration of the issue of bullying and for a better understanding of the legal implications of bullying'. And in July 2013, the National Centre Against Bullying (NCAB) hosted a symposium on 'Bullying, Young People and the Law'. What, if anything, has changed in the intervening years? Leading researchers in the field (e.g., Campbell et al., 2010; Butler et al., 2011) have led the way in researching the issue.

There have been few criminal prosecutions of young people involved in school bullying and only the state of New South Wales has legislation specifically directed at bullying (Campbell et al., 2010). Key issues confronting lawmakers, education authorities and schools relate to the matter of duty of care and the age at which an individual is determined to be criminally liable for her/his actions. In Australia the age has been established at 10 years, meaning that a child under this age cannot be found criminally liable but young people 10–14 years of age may be found criminally liable if it can be proven beyond reasonable doubt that the young person knew that they should not have committed the offence. Beyond 14 years of age, the young person is deemed to have the requisite capacity and is criminally liable for his or her conduct (Campbell, Butler and Kift, 2008).

Campbell et al. (2010, p. 242) also noted that 'The law in Australia in many ways has not kept pace with advances in technology and this is true for cyberbullying'. The debate regarding the need to enact legislation addressing bullying including the emergent forms of cyberbullying takes into account whether civil and not criminal law is the path to follow, the fact that cyber offences such as stalking may already be covered by existing laws, and whether bullying is rightly considered as a disciplinary or educational matter rather than a criminal act. The most recent Federal Government policy rejected the idea of pursuing a national law against cyberbullying.

The National Safe Schools Framework The NSSF aimed to raise awareness of the importance of a shared vision of physical and emotional safety and well-being for all students in Australian schools. A study by the NSSF involving 7,418 students aged 9 to 14 years old and 453 teachers from 106 representative schools was undertaken to determine teachers' perceptions about the extent of implementation of the NSSF, their teachers' capacity to address student bullying and students' reports of bullying in their school (Cross et al., 2011). It was concluded that the NSSF required greater implementation support and that teachers required further training to implement the guidelines. While the majority of respondents (90%) reported that their school had a policy that addressed bullying, over 25% did not know its contents. Many school administrators reported anecdotally having limited time or insufficient resources to engage the whole-school community in policy development.

The Melbourne Declaration on Educational Goals for Young Australians This provided the basis for a revision of the NSSF. By way of brief background, in 2008 the 'Melbourne Declaration' was issued by the Ministerial Council on Education, Employment, Training and Youth Affairs and emphasised the goal of improving educational outcomes for all young Australians as central to the nation's social and economic prosperity and also the need to enable young people to live fulfilling, productive and responsible lives. The paper sets out goals to achieve higher standards in the Australian education system (www.mceecdya.edu.au/ verve/_resources/national_declaration_on_the_educational_goals_for_ young_australians.pdf). The Declaration informed the revised version of the NSSF and its guiding principles. The vision is underpinned by guiding principles about safe, supportive and respectful school communities. These guiding principles emphasise the importance of student safety and wellbeing as a prerequisite for effective learning in all school settings. The revised version of the NSSF was launched in 2011 by the Federal Minister for Education (http:// education.qld.gov.au/studentservices/behaviour/resources/nssf.html).

To support the framework the government annually funds the Safe and Supportive School Communities (SSSC) Committee and the associated Bullying. No way! (http://bullyingnoway.gov.au/). This national mechanism is used to share information, resources and successful practices to address bullying, harassment and violence in schools. In accordance with the NSSF, schools are encouraged to adopt evidence-based, whole-school programs to improve the social and emotional health of young people in schools. The issue of the implementation of the framework in schools and the resourcing and teacher training in bullying prevention remains a matter of ongoing concern in Australian schools. Presently there is also a lack of evidence-based anti-bullying interventions suited to the Australian school setting although Rigby (2010) has provided a comprehensive review of general approaches used in Australian schools.

New Zealand

Bullying crises as impetus for change In 2007, a number of extreme bullying incidents occurred at Greater Wellington's Hutt Valley High School. On one occasion, six students attacked nine of their classmates, throwing them to the ground, ripping their pants off and violating them with screwdrivers, pens, scissors, branches, drills and pencils. One student was beaten unconscious; another burnt with a lighter. The various processes undertaken to deal with the problem became complicated and sometimes inappropriate and ineffective. This case was not only distressing and harmful for those victimised; it was symbolic of the inability of many schools throughout New Zealand to deal with bullying and criminal violence. It resulted in a critical report by the Ombudsman (McGee, 2011) to the House of Representatives. Currently, all schools are self-governing; although having a bullying policy is not mandatory, National Administrative Guideline 5 (NAG5) states that all boards of trustees must provide a safe physical and emotional environment for their students.

Despite some damning research about bullying in New Zealand (see Chapter 3) and the Hutt Valley High School case, various organisations (e.g., NetSafe, Ministry of Education, New Zealand Police) have been proactive and creative over the last two decades in their efforts to address school bullying, albeit these approaches have been somewhat piecemeal.

Currently, there are no laws in New Zealand specific to bullying as it is not considered to be a criminal offence. Therefore, bullying behaviours are unlikely to be dealt with by police unless they are considered under the umbrella of criminal offences such as physical abuse, assault or harassment. Furthermore, the National Administrative Guideline 5 (NAG5) from the Ministry of Education requires every school's board of trustees to provide a safe physical and emotional environment for students, but schools are not required to have a specific anti-bullying policy (see Chapter 3).

In May 2012 New Zealand's chief coroner proposed law changes targeting cyberbullying, arguing that bullying by text messaging or on social media sites was contributing to New Zealand's high rate of youth suicide, that it was often a background factor in suicide cases before coroners, of attempted suicides, and of incidents of self-harm. In response, the Minister of Justice directed the Law Commission to write a position paper on cyberbullying. The document *Harmful Digital Communications: The adequacy of the current sanctions and remedies, Wellington, August 2012* was the response. The subsequent *Harmful Digital Communications Act* came into force in 2015 and includes penalties for inciting suicide, even if that other person does not commit or attempt to commit suicide (up to 3 years jail) and for causing harm by digital communication (up to 2 years jail or a fine of up to $50,000).

Anti-bullying initiatives In the early 1990's three major anti-bullying initiatives were developed in New Zealand: The Ministry of Education's *Managing Anger: Eliminating Violence;* The New Zealand Police's *Kia Kaha*; and The Peace Federation of Aotearoa's *Cool Schools Peer Mediation Program.* The latter two are still in use and are examined here.

Kia Kaha: This program aims to increase assertiveness and self-esteem in students and was launched in 1992. The program is comprised of four separate age-related kits containing a range of useful paper and ICT resources that explain the nature of bullying and how to deal with it. These lessons are implemented by classroom teachers. All teachers involved in *Kia Kaha* have the opportunity to plan with the Police Education Officer and determine the dates and times of their *Kia Kaha* lessons. Overall, the program focuses on improving self-esteem and assertiveness in students. Critical evaluations of *Kia Kaha* (see Sullivan 1998, 2005; Raskauskas, 2007) have made suggestions for improvements to the program. As a result, the New Zealand Police have modified and improved *Kia Kaha* (www.police.govt.nz/advice/personal-and-commu nity-advice/school-portal/resources/successful-relationships/kia-kaha)

Cool Schools Peer Mediation Program: This program teaches children and young people how to assess and resolve conflict and to then practice what they have learned as peer mediators in their schools. The program involves a whole-staff training day where teachers are expected to learn skills to then utilize in their classrooms. Following staff training, student peer-mediators are chosen through an application process; the student peer-mediators are then trained to assist their peers in conflict resolution. The Ministry of Education (Murrow et al., 2004) carried out an evaluation of seventeen schools that were using *Cool Schools* and found that generally teachers and students were positive about the program and as staff gained experience, their effectiveness in addressing the problems improved. They also noted that being well prepared led to greater success and the program appeared most effective in reducing student conflict when integrated into the school's behaviour management plan. Furthermore, *Cool Schools* was found to be particularly effective when used as a mediation tool in low-SES schools. However, when commitment and expectations varied amongst teachers, this was shown to be a barrier to the program's success in some schools (www.peace.net.nz/index.php?pageID=24).

Current developments It is possible that significant and nationally mandated progress has been thwarted by the independence of New Zealand schools. For example, although the arguments to change education law so that all schools were required to have a bullying policy were very strong, particularly in light of the stance of the educational unions and the Ombudsman, they did not succeed. However, despite this setback, what has been emerging is a strong, multi-faceted voice providing direction, creative ideas and constructive processes and frameworks for addressing school bullying.

As an example of this collective voice the Human Rights Commissioner initiated the cross-sector Bullying Prevention Advisory Group in 2013, which included representatives from a number of government departments, advisory groups, teacher's associations and NGOs. The group produced a publication called *Bullying Prevention and Response: A Guide for Schools* (2014). The document has been situated as part of the Ministry of Education's Positive Behaviour for Learning initiative (http://pb4l.tki.org.nz) and a copy of the report has been sent to every public school in New Zealand. It remains to be seen what sort of impact, if any, this comprehensive guideline will have on bullying within New Zealand.

However given New Zealand's relatively small population and single government, once momentum builds there is the potential to have a national impact. For example, in response to a call for more in-service training for teachers in the area of bullying prevention (Green et al., 2013), Accent Learning (professional development unit and part of Victoria University of Wellington) has formulated an agreement with Professor Christina Salmivalli (University of Turku, Finland) to implement the KiVa program in New Zealand schools.

Australasia: summary There are important differences in how the issue has been addressed in Australia and New Zealand. Australia is one of the few countries in the world to have in place a national framework (National Safe Schools Framework) within which to consider the issue of the bullying of young people in our schools. However, a great deal more remains to be done particularly around the key issues of pre-service teacher training that properly address the issue of bullying and the links between bullying and poor mental health outcomes. In contrast, although New Zealand's approach to addressing bullying to date has been persistent and creative it has suffered from a lack of national support. However, recent developments including the cross-sector advisory group and the assent of the *Harmful Digital Communications Act (2015)* signify a move in the right direction.

Overviews and meta-analyses of large-scale interventions

There have been several reviews and meta-analyses of anti-bullying program evaluations. Ttofi and Farrington (2011) reported a meta-analysis of 44 school-based intervention programs carried out over some 25 years; these were international, but all coming from Europe, North America and Australasia, except for one from South Africa. They found that on average, the programs reduced bullying others by around 20–23% and victimisation by around 17–20%. Ttofi and Farrington also examined, across programs, which program components were most associated with success. For reducing bullying rates, these were parent training/meetings, improved playground supervision, disciplinary methods, school conferences, information for parents, classroom rules, classroom management and teacher training. For reducing victim rates, these were use of videos, disciplinary methods, parent training/meetings and cooperative group work; however, work with peers was associated with a significant increase in victimisation.

Their overall conclusion of reductions of around 20% or more appears a robust finding, and quite encouraging. The conclusions drawn about individual component effectiveness are important, but may be less robust. Smith, Salmivalli and Cowie (2012) argued that their analysis was (inevitably) limited historically in that methods of intervention have been and still are being developed and changed. They also queried the conclusion about the ineffectiveness of work with peers (which may depend very much on what kind of peer support is used), and also a conclusion that programs worked better with older children (which is contrary to experience with OBPP and KiVA, and seems to have arisen from between-program rather than within-program comparisons).

Conclusions

Over the last two decades a range of anti-bullying interventions have become available, and are disseminated and widely employed, in schools in western industrialised countries. Reviews suggest that these have had some success and are worthwhile in terms of reducing suffering and ultimately enhancing school climate and good citizenship. There is still much to be learnt, particularly about the effectiveness of specific intervention components. One area of continuing controversy is the relative effectiveness of more sanctions-based or disciplinary approaches, compared to non-punitive approaches (with restorative approaches perhaps located between these). Another area of debate is whether we should pursue 'bullying-focussed' solutions, or work generally on relationships and school climate and improve 'convivencia' – a Spanish word that is the opposite of bullying and implies respect and co-existence. Finally, cyberbullying provides new challenges, as being a relatively new form of bullying with its own characteristics and somewhat different modes of effective intervention (see Mora-Merchan and Jäger, 2010). Although evaluations of interventions for cyberbullying help schools and organisations to develop more effective e-safety resources, the biggest challenge is to keep up with the rapid speed of evolution of new technologies; social networks and apps.

Despite continuing challenges, school bullying is an area where research and practice have gone hand in hand over recent years, with good evidence that the outcomes have improved pupil well-being and happiness.

REFERENCES

Banerjee, R., Robinson, C. and Smalley, D. (2010). *Evaluation of the beatbullying peer mentoring program*. Report for Beatbullying. Falmer: University of Sussex.

Bauer, N. S., Lozano, P. and Rivara, F. P. (2007). The effectiveness of the Olweus bullying prevention program in public middle schools: A controlled trial. *Journal of Adolescent Health*, 40, 266–274.

Blatchford, P. (1998). *Social life in school: Pupils' experiences of breaktime and recess from 6 to 16*. London: Routledge.

Boulton, M. J. and Flemington, I. (1996). The effects of a short video intervention on secondary school pupils' involvement in definitions of and attitudes towards bullying. *School Psychology International* 17, 331–345.

Bowles, R., Reyes, M. G. and Pradiptyo, R. (2005). *Safer schools partnerships*. Report for the Youth Justice Board. York: University of York.

Brown, E. C., Low, S., Smith, B. H. and Haggerty, K. P. (2011). Outcomes from a school-randomized controlled trial of Steps to Respect: A Bullying Prevention Program. *School Psychology Review*, 40, 423–443.

Butler, D., Kift, S., Campbell, M., Slee, P. T. and Spears, B. (2011). School policy responses to cyberbullying: An Australian legal perspective. *International Journal of Law and Education*, 16, 7–28.

Campbell, M. A., Butler, D. and Kift, S. (2008). A school's duty to provide a safe learning environment: Does this include cyberbullying? *Australian and New Zealand Journal of Law and Education*, 13, 21–32.

Campbell, M. A., Cross, D., Spears, B. and Slee, P. (2010). *Cyberbullying- legal implications for schools*. CSE Occasional Paper, 118. Melbourne: CSE.

Commonwealth of Australia (1994). *Sticks and stones: A report on violence in schools*. Canberra: Australian Government Publishing Service. http://catalogue.nla.gov.au/Record/143978

Cowie, H. and Smith, P. K. (2010). Peer support as a means of improving school safety and reducing bullying and violence. In Doll, B., Pfohl, W. and Yoon, J. (Eds.), *Handbook of youth prevention science* (pp. 177–193). New York: Routledge.

Cowie, H., Smith, P. K., Boulton, M. J. and Laver, R. (1994). *Co-operative group work in the multi-ethnic classroom*. London: David Fulton,

Craig, W. M., Pepler, D. J. and Atlas, R. (2000). Observations of bullying in the playground and in the classroom. *School of Psychology International*, 21, 22–36.

Cross, D., Epstein, M., Hearn, L., Slee, P. T., Shaw, T., Monks, H. and Schwartz, T. (2011). National safe schools framework: Policy and practice to reduce bullying in Australian schools. *International Journal of Behavioural Development*, 35, 398–404.

Davidson, J, Martellozzo, E. and Lorenz, M. (2009). *Report 2: Evaluation of CEOP ThinkUKnow Internet Safety Program and Exploration of Young People's Internet Safety Knowledge*. Kingston University.

DCSF (2007). *Safe to learn: Embedding anti-bullying work in schools*. London: Department of Children, Schools and Families.

DfE (1994). *Bullying: Don't suffer in silence: An anti-bullying pack for schools*. London: HMSO.

(2013). *Preventing and tackling bullying: Advice for head teachers, staff and governing bodies*. Available online at www.education.gov.uk/publications ref: DFE-00292–2013

DfES (2nd edn. 2000; revised 2002). *Bullying: Don't suffer in silence. An anti-bullying pack for schools*. London: HMSO.

Education and Inspections Act (2006). London: HMSO. Available at www.legislation.gov.uk/ukpga/2006/40/contents

Edwards, D., Hunt, M. H., Meyers, J., Grogg, K. R. and Jarrett, O. (2005). Acceptability and student outcomes of a violence prevention curriculum. *Journal of Primary Prevention*, 26, 401–418.

Eisner, M. and Malti, T. (2012). The future of research on evidence-based developmental violence prevention in Europe – Introduction to the focus section. *International Journal of Conflict and Violence*, 6, 166–175.

Espelage, D. L., Low, S., Polanin, J. R. and Brown, E. C. (2013). The impact of a middle school program to reduce aggression, victimization, and sexual violence. *Journal of Adolescent Health*, 53, 180–186.

Fekkes, M., Pijpers, F. I. M. and Verloove-Vanhorick, P. S. (2006). Effects of antibullying school program on bullying and health complaints. *Archives of Pediatrics and Adolescent Medicine*, 160, 638–644.

Frey, K. S., Nolen, S. B., Edstrom, L. V. and Hirschstein, M. K. (2005). Effects of a school-based social-emotional competence program: Linking children's goals, attributions, and behavior. *Journal of Applied Developmental Psychology*, 26, 171–200.

Frey, K. S., Hirschstein, M. K., Edstrom, L. V. and Snell, J. L. (2009). Observed reductions in school bullying, nonbullying aggression, and destructive bystander behavior: A longitudinal evaluation. *Journal of Educational Psychology*, 101, 466–481.

Frey, K. S., Hirschstein, M. K., Snell, J. L., Edstrom, L. V., MacKenzie, E. P. and Broderick, C. J. (2005). Reducing playground bullying and supporting beliefs: An experimental trial of the Steps to Respect program. *Developmental Psychology*, 41, 479–491.

Green, V. A., Harcourt, S., Mattioni, L., & Prior, T. (2013). *Bullying in New Zealand schools: A final report*. Wellington, New Zealand: Victoria University of Wellington. Retrieved Nov 9, 2015 from www.victoria.ac.nz/education/ pdf/Bullying-in-NZ-Schools.pdf

Hanewinkel, R. (2004). Prevention of bullying in German schools: An evaluation of an anti-bullying approach. In P. K. Smith, D. Pepler and K. Rigby (Eds.), *Bullying in schools: How successful can interventions be?* (pp. 81–97). Cambridge: Cambridge University Press.

Harmful Digital Communications Act, No. 63. (2015). Retrieved Nov 12, 2015 from www.legislation.govt.nz/act/public/2015/0063/latest/whole.html

Hoglund, W., Hosan, N. and Leadbeater, B. (2012). Using your WITS: A 6-year follow-up of a peer victimization prevention program. *School Psychology Review*, 41, 193–214.

Houlston, C. and Smith, P. K. (2009). The impact of a peer counseling scheme to address bullying in an all-girl London secondary school: A short-term longitudinal study. *British Journal of Educational Psychology*, 79, 69–86.

Houlston, C., Smith, P. K. and Jessel, J. (2009). Investigating the extent and use of peer support initiatives in English schools. *Educational Psychology*, 29, 325–344.

Huesmann, L. R. and Guerra, N. G. (1997). Children's normative beliefs about aggression and aggressive behavior. *Journal of Personality and Social Psychology*, 72, 408–419.

Huitsing, G. and Veenstra, R. (2012). Bullying in classrooms: participant roles from a social network perspective, *Aggressive Behavior*, 38, 494–509.

Humphrey, N., Kalambouka, A., Bolton, J., Lendrum, A., Wigelsworth, M., Leenie, C. and Farrell, P. (2008). *Primary social and emotional aspects of learning (SEAL): Evaluation of small group work*. DCSF RB064. London: DCSF.

Humphrey, N., Lendrum, A. and Wigelsworth, M. (2010). *Social and emotional aspects of learning (SEAL) program in secondary schools: A national evaluation. DFE-RB049.* London: DfE.

Hasebrink, U. (2014). *Children's changing online experiences in a longitudinal perspective.* London: EU Kids Online. www.eukidsonline.net

IOM (Institute of Medicine) and NRC (National Research Council) (2014). *Building capacity to reduce bullying: Workshop summary.* Washington, DC: The National Academies Press.

Kärnä, A., Voeten, M., Little, T., Poskiparta, E., Kaljonen, A. and Salmivalli, C. (2011a). A large-scale evaluation of the KiVa anti-bullying program: Grades 4–6. *Child Development*, 82, 311–330.

Kärnä, A., Voeten, M., Little, T., Alanen, E., Poskiparta, E. and Salmivalli, C. (2011b). Going to scale: A nonrandomized nationwide trial of the KiVa antibullying program for comprehensive schools. *Journal of Consulting and Clinical Psychology*, 79, 796–805.

Kärnä, A., Voeten, M., Little, T., Alanen, E., Poskiparta, E., and Salmivalli, C. (2012). Effectiveness of the KiVa antibullying program: Grades 1–3 and 7–9. *Journal of Educational Psychology*, 105, 535–551.

Leadbeater, B., Hoglund, W. and Woods, T. (2003). Changing contexts? The effects of a primary prevention program on classroom levels of peer relational and physical victimization. *Journal of Community Psychology*, 31, 397–418.

Leadbeater, B. and Sukhawathanakul, P. (2011). Multicomponent programs for reducing peer victimization in early elementary school: A longitudinal evaluation of the WITS Primary program. *Journal of Community Psychology*, 39, 606–620.

Limber, S. P., Nation, M., Tracy, A. J., Melton, G. B. and Flerx, V. (2004). Implementation of the Olweus Bullying Prevention Program in the Southeastern United States. In P. K. Smith, D. Pepler and K. Rigby (Eds.), *Bullying in schools: How successful can interventions be?* (pp. 55–79). Cambridge: Cambridge University Press.

Livingstone, S., Haddon, L., Görzig, A. and Ólafsson, K. (2011). *EU Kids Online II: Final Report.* LSE, London: EU Kids Online.

McGee, D. (Ombudsman) (2011). Complaints arising out of bullying at Hutt Valley High School in December 2007. (*Presented to the House of Representatives, 2011*). Retrieved November 6, 2015 from www.ombudsman.parliament.nz/resources-and-publications/latest-reports

Melbourne Declaration of Educational Goals for Young People (2008). *Ministerial Council on Education, Employment, Training and Youth.* Carlton: Victoria.

Menesini, E., Nocentini, A. and Palladino, B. E. (2012). Empowering students against bullying and cyberbullying: Evaluation of an Italian peer-led model. *International Journal of Conflict and Violence*, 6, 313–320.

Mora-Merchan, J. and Jäger, T. (Eds.) (2010). *Cyberbullying: A cross-national comparison.* Landau: Verlag Emprische Padagogik.

Murrow, K., Kalafatelis, E., Fryer, M., Ryan, N. and Dowden, A. (2004). *Report to the Ministry of Education: An evaluation of three programs in the innovations funding pool - Cool schools*, Wellington: Research Division of the Ministry of Education.

Netsafe: The Internet Safety Group. (2005). *The text generation: Mobile phones and New Zealand youth*. Auckland: Netsafe www.cyberbullying.org.nz/

Ofsted (2003). *Bullying: Effective action in secondary schools*. London: OFSTED.
(2012). The framework for school inspection: Guidance and grade descriptors for schools in England under section 5 of the Education Act, from January 2012. Ref: 090019. www.ofsted.gov.uk/resources/110128

Olweus, D. (1999). Sweden. In Smith, P. K., Morita, Y., Junger-Tas, J., Olweus, D., Catalano, R. and Slee, P. (Eds.), *The nature of school bullying: A cross-national perspective* (pp. 7–27). London and New York: Routledge.

Olweus, D. and Limber, S. (2010). The Olweus Bullying Prevention Program: implementation and evaluation over two decades. In S. Jimerson, S. Swearer and D. Espelage (Eds.), *Handbook of bullying in schools: An international perspective* (pp. 377–401). New York: Routledge.

Pack, C., White, A., Racynski, K. and Wang, A. (2011). Evaluation of the Safe School Ambassadors Program: A student-led approach to reducing mistreatment and bullying in schools. *Clearing House*, 84, 127–133.

Paul, S., Smith, P. K. and Blumberg, H. H. (2012). Revisiting cyberbullying in schools using the Quality Circle approach. *School Psychology International*, 33, 492–504.

Pikas, A. (1989). A pure concept of mobbing gives the best results for treatment. *School Psychology International*, 10, 95–104.
(2002). New developments of the Shared Concern Method. *School Psychology International*, 23, 307–336.

Raskauskas, J. (2007) *Evaluation of the Kia Kaha Anti Bullying Program for students in years 5–8*. Wellington: New Zealand Police.

Rigby, K. and Griffiths, C. (2010). *Applying the method of shared concern in Australian schools: An evaluative study*. Canberra: Department of Education, Employment and Workplace Relations. www.deewr.gov.au/schooling/nationalsafeschools/pages/research.aspx

Rigby, K. and Smith, P. K. (2011). Is school bullying really on the rise? *Social Psychology of Education*, 14, 441–455.

Robinson, G. and Maines, B. (2007). *Bullying: A complete guide to the Support Group Method*. Bristol: Lucky Duck Publishing.

Rubin-Vaughan, A., Pepler, D., Brown, S. and Craig, W. (2011). Quest for the Golden Rule: An effective social skills promotion and bullying prevention program. *Computers and Education*, 56, 166–175.

Salmivalli, C., Kärnä, A. and Poskiparta, E. (2010). From peer putdowns to peer support: A theoretical model and how it translated into a national anti-bullying program. In S. Jimerson, S. Swearer and D. Espelage (Eds.), *Handbook of bullying in schools: An international perspective* (pp. 441–454). New York: Routledge.

Samara, M. and Smith, P. K. (2008). How schools tackle bullying, and the use of whole school policies: changes over recent years. *Educational Psychology*, 28, 663–676.

Sapouna, M., Wolke, D., Vannani, N., Watson, S., Woods, S., Schneider, W., Enz, S., Hall, L., Paiva, A., Andre, E., Dautenhahn, K. and Aylett, R. (2009). Virtual learning intervention to reduce bullying victimization in primary school: A controlled trial. *Journal of Child Psychology and Psychiatry*, 51, 104–112.

Sellman, E., Cremin, H. and McCluskey, G. (Eds.), (2013). *Restorative approaches to conflict in schools: Interdisciplinary perspectives on whole school approaches to managing relationships*. London: Routledge.

Slaby, R. G. (2005). The role of the bystander in preventing bullying. *Health in Action*, 3(6). http://hhd.org/sites/hhd.org/files/bystander.pdf.

Slee, P. T. and Ford, D. (1999). Bullying is a serious issue – it is a crime! *Australian and New Zealand Journal of Education and Law*, 4, 23–39.

Smith, B. H. and Low, S. (2013). The role of social-emotional learning in bullying prevention efforts. *Theory Into Practice* 52, 280–287.

Smith, P. K., Cowie, H. and Sharp, S. (1994). Working directly with pupils involved in bullying situations. In P. K. Smith and S. Sharp (Eds.), *School bullying: Insights and perspectives* (pp. 193–212). London: Routledge.

Smith, P. K., Howard, S. and Thompson, F. (2007). Use of the Support Group Method to tackle bullying, and evaluation from schools and local authorities in England. *Pastoral Care in Education*, 25, 4–13.

Smith, P. K., Kupferberg, A., Mora-Merchan, J. A., Samara, M., Bosley, S. and Osborn, R. (2012). A content analysis of school anti-bullying policies: A follow-up after six years. *Educational Psychology in Practice*, 28, 61–84.

Smith, P. K., Salmivalli, C. and Cowie, H. (2012). Effectiveness of school-based programs to reduce bullying: a commentary. *Journal of Experimental Criminology*, 8, 433–441.

Smith, P. K., Pepler, D. J. and Rigby, K. (Eds.) (2004). *Bullying in schools: How successful can interventions be?* Cambridge: Cambridge University Press.

Smith, P. K. and Sharp, S. (Eds.) (1994). *School bullying: Insights and perspectives*. London: Routledge.

Spiel, C., Salmivalli, C. and Smith, P. K. (2011). Translational research: national strategies for violence prevention in school. *International Journal of Behavioral Development*, 35, 381–382.

Strohmeier, D. and Noam, G. G. (Eds.) (2012). Evidence-based bullying prevention programs for children and youth. *New Directions for Youth Development*, 133, Spring (whole issue).

Sullivan, K. (1998). *An Evaluation of Kia Kaha, the New Zealand Police's resource kit about bullying for students, teachers and parents*. Wellington: New Zealand Police.

    (2005). *A critique and formative evaluation of Kia Kaha: Our place, the New Zealand Police's anti-bullying program for secondary schools*. Wellington: New Zealand Police.

Thompson, F., Robinson, S. and Smith, P. K. (2013). An evaluation of some cyberbullying interventions in England. In M. L. Genta, A. Brighi and A. Guarini (Eds.), *Cyberbullismo: Ricerche e strategie di intervento (Cyberbullying: Research and intervention strategies)* (pp. 136–153). Milano: Franco Angeli.

Thompson, F. and Smith, P. K. (2011). *The use and effectiveness of anti-bullying strategies in schools*. DFE-RR098. London: DfE.

Ttofi, M. M. and Farrington, D.P. (2011). Effectiveness of school-based programs to reduce bullying: a systematic and meta-analytic review. *Journal of Experimental Criminology*, 7, 27–56.

Wolfe, D. A., Crooks, C., Jaffe, P., Chiodo, D., Hughes, R., Ellis, W., Sitt, L. and Donner, A. (2009). A school-based program to prevent adolescent dating violence. *Pediatrics and Adolescent Medicine*, 163, 692–699.

Wolfe, D. A., Crooks, C. V., Chiodo, D., Hughes, R. and Ellis, W. (2012). Observations of adolescent peer resistance skills following a classroom-based healthy relationship program: A post-intervention comparison. *Prevention Science*, 13, 196–205.

Young, S. (1998). The Support Group approach to bullying in schools. *Educational Psychology in Practice*, 14, 32–39.

Youth Justice Board (2004). *National evaluation of the restorative justice in schools program*. Youth Justice Board Publication, Number D61. London: Youth Justice Board.

16   Actions against *ijime* and *net-ijime* in Japan

Tomoyuki Kanetsuna and Yuichi Toda

The history of actions on *ijime* in Japan started back in 1985, rather independently from the rest of the world. The first research studies followed a tragic chain of suicides of children, who claimed in their suicide notes that being victims of *ijime* had led them to take their own lives. These suicides gave the society a huge shock and put a spotlight on the ferocious nature of *ijime*, which came to be seen as one of the biggest social problems in Japan (for more detail, see Chapter 4). This was the beginning of three decades of activity. Since then, there have been a large number of studies aiming to uncover its nature, and different attempts to tackle the problems by the government, local boards of education, schools and academics.

In this chapter, we introduce major actions taken by the government over the last thirty years, and some recent actions taken by local boards of education as well as by individual schools and academics against *ijime* and *net-ijime* (cyberbullying) in Japan. We also discuss a number of agendas and implications that should be addressed for future studies and practices.

Actions by the Government

Initially, major attempts by the government were centred on a series of official meetings held by the Ministry of Education, Culture, Sports, Science and Technology (MEXT) who gave suggestions, appeals and orders to local prefectural governors, local boards of education and individual schools.

The MEXT first convened an expert meeting on problematic behaviour of children in 1985 so as to deal with the serious situation of the *ijime* problem. This expert meeting aimed to examine the actual conditions of *ijime* at school and to discuss long-term and comprehensive solutions to the problem. However, in view of the urgency of the situation, they decided to release an immediate appeal to everyone involved in education. In this appeal, some basic understandings concerning *ijime* were put forward, namely that *ijime* is:

(1) a serious problem that strongly and negatively influences children both physically and psychologically;
(2) closely associated with psychological weakness of children today;
(3) often rooted in peer relationships at school, and thus teachers' guidance is very important;
(4) strongly related to family relationships and thus parental discipline is very important; and
(5) in order to tackle the *ijime* problem, both immediate steps and long-term measures are needed.

Besides these five basic shared understandings, the MEXT proposed a clear definition of *ijime*, and a strong policy against it: 'it is never ever tolerated for one person to inflict *ijime* on another' (MEXT, 1985). Furthermore, based on these understandings, a number of priority policies were presented to tackle the problem by schools, local boards of education and parents and family members. In this year (1985), the government for the first time added *ijime*-related items to their 'annual fact finding survey on problematic behaviour in schools', so as to examine the actual conditions of *ijime* at school. After these actions by the MEXT, the decreasing figures found in their annual surveys from the late 1980s to the early 1990s led people to think that the *ijime* problem had subsided; though some experts issued a warning to society not to be too optimistic about the situation and to make continuing efforts to reduce *ijime* (e.g., Taki, 1992).

As though these warnings by some experts were justified, the problem of *ijime* once again caught people's attention from 1994 to 1995, following tragic suicides of children due to *ijime*; this has been considered as the second phase of *ijime* movement in Japanese society (Morita, 2006). During this period, the government once again held official meetings and conferences of experts to discuss measures to tackle the *ijime* problem, and a number of suggestions, appeals and comprehensive guidelines were released (MEXT, 1994; 1995; 1996a, b). In these appeals and guidelines, the government particularly emphasised two important points. Firstly, they stressed that *ijime* can be found in any class of any school, so that schools should never assume that there would be no *ijime* in their school. This was important because, in order to avoid damaging their reputation, schools had long been reluctant to or negative about reporting *ijime* cases to local boards of education, and this tendency for schools to keep quiet about *ijime* cases made it even more difficult to tackle the problem.

Secondly, the government stressed that 'perpetrating *ijime* behavior must not be allowed by any means, and schools should always consider matters from the victims' side' (MEXT, 1995). This announcement was important, as schools had long been negative about questioning perpetrators over the responsibility for their *ijime* behaviour, and they put more effort on saving or caring for the victims of *ijime* rather than imposing punishment on behaviours of perpetrators (Morita, 2006). One of the examples of this trend is the introduction of school counsellors. In 1995, the government started sending school counsellors mainly to local state junior-high schools to help students – not only for dealing with *ijime* problems but also for handling various other problems. At the beginning, about 150 schools had school counsellors, but today more than 10,000 schools have school counsellors on a regular basis. However, there was an argument within society that this emphasis just on saving the victims needed more reflection, and the government started to stress the need to implement more thorough and severe guidance against perpetrators of *ijime* (Morita, 2006).

The third phase of the *ijime* problem came about ten years later, from around 2006 to 2007, again when a chain of child suicides caught the attention of people and the mass media, which have played an important role to make people aware the problem of *ijime*. At the same time, because of the rapid and widespread growth of mobile phone use and internet access among school children, the problem of cyberbullying or *net-ijime* also became a focus of attention. In these years, a number of official meetings and conferences of experts were once again held, and urgent appeals, policies and guidelines were again sent to local boards of education and individual schools (MEXT, 2006a,b,c,d). The contents of these appeals and guidelines were very similar to those previously proposed in the mid-1990s. However, the recommended actions against perpetrators became more severe, including punitive measures such as in- and out-of-school suspensions; though these severe measures against perpetrators of *ijime* brought on a debate over the pros and cons of such an approach. In addition, the guidelines proposed during these years included recommended actions against *net-ijime* including implementation of internet and media literacy education to school children (e.g. MEXT, 2007; 2008).

In October 2011 a tragic suicide case of a junior-high school boy in Shiga prefecture, due to his being a victim of severe *ijime*, again caught the public and media attention. This case, however, drew public attention not only due to the severity of the *ijime*, but also because of the negative response of the school and the local board of education, who were considered to be trying to cover the case up from the public eye. Following another huge debate on the topic in society after this case, the MEXT proposed an 'Anti-*ijime* Action Plan' in September 2012. This was followed by the enactment of an 'Act of Promotion of Bullying Prevention' in June 2013 and the development of a 'Basic National Policy on Bullying Prevention' in October 2013 (MEXT, 2012; 2013a, b). These recent series of actions against *ijime* by the government could be seen as a reflection of what they overlooked or learned from the previous thirty years history of activity. What they had done about *ijime* during that long period was mostly limited to notifications and announcements to the local boards of education and school governors; the creation of specific measures to implement in schools was entrusted to individual schools (MEXT, 2012). Taking this reflection as a stepping-stone to more successful prevention and intervention against *ijime*, the new Action Plan emphasised an active involvement of the government by strengthening cooperation with relevant organisations. The Action Plan included:

(1) the establishment of an advisory committee for *ijime* within the Ministry, consisting of a number of experts from various fields including lawyers, psychiatrists, ex-police officers and academic researchers;
(2) the establishment of support teams for *ijime* within the local boards of education, again consisting of a number of experts from various different fields;
(3) improving systems for support and counselling of children by increasing the number of school counsellors and school social workers dispatched to schools; and
(4) the revision of rules and systems related to the problem of *ijime*, particularly strengthening cooperation with external organisations including the police and social welfare services (MEXT, 2012).

As this Action Plan, along with the 'Act of Promotion of Bullying Prevention' and the 'Basic National Policy of Bullying Prevention' have recently been implemented, local prefectural governors, boards of educations, as well as individual schools all over Japan are now trying hard to organise the action teams and to develop each level of basic policy for *ijime* prevention, as required by the National Policy and the Act of Promotion of Bullying Prevention. An evaluation of these actions by the government has not yet been conducted, and there is a need to carefully track the effects of these actions.

Actions against *ijime* at school

As discussed so far, for the last three decades the concrete actions against *ijime* at school have mostly been entrusted to individual schools. As a result, schools have been trying various psycho-educational programs, mostly imported from western countries (such as assertiveness training, social skills education and stress management). However, particularly in the earlier years, these programs were often transplanted into classes without adequate checks or modification to see if they fitted in with the system and climate of schools in Japan. This often resulted in such programs not being as effective as expected. Furthermore, because these programs were implemented by influential researchers and practitioners, conflicts sometimes happened between groups recommending different programs and approaches. In some regions, a local board of education would try to implement a certain program into every school in their jurisdiction; yet often, despite huge efforts by teachers, it worked only for a few years, and then evoked complaints by a majority of teachers against the top-down implementation by the local board of education.

It is clearly important to consider carefully the preparation of a sequence and combination of practices suitable to Japanese school systems, and to the climates of individual schools and classes. Taki (2002) presented an oblique model, which classified individual school practices into a matrix with two oblique dimensions: 'teacher-led vs. student-led' approaches, and 'intervention vs. prevention'. Student-led prevention and intervention are often found to be difficult to implement, for students themselves as well as for teachers and school staff, yet their impacts are often found to last longer and to be more effective than teacher-led practices. One of the most difficult but important issues to be considered about student-led approaches is how to guarantee the implementation of children's initiatives. As one teacher said: 'If we teachers change students' decisions after letting them decide, they don't trust us nor think independently anymore. That's why we staff discuss thoroughly which aspects are to be decided by students before letting them think and decide'.

In addition to the above two dimensions put forward by Taki (2002), we would like to propose two more practice dimensions: 'class-based vs. school-based (inter-class-based) vs. inter-school-based', and 'sporadic vs. systematic'.

Ijime in Japan is often described as a group phenomenon, in which students belonging to the same social group, like a class at school, use *ijime* as a tool to maintain their group cohesiveness (see also Chapter 4). Morita and Kiyonaga (1986; 1994) explained this as 'the interaction process of homogeneity within a class' whereby students who do not share the same values, attitudes, interests or social background with other children in the class, will be labelled as 'heterogeneous' and targeted as victims of *ijime*. In such an environment, perpetrators of *ijime* often find themselves as enforcers of 'justice' and believe that they have the right to enforce sanctions against such 'outsiders'. This in turn strengthens the reluctance of the targeted victim to seek help; this is because of the difficulty in finding external help as well as the fear of the on-going *ijime* getting even worse (Kanetsuna, Smith and Morita, 2006). Furthermore, the reluctance of other members of the group to intervene in the situation or to inform the class-teacher would be strengthened, since such *ijime* behaviour often quickly spreads to the whole classroom, and it becomes one of the temporary fashions of the class.

At this stage, other non-involved members of the class find themselves under pressure to choose which side they stand by. The answer is most likely to be the perpetrators. Thus, an important question is how to create a situation whereby those defenders who wish to help victims can do so safely, without any risk of becoming a new target of *ijime*. This can partly be managed by strengthening the 'anonymity' of the actions against *ijime*. For example, school-based actions would be more anonymous than class-based actions, because it would be difficult for perpetrators to identify the defenders of the victim. In this sense, inter-school-based practices would be even better.

However, as discussed above, schools are often made to try independently to follow the national policies, guidelines and appeals. As a result, many actions and practices implemented over the last three decades lapsed into something imported, teacher-led, class-based and sporadic. For more effective prevention and intervention against *ijime*, we should set out to implement actions that are originally designed for the systems and climates of schools and classes in Japan, and that should be more student-based and school-based or even inter-school-based, and be designed as more systematic in their implementation.

One of the major practices against *ijime* at school in Japan is 'peer support scheme' (Toda, 2005; Toda and Ito, 2005). Among various types of peer support (peer counselling, peer mediation, peer tutoring, etc; see also Chapter 10), Kawata (1996) introduced an original Japanese type of peer support named 'On Paper Method' or 'Q&A Handout Method' implemented in a junior high school in Kanazawa city. Following this practice by Kawata, Toda (2005) implemented the 'Q&A Handout Method' to a linked elementary and junior high school in Tottori Prefecture. In this Tottori practice, the members of the peer support team were constituted from both elementary and junior high school students, and because of this vertical or multi-age inter-school-based approach it is even more anonymous compared to the original Q&A Handout Method by Kawata which was a single school approach.

In this Tottori method, very similar to the one by Kawata, students are allowed to write their concerns anonymously or using a pen-name and post them into a box, which will be opened by teachers who are responsible for the activity, usually a school nurse and a few other supporting teachers. This group of teachers read and decide whether the concern should be handed to peer supporters, or handled by teachers due to its urgency and/or severity. If sharing the concern is regarded as safe and useful for the students, the teachers rewrite the original message to conceal the handwriting and private information, and hand it to a group of peer supporters. The peer supporters then read and write their replies to the concerns reflecting their own experiences and opinions, under the careful supervision of the supporting teachers. The replies that are judged adequate are printed on the Q&A handout to be delivered to all members of the school (Toda, Nishiumi and Yoshida, 2003). This method tries to share concerns and advice within the school in order to nurture an attitude of mutual support in the community.

This Q&A Handout Method can be considered as a 'program-oriented' practice, which is expected to be repeatedly implemented in various different school and class settings. In other words, this is a 'whenever, wherever, and whoever' practice. A 'project-oriented' practice, on the other hand, can be considered as a 'one-off and order-made' practice for a particular setting. As such, it is not expected to be widely distributed but focuses more on solving a problem that a particular school or a class is faced with. This 'program vs. project' dimension is related to the 'systematic vs. sporadic' dimension. As discussed above, a program-oriented approach is expected to be implemented in various different settings and it should therefore be more systematic in organisation, while project-oriented approach is a 'one-off' practice and should therefore be sporadic in nature.

An example of such a 'project-oriented' practice was reported by Kanetsuna and Toda (submitted). This project was conducted at a junior-high school in Hyogo prefecture between 2007 and 2008, funded by the local board of education. The project had three essential principles: a whole-school (inter-class-based) approach whereby students in every class of every grade participated in the project; a student-led approach in which besides the training sessions of teachers and parents, actual activities within the school were mostly conducted by the student committee; and a multipurpose approach in which, while the core aim was to tackle *ijime*, it also aimed for career education for students.

The project started by building a project team within the school whose members included teachers, parents, students and local representatives. The team then set a goal for the project, which was to raise awareness within the school and change attitudes towards the problem of *ijime* among teachers, parents and students. In order to achieve this goal, teachers took a series of training sessions conducted by university professors. Parents were given a series of newsletters, which explained what *ijime* is, how they can detect whether their children might be involved in any *ijime* situation and how they should deal with it by themselves, and together with teachers. A committee of students was elected on a representative basis, ideally one or two students per class, though in reality it was often elected by an up-or-down vote for students chosen by class teachers; this committee led various activities within the school. They first collected opinions on *ijime* from students in order to understand the general perceptions of *ijime* among the students. They then made a slogan for prevention, and designed a stop-*ijime* sign. Finally, as a culmination of two-years of the anti-*ijime* project, they produced some video footage for awareness raising of anti-*ijime*, with English and Japanese subtitles so that it can be distributed all over the world (www.youtube.com/watch?v=ZW92_9SYb-0).

One of the characteristics of this project was the support it received from a number of professionals from various different fields, including academic researchers from both in and outside Japan as well as experts of film production and theatre arts. These professionals not only gave advice to the students and supported their activities, but also provided some excitement for their involvement in the project, and helped give them a positive attitude to anti-*ijime* work. This part of the project was exactly what 'project-oriented' means, as this particular school had a problem of low self-esteem and low levels of motivation among students. Yet by meeting and working with those professionals, students gained self-esteem and started to be actively involved in anti-*ijime* work.

The effect of the project on the number of reported *ijime* cases, however, varied depending on the grades and classes, and the energy and effort the different groups of students put into it; those who were not a member of the committee involved in anti-*ijime* activities were considered merely passively as a target to change their attitudes towards *ijime* and actions against it. Thus, an effect of the project was a split between those who gave approval to activities of the committee and those who did not. However, one of the positive outcomes of the project was that after it finished, attitudes towards the activities of the student committee became much more positive and many more students hoped to become one of the members of the committee and get involved in anti-*ijime* actions within the school.

Takeuchi (2010) reported another student-led practice based on a peer-support scheme to tackle *ijime*. This was an inter-school-based approach involving twelve state-funded junior high schools in Osaka, conducted as a part of a 'school summit' held regularly by the student committees of these twelve schools. The 'school summit' was first organised in August 2007, under the supervision of the teachers who play an advisory role for each committee, aiming at discussing various problems among students, and the problem of *ijime* and *net-ijime* were considered as one of the themes to be taken for serious discussion. Members of the school summit decided to make a drama on the theme of *ijime* and *net-ijime* to highlight its seriousness, and the play was made and acted by themselves with minimal backup from the advisory teachers.

Takeuchi (2011) reported that the drama vividly expressed severe peer-relationship difficulties and made a strong impact on both teachers and students. This drama played by the members of the summit was edited for DVD and distributed to all primary and junior high schools around the region to be used for anti-*ijime* activities. Takeuchi (2012) reported that according to the statistics by the local government, there was a reduction of about 25% in recognised *ijime* incidents in 2011 in the region compared to the figure in 2007. Although the summit and their activities such as the play they made was not the only reason for this reduction, a student-led horizontal inter-school-based approach to tackle *ijime* and *net-ijime* can still be considered to work very effectively. Another strong point of this inter-school-based approach is that, even if one school falls into a serious situation and cannot recover by itself, other schools can work together with it to deter or stop *ijime* or at least make the situation better.

Non-school based approach

Miyakawa et al. (2013) reported a non-school based approach using bulletin board system (BBS) on internet. The first online support using BBS on internet in Japan appeared in the early 1990s, and the numbers gradually increased during the 2000s. Today, there are a huge number of different kinds of online support sites for victims of *ijime,* as well as for those affected by other school and family problems, run by either the local governments or private sectors (Miyakawa et al., 2013). Miyakawa himself administers one such online support site, where anyone can freely write, and read others' queries and advice. One of the big advantages of such online support by the BBS on internet is that children can ask for support without writing their own names, so that they do not have to worry about revenge from perpetrators or becoming a new target of *ijime* themselves. However, generally, the only support they can receive from these online support sites is advice on what to do but not actual intervention, and so it may be more useful if such online supports can thoughtfully be connected with actual interventions at school.

Actions against *net-ijime* at school

Actions against *net-ijime* in Japan mainly started around 2006, following the rapid and widespread use of mobile phones and internet access among children. In this year, the MEXT first included *net-ijime* related items in their annual survey on problematic behaviour. According to the latest survey on internet use among youth, carried out in 2013, more than 35% of primary school pupils, 50% of junior-high school and 97% of high school students have a mobile phone, and among these, about 10% of primary pupils, 50% of junior-high and 80% of high school students use a smart-phone. Most of those who use a smart-phone report having access to internet (Cabinet Office, 2014).

There have been various different approaches to tackling *net-ijime*. These have included teaching internet literacy and morals to children, making rules and strict monitoring of their usage of internet and encouraging efficient use of internet filtering services for their computers and mobile phones (Miyakawa et al., 2013). However, these adult-led approaches seem to have clear limitations and cannot be a total solution of the problem.

Takeuchi and Abe (2013) introduced a vertical inter-school-based peer-support type practice. In this practice, trained university students were sent to facilitate discussions among high school students on internet violence and to provide the knowledge of what is and is not illegal and/or dangerous. Doing such student-led type of activities, Takeuchi emphasised the importance for teachers to trust students and to have a collaborative stance with them, regardless of the types of schools that implemented the activity. As there have not yet been many student-led approaches for prevention of *ijime* and *net-ijime* in Japan, active use of such an approach would be expected.

Another practice for tackling *net-ijime* can be found in the field of educational technology. Ishihara (2011) reported the use of 'information study note' as a moral lesson practice in elementary schools. The information study note is a kind of digital educational material for learners of information education that can be used under free internet access environment. It was developed following the 'Future School Project' led by the Ministry of Internal Affairs and Communication (MIAC). This future school project started in 2010 and aimed at promoting the active use of information communication technology (ICT) in education. Traditionally, children can use computers and access internet only at a computer specialised classroom in a school. However, the 'Future School Project' allowed all children to have an information terminal such as a tablet computer, and to actively use such mobile computers in normal subject classes. The MIAC also promoted a vision of information technology in education in 2011; this had three aspects, namely 'active use of ICT to the curriculum subjects', 'information education', and 'informatization (computerization) of school affairs'.

The information study note was developed to cover the first and the second aspects of the vision of the MIAC, and is constituted of five different study units: 'character input', 'information gathering', 'intellectual property education', 'information ethics' and 'information security'. These units are based on the course of study published by the MEXT, and the unit on 'information ethics' is especially relevant to the problem of *net-ijime*. At an introductory session, in order for students to be interested in the topic and aware of the problem, animated teaching materials are used, and after they have learned the pros and cons of internet chatting (for instance) with these animated materials, students are then given an opportunity to actually experience internet chatting with their tablet computers. At first, students are told to chat to each other with their real name open, and after a while when they understood what internet chatting was like, students were told to chat to each other with nicknames so that it appeared to be anonymous. Ishihara (2011) reported that even when students were told to chat anonymously, they continued to chat as if they were chatting with their real name open; however, after a while, their comments in the chat became a bit loose or too relaxed when they got used to being anonymous.

The information study note has a function of displaying real names of participants whenever teachers wanted. Teachers use this function when they feel the conversation in a chat room is becoming too loose or relaxed, and students suddenly realised that they were actually not anonymous. This function is for teaching students that anonymity in the internet is limited, and it is always possible for the administrator of a particular internet site or internet provider to track back and identify who wrote a particular comment on a particular internet site. This is very important for students to learn how to use computers and internet not only technically but also ethically so that they can understand what kind of behaviours on the internet can escalate to *net-ijime*.

While there are lessons specialised for ICT in junior-high and high schools in Japan, there is not such a class in elementary schools yet, though more and more elementary pupils use smart-phones, and it is therefore important to use such material as the information study note to give younger children an opportunity to learn about ICT and its proper use.

Issues to be addressed for actions against *ijime* / *net-ijime* in Japan

In order for effective and successful intervention for and prevention of *ijime* at school, it is not only crucial to consider how we design and implement practices, but also how we evaluate such practices including the interpretation of evaluation outcomes. For example, *ijime* is generally considered a group phenomenon, yet many evaluation studies of actions against *ijime* only use overall increase or decrease in numbers of victims and perpetrators as an index to examine its effectiveness. Toda, Strohmeier and Spiel (2008) argued the importance of evaluating the effectiveness of any anti-*ijime* practices not only on a whole-school basis but also on an individual class basis, by focusing on the process of collectivisation of perpetrators and disempowerment of victims. In order to manage this, Toda et al. (2008) introduced two new indices to assess the severity of *ijime*. One is to calculate the ratio of bullies and victims within a class (the B/V ratio). A second is the number of 'helpless victims'; this can be calculated by subtracting those who cannot fight back against perpetrators or seek any social help from others, from all reported victims.

They argued that *ijime* conducted in a stable group, as is most often the case in Japan, would be predicted to start at a low frequency, with less harmful negative behaviours carried out and with many victims involved, and with the bully/victim ratio therefore likely to be 1.0 or below. However, after a certain period of time, a particular pupil would be singled out as a fixed victim and the aggressive acts would be repeated towards the same target, and at the same time, more aggressors would join in. In this case, the bully/victim ratio rises above 1.0, and it becomes much more difficult for the victim to escape from the situation. This ratio has a practical utility: as there would be few classes with no victims / perpetrators, it can be difficult to decide which class should be focussed on first for intervention efforts; however, assuming we can trust most replies to questionnaires and compare the B/V ratio between different classes, we may be able to decide the order of priority (Toda and Kanetsuna, 2011; Kanetsuna and Toda, submitted).

Of course, we should not rely too much on questionnaire research to evaluate the effectiveness of any actions against *ijime*. It can sometimes be hard to draw a whole picture of the situation merely from the questionnaire outcomes, and a more detailed picture can be obtained by using alternative measures such as peer-nomination and networking analysis – procedures which have come to be considered as 'standard' in western countries. However, it is very difficult to apply such measures at schools in Japan, mostly for ethical reasons, and instead of these measures, B/V ratio and 'the number of helpless victims' are good alternative indices to utilize the limited source of data effectively for prevention and intervention of *ijime* at school.

Regarding *net-ijime*, one of the issues to be considered is the characteristic of anonymity on the internet. Use of online social media such as BBS, weblog, and various kinds of social networking services is increasing, especially among young people, and about 70% of those using such online social media in Japan prefer anonymous communication (Internet White Paper, 2008). The MEXT (2008) claimed that such anonymity in internet communication makes it easy for children to become both victims and perpetrators of *net-ijime*. In fact, given such anonymity in use of the internet, it may be too narrow a focus to pick on *net-ijime* as the only problem on the internet; instead, we should take a broader perspective on cyber-related problems. For example, if we can be sure that the victim and the perpetrator(s) of *net-ijime* are students belonging to the same social group, it can be treated as a case of *net-ijime*, but in reality, there is always the possibility that many other unknown persons even including adults are involved in the case. This is one of the reasons for the difficulty of intervention against *net-ijime*, and how we intervene and how we evaluate such interventions are issues to be solved by future studies.

Conclusions

In this chapter, we have introduced and discussed various different actions and approaches against *ijime* and *net-ijime* in Japan. Over the last three decades, actions against *ijime* in Japan can be regarded as rather sporadic. One of the reasons for this may be the stance of the Japanese government on action against *ijime*. While a large number of appeals, policies and guidelines have been released, no materials and programs have been distributed. Instead, the concrete actions against *ijime* have been entrusted to individual schools, partly due to the difficulties of top-down implementation of practices against *ijime* at school. In such a situation, implementation of any practice against *ijime* has only been conducted in some pioneering schools by some academic researchers and practitioners.

However, given the seriousness of the situation of *ijime* and *net-ijime* at schools in Japan, there is a need to disseminate effective approaches – such as those introduced in this chapter – to all schools in Japan. Because there is no particular top-down nationwide program against *ijime* and *net-ijime* in Japan, it may be time-consuming to achieve this. Yet if we can meaningfully connect those practices implemented sporadically all over

Japan, and properly evaluate them, we can create original, student-led, effective and long-lasting practices suited for the systems and climates of schools and classes in Japan. To do this, the active involvement of academic professionals and societies should also be very important, not only for proposing and evaluating practices but also for the training of both trainee and active teachers in their implementation.

REFERENCES

Cabinet Office (2014). *The results of internet environment survey among youth 2013* (in Japanese). www8.cao.go.jp/youth/youth-harm/chousa/h25/net-jittai/pdf/kekka.pdf. (Retrieved Nov 11, 2015).

Internet White Paper (2008). Internet Association Japan.

Ishihara, K. (2011). Trial and practices of information study note. *Proceedings of Japan Society for Educational Technology*, 27, 339–340.

Kawata, H. (1996). To enable children to collaborate to keep them healthy. *Journal of the Junior High School of the Faculty of Education, Kanazawa University*, 39, 137–155.

Kanetsuna, T., Smith, P. K. and Morita, Y. (2006). Coping with bullying at school: Children's recommended strategies and attitudes to school-based interventions in England and Japan. *Aggressive Behavior*, 32, 570–580.

Kanetsuna, T. and Toda, Y. (submitted). Applying three different indices to evaluate an antibullying project: a four time-point survey in a junior high school.

Ministry of Education, Culture, Sports, Science and Technology (1985). *Appeals for thoroughness of guidance on ijime problem* (in Japanese). www.mext.go.jp/b_menu/hakusho/nc/t19850629001/t19850629001.html. (Retrieved Nov 11, 2015).

(1994). *Urgent appeal released by anti-ijime emergency meeting* (in Japanese). www.mext.go.jp/b_menu/hakusho/nc/t19950313001/t19950313001.html. (Retrieved Nov 11, 2015).

(1995). *For measures to be taken for the immediate resolution of the ijime problem* (in Japanese). www.mext.go.jp/b_menu/hakusho/nc/t19950313001/t19950313001.html. (Retrieved Nov 11, 2015).

(1996a). *To protect the irreplaceable lives of children – an anti-ijime emergency appeal by Minister of Education.* Tokyo: Ministry of Education, Culture, Sports, Science and Technology.

(1996b). *Report of the experts meeting on behavior problems of students – for a comprehensive approach on the ijime problem* (in Japanese). www.mext.go.jp/b_menu/hakusho/nc/t19960726001/t19960726001.html. (Retrieved Nov 11, 2015).

(2006a). *For thorough actions against ijime problem* (in Japanese). www.mext.go.jp/a_menu/shotou/seitoshidou/06102402/001.htm. (Retrieved Nov 11, 2015).

(2006b). *Points of efforts and basic understanding of ijime problem at school* (in Japanese). www.mext.go.jp/a_menu/shotou/seitoshidou/06102402/002.htm. (Retrieved Nov 11, 2015).

(2006c). *Education rebuilding council report: Urgent proposal to ijime problem for educators and the nation* (in Japanese). www.kantei.go.jp/jp/singi/kyouiku/dai3/siryou3-1.pdf. (Retrieved Nov 11, 2015).

(2006d). *Urgent proposal to ijime problem: Report of the council for creating systems that protect and nurture children* (in Japanese). www.mext.go.jp/b_menu/shingi/chousa/shotou/040/toushin/06120713.htm. (Retrieved Nov 11, 2015).

(2007). *Primary report of the council for creating systems that protect and nurture children: Establishment of a system for early detection and appropriate response to ijime problem – aiming at school and local communities with warmth* (in Japanese). www.mext.go.jp/b_menu/shingi/chousa/shotou/040/toushin/07030123.htm. (Retrieved Nov 11, 2015).

(2008). *Secondary report of the council for creating systems that protect and nurture children: To protect children from 'net-ijime' – let's review the way of using mobile phone and internet* (in Japanese). www.mext.go.jp/b_menu/houdou/20/06/08061612/002.htm. (Retrieved Nov 11, 2015).

(2012). *Comprehensive policy for anti-ijime and school safety: In order to protect children's lives* (in Japanese). www.mext.go.jp/component/a_menu/education/detail/__icsFiles/afieldfile/2012/09/05/1325364_1_1.pdf. (Retrieved Nov 11, 2015).

(2013a). *Act of Promotion of Bullying Prevention* (in Japanese). www.kantei.go.jp/jp/singi/kyouikusaisei/dai10/sankou2.pdf. (Retrieved Nov 11, 2015).

(2013b). *Basic National Policy on Bullying Prevention* (in Japanese). www.mext.go.jp/a_menu/shotou/seitoshidou/1340770.htm. (Retrieved Nov 11, 2015).

Miyakawa, M., Takeuchi, K., Aoyama, I., and Toda, Y. (2013). Problems and support practice in the Internet. *Studies on Education and Society*, 23, 41–52.

Morita, Y. (2006). *What is bullying-the problem of classroom, the problem of society*. Tokyo: Chuoukoronshinsha.

Morita, Y. and Kiyonaga K. (1986; 2nd edn. 1994). *Ijime: Kyousitsu no Yamai [Ijime: the disease of the classroom]*. Tokyo: Kaneko Shobo.

Takeuchi, K. (2010). A practical study of peer support programs by school council of all junior high schools in a city: Focus on a play which aims to eradicate cyber bullying; by Osaka Pref. Neyagawa City Junior High School Students Summit (in Japanese). *Japanese Journal of Peer Support*, 7, 19–27.

(2011). Children's own initiative to change their school: A glimmer of hope after a tragic incident. In R. H. Shute, P. T. Slee, R. Murray-Harvey and K. L. Dix (Eds.), *Mental health and wellbeing: Educational perspectives* (pp. 347–350). Adelaide: Shannon Research Press.

(2012). Study of countermeasures to mobile phones and internet problems by peer support scheme: Efforts of cyberbullying eradication by junior-high school students summit (in Japanese). *Proceedings of Japanese Society of Educational Psychology*, 54, 247.

Takeuchi, K. and Abe, K. (2013). 'Smart' online violence in Japan and the United States: Discussing the similarity/difference of them and applicability of inter-school peer support system. *Japanese Journal of Educational Practices on Moral Development*, 8, 28–31.

Taki, M. (1992). The empirical study on the occurrence of 'ijime' behavior: The verification of the causal hypotheses using the questionnaire panel survey (in Japanese). *Japanese Journal of Educational Sociology*, 50, 366–388.

   (2002). A study on the philosophy and the method of guidance and counselling in Japanese schools – guidance and counselling model and the three approaches (in Japanese). *Japanese Journal of the Study of Guidance and Counselling*, 1, 76–85.

Toda, Y. (2005). Bullying and peer support systems in Japan: Intervention research. In D. Shwalb, J. Nakazawa and B. Shwalb (Eds.), *Applied developmental psychology: Theory, practice, and research from Japan* (pp. 301–319). Information Age: Greenwich, CT.

Toda, Y. and Ito. M. (2005). Some variations of peer support in Japan. *Peer Support Networker*. http://peersupport.ukobservatory.com/ (Retrieved Nov 11, 2015).

Toda, Y. and Kanetsuna, T. (2011). The evaluation of anti-bullying programs led by student committee. 15th European Conference of Developmental Psychology, Bergen, Norway.

Toda, Y., Nishiumi, M. and Yoshida, H. (2003). The evaluation of 'on paper method' peer support practice in an elementary school (in Japanese). *Annual Report of Centre for Educational Research and Practice, Faculty of Education and Human Sciences* 2. Niigata University .

Toda, Y., Strohmeier, D. and Spiel, C. (2008). Process model of bullying. In T. Katoh and H. Taniguchi (Eds.), *Darkside of interpersonal relationships* (pp. 117–131). Kyoto: Kitaohji-Shobo. (original in Japanese)

17 Intervention programs in South Korea

Keumjoo Kwak

School violence is a serious social issue in South Korean society, and schools and the government are searching for effective and proactive measures to actively intervene and prevent school violence. This chapter will review the current intervention programs uniquely designed and developed for use in South Korean schools. While bullying (*wang-ta*) is a serious concern, prevention programs specifically for bullying alone have not been developed yet. In South Korea, prevention programs for overall school violence have been developed, and bullying (*wang-ta*) is included as part of the program content. Therefore, these classroom programs in general focus on changing the climate of classroom and the environment within school. For example, "Harmony" is one of the most recently developed school violence prevention programs for school students. The contents of the intervention and prevention programs developed in consideration of the South Korean culture will be reviewed in terms of the intervention and prevention topics, the target audience (victim, perpetrator, outsider, and teacher), the multimedia resources, the incorporation of the current Korean school violence laws, and how the programs are enforced for proper and effective use. New and improved programs are being developed and the follow up program for "Harmony" targeting different aspects of school violence is in progress.

History of intervention programs in South Korea

In South Korea, school violence including *wang-ta* has been a serious social issue (Kwak, 2006). Victim and perpetrator rates for school violence (*wang-ta*) are continuously rising, the age of experiencing school violence is getting as low as elementary grade, and perpetrators of school violence are showing a tendency of growing insensitivity to violence (W. Jung, 2012; and see Chapter 5).

In countries such as the United States, Norway, and Canada, a nationwide scale of research on determining the causes of increase and decrease of school violence, and making efforts to reduce it, have been ongoing since the 1970s (see Chapter 15). From the 1980s, while national levels of school violence prevention programs have been propelled in foreign countries (Kwak et al., 2005), the history of understanding the status, countermeasure preparation, and development of school violence prevention program in South Korea is relatively short.

As the severity of school violence became prominent, on December 29, 2003, South Korea revised the *School Violence Prevention and Countermeasure Act*. Through an extensive procedure involving a total of seven revision processes and basic plan establishments/enforcements, the country made an effort to eradicate bullying through policies (Kwak, 2011). Furthermore, school violence prevention programs reflecting on aspects of policy, the characteristics of *wang-ta*, and South Korea's educational environment, are under development by researchers.

The status of school violence prevention program in South Korea

Prevention types

Though the definition of *prevention* is controversial, it can be distinguished into three types according to various researchers (Caplan, 1964; Durlak, 1995; Jeong et al., 1997). Primary prevention is an indirect and overall prevention process for people who do not have problems at the present time. This prevention is not a specialized treatment or counseling for people who have social, psychological, or physical problems, but implementations taking place in schools or institutions/agency by means of social policy (Weissberg and Greenberg, 1998). In order to reduce existing disorders and illnesses, secondary prevention directly acts on potential risk factors. That is, by investigating behavioral and emotional symptoms in the early stage, the potential to develop into a severe psychological disorder may be reduced (Kwak, 1999). Tertiary prevention is aimed at people who have already developed disorders. The purpose of the tertiary prevention is to maximally reduce other results due to the disorders and to rehabilitate people to readapt to social life. The tertiary prevention is closer to the means of rehabilitation than prevention (Weissberg and Greenberg, 1998). In South Korea's earlier school violence prevention programs, prevention programs for elementary, middle, and high school students that strongly reflected the characteristics of primary prevention were most abundant. Subsequently, tertiary prevention programs that focused mainly on victims and perpetrators were developed (Jang, 2005; Kwak, 2011).

Prevention program categories

The previous domestic prevention programs mostly dealt with overall school violence. This includes various types such as physical aggression, *wang-ta*, cyber aggression, verbal aggression, etc., or *gipdan-ttadolim* (*wang-ta*). In 2008, the *School Violence Prevention and Countermeasure Act* was revised and sexual violence was introduced as a subcategory of school violence. Subsequently, prevention programs for sexual violence have been developed in recent years.

*Program target subject, structured factors,
and implementation method*

The school violence (*wang-ta*) prevention programs developed in South Korea have mostly been targeted at middle schools, or combined years (elementary-middle school years, middle-high school years, elementary-middle-high school years). However, as if reflecting the inclination of experiencing bullying at a younger age, many prevention programs developed in the mid and late 2000s were directed at elementary school students (Kwak, 2012). Most of South Korea's previous school violence prevention programs have focused on the victims, while programs that targeted perpetrators were largely based on mediation (Kwak, 2012).

Most of the school violence prevention programs in South Korea were school-based implemented programs. Program contents were mainly on understanding others, developing interpersonal skills, resolving conflict, expressing oneself, and anger management. Many programs utilized videos.

Prevention programs in South Korea

Representative programs among current South Korean prevention programs are described in detail below.

Prevention programs for all students

HELP-ing Program: HELP-ing (HELP-ing: Help Encourage yourself as a Leader of Peace-ing!) program (Kwak et al., 2005) is targeted at the bystander group that constitute most school members and are at the core of solving the problem. In order to change the lack of awareness, responsibility, and action that bystanders usually show in violent situations, the program aimed to help bystanders develop social perception skills such as self-perception and coping skills. Reflecting South Korea's educational environment, prevention programs were developed to be implemented in a relatively short period for typical students. Prevention programs for elementary students (40 minutes) and middle school students (45 minutes) were each administered through one, two, four, or eight sessions according to the school environment (Kwak, 2006).

To study the implementation effect of the prevention program, training groups attended the program one to two sessions per week for a total of eight sessions, while control groups attended typical class lessons. The participants – 325 students in the training group and 330 students in the control group – were recruited from two elementary and middle schools in Seoul and Gyeonggi-do. Training and control classes were held within each school. Pre- and post-test results of the training and control groups' experience of school violence indicated that in the case of *gipdan-ttadolim,* the levels of both victimization and perpetration of the elementary and middle school students of the training group decreased more than was the case in the control group. In addition, the training group, compared to the control group, showed a decrease in cyber aggression (perpetrators only), damaging belongings (victims), and *gorophim* (harassment) (see Tables 17.1 and 17.2; Kwak, 2006).

In the case of changes in perception and attitude, the interaction effect of the test results (pre- and post-test) and the group (control and training) on peer pressure (pressure to act antisocial behaviors such as *wang-ta* or delinquency), peer conformity (conforming to antisocial or violent behaviors), perception of *wang-ta* (accurate awareness of what behaviors constitute as *wang-ta*), unmoral language use (describing aggressive behavior in neutral language), irresponsibility (not holding responsibility of one's aggressive behavior), and moral justification

Table 17.1 *Mean perpetration scores for pupils in training and control groups at pre- and post-test in evaluation of HELP-ing program (from Kwak, 2006).*

	Group			
	Training		Control	
	Pre-	Post-	Pre-	Post-
Type	*M (SD)*	*M (SD)*	*M (SD)*	*M (SD)*
Gipdan-ttadolim	1.35 (0.69)	1.16 (0.61)	1.29 (0.53)	1.29 (0.67)
Gorophim [harassment]	1.12 (0.47)	1.07 (0.58)	1.10 (0.59)	1.13 (0.63)
Cyber aggression	1.08 (0.72)	1.07 (0.58)	1.09 (0.63)	1.12 (1.7)

Table 17.2 *Mean victimization scores for pupils in training and control groups at pre- and post-test in evaluation of HELP-ing program (from Kwak, 2006).*

	Group			
	Training		Control	
	Pre-	Post-	Pre-	Post-
Type	*M (SD)*	*M (SD)*	*M (SD)*	*M (SD)*
Gipdan-ttadolim	1.26 (0.89)	1.17 (0.50)	1.20 (0.67)	1.23 (0.48)
Damaging belongings	1.23 (0.68)	1.15 (0.66)	1.13 (0.74)	1.19 (0.47)
Cyber aggression	1.21 (0.47)	1.17 (0.66)	1.27 (0.74)	1.21 (0.68)

Table 17.3 *Mean perception and attitude scores for pupils in training and control groups at pre- and post-test in evaluation of HELP-ing program (from Kwak, 2006)*

	Group			
	Training		Control	
	Pre-	Post-	Pre-	Post-
Type	*M (SD)*	*M (SD)*	*M (SD)*	*M (SD)*
Peer pressure	1.84 (0.90)	1.43 (0.47)	1.91 (0.71)	1.87 (0.21)
Peer conformity	2.47 (0.75)	2.03 (0.15)	2.28 (0.27)	2.07 (0.83)
Perception of wang-ta	2.02 (0.51)	2.53 (0.35)	2.03 (0.24)	2.03 (0.63)
Unmoral language use	1.71 (0.13)	1.56 (1.85)	1.73 (0.45)	1.69 (0.83)
Irresponsibility	2.07 (0.50)	1.90 (0.95)	2.09 (0.65)	2.07 (1.14)
Moral justification	2.14 (0.60)	1.97 (0.24)	2.14 (0.35)	2.15 (0.45)

(justifying their aggressive behavior as moral) indicated that the training group improved on all these measures, and significantly more so than was the case in the control group (see Table 17.3).

Overall then, some positive outcomes of this prevention program have been established (see also Kwak, 2006).

***Harmony Program*:** This program is one of the newest programs still in progress, which was first implemented in July 2012 across fifteen schools (Park, 2013). The Ministry of Education, Science and Technology developed this program to prevent school violence and to create a harmonious environment by improving empathy and communication skills of students, teachers, parents, and all school members. Furthermore, it was also developed as a modular program so that it may be applied selectively based on each school's unique characteristic and condition. As of August 2013, the Ministry of Education, Science and Technology developed a total of thirty-six programs separated by modules (empathy, communication, bullying awareness, and management), class levels (early elementary school, later elementary school, middle school, and high school), student version, teacher version, and parent version (Park, 2013). Specialists appointed by the Ministry of Education, Science and Technology developed and administered customized programs that reflected each school's characteristics and conditions. In addition, they appointed masters and doctoral-level counselors to execute the programs. The program took into account the psychological trait and school violence tendency of the student's developmental stage. However, to improve the applicability of the program to the school field, the finalized program was constructed focusing relatively more on the class teacher.

More specifically, the program for students utilized activities such as group counseling and art therapy to improve their psychological characteristics such as empathy, anger management, and communication abilities (Park, 2013). The program was implemented across six sessions for a total of twelve hours. Programs for teachers and parents were implemented from one to six hours on contents such as communicating with students/children, coping strategies of problem behaviors, and countermeasures for school violence. Results revealed that the program had positive effects such as improvements in students' relationship with peers and improvement in teacher's understanding of students.

The Ministry of Education, Science and Technology plans to administer thirty-six additional programs that deal with self-esteem, emotion regulation, conflict resolution modules separated by class levels, student version, teacher version, and parent version (Park, 2013). Furthermore, it is hoped that the program will be administered progressively and systematically to all elementary, middle, and high schools to prevent bullying.

Siubou Program (Give a glance at your friend, give a warm helping hand to your friend): The Siubou program, (Ministry of Education and Human Resources Development, Research Person in Charge: Kwak, 2006) tackled the cause and effects of school violence at the cognitive, emotional, and behavioral level (primary prevention) and examined school violence from the aspect of secondary prevention. Elementary and middle school students were given 10-minute clips of audiovisual materials over 10 sessions, to the entire class, to enhance the delivery of the program content (Kwak, 2006). The entire session consists of three phases:

- personality development (including human rights, communication, interpersonal relationships, and altruistic behavior); this aims to help students effectively handle social issues such as impulsive behaviors and emotions, and both trivial and serious conflicts in interpersonal relationships;
- school violence prevention (including culture of violence); this aims to awaken the attention of students to the addictive and risky violence culture in everyday life, and promote students' ability to control these aspects of their lives;
- bullying management (including verbal abuse, physical violence, extortion, *gipdan-ttadolim*, and cyber aggression); examples of bullying cases are presented as well as management skills that students can familiarize themselves with (Kwak, 2006).

The Siubou program differentiates itself from other prevention programs in that researchers considered the developmental aspects when producing this program. This program could be applied to a large extent as it embraces unique characteristics of the South Korean educational environment and school violence. Furthermore, the program includes appropriate materials relevant to cyber aggression (Kwak, 2006).

I Can Make a Difference! Program: This prevention program is based on literature reviews of domestic and foreign questionnaire surveys (program demands and suggestion survey) (Kwak, 2011). It is a follow-up program of the 2005 Siubou prevention program (Kwak, 2006) and is a 2011 version program for elementary grade students on bullying prevention program (Kwak, 2011).

Since the Siubou Program simply consists of audiovisual materials, it is difficult to apply in the classroom environment. In addition, the Siubou Program is only 7 to 10 minutes long and may fail to effectively deliver the main message; therefore, in order to remedy this drawback, the "I Can Make a Difference" prevention program was developed. The program consists of ten 40-minute sessions; activity sheets and various audiovisual materials are used to inform cognitive, emotional, and behavioral aspects from the developmental perspectives. Furthermore, based on the revised Act (p.351) and society's concern of school violence, this program specifically focuses on verbal abuse and sexual violence. In addition, a separately provided instructor's form presents information on theoretical explanations on school violence so that additional training is not required for instructors to administer this program. Therefore, administration of the program by the schools is easily done (Kwak, 2011).

The student's version is different for lower-level students (elementary grades 1 to 3), and higher-level students (elementary grades 4 to 6). However, when administering questionnaire surveys, elementary grades 1 to 2 were classified as lower level and grades 3 to 6 were classified as higher level. The explanation as to why lower-level and higher-level classifications are made this way is that from the cognitive developmental approach, the developmental period of grades 1 to 3 is from the pre-operational stage to early concrete operational stage; the developmental period of grades 4 to 6 is from the middle concrete operational stage to early formal operational stage; in the transitional period from grades 3 to 4, as students learn societal obedience-adaptation, criticism and separation from social groups, and social skills such as break away-competition-collaboration, they mock or criticize other students' new or different aspects (You, 2003; as cited in Kwak, 2011); in the developmental stage of grade 4, students increase in their conformity to peer groups (Wilt, 1959).

By focusing on conscience, courage, communication skills, sympathy, and personality education, this program intended to teach what school violence, *wang-ta*, verbal aggression, cyber aggression, and sexual violence are. Not only did the program simply teach what they are, but also encouraged students to personally realize why such behaviors are bad and motivate them to change. The main purpose of this program was to raise students who can lead in the prevention and change of school violence (Kwak, 2011).

Reach out your hands Program: This program is a middle-school form follow-up of the 2005 Siubou Program (Kwak, 2006) and its contents are closely connected with the 2011 "I Can Make a Difference" program. The program (Kwak, 2012) is aimed at middle school students and therefore, considers their cognitive, emotional, behavioral, and developmental characteristics. It is administered through a total of eight sessions, each session consisting of audiovisual materials and activity sheets. It treats topics on personality development, school violence awareness, verbal abuse prevention, cyber aggression prevention, *gipdan-ttadolim* prevention, and sexual violence prevention.

In order to effectively deliver the core messages of the program, various methods such as explaining fundamental psychological theories through experiments, presenting true case examples and various press releases, and presenting examples of cases that may occur in daily life were used. In an effort to help students understand the difference between truth and opinion in an interactive manner, narrator animations were incorporated for each method. By utilizing animations, students may perceive the negative aftermath of violence and coping skills in an easy and interesting but also in a serious manner. In addition, by explaining school violence through case examples that may readily occur in daily life, personality development (considered of essential importance in school violence prevention) was also intended to be handled.

To distinguish itself from other prevention programs, this program not only focused on perpetrators and potential perpetrators, but also included victims and bystanders. It aimed to introduce practical coping skills and changes of attitudes about bullying in the entire middle school populations. Through discussion of issues around middle school students' school violence and prevention, this program intended to raise awareness about the severity of school violence. When developing prevention and coping skill methods on school violence, especially physical violence, sexual violence, *wang-ta,* verbal abuse, extortion, and cyber aggression, the program considered the adolescents' developmental stage. Furthermore, in order to develop effective learning methods for the entire target subjects, it was based on psychological theories.

In addition to the student's version of the program, a teacher's version that provides program information and instructions was also developed. Therefore, not only can one expect to see preventive effects at the student level but also anticipate such effects at the school level. For instructors to readily implement the program, practice guidelines that include each session's purpose, theoretical basis and background, information, activity sheet explanation, and so forth are provided. Therefore, instructors are not required to take further professional training and may readily administer the program in the classroom setting.

By treating topics on personality development and developmental aspects, the program aims to distinguish itself from other prevention programs. It considers risk factors, potential factors, and protective factors of adolescents' aggressive behavior attributional styles established by literature reviews of previous research studies. In addition, middle school students' characteristics related to school violence are also considered as an important factor. The potential of middle school students being involved in school violence or *wang-ta* is considerably higher than other grade students; the extent of harmful consequences for victims is much more critical and may even lead to suicide. Therefore, this program focuses greatly on enhancement of thinking skills, cognitive skills, and social perspective taking skills. By directly participating in brainstorming activity, debate and discussion activity, and role-playing activity, students may further develop and enhance their perceptions and social perspective taking skills.

While this program has distinguished surveys based on the lower-level student's and higher-level student's developmental period, differentiating the program's content itself may be expected to be more effective. Lower-level student's program may be modified to make it easier and more fun, strengthen its humanistic education, and focus on prevention of victimization. On the other hand, higher-level student's program may present more practical cases related to school violence and focus on both prevention of victimization and perpetration (Kwak, 2012).

KEDI School Violence Prevention Program: This program was developed by the Korean Educational Development Institute (KEDI) from the perspective of preventive science to reduce personal and environmental risk factors that expedite school violence occurrence. Its intention to strengthen personal and environmental protective factors suppressing school violence extends to preventing and eradicating school violence. Considering the developmental level of elementary students, this program consists of accessible materials and information, as well as lively animations and audio-visual clips to induce students' interest and amusement. Especially, because instructors ask students to only watch audio-video clips, this program has an advantage of being easy to implement. The program consists of four sessions and focuses on emotional intelligence and problem solving skill enhancement (Ministry of Education, Science and Technology and Ministry of Justice, 2009). The program may enhance its effectiveness by utilizing other materials such as activity sheets or organizing discussion sessions so that students may actively think about what they have learned and apply it to their daily situations.

Prevention programs for victims and bullies

KEDI school violence victim student cure and perpetrator student lead program: KEDI developed and disseminated this perpetrator student lead program ("Again! One Decision") and victim student program ("It's a New Start"). This program revised previous prevention programs' drawbacks, reflected on advice given by specialized (visiting) counselors and site specialists, and developed a program for 7th (middle school second year) through 10th grade (high school second year) students. The program consists of seven sessions: excluding session one and session seven, sessions two to six are comprised of "basic programs" that are mandatory and "advanced programs" that consist of more in-depth information. It may be administered over a minimum of seven courses to a maximum of twelve courses. The program information consists of interpersonal relationship skill enhancement, anger-stress management, conflict resolving skill enhancement, community consciousness development; role-play activity, video watching, volunteering, cooperation games, and drawing activities are utilized to acquire the above information (Ministry of Education, Science and Technology and Ministry of Justice, 2009).

The content of each session consists of introduction, development, and closing phases and lasts around 90 minutes. In the case of basic programs, sessions are comprised so that they may be administered in a short period. Basic programs consist of relatively simpler information than the advanced programs so they may be of easier use in school settings. Generally prevention program periods in schools run from 45 minutes to 50 minutes. Therefore, in such cases focusing on either one to two mandatory sessions of the basic programs is recommended. The advanced programs are able to be used in related professional organizations or centers, and thus some teachers need to take this into consideration when using the programs. Since this program distinguishes materials for victim students and for perpetrator students, it is advantageous for instructors to choose specific programs on the type of students accordingly (Ministry of Education, Science and Technology and Ministry of Justice, 2009). The program may be enhanced by ensuring that the teachers are well-trained to administer the advanced programs. Providing set guidelines and training to teachers will help them to manage the program in a more efficient manner.

Rainbow Program: With the support of the Government Youth Commission, the Foundation for Preventing Youth Violence developed a program for elementary, middle, and high school students in 2002. This program introduces various manuals that may be of great use in school environments and youth organizations. The program information consists of growing the strength of the mind, sharing interest and love, practicing counseling a friend, discerning school conflict, sharing experience with a senior student, and raising hope. Each topic is comprised of reading books, watching videos, and doing topic-related activities. This program assists school violence victim students to positively overcome their psychological wounds; its main purpose is to reduce violent cases within the school zone so that no more students may be victims of the school violence. The program is implemented in either for camp-use (2 nights, 3 days weekend camp) or for school-use (10 weeks group counseling, 2 hours per session). In the case of camp-use, the program consists of 3 instructors per 20 to 30 students and in the case of school-use, the program consists of 1 instructor per 8 to 10 students (Moon, 2006).

Through various intelligence, emotional intelligence, and problem solving skill development, the Rainbow Program aims to tackle the root causes of school violence; its effectiveness is enhanced through the educational procedure plan of diagnosis, eradication, and evaluation. Experience-centered activities such as computer activity, writing journal, and watching videos increase students' motivation. Students enjoy their experiences through expressing personal thoughts on the internet bulletin board, watching videos, role-playing activity, completing animation, and other various activities; in addition, psychologists and instructors participate through group counseling (Ministry of Education, Science and Technology and Ministry of Justice, 2009). The program may be enhanced by tailoring its contents based on the students' developmental stage. For example, parent education may be supplemented for elementary students' program so that the parent's attention and support may foster the student to apply his or her knowledge of school violence prevention in daily situation.

Let's Play Friend Program: The purpose of this program is to support students in discussing their experience as victims of school violence, to understand the cause of school violence, search for new solutions, and to enhance interpersonal skills through familiar media and psychodramas. Target participants are students who are having difficulty in forming and maintaining interpersonal relationships with others from 5th grades to 8th grades (middle school second year). The program is a six-months course consisting of two stages: the first stage is a two nights, three days long basic-course camp, and the second stage is a five-months course group counseling, one session per month (Ministry of Education, Science and Technology and Ministry of Justice, 2009; Moon, 2006).

Students receive continuous treatment through camp activities and counseling sessions, and also experience changes in emotional, cognitive, and behavioral aspects. In addition, in the procedure of producing movies with peers, students experience a sense of accomplishment. In the two nights, three days camp, students receive group counseling and psychodramas through videos and also produce movies with 6 mm digital camcorders (Ministry of Education, Science and Technology and Ministry of Justice, 2009).

In this program, by personally writing stories and producing their own media productions with peers, students experience enjoyment and accomplishment. The experience of forming relationships with other peers and the counselor's enthusiastic support enhances students' self-esteem. In addition, regular meetings with peers who participated in the camp help maintain their friendship as well as the effectiveness of this program (Ministry of Education, Science and Technology and Ministry of Justice, 2009). The program may be enhanced by making sure in follow-ups that the peers participate in regular meetings after the camp session.

Specialized Program for Bullies: In order to prevent recurrence of school violence and to help students develop as healthy members of the society, the Foundation for Preventing Youth Violence developed this program in 2002. The program is a one to two weeks' course of educating five to six students. It includes psychological diagnosis, group programs, individual counseling, and bullying prevention education (Ministry of Education, Science and Technology and Ministry of Justice, 2009).

The goal of the "specialized program for perpetrator students (Foundation for Preventing Youth Violence)" is for students to perceive situations where aggressive tendency or conflict may rise, help reduce aggressiveness that may be displayed in daily situations, and help develop problem-solving behaviors through appropriate verbal expressions. In addition, practicing appropriate problem-solving skills and reducing inappropriate problematic social behaviors may promote emotional and psychological stability (J. Jung, 2009).

Psychological tests, group programs, individual counseling sessions, bullying prevention education, compliment journals, reading, volunteering, and visiting organizations are main components of the program. The program is tailored to each student's situation and personality. After completion of the program, counseling sessions with the instructor help maintain care for the students. The program consists of five sessions (Ministry of Education, Science and Technology and Ministry of Justice, 2009).

Conclusions

Though the history of development of prevention programs in South Korea is relatively short compared to that in some foreign countries, such programs are now continuously being developed and revised. As can be seen, such prevention programs have focused on curriculum work that raises awareness of school violence, and works on psychological attributes of perpetrators, victims, and bystanders. Prevention programs in South Korea focusing on overall school violence and school-based implementation programs for victim and perpetrator students are being developed. However, despite this effort, the severity of the school violence continues to be a critical social issue. Therefore, while development of prevention programs basing its foundation on research studies on the characteristics of *wang-ta* is important, revision and implementation of the programs are also essential (Kwak, 2006).

Overall, evaluations of the effectiveness of current programs are needed. Of the various programs reviewed in this chapter, only two – the HELP-ing Program and the Harmony Program – have received any evaluation. Such evaluations are necessary so that further revisions may improve the quality of the programs, and resources devoted to those shown to be effective. During the process of developing and then revising prevention programs, awareness that school violence or *wang-ta* should not be permitted needs to be spread out through the related organizations' systematic development and long-term plans (Kwak, 2008).

REFERENCES

Caplan, G. (1964). *Principles of preventive psychiatry*. New York: Basic Books.

Durlak, J. A. (1995). *School-based prevention programs for children and adolescents*. Thousand Oaks, CA: Sage.

Jang, K. (2005). 민속놀이를 활용한 초등학생 학교폭력 예방 프로그램 개발 연구 [Study on elementary school students' school violence prevention program development using traditional games]. 숙명여자대학교 석사학위 청구논문 [Seoul: SookMyung Women's University Master's degree Dissertation].

Jeong, H., Lee, S., Kim, E., Park, H., Shin, H. and Kang, S. (1997). 청소년문제 예방을 위한 학교정신건강 프로그램의 개발 [The development of school mental health program for adolescent problem prevention]. 한국임상심리학회 [Seoul: *Korean Psychological Association Division of Clinical Psychology*], 42–70.

Jung, J. (2009). 학교기반 학교폭력 예방프로그램의 효과성 분석에 관한 연구 [Study of the effectiveness analysis of school based school violence prevention programs]. 한양대학교 행정-자치대학원 석사학위 청구논문 [Seoul: Hanyang University Graduate School of Public Administration Master's degree Dissertation].

Jung, W. (2012). 학교폭력의 실태 및 대응방안 [The actual condition and solution of school bullying and violence]. 한국범죄심리연구 [*Korea Criminal Psychology Research*], 8, 177–195.

Kwak, K. (1999). 학교폭력 및 왕따 예방프로그램(1): 개관 [A review of selected violence prevention programs in the schools]. 한국심리학회지: 사회문제 [*Korean Journal of Psychology: Social Issue*], 5, 105–122.

(2005). 학교폭력 예방 프로그램 개발에 관한 연구 [Research on the development of school violence prevention program]. KT&G 복지재단 결과보고서 [Seoul: KT&G Social Welfare Foundation Report].

(2006). 한국의 왕따 및 학교폭력: 특징과 한국형 예방프로그램 [Korean wang-ta and school violence: characteristics and prevention program]. 한국심리학회 [Seoul: *Korean Psychological Association*], 134–135.

(2008). 한국의 왕따와 예방프로그램 [Korean society and educational achievement: The flipside of achievement-delinquency among Korean adolescents: Korean wang-ta: characteristics and prevention program]

한국심리학회지: 사회문제 [*Korean Journal of Psychology: Social Issue*], 14, 255–272.

(2011). 학교폭력(성폭력) 예방 프로그램 개발 최종 보고서 [School violence (sexual violence) prevention program development final report]. 교육과학기술부. [Seoul: Ministry of Education, Science and Technology].

(2012). 중등 학교폭력 예방 교육자료 개발 최종 보고서 [Middle-school school violence prevention development final report] . 교육과학기술부[Seoul: Ministry of Education, Science and Technology].

Kwak, K., Kim, D., Kim, H., Koo, H. and National School Violence Countermeasure Council (2005). 학교폭력 예방 프로그램 개발에 관한 연구 [Research on the development of school violence prevention program]. 교육과학기술부 일반과제 보고서 [Seoul: Ministry of Education, Science and Technology Report].

교육과학기술부, 법무부 [Ministry of Education, Science and Technology and Ministry of Justice] (2009). 굿바이! 학교폭력 [Goodbye! School violence] : 학교폭력과 성폭력 예방 및 대처 가이드북 [School violence and sexual violence prevention and management guidebook. Seoul: Ministry of Education, Science and Technology Report].

Moon, Y. (2006). 학교폭력 예방과 상담 [*School violence prevention and counseling*]. 서울: 학지사 [Seoul: Hakjisa].

Park, H. (2013). 학교폭력 예방정책의 추진 현황과 과제 [School violence prevention policy's present condition and task]. 한국교육개발원 [Seoul: Korean Educational Development Institute].

Weissberg, R. P. and Greenberg, M. T. (1998). School and community competence-enhancement and prevention programs. In W. Damon and N. Eisenberg (Eds.), *Handbook of child psychology* (5th edn.). New York: John Wiley and Sons.

Wilt, M. E. (1959). *Creativity in the elementary school*. NY: Appleton-Century-Crofts.

18 Interventions against bullying in mainland China

Wenxin Zhang

As in other nations or cultures, school bullying is a prevalent phenomenon in mainland China (see Chapter 6). Approximately 25% of primary school students and 15% of middle school students have been found to be involved in regular interactions as either bullies or victims in mainland China (Zhang, 2002; and Chapter 6). There is evidence that both bullies and victims are confronted with a range of maladjustment issues: externalizing problems, internalizing problems, and even suicide (Cheng et al., 2010; Ji et al., 2011; Wang et al., 2012). There is a great need for effective bullying intervention programs to tackle school bullying and victimization in mainland China.

Since the development and implementation of the Olweus Bullying Prevention Program in Norway (Olweus, 1991, 1993), several major bullying intervention projects have arisen, including the PEACE Pack in Australia (Slee, 2001), the Sheffield Bullying Prevention Project in England (Smith et al., 2004), the Steps to Respect program in United States (Committee for Children, 2001), and the Donegal Primary Schools Anti-Bullying Intervention Project in Ireland (O'Moore and Minton, 2004) (see also Chapter 15). Given the cultural variations in characteristics of school bullying, these projects all have their unique features, although they all have some resemblance to the Norwegian model. They provide models and important implications for the development of bullying prevention programs in China.

Research on bullying began relatively later in China than in many western nations, and consequently, Chinese bullying intervention programs have been limited. Although peer bullying was specifically prohibited according to the *Regulations of Primary and Middle School Students* issued by the Ministry of Education (Ministry of Education, 2004), no government-sponsored bullying intervention programs were reported or implemented till the end of the twentieth century. However, we hold positive attitudes toward intervention against school bullying. It is fortunate to find that Chinese children reported higher levels of attitudes against bullying than their English counterparts (Ji et al., 2003;

and Chapter 9). In fact, the spirit of benevolence is thoroughly emphasized in Chinese moral systems. As a result, Chinese culture holds strongly negative attitudes toward bullying behavior, which means that the peers, parents, and teachers would be more likely to be inspired to prevent bullying behavior. However, intervention studies in China are scarce, and such efforts have only begun during the past decade.

In mainland China, since the prevalence of bullying in Chinese schools had been reported (Zhang, 2002), attention to bullying problems among children and youth has increased dramatically among the researchers, educators, and the general public. To explore the intervention model and strategies of school bullying applicable to Chinese schools, Zhang and his colleagues conducted a five-week intervention program with an action research method in a primary school in Jinan in the winter of 2000 (Ju, Wang, and Zhang, 2009; Zhang and Ju, 2008). This represented the first attempt at bullying-intervention in mainland China.

The goals of the program were (a) to help the participating school reduce the incidence of bullying and build a more respectful, cooperative, helpful, and safe classroom and school atmosphere, through this interventions in which students interacted with their peers and classmates in positive and proper ways and (b) to explore practical intervention strategies to tackle school bullying problems that can be generalized into Chinese primary and junior high schools.

Research design

The program adopted the conceptual structure and procedures of action research for the intervention program, but also used the experimental design of the experiment-control group with pre- and post-test. Both the experimental group and control group received pre- and post-test by questionnaire survey.

The intervention lasted for five weeks. The basic procedure designed for a five-week program contained three steps.

> *Step one:* Teacher training. To some extent, teachers work as practitioners and play a key role in action research, so it was necessary for them to master the relevant knowledge and skills that would be used for the intervention through a training program before the intervention actually started. For the purpose of the present intervention, the training program designed for the participating teachers involved four types of content: (1) basic knowledge of the procedure and methodology of educational research; (2) knowledge of school

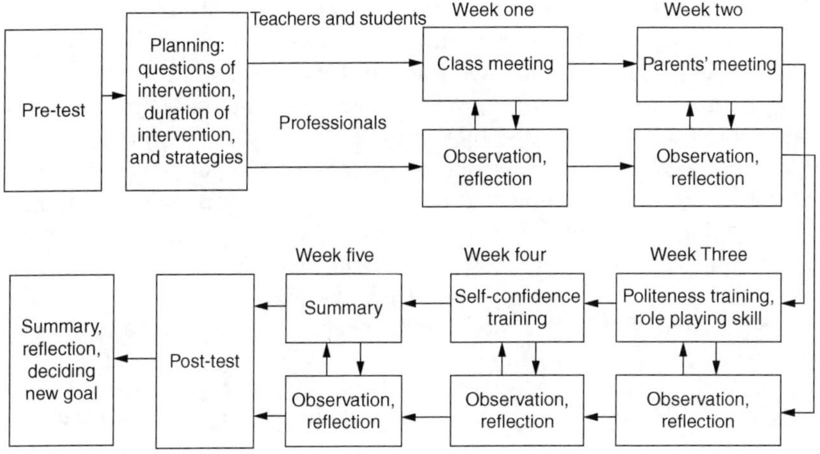

Figure 18.1 The process of intervention and activity arrangement in the intervention program in mainland China.

bullying; (3) action research; and (4) intervention skills, including brain storming, quality circle, self-confidence training, role-playing, and so on.

Step two: Designing a five-week intervention program. The intervention program was located basically at the class level. Intervention at the individual level, both for the victims and the bullies were nested into the interventions at class level.

Step three: Implementing the intervention program. The intervention program of each week was conducted in accordance with the model of action research: Planning-Action-Observation-Reflection, which is illustrated in Figure 18.1.

Participants

The participants were 354 students of grade 3 and 5 five (about age 9 to 11 years) from a primary school in Jinan City, capital of Shandong Province, China. Within each grade, two classes were randomly assigned as the experimental group ($n = 233$), and the other two were assigned as the control group ($n = 121$).

Evaluation of intervention

According to the result of the investigation prior to the intervention and also interviews with teachers and students, bullying/victimization among students took place not only within the school setting but also more frequently and seriously on the children's way to school and the way back home. Evaluations of the intervention effect in both settings were evaluated respectively via the following two different measures.

***Questionnaire on bullying/victimization*:** The Bullying/Victimization Questionnaire designed by Olweus (1993) is a self-report questionnaire that has been widely used in research of school bullying in different cultures. A modified Chinese version of this questionnaire was made by Zhang, Wu, and Jones (1999). Questions were used to assess the incidence and severity (frequency) of bullying/victimization on the way to school and on the way back home from school.

***"My Life in School" checklist*:** A checklist was developed to investigate the children's experience of bullying/victimization in the whole school settings (not only limited to their experiences on the way to school and the way back home) based upon the "My Life in School" checklist by Arora (1994). The participants completed this checklist on a weekly basis. With this measure, the researchers and participating teachers were able to learn about the situations of the bullying/victimization (including what happened to the children both within the school and out of school) and make timely judgments of the effects of the interventions.

***Open-ended questions*:** children were also asked about changes in their feelings concerning school life after the intervention.

Results

Percentage of children being victimized on the way to school and on the way home from school

The findings are shown in Figures 18.2 and 18.3. After the intervention, the percentage of children who reported being bullied "at least once or twice" during the course of the past five weeks on their way to school, which was 32% before intervention in the experimental group, dropped to 14%, and children who reported being bullied "often" or more frequently dropped from 10% to 5%. The corresponding reductions in the control group were from 37% to 22%, and 11% to 5%, respectively (Figure 18.2).

In terms of the incidence of being bullied on the way back home from school, the percentage of children in the experimental group who reported being bullied "at least once or twice" dropped from 35% to 17%, and for those bullied "often" or more it dropped from 11% to 8%. The corresponding reductions in the control group were from 45% to 38%, and 10% to 9%, respectively (Fig. 18.3).

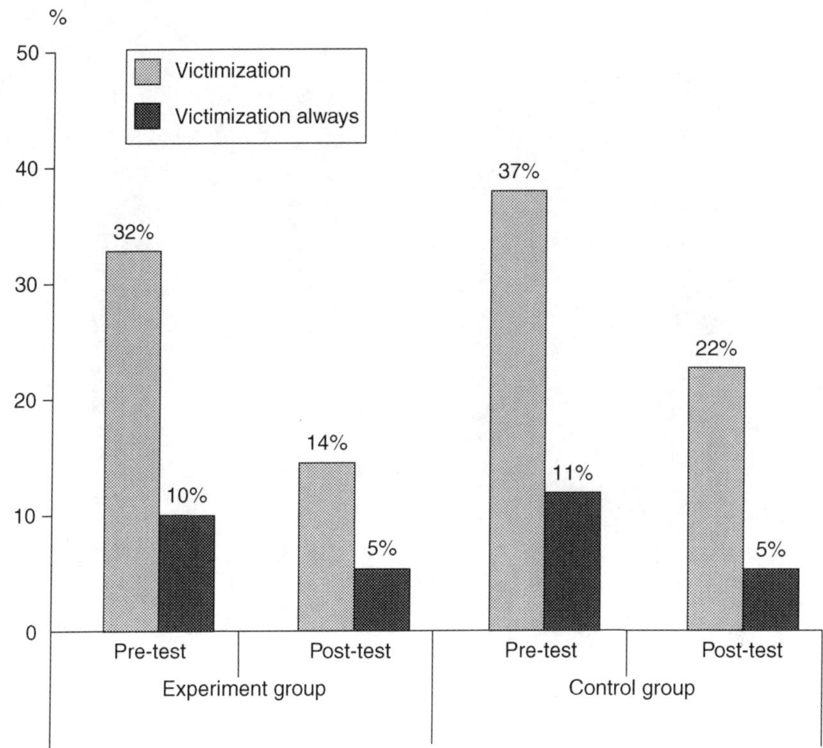

Figure 18.2 Changes in the percentage of children who reported being bullied on their way to school.

The number of students who reported being bullied on the way to school and on the way home reduced to some extent from the pre-test to the post-test, both in the experimental group and the control group. However, for the experimental group this reduction was of the order of 50%, both on the way to school and on the way home, and this was a significantly greater reduction than that seen in the control group.

Severity of children being bullied on the way to school and on the way back home from school

The changes in the reported severity (frequency) of peer victimization were used as an alternative way to further evaluate the effects of the intervention program. The means and standard deviations of severity of being bullied, both on the way to school and on the way back home are

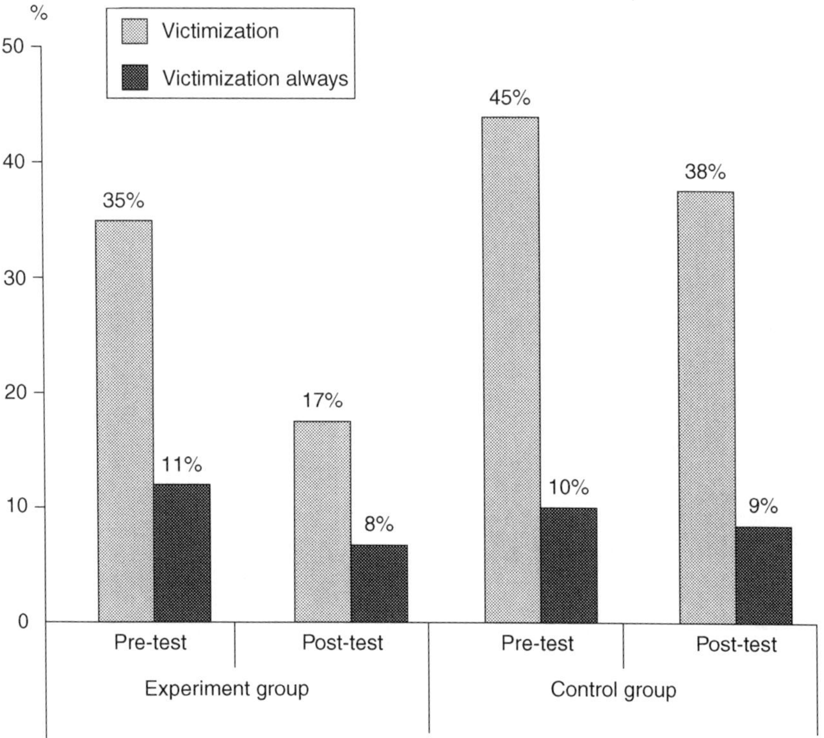

Figure 18.3 Changes in the percentage of children who reported being bullied on their way back home from school

shown in Table 18.1, for both the experimental and control groups. At pre-test data analysis indicated that the severity of being bullied for the children in the experimental and control groups did not differ significantly, either for going to school ($t = -0.139$, $p>0.05$), or back from school ($t = -0.486$, $p>0.05$). At post-test, the severity of being bullied on the way to school was still similar between the experimental and control groups ($t = -1.057$, $p>0.05$). However, on the way back home, children in the experimental group suffered much less victimization than those in the control group ($t = 2.58$, $p<0.05$). Paired samples t-tests of the mean scores at pre-test and post-test showed declines on the way to school in both experimental ($t = 4.54$, $p<0.01$) and control ($t = 3.19$, $p<0.01$) groups. However, for severity of being bullied on the way home, there was a significant reduction for children in the experimental group ($t = 3.86$, $p<0.01$), but no significant difference for the control group.

Table 18.1 *Mean severity (frequency) score of victimization on children's way to school and way back home from school.*

	Experiment group				Control group			
	Way to school		Way from school		Way to school		Way from school	
	M	*SD*	*M*	*SD*	*M*	*SD*	*M*	*SD*
Pre-test	1.57	1.08	1.58	1.03	1.59	1.00	1.64	0.93
Post-test	1.24	0.72	1.30	0.81	1.32	0.73	1.55	0.91

In summary, the intervention had some success in reducing the frequency and severity of being bullied by peers, on the way to school and especially on the way home.

Victimization in the school setting

Figure 18.4 shows changes in reports of being victimized in the experimental group children (in grades three and five separately), over the five weeks of the intervention. As can be seen, the mean scores for reported victimization decreased continuously from an average of 2.21 in week one to an average of 1.96 in week four. Results of a repeated measure Analysis of Variance (ANOVA) indicated that changes in scores of being bullied between successive weeks were significant ($F_{4,800} = 66.67$, $p<0.001$); further analysis indicated significant differences from week to week, up to week four, but no difference between week four and week five. There was no significant interaction between week and gender ($F_{4,800} = 1.49$, $p>0.05$). Although the downward trend in Figure 18.4 is evident at both grade three and grade five, there was a significant interaction between week and grade ($F_{4,800} = 6.70$, $p<0.001$). This interaction was found mainly between weeks one and two, where the frequency of victimization declined more rapidly for third graders than fifth graders; and between weeks four and five, where the frequency of victimization decreased further among third graders, but slightly increased among fifth graders.

In summary, experiences of victimization decreased rather steadily through the intervention period, for both boys and girls and for both grade levels; but the effects were most consistent among the third graders.

Changes in students' feelings after intervention

In response to questions about changes in their feelings concerning school life after the intervention, most students gave answers like

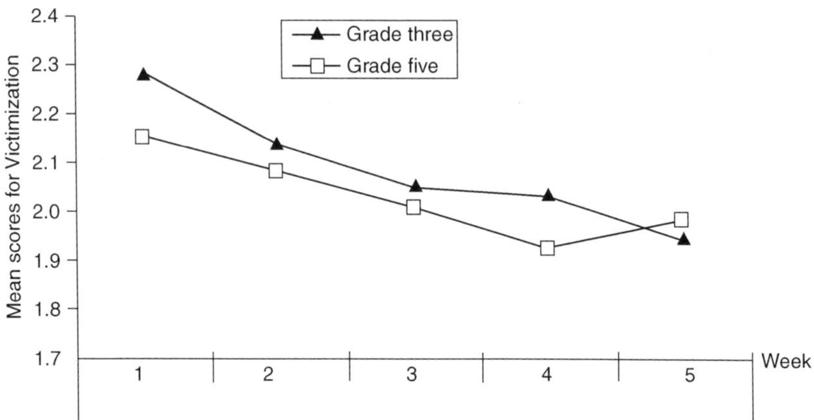

Figure 18.4 Changes of victimization in experimental group (grades three and five), by week, during intervention

"There is a decrease in the number of victims," "The number of bullies is going down," "I am bullied by others much less than I used to," "Civilized habits are getting more popular than before in our class," "Teachers now pay more attention to our life in school," "I can complain freely," "I can say anything in my mind," "I feel that school teachers and counselors are concerned about the bullying and victimization problem a big issue," "I feel good" and so on. These answers in general indicated that the intervention brought about a positive influence on students' feelings.

Discussion

Through a five-week intervention, a remarkable reduction was observed in both the incidence (namely, proportion of victims) and the extent of the severity (frequency) of victimization among the students of the experimental group both on the way to school and on the way home. The proportion of victims dropped by as much as 50 percent, and severity of peer victimization also reduced significantly. At the same time, through experimental intervention, positive changes also took place with regard to the bullying problem in the school setting as indicated by the reduction of the severity of peer victimization. The extent to which children reported being bullied in school declined continuously during the first four weeks of the intervention, among the experimental group. The participants reported that they felt safer after the intervention, the classroom atmosphere became more positive, and their satisfaction with school increased. This demonstrated that the intervention produced very positive effects on reducing the problem of bullying in the school.

A decline of the incidence of peer victimization on the way to school or on the way home was also observed between the pre- and post-test among the children in the control group, who did not receive the intervention; although the degree of decline in the control group was much less than that in the experimental group. Moreover, the severity level of victimization on the way to school also declined significantly among students of the control group. This may in large part be attributed to the spread or diffusion of the experimental treatment to the control group. Since all of the teachers in the same grade shared one office room, and the experimental and control classes were in neighboring classrooms, the effect of the intervention could easily have produced a spread effect on the teachers and the students of the control group. A similar phenomenon was also observed in previous studies (Smith and Shu, 2000; Olweus, 1991).

The results of this study indicated that the effect of the intervention, although found for both grade levels, brought about a greater reduction in the incidence of victimization in third graders than in fifth graders; the intervention program was more effective among younger children than among older children. This differentiation of intervention effect by age may be associated with changes in the characteristics of those children involved in bullying/victimization episodes. Some researchers have found that with an increase of age, bullies are increasingly inclined to rationalize their own bullying behavior when an episode occurs, such as considering victims to be withdrawn, unvalued or deserved, while bystanders give less help to victims and the victims request less aid from others. Such changes in the characters of bullies, bystanders and victims with age, may increase the difficulties of changing their behavior and thereby constrain the actual effect of the intervention.

Given that the goal of the present study was to help the school tackle the problem of school bullying, the methodology of action research seems to be the right choice for the intervention program. This methodology focuses on the change in the target behaviors in real situations. However, from the methodological point of view, while action research usually has good ecological validity, it has been criticized for a lack of scientific rigorousness or lower internal validity of research. This program adopted the conceptual structure and procedures of action research for the intervention program, but also used the experimental design of the experiment-control group with pre- and post-test. It is expected that such a combination of the advantages of action research and experimental design will help to overcome the shortages of each independent approach and help keep both a relatively high external and internal validity of the intervention research.

Although this intervention study produced very inspiring positive effects on reducing the incidence and severity of children's victimization by peers both in the school setting and on the way to school and back home from school, it is not without limitations. First of all, the intervention strategies of this study were designed mainly for bullying/victimization at a group level or classroom level; it was to a much less degree an individual-oriented program that focused on the intervention with typical bullies and victims. To the extent that bullying/victimization is both an individual and group process, it is important to pay more attention to how to use various psychological skills in intervening with typical bullies and victims on an individual level. Secondly, the social contexts of the children, including family, school, peer, social network, and so on, all have influences upon the incidence and development of children bullying. Therefore, an integrated model of intervention that can integrate the resources in family, school, peer, and community should be a direction for research in this area. A last but not least issue concerns the long-term effect of the intervention. The evaluation of the intervention effect in the present program was based upon the concurrent assessment of intervention effect, and information of the long-term effect of the intervention is still lacking. Future researchers should consider the assessment for the long-term effect of such intervention programs.

REFERENCES

Arora, C. M. J. (1994). Measuring bullying with the 'life in school' checklist. *Pastoral Care in Education*, 12, 11–15.

Cheng, Y., Newman, I. M., Qu, M., Mbulo, L., Chai, Y., Chen, Y., and Shell, D. F. (2010). Being bullied and psychosocial adjustment among middle school students in China. *Journal of School Health*, 80, 193–199.

Committee for Children (2001). *Steps to Respect: A bullying prevention program*. Seattle, WA and www.cfchildren.org.

Ji, L. Q., Chen, L., Xu, F. Z., Zhao, S. Y., and Zhang, W. X. (2011). A longitudinal analysis of the association between peer victimization and patterns of psychosocial adjustment during middle and late childhood (in Chinese). *Acta Psychologica Sinica*, 43, 1151–1162.

Ji, L., Zhang, W., Jones, K. and Smith, N. (2003). A comparison of children's attitudes towards bullying between Chinese and British children (in Chinese). *Studies of Psychology and Behavior*, 1, 122–127.

Ju, Y. C., Wang, S. Q., Zhang W. X. (2009). Intervention research on school bullying in primary schools. *Frontiers of Education in China*, 4, 115–116.

Ministry of Education (2004). *Notification on the publication of the regulations of primary and middle school students*. Retrieved Nov 9, 2015 from www.moe.gov.cn/publicfiles/business/htmlfiles/moe/s3325/201001/81948.html

O'Moore, A. M. and Minton, S.J. (2004). Ireland: The Donegal Primary Schools anti-bullying project. In P.K. Smith, D. Pepler, and K. Rigby (Eds.), *Bullying in schools: How successful can interventions be?* (pp. 275–288). Cambridge: Cambridge University Press.

Olweus, D. (1991). Bullying/victim problems among school children: Basic facts and effects of a school based intervention program. In D. J. Pepler and K. H. Rubin (Eds.), *The development and treatment of childhood aggression* (pp. 411–448). Hillsdale, NJ: Erlbaum.

(1993). *Bullying at school: What we know and what we can do*. Oxford: Blackwell.

Slee, P. T. (2001). *The PEACE Pack: A program for reducing bullying in our Schools* (3rd edn.). Adelaide, Australia: Flinders University.

Smith, P.K. and Shu, S. (2000). What good schools can do about bullying: Findings from a survey in English schools after a decade of research and action. *Childhood*, 7, 193–212.

Smith, P. K., Sharp, S., Eslea, M. and Thompson, D. (2004). England: The Sheffield project. In P. K. Smith, D. Pepler, and K. Rigby (Eds.), *Bullying in schools: How successful can interventions be?* (pp. 99–124). Cambridge: Cambridge University Press.

Wang, H., Zhou, X., Lu, C., Wu, J., Deng, X., Hong, L., Gao, X., and He, Y. (2012). Adolescent bullying involvement and psychosocial aspects of family and school life: A cross-sectional study from Guangdong province in China. *PLoS One*, 7, e38619.

Zhang, W. X. (2002). Prevalence and major characteristics of bullying/victimization among primary and junior middle school children (in Chinese). *Acta Psychologica Sinica*, 34, 387–394.

Zhang, W. X. and Ju, Y. C. (2008). Intervention research on bullying of pupils in primary schools (in Chinese). *Educational Research*, 30, 95–99.

Zhang, W. X., Wu, J. F., and Jones, K. (1999). The modification of a Chinese version of the Olweus Bully/Victim Questionnaire (in Chinese). *Psychological Development and Education*, 15, 7–11.

Siu Fung Lin and Chi Leung Lai

Hong Kong has been affected by both Western and Chinese culture for over one hundred years. However, until recently schools in Hong Kong have adopted a traditional Chinese way to handle school bullying. Punitive measures such as de-meriting the students involved, informing parents and suspension from schools have long been used. One reason for this may be that some school personnel are afraid that school bullying could be closely related to triad society and related gang activities; according to the Hong Kong Police (2003), 141 people were arrested and charged with triad-related offences through under-cover operations in several secondary schools from 1999 to 2001.

Many Western countries have been using anti-bullying strategies such as whole-school approach, peer mediation and anger-management curricula. However, a survey by Wong and Lo (2002) found that not many teachers and principals in Hong Kong understood these concepts and made little or no attempt to adopt them. Informal interviews with experienced and senior schoolteachers confirmed that they were given zero guideline or guidance as to how to handle school bullying before 2000.

In fact, school bullying was never discussed in a high profile way and was even considered as a kind of taboo topic – something shameful for the school if it happened. No history of school bullying intervention can be found in Hong Kong before the school year 2004–2005. However, some severe cases of bullying in 2003 raised public concern and opened up discussion (see Chapter 7). The year 2004 marked a beginning of awareness of school bullying as a general problem. Only in the last decade have programs and guidelines for dealing with school bullying been developed by governmental authorities, NGOs, and local practitioners (see Fung and Wong, 2007; EMB 2004; EDB 2008; 2012; Caritas Website www.ghs.edu.hk/sec/panel/ict/Project/12–13/F2_Web/2E_23/web/aricle_d.html).

Legislative effort and responsibilities of the Education Bureau (EDB)

In February 2004, the Legislative Council, in response to a series of bullying events, held a meeting specifically on school bullying and proposed research into the issue. In March 2004, an information document on bullying was disseminated. The EDB summarised mostly Western studies on characteristics of bullies and victims, aggressive behaviours and parenting style and teachers' perceptions and attitudes towards bullying (Legislative Council, March 2004). It produced a set of resources for schools, taking the stance that school bullying is not to be tolerated (zero-tolerance), and reminding schools to adopt a school-based whole-school approach in combating and preventing bullying. School-based programs are to be monitored by school boards.

Following a second wave of bullying incidents in 2008–9 (see Chapter 7), the Education Bureau commented that it was important how adults, and in the case of a school setting, the teachers, handled it. EDB reported that in 2008–9 more than forty workshops were conducted, training approximately 3,500 teachers how to identify, handle and prevent school bullying. Another resource pack was distributed to schools for the promotion of anti-bullying work (*Wen Wei Pao*, 28 January, 2010). EDB also proposed that Educational Psychologists, School Development Officers of the Regional Education Offices and the Guidance and Discipline Section should provide consultation and on-site support with reported school bullying cases. In another special meeting on School bullying (LC Paper No. CB(2) 1034/07–08(01), February, 2008), it reiterated zero-tolerance to school bullying, that more counselling staff would be deployed to primary schools, and that a 'one school, one social worker' policy at secondary schools would stay.

An extra 1,000 program workers were hired to assist school social workers in conducting activities for secondary students. Activities were designed to develop the psychological and physical well-being and potential of students at secondary level. Lifeskills training was also introduced in the school curriculum. The EDB has commissioned local tertiary education institutions to provide training courses to school teachers. The curriculum of the in-service course for school guidance officers and counselling team teachers has a 3-hour lecture on school bullying among adolescents and may include specific intervention strategies. In the 2011–12 school year, anti-bullying days/ weeks were launched and participating schools were supported with promotional materials with a core message that bullying in any form is not tolerated.

Home-school co-operation was also encouraged; parent-teacher associations were set up and parent education courses organised by NGOs. The content of these courses includes how to handle children with behavioural problems and how to support children against bullying. Leaflets were distributed to parents about the promotion of harmonious school environments ('Help your child to establish harmonious peer relationships in school'; Legislative Council, 2008).

In response to the new and seemingly fast growing phenomenon of cyberbullying (see *China Daily* Hong Kong Edition, 2 June, 2010), the Hong Kong Federation of Youth Groups joined with fourteen other NGOs and in 2009 launched an Internet Education Campaign: 'Be Net-wise'. The campaign was supported by the Office of the Government Chief Information Officer and sponsored by the Hong Kong Government. Also, the Office of the Privacy Commissioner for Personal Data (PCPD) has published the Personal Data (Privacy) Ordinance Liberal Studies Teaching Kit, to act as a resource pack for secondary teachers to teach students how to protect their personal data (see www.pcpd.org.hk/youthprivacy/teaching-resources.html).

Suggestions were given on cyberbullying based on Bhat, Chang and Linscott (2010): (a) a definition of cyberbullying and behavioural examples of types of actions that constitute cyberbullying; (b) knowledge and understanding of the types of ICT used to cyberbully; (c) roles in cyberbullying, including that of active cyberbully, secondary cyberbully, observer and target and what actions each one can take to prevent cyberbullying (a clear list of do's and don'ts); (d) specific safety and reporting features associated with each type of technology; (e) specific actions students should take if they are cyberbullied, such as taking screen shots, printing evidence, speaking to trusted adults and not retaliating as this often escalates the cyberbullying; (f) behavioural examples of types of actions that are to be taken to curb cyberbullying; (g) understanding the detrimental psychological, social and academic effects of cyberbullying experienced by targets of such attacks; (h) reporting procedures for cases of cyberbullying and encouragement of observers to step forward to stop the harassment and (i) clear consequences for those who engage in cyberbullying.

We now describe some specific intervention measures used in Hong Kong schools.

Intervention measures

Building Harmonious School Environments Together
「和諧校園齊創建」 *2004*

This resource package was prepared by the EDB in 2004. It was initially in the format of a CD, distributed to all schools but usually, kept and circulated amongst the counselling team. The package aimed at improving human relationship education and it's slogan was「承責改進法」 'Be responsible and improve'. Teachers were required to stop bullying behaviours and help students solve the problem with five propositions: (1) revisit the situation, (2) evaluate personal responsibility, (3) bear responsibility, (4) improve and (5) work towards harmony. The program adopted ideas from Solution-Focused Therapy (Metcalf, 1995/2008; Huicheng He 何會成, 2003; Jialing Wu, 吳家玲, 2003), the No Blame Approach (Maines and Robinson, 1992; Sullivan, 2000) and the Pikas Method of Shared Concern (Pikas, 1989, 2002; Sullivan, 2000). Teachers were advised to develop and use counselling skills and follow a five-step process with bullying incidents: (1) Interview the bully(ies), (2) interview the victim(s), (3) train other parties involved including bystanders and prepare them to discuss together, (4) reconciliation and (5) follow-up.

This package is thus far the most comprehensive available and ready for use by any teacher. It contains eight major sections:

(1) Philosophy and theoretical postulates: an orientation to the definitions of bullying and worldwide recognition of the issue; there are cases presented in drama to illustrate what constitutes school bullying, roles in bullying and types of bullying.

(2) Assessment: three questionnaires ready-made for schools to perform school-based evaluations – a simple questionnaire in Chinese language modified from Sharp and Smith (1994), data input method and analysis; a teacher observation form and reports from classmates modified from (吳徐玉儀、蔡黎惠賢、曾惠美、張春儀、李馮秀華及胡杏芳; Yuk Yi, Tsui; Wai Yin, Lai; Wai-mei, Tsang; Chun Yee, Tjon; Sau Wa, Fung; Hang Fong, Wu. [2002]).

(3) School policy: the concept of Whole School Approach as used in western countries (Olweus, 1991; Chazan, Laing and Davies, 1994; Smith et al., 1999; Newman, Horne and Bartolomucci, 2000) and steps towards a successful implementation.

(4) Dealing with the bullying case「承責改進法」'Bearing the responsibilities and improve', exemplified with case studies in written form and with videos for demonstrations of skills and steps.

(5) Follow up package: supports and follow up work needed for both bullies and victims at the class level, activities with instructions provided in detail.

(6) Prevention: seventeen lesson plans with objectives and activities on concepts like against bullying, love and respect, be fair and cooperative. There are worksheets designed for download and for immediate use by school teachers, and stories prepared for discussion and personal reflection.

(7) Teacher training: sets of materials designed for school-based training or self-use.

(8) Resources: a list of books, articles and related web sites for further use and/or references.

It is a simple-to-use pack with concepts illustrated in interesting ways. However, the resource pack and suggestions from the EDB posed some difficulties: the pack is only available in Chinese language and not available in any other languages, therefore English and other language speaking children and teachers have no chance to use it; the 'whole school approach' was not so clearly explained to those who are unused to the idea – the suggestions were sound but would need a special working group to implement all year through and involved all parties in the school; skills and strategies were introduced to teachers for handling or preventing school bullying in the format of worksheets and stories provided; however, demonstrations and some training for inexperienced teachers would be more desirable – ongoing training workshops should be provided for the use of this package; 'school monitoring' in a broad sense without specific guidelines would be difficult for schools to follow; and 'reminding' would not help any school or teacher to enforce anything in addition to a normal teaching load or routine.

This 2004 package was revised and re-issued in 2010.

Building Harmonious School Environments Together – zero tolerance of bullying in schools「和諧校園齊創建 - 校不容凌」*2010*

This new version of the 'Building Harmonious School Environments Together' became an online resource. It has added material in three areas: drama for preventive measures, parental guidance, and dealing with cyberbullying. Yet, it is still in Chinese language only and no English version is available for non-Cantonese-speaking school children and teachers.

The drama section, with reference to Neelands and Goode (1990), provides skills for preparing teachers in running eight sessions for Primary level and four sessions for Secondary level. All have the same objectives, leading children to experience and reflect on the three roles played in a bullying scenario. All the dramas were designed with an open ending, allowing students to play a different role (bullies, victims and bystanders) and leading to different endings according to the actions they take. This is to help them think, feel and then understand another's situation.

The parental guidance part was a crucial section missing in the earlier version. Without educating the parents, it is difficult to gain their cooperation and their awareness of the issues concerned. This can be a foundation of prevention. These guidelines included basic understanding of the nature of bullying and its consequences on the child, parental observation, identifying and discussing with the child and school about bullying, how to deal with the immediate situation and how parents can encourage good behaviour in their children in their everyday life.

A one-page guideline on cyberbullying prevention was given in the session 'dealing with school bullying' in the package and also integrated in 'types of bullying' for parents.

The package is supplemented with ready-made materials for teachers, such as Stories for Assemblies with a theme on anti-bullying cases, and worksheets designed for student reflection. Although these do not provide an exhaustive list of stories for the full year, it is a comprehensive and usable set of materials that sets a very good example for teachers to follow when preparing for assemblies. Practical and useful documents are provided: lists of to-do checklists, flow chart for handling bullying cases, bully records and guidelines for counselling bully cases with detailed advice. These materials and resources would definitely help those who may not have the opportunity to attend special training in the area and who are overwhelmed with the situation and other workloads.

Project CARE: Child and Adolescents at Risk Education
「有教無戾 2006–2011

With support from the Quality Education Fund in 2006, the project CARE launched a one-year program in ten secondary schools. It adopted an Ecosystemic Model with children level, school and teacher level, peer and parent level and involved social workers, school counsellors, school teachers, school children and their parents. Two school talks were arranged for children on educating their understanding of school bullying, two training workshops for teachers and school management, and two talks for parents on parenting issues and their knowledge of children's emotions. Triangulation of data/information from teacher observation, parent interviews and student interviews was used for the identification of bullying, and group interventions were provided for both aggressors and victims. Ten sessions of Cognitive-Behavioural Therapy / Attribution training were conducted which included re-building self-image, self-confidence, assertiveness training, anger management, effective communicating and building relationships with others and conflict resolution skills.

Adopting Crick and Dodge's (1996) framework on aggression, school bullying incidents were categorised as proactive aggression or reactive aggression. The roles of bullies were then categorised as proactive aggressor or reactive aggressor according to their intention; while victims were categorised as aggressive victim or passive victim based on their characteristics (Fung and Wong, 2007). The assessment tools were the Child Behavior Checklist Youth Self-Report (CBCL-YSR) (Achenbach, 1991); the Reactive and Proactive Questionnaire (RPQ) (Raine et al., 2006); and the Peer Victimization Questionnaire (PVQ) (Lopez, 1997; see Lopez and DuBois, 2005). Since the reactive aggressor and passive victim roles were most numerous, they were selected for the core training for the ten intervention sessions. There are two sets of intervention program designed for these two types of participants.

The program for reactive aggressors adopted a cognitive and behavioural therapy approach and implemented ABC (Activating event, Belief and Consequence) as a core. The first 2 sessions were for self and group goal setting, and exploring the 5 senses. There followed 5 sessions on ABC training, 1 session on understanding emotions and emotional management, 1 session on 'I' message and a last session integrating ABC and the use of 'I' messages. The program was structured with ready-made worksheets for a group no bigger than 8 people. Each session was 1.5 hours, a reasonable duration for 11- to 18-year olds and for a group discussion. However, the core teaching of the ABC model was brief for understanding, sharing and reflecting in only about half an hour in session 3. The worksheets were all open-ended exercises that require very experienced counsellors to direct group members towards achieving the goals. Also, the exercises were rather general; effective use of content analysis from individual interviews so that the exercises focused on participants' problems in their everyday encounters and targeted at the characteristics of reactive aggressors might be more useful.

The program for passive victims stemmed from attribution theory (Heider, 1958), including hostile attribution bias, situational attribution, and dispositional attribution. There were altogether 10 sessions; 2 on sense of security, 1 on self-esteem and the remaining 7 on rational and irrational attributions. Sessions were conducted in groups with video presentations that were analysed and discussed.

The intervention program was provided step-by-step guidance towards building a rational belief system. The content is rich and deserves additional training sessions for the process of change to happen and consolidate. The idea of using case studies for learning these concepts was excellent; however, the cases used were in a broad range of experiences such as parent-child conflicts, love and dating issues, sibling rivalries, football match etc. Only a few scenarios were related to the role of a victim.

An evaluation of the project was made by giving children pre- and post-test performances on stress coping (home interview with child, Dodge, Bates and Pettit, 1990), anger control (Anger-self-report, Zelin, Adler and Myerson, 1972), level of depression and anxiety (CBCL-YSR), inattentive behaviours in class and aggressive behaviours (teachers' interview and observation). Over a 3-month period, data from 41–47 aggressors showed significant declines on anger level, aggressive behavioural levels, and inattentive behaviours in class. Data from 65–71 victims showed significant declines in anxiety/depression, victimisation scores, social exclusion scores and inattentive behaviours in class (Fung and Wong, 2007). However, there was no mention of any no-treatment control, so there could have been other factors that affected the decline of aggressive behaviours.

In July 2009, the program received further funding from the Quality Education Fund for another 3 years to extend the intervention to another 10 secondary schools and 10 primary schools. Therefore, another analysis was done for the project: 5,025 students from ten secondary schools completed measures including the CBCL-YSR and the RPQ; 63 students (38 males and 25 females) aged 11 to 17 years old who displayed proactive aggression were randomly assigned to a one and a half hours cognitive-behavioural group. Due to the very high attrition rate, the final sample used in the analysis included 46 students (29 males and 17 females). Scores were compared at initial screening, post-test and follow-up assessments at 3 months, 6 months, 1 year and 2 years. Proactive, reactive and physical aggression scores significantly decreased (except for verbal aggression), but levels of empathy failed to increase after the intervention. However, qualitative analyses showed that after intervention, students demonstrated much empathic understanding, for example, 'he had his reasons' or 'he may have felt frustrated' (Fung, 2011).

A further study of CARE was done in 2012. From 5,089 students, 269 aggressive victims were identified; of these, 68 (48 boys and 20 girls) aged 11 to 16 were randomly assigned to 10 cognitive-behavioural groups. They received sessions on cognitive distortions, emotional skill deficits, and behavioural regulation impairments. Of these, 39 completed a one-year follow-up assessment. Scores on reactive aggression, aggressive behaviour, and various forms of victimisation (physical, verbal and social exclusion) declined significantly over time (post-test, six months, and one year), as did levels of anxiety/depression, trait anger and anger expression (but not anger control) (Fung, 2012). Again, there appears to have been no no-treatment control.

The CARE program is a costly intervention. Although screening was done in a massive scale (over 5,000 pupils per cohort), only 13% fell into their selected proactive aggressor and reactive victim categories, although many of the exercises could be useful in a whole-school approach. Another issue with CARE is that cyberbullying was not considered. The value of this pioneer study is the positive significant outcome that gives a direction to help proactive aggressors and reactive victims in schools. For the benefit of both schoolteachers and students, a simplified version of the CARE program would be helpful. Perhaps ten sessions could be used by class teachers for general education purposes. It would certainly help to promote everyday interactions without aggression and negative attributions. That would serve as an effective preventative as well as intervention measure.

P.A.T.H.S. to Adulthood 2004–8, 2009–12, 2013–now

A citywide inclusive Youth Enhancement Scheme, 'P.A.T.H.S. (Positive Adolescent Training through Holistic Social Programs to Adulthood) was jointly launched by the Research Team (academics from 5 universities), Social Welfare Department and Education Bureau and funded by the Hong Kong Jockey Club in 2004–2008. Altogether 198 secondary schools participated in 2005 and an evaluation of its effectiveness was done. The scheme aimed to promote the holistic development of adolescents at Secondary level. The curriculum adopted incorporates fifteen psychological constructs including sexuality, internet addiction, substance abuse and bullying, with an attempt to promote students' psychosocial competencies (Shek, Ma and Sun, 2011). The original phase was from 2004 to 2008, with an extension phase from 2009 to 2012 and a further extension to make it a community-based program for non-participating schools and junior forms commencing from 2013 until now.

In P.A.T.H.S., there are Tier 1 and Tier 2 Programs. The Tier 1 Program is for every student in Secondary 1 to Secondary 3, with normally 20 hours at each grade with 40 teaching units. The program includes bonding, resilience, social competence, emotional competence, cognitive competence, behavioural competence, moral competence, self-determination, spirituality, self-efficacy, clear and positive identity, beliefs in the future, recognition for positive behaviour, opportunities for prosocial involvement and fostering prosocial norms. One out of five students who have psychosocial needs were selected to the Tier 2 Program.

One aim of Tier 1 was to use a preventative measure to handle bullying by training students' skills of bonding and relationship with others. It can be part of the developmental guidance curriculum in classroom. The objectives were to create a warm school environment with harmony and respect to each other. Students learn how to show compassion, tolerance and forgiveness to others. This program can be part of the whole school approach in which all teachers and peers and other staff can support the building of a safe and caring school culture in which bullying cannot exist.

Evaluation of the scheme showed consistently that P.A.T.H.S. was effective in promoting an overall positive youth development including tackling school bullying (Shek et al., 2008; Shek and Sun, 2008; Shek and Ng, 2009a,b,c; Shek, 2010; Tsang et al., 2010; Shek and Sun, 2010).

Be Net-wise 2009–10

A year-long Internet Education Campaign, 'Be Net-Wise', initiated by the Hong Kong Government, and coordinated by the Hong Kong Federation of Youth, was launched between September 2009 and August 2010. The aim was to promote and enhance safe and responsible internet activities, and raise awareness of net safety amongst young people, so as to develop good practices when using the internet. Be Net-wise is a City-Wide Internet Education Campaign, targeted at Primary and Lower Secondary school children, school teachers and parents. Activities include mass level education and individual and family support. At mass level, the public were educated via exhibitions, talks and workshops, web games and resources for youth posted on the internet, resources for teaching and multi-media competitions. At a personal and family level, the campaign provided a family service support centre and home visits, and trained ambassadors provided hotline support. Parents were educated, not only on general and basic knowledge on internet and safe internet usage, but also on children's developmental capability and ability to understand and use the internet properly and safely. The guideline for parental guidance was very thorough, described according to developmental stages (5–7 years, 8–12 years, 13–17 years and 18 years or above).

A research study was carried out in April–May 2010; this involved 18 secondary schools with 2,981 questionnaires collected from students, plus interviews with academics, council members, social workers, educational practitioners and representatives from the Hong Kong Internet Society. The study found substantial prevalence of cyberbullying and compared with studies done earlier, the trend was on the rise (see Chapter 7); based on features of cyberbullying identified, they made recommendations for more research; for media literacy education in schools, including guidelines for students in handling cyberbullying; requirements for network suppliers to set up rules of safe internet use; and provision of detailed guidelines to parents and educators as a basic and essential preventive measure (Hong Kong Federation of Youth Groups and Office of the Government Chief Information Officer, 2010).

English-speaking schools in Hong Kong

None of the above programs provided support or intervention for non-Cantonese-speaking school children in Hong Kong. Most of the English schools are privately owned and not under the EDB. These schools charge large school fees and take pupils from well-off families. They are rather independent in their school management, finance and education policies, including on handling school bullying.

However a few government-owned English-speaking schools (primary and secondary) take children of minorities living in Hong Kong, mainly from the Philippines, Pakistan, India, Korea, Taiwan and some local children returning from other countries. These children cannot read or write in Chinese. How do these schools cope with bullying?

One of these government English-speaking primary schools adopted the 'Don't laugh at me' program from the United Kingdom/United States (Roerden, 2000) and made it a whole school approach. The basic structure of the program was on four major themes: expressing feelings, caring and cooperating, resolving conflicts and celebrate diversity. These schools spent class time on using the program, held an anti-bullying week, taught all children in the school to sing the song 'Don't laugh at me' and children were taught how to respond to bullying in various forms via lyrics of the song, that is, simply say, 'don't laugh at me', 'don't call me names'. Assemblies using bullying as themes were held with dramas and role-plays. Individually, teachers all got involved in counselling pupils and helping them to resolving conflicts. It was found to be helpful and effective by both school teachers and children, over a year-long intervention. The song is easy to pick up and the lyrics are educational on anti-bullying.

A comparison of different approaches

Four international secondary schools using the British National Curriculum each tried a different approach, over seven months of a school year (Wurf, 2012). The four approaches were

(1) a Curriculum intervention was adopted across the whole year 7. It involved role-play, class discussions, cooperative learning activities and worksheets, with objectives that students would be able to define bullying, differentiate types of bullying, identify bullying situations and therefore protect themselves and avoid bullying happening.

(2) Pikas's Method of Shared Concern (1989, 2002); when incidents of bullying occurred, the five phase model was used: teacher talks with student(s) to elicit a constructive solution, teacher shows empathy and options for mediation, teacher monitors the commitment of mediation and how the bullying should stop, teacher meets all parties involved and they come to an agreement among them for prevention, and follow up meetings to ensure bullying does not happen anymore.

   Also, across the whole of year 7 (secondary one), the Pikas method was used together with the Curriculum intervention and increased supervision and monitoring within and outside class.

(3) a Whole School approach. An assembly was held with a summary of the pre-test results. Students were invited to get involved in setting up an anti-bullying school policy and this raised their awareness and concern. Over a subsequent three-week period, they had lessons conducted by class teachers, with a video on bullying and class discussions; group exercises to identify types of bullying in their school, and to suggest solutions; and role play activities with worksheets on possible responses to bullying. The school used existing disciplinary procedures for the management of bullying incidents and did not implement any mediation or monitoring procedures.

(4) a Control school where no special intervention took place.

At each school, a pre-test took place at the end of the first term while a post-test happened at the end of the year. The English version of the Olweus (1991) questionnaire was used to identify the incidence of bullying. A total of 545, year 7 pupils from 21 classes in the four schools (equivalent to Secondary 1 in the mainstream) participated, with a 7-month follow up after intervention.

A systematic comparison on students' self-reports of both bully and victim roles in the four schools found the Whole School approach the most effective with a highly significant reduction in school bullying. The next most effective was the combination of Curriculum and Pikas method across year 7. However, the Pikas method on its own was ineffective, with some increase in bullying at post-test while bully rate was the highest in the control school (Wurf, 2012).

The apparent lack of effectiveness of the Pikas approach on its own suggests that students who committed bullying noticed that there was no disciplinary consequences and only talks and agreements. The findings also suggest the importance of curriculum for changing students' attitudes; and a curriculum might have helped to have a consensus amongst all parties in the whole school ecosystem. Wurf agreed with Ttofi and Farrington's (2011) meta-analysis (see also Chapter 15), that combining approaches together in an anti-bullying intervention leads to higher success rates.

Using a Restorative Whole-school approach

Wong et al. (2011) reported intervention work with 4 schools in 2004–06. The schools were offered training in a restorative program (see p.307). This involved anti-bullying policies, workshops and talks for parents, mediation services for resolving conflicts for students, peace education and training programs for school staff. One school was judged to have fully implemented this, two to have partially implemented it, and one did not implement any of the activities. Altogether 1480 students aged 13–15 years participated. Pre- and post-tests were conducted with a 15-month interval. Amongst a range of attitudes and behaviours measured, personal experiences of four types of bullying perpetration were assessed by 12 items with a 4-point scale. Reduction of bullying was greatest in the school that fully adopted restorative practices, and less but still significant in the two schools that partially adopted it; whereas bullying got significantly worse in the one school that did not implement the program. There were some corresponding changes in empathic attitudes and self-esteem.

Children with special needs

Children with special needs are more vulnerable to bullying because of their learning difficulties or their social and emotional problems. However, their vulnerability is often ignored, and they may receive little protection against bullying (Whitney, Smith and Thompson, 1994). Coping strategies of children with various special needs may need teachers who specialise in that particular area to help. Thus, school bullying concerns should be included in pre- and in-service training courses in Special Needs. Although the P.A.T.H.S. program extended their service to special schools in 2006–7, it was only advising special schools to modify their Tier 1 to suit their own needs.

Suggestions for future directions

In the next sections, we offer some suggestions for future directions in Hong Kong.

Localize coping strategies for Chinese school children

Coping strategies in response to bullying are an important component to consider. Kristensen and Smith (2003) investigated 9–16 year old children in Denmark and found that they preferred approach to avoidance strategies. Nevertheless, research in Hong Kong has found that school children generally prefer the use of avoidance to approach strategies (Fung, 2007, Wong et al., 2002). Unfortunately, the research evidence suggests that avoidance strategies (such as trying to ignore the problem) are not often successful. It is culturally entrenched that Chinese do not tend to confront, and assertiveness is an ideology that is never mentioned in our formal and informal education. In fact, it is hard to find the exact word to translate 'assertiveness' into Chinese language. As such, language itself reflects how difficult it is if we wish to teach our school children to be assertive and to approach the problem rather than avoid it.

The approach strategies need to be adjusted and not directly imported from western studies. Also, our schools and other authorities need to have monitoring and supervisory system ready so that children will feel comfortable and confident in using approach strategies and reporting bullying; for example, setting up a regular weekly or monthly checking initiated by the class teacher or guidance teacher; or making use of a post box for reporting, for both victims and bystanders; or, making use of a chat room, email account or mobile number for students to call/message for help.

Legal education

Our education system has not encouraged us to explore our human or legal rights in our community and society. Again, like the absence of assertiveness, it is another characteristic of a collective society. It is time for us to inform our younger generations what their legal rights and responsibilities are, especially as regards personal safety, personal data protection, respect for copyright, privacy and confidentiality. The law on child protection should be noted too, especially with very high rates of web surfing and browsing social networking sites among our young people (Xu, 2010).

Traditional or Confucius value re-visited – forgiveness

What have we learned from the International Schools' experience? An awareness of the values of forgiveness and respect. According to the CARE program, most of the bullies were proactive ones who have chosen to take revenge when hurt by their offenders. Consistent with an earlier study with American children by Hepp-Dax (1996), Hui and Chau (2009) found forgiveness intervention effective with Hong Kong Chinese children adopting Enright and Coyle's (1998) process model. It is an eight-week intervention and led to children's attitude change in forgiveness towards offenders, and had positive effects on overall psychological well-being. When it becomes a strategy for conflict resolution, children will choose not to retaliate and cut the chain of any further bullying act. It is a component included in P.A.T.H.S. Forgiveness is not a value new to our culture but a deeply entrenched Chinese traditional value. Therefore, integrating forgiveness as a component in the school curriculum could be helpful with the intervention and prevention of bullying.

Media literacy education

We are living in an era of global citizenship and netizen-ship. Our schoolchildren were born with all kinds of media around them and are considered the first generation of netizens. With high exposure to the media, it is essential that they are able to analyse, evaluate, screen and select information they want, including rejecting bullying. When school children become conscious of the author of the messages, purposes and examine the techniques and point of view of the sender, they would become an informed netizen and be net-wise. Bhat et al., (2010) together with Potter (2001) would be a good introduction to the issue, and integrating some sessions into the liberal studies in both our lower and upper secondary curriculum could be a good idea.

Parent education

If school bullying is a systemic and a complex process of social inter-actions that involves bullies, victims, peers, adults, parents and school as well as home environments (Vreeman and Carroll, 2007), cyberbullying increases the level of complication. School has been a major platform and provider of intervention and prevention in the past decade; however, parent education needs to be our next target, to educate, support and collaborate with parents in helping them manage the fast growing media use of their children and the increased difficulties in tackling cyberbully-ing and safety on the internet.

Teacher's perceptions

Teachers' perceptions and knowledge about school bullying need to be increased via in-service training. Regular workshops on handling bullying incidents, counselling students and communicating with parents would be beneficial. Sharing the difficulties and successes in the adoption of a whole school approach would be a good way to provide continual support and advice.

Summary of the situation in Hong Kong

Notwithstanding all the programs devised, teachers find it hard to iden-tify, tackle and prevent school bullying in Hong Kong. The workload of teachers has been on the increase in the last decade, due to frequent school reforms. Teachers have not been prepared psychologically, cogni-tively and practically to handle school bullying. Either, they choose to ignore the problem, if it has not escalated to the extent that they need to get police involved; or they choose to suppress it by force, leaving the problems and relationships unresolved. Schools with special needs chil-dren have problems using these programs.

Citywide concern about and attention to tackling school bullying, by both government and the research community, usually peaks soon after media reports of appalling incidents. The individual projects and collect-ive efforts on prevention and intervention programs need to be main-tained and built on. We have some solid and useful recommendations from specialists and study reports, but there remains a lack of centralised support and funding, with little or no collaboration amongst different disciplines, occupations and roles involved: schools, teachers, parents, Education Bureau, scholars, Universities, NGOs, police, social workers, the legal sector and technology sector. Many schools still refuse to admit the existence of bullying, this perhaps being an issue of the Chinese concept of losing face, together with the fear of adverse effects on school reputation; however, this can be changed if schools see bullying as a psychosocial and general relationship problem instead of a quality problem. Zero case report is different from zero tolerance. As a way forward, we need to go beyond zero tolerance of bullying in schools and be prepared for the challenges of cyberbullying. We need to equip not only our children, but also our parents and teachers with enhanced everyday skills to face this and other challenges.

REFERENCES

Achenbach, T. M. (1991). *Integrative guide for the 1991 CBCL/4-18, YSR and TRF profiles*. Burlington: Department of Psychiatry, University of Vermont.

Bhat, C. S., Chang, S-H and Linscott, J. A. (2010). Addressing cyberbullying as a media literacy issue. *New Horizons in Education*, 58, 34–43.

Chazan, M., Laing, A. F. and Davies, D. (1994). *Behavioural difficulties in middle childhood*. Bristol: Falmer Press.

China Daily, Hong Kong Edition (2 June, 2010). One in every ten Hong Kong students' victims of Internet bullying.

Crick, N. R. and Dodge, K. A. (1996). Social information-processing mechanisms in reactive and proactive aggression. *Child Development*, 67, 993–1002.

Dodge, K. A., Bates, J. E. and Pettit, G. S. (1990). Mechanisms of violence. *Science*, 250, 1678–1683.

EDB (2008). Legislative Council Panel on Education, *Information Note on Bullying in Schools*. LC Paper No. CB(2)1034/07–08(01). Hong Kong Government.

 (2012). Press Releases of the Legislative Council Panel on Education, Hong Kong Government. 19 December, 2012..

EMB (2004). Legislative Council Panel on Education, Bullying in Schools, LC Paper No. CB(2) 1770/03–04. Hong Kong Government.

Enright, R. D. and Coyle, C. T. (1998). Researching the process model of forgiveness within psychological interventions. In E. L. Worthington Jr. (Ed.), *Dimensions of forgiveness: Psychological research and theological perspectives* (pp. 139–161). Philadelphia: Templeton Foundation Press.

Fung, A. L. C. (2007). A qualitative evaluation of social-cognitive changes in children with reactively aggressive behaviors. *Journal of School Violence*, 6, 45–64.

 (2011). Group treatment of reactive aggressors by social workers in a Hong Kong school setting: A two-year longitudinal study adopting quantitative and qualitative approaches. *British Journal of Social Work*, 42, 1–23.

 (2012). Intervention for aggressive victims of school bullying in Hong Kong: A longitudinal mixed-methods study. *Scandinavian Journal of Psychology*, 53, 360–367.

Fung, A. L. C. and Wong, J. L. P. (2007). *Project C.A.R.E.: Children and adolescents at risk education*. Hong Kong: Hong Kong Christian Service.

Heider, F. (1958). *The psychology of interpersonal relations*. New York: Wiley. Hepp-Dax,

Hepp-Dax, S. H. (1996). Forgiveness as an educational goal with fifth-grade inner-city children. Doctoral dissertation, Fordham University. *Dissertation Abstracts International A*, 57, 4235.

Hong Kong Federation of Youth Groups and Office of the Government Chief Information Officer (2010). Report of the 'Be Net Wise' Internet Education Campaign.

Hong Kong Police. (2003). Operations. Police Review 2000 & 2001. Available at www.info.gov.hk/police/aa-home/review

Hui, E. K. P. and Chau, T. S. (2009). The impact of a forgiveness intervention with Hong Kong Chinese children hurt in interpersonal relationships. *British Journal of Guidance and Counselling*, 37, 141–156.

Kristensen, S. M. and Smith, P. K. (2003). The use of coping strategies by Danish children classed as bullies, victims, bully/victims, and not involved, in response to different (hypothetical) types of bullying. *Scandinavian Journal of Psychology*, 44, 479–488.

Legislative Council (2004). Referring to the Administration's response to his questions on bullying in schools. LC Paper No. CB(2)1770/03–04 (01). Hong Kong Government.

(2008). An information note on bullying in schools provided by the Administration. LC Paper No. CB(2)1398/07–08. Hong Kong Government.

Lopez, C. (1997). *Peer victimization: Preliminary validation of a multidimensional self-report measure for children and young adolescents*. Unpublished Master's thesis. University of Missouri-Columbia, U.S.A.

Lopez, C. and DuBois, D. L. (2005). Peer victimization and rejection: Investigation of an integrative model of effects on emotional, behavioral, and academic adjustment in early adolescence. *Journal of Clinical Child and Adolescent Psychology*, 34, 25–36.

Maines, B. and Robinson, G. (1992). *The no blame approach*. Bristol: Lucky Duck.

Metcalf, L. (1995/2008). *Counseling toward solutions: A practical solution-focused program for working with students, teachers, and parents*. Hoboken, N.J.: Wiley.

Neelands, J. and Goode, T. (1990). *Structuring drama work: A handbook of available forms in theatre and drama*. Cambridge: Cambridge University Press.

Newman, D. A., Horne, A.M. and Bartolomucci, L. (2000). *Bully busters: A teacher's manual for helping bullies, victims and bystanders*. Champaign, IL: Research Press.

Olweus, D. (1991). Bully/victim problems among schoolchildren: Basic facts and effects of a school based intervention program. In D. J. Pepler and K. H. Rubin (Eds.), *The development and treatment of childhood aggression*, pp. 411–448. Hillsdale, NJ: Erlbaum.

Pikas, A. (1989). A pure concept of mobbing gives the best results for treatment. *School Psychology International*, 10, 95–104.

(2002). New developments of the shared concern method. *School Psychology International*, 23, 307–326.

Potter, W. J. (2001). *Media Literacy*. Thousand Oaks: Sage Publications.

Raine, A., Dodge, K., Loeber, R., Gatzke-Kopp, L., Lynam, D., Reynolds, C., Stouthamer-Loeber, M. and Liu J. (2006). The reactive–proactive aggression questionnaire: differential correlates of reactive and proactive aggression in adolescent boys. *Aggressive Behavior*, 32, 159–171.

Roerden, L. P. (2000). *Don't laugh at me – Teacher's guide*. Operation Respect, Inc. and Educators for Social Responsibility.

Sharp, S. and Smith, P.K. (Eds.) (1994). *Tackling bullying in your school: A practical handbook for teachers*. London: Routledge.

Shek, D. T. L. (2010). School drug testing: A critical review of the literature. *Scientific World Journal*, 10, 356–365.

Shek, D. T. L., Ma, H. K. and Sun, R. C. F. (2011). Development of a new curriculum in positive youth development program: The Project P.A.T.H.S in Hong Kong. *Scientific World Journal*, 11, 2207–2218.

Shek, D. T. L., Ma, H. K., Sun, R. C. F. and Lung, D. W. M. (2008). Process evaluation of the Tier 1 program (Secondary 1 curriculum) of the Project P.A.T.H.S.: findings based on the full implementation phase. *Scientific World Journal: TSW Holistic Health and Medicine*, 8, 35–46.

Shek, D. T. L. and Ng, C. S. M. (2009a). Subjective outcome evaluation of the Project P.A.T.H.S. (Secondary 2 Program): Views of the program participants. *Scientific World Journal*, 9, 1012–1022.

(2009b). Secondary 1 program of Project P.A.T.H.S.: Process evaluation based on the co-walker scheme. *Scientific World Journal: TSW Child Health and Human Development*, 9, 704–714.

(2009c). Qualitative evaluation of the Project P.A.T.H.S.: Findings based on focus groups with student participants. *Scientific World Journal: TSW Child Health and Human Development*, 9, 691–703.

Shek, D. T. L. and Sun, R. C. F. (2008). Evaluation of Project P.A.T.H.S. (Secondary 1 Program) by the program participants: Findings based on the Full Implementation Phase. *Adolescence*, 43, 807–822.

(2010). Subjective outcome evaluation based on secondary data analyses: The Project P.A.T.H.S. in Hong Kong. *Scientific World Journal*, 10, 224–237.

Smith, P. K., Morita, Y., Junger-Tas, J., Olweus, D., Catalano, R. and Slee, P. (Eds.). (1999). *The nature of school bullying: A cross-national perspective*. London and New York: Routledge.

Sullivan, K. (2000). *The anti-bullying handbook*. New York: Oxford University Press.

Tsang, K. M., Hui, E. K .P., Shek, D. T. L. and Law, B. C. M. (2010). Subjective outcome evaluation of the Project P.A.T.H.S.: Findings based on the perspective of the program implementers (Secondary 1 program). *Scientific World Journal: TSW Child Health and Human Development*, 10, 201–210.

Ttofi, M. M. and Farrington, D. P. (2011). Effectiveness of school-based programs to reduce bullying: A systematic and meta-analytic review. *Journal of Experimental Criminology*, 7, 27–56.

Vreeman, R. C. and Carroll, A. E. (2007). A systematic review of school-based interventions to prevent bullying. *Archives of Pediatrics and Adolescent Medicine*, 161, 78–88.

Wen Wei Pao 香港文匯報 (28 January, 2010). 校園欺凌案上學年三百宗-(over 300 school bullying incidents in the first school term in HK).

Whitney, I., Smith, P. K. and Thompson, D. (1994). Bullying and children with special educational needs. In P. K. Smith and S. Sharp, (Eds.), *School bullying: Insights and perspectives* (pp. 213–240). London: Routledge.

Wong, D. S. W., Cheng, H. K., Ngan, R. M. H. and Ma, K. (2011). Program effectiveness of a Restorative Whole-School Approach for tackling school bullying in Hong Kong. *International Journal of Offender Therapy and Comparative Criminology*, 55, 846–862.

Wong, D. S. W. and Lo, T. W. (2002). School bullying in secondary schools: Teachers' perceptions and tackling strategies. *Educational Research Journal*, 17, 253–272.

Wurf, G. (2012). High school anti-bullying interventions: An evaluation of curriculum approaches and the Method of Shared Concern in four Hong Kong International Schools. *Australian Journal of Guidance and Counselling*, 22, 139–149.

Xu, Z. (2010). *WAVNet: Wide-area virtual networks for dynamic provisioning of IaaS*. Unpublished Master's Thesis. Hong Kong: The University of Hong Kong.

Zelin, M. L., Adler, G. and Myerson, P. G. (1972). Anger self-report: An objective questionnaire for the measurement of aggression. *Journal of Consulting and Clinical Psychology*, 39, 340.

何會成、劉翠玲等（2003）。《尋解導向治療-進深篇》。香港：香港明愛家庭服務。[Huicheng He; Cuiling Liu (2003) Solution-focused therapy. Practice and reflections II. Hong Kong Caritas Family Service]

吳家玲、何會成等（2003）。《尋解導向治療-初探篇》。香港：香港明愛家庭服務。[Jialing Wu, Huicheng He. (2003) Solution-focused therapy. Practice and reflections I. Hong Kong Caritas Family Service.]

吳徐玉儀、蔡黎惠賢、曾惠美、張春儀、李馮秀華及胡杏芳（2002）。《愛的教育:輔導成長,發展生命課程》香港:香港大學課程與教育學系。[Yuk Yi, Tsui; Wai Yin, Lai; Wai-mei, Tsang; Chun Yee, Tjon; Sau Wa, Fung; Hang Fong, Wu. (2002), Love education: Enhancing Developmental Guidance. Department of Curriculum and Education. University of Hong Kong.]

Part V

Conclusions

20 Reflections on bullying in eastern and western perspectives

Peter K. Smith, Keumjoo Kwak and Yuichi Toda

This book set out with the aim of comparing the research traditions on *bullying*, or similar concepts such as *ijime*, or *wang-ta*, in eastern and western societies. How similar are the findings? What direct comparisons have been made across cultures? And what are the implications for intervention strategies? In this final chapter, we review the contributions in the book and venture some answers, albeit provisional, to these questions.

As the first part of the book shows, there are now substantial traditions of research in both eastern and western cultures, on bullying, or on behaviours such as *ijime, wang-ta* and *qifu*, which share many characteristics of *bullying*. These traditions of research have had some autonomy, but have also influenced each other. Broadly, a western tradition originating mainly in Scandinavia has, over the last thirty years, spread throughout much of continental Europe, as well as commonwealth countries such as Canada, Australia and New Zealand. The research tradition in the USA has developed more from work on victimisation, over the last twenty years. There has nevertheless been much mutual influence between researchers in North America, Europe and Australasia, as evidenced by, for example, the use of the Olweus intervention program in the USA, piloting of the KiVa program in New Zealand and use of the Pikas method in Australia.

The most vigorous autonomous tradition in eastern countries has arguably been that on *ijime* in Japan, although work in South Korea, to some extent influenced by Japan, also has quite a long history. Research in mainland China has been less extensive, but growing; and there has been considerable research in Hong Kong, perhaps influenced by its status as a British colony until 1997. Some of the research in these eastern countries has been influenced by western concepts and used western-based instruments, such as the Olweus questionnaire; and indeed has sometimes imported western interventions such as the Olweus program (see Chapter 18).

Is there a meaningful convergence here? Does such a coming together of research traditions imply an *absolutist* view of bullying (as defined in Chapter 11)? There do seem to be some important differences between bullying-like phenomena in western and eastern cultures, which might warn against this. This is the topic that this book has set out to explore. However as editors, while warning against the dangers of absolutism, we also reject a purely *relativist* position (as defined in Chapter 11). We do believe that there are important similarities in the phenomena, enough that we can usefully bring them together to compare in one set of chapters. Thus, we adopt what Guillaume and Funder (Chapter 11) designate as a *universalist* position.

Some similarities in the phenomena

The concepts of *bullying, victimization, ijime, wang-ta* and *qifu* do share criteria related to intentional harm done to someone, by another or others in some position of relative power. As such, this is distinct from aggressive fighting which is a more commonplace human phenomenon. This imbalance of power, or the difficulty of the victim being able to defend themselves, has been widely recognised as a reason why such phenomena should be taken seriously. There is a societal obligation to intervene in what is an unfair situation that does harm to the victim (and others).

Furthermore, many characteristics of bullying-like phenomena are similar across all countries studied. These include the types of bullying seen, and to some extent, their relative frequency; typical age changes; gender differences in frequency and types; and the outcomes for those involved.

The main types have been verbal, physical, indirect relational (rumour spreading) and social exclusion (which can be direct or indirect). More recently, cyber bullying (or *net-ijime*, etc) has become prominent – the internet revolution and the growth of interest in social networking sites in middle childhood and adolescence being a worldwide phenomenon. Even the relative frequency of these types shows some common patterns – for example, verbal bullying is generally most frequent (e.g., Northern Ireland, Chapter 1, Table 1.2; South Korea, Chapter 5, Table 5.2; Hong Kong, Chapter 7, Table 7.1). Age changes generally show some decrease in victim rates through the adolescent years; for example, Smith, Madsen and Moody (1999) showed this for Japan as well as several western countries. Also, gender differences are often replicated, with boys being more involved in physical types of bullying, and girls more in relational.

In addition, studies in different countries all show negative consequences associated for being a victim of bullying. A decade ago, Eslea and colleagues (2003) compared data from Japan, mainland China and seven European countries. Examining associations with liking playtime, being alone at playtime and having few good friends in class, they reported that 'victims were significantly worse off on all the measures in all the samples where a difference was found' (25 out of 27 comparisons; Eslea et al., 2003, p. 78). Studies also consistently show victims being more at risk for emotional health problems such as anxiety and depression, whether in western countries (Chapters 1, 2 and 3) or eastern countries (Chapters 4, 5, 6 and 7).

Schwartz and colleagues carried out a series of studies of correlates of victimisation in eastern cultures. Schwartz, Chang and Farver (2001) examined peer group victimisation in a Chinese primary school. The correlates of victimisation, such as poorer academic functioning, submissive-withdrawn behaviour and aggression, suggested to them 'considerable similarity in the processes underlying peer group victimization across Chinese and Western cultural settings' (p. 520); and subsequently, in a similar study in Hong Kong schools, Tom et al. (2010) stated that they were 'able to replicate the behavioral and academic correlates of peer victimization from past research conducted in the West and mainland China with children in Hong Kong' (p. 35). A study at a primary school in South Korea by Schwartz et al. (2002) also found 'considerable similarity in the social processes underlying peer group victimisation across South Korean and Western cultural settings' (p. 113).

Some differences in the phenomena

Despite many similarities, it is clear that there are a number of important differences too. These have emerged in previous definitions and descriptions, and through a limited number of direct comparisons, some of these reported in Chapters 8, 9, 10, 13 and 14.

Definitional issues and language terms

Although similar enough to relate together, terms such as *bullying, ijime, wang-ta* and *qifu* are not identical in meaning. Thus, Morita (1985) defined *ijime* as 'A type of aggressive behavior by which someone who holds a dominant position in a group-interaction process, by intentional or collective acts, causes mental and/or physical suffering to another inside a group'. This definition places more emphasis on the group nature of the phenomenon, than do usual definitions of *bullying* (see Chapter 1). The Korean term *wang-ta* means severe exclusion or an excluded person (see Chapter 5), thus inevitably emphasising this type of behaviour, even if physical attacks are not excluded from the phenomenon. Whereas in China, *qifu*, described as the closest counterpart of *bullying* in Chapter 6, is considered as 'a kind of behavior to intimidate, oppress, or embarrass others with an arrogant attitude and in unreasonable ways', clearly emphasising the imbalance of power involved as the main criterion.

Types of bullying, who bullies whom and where bullying happens

It is commonly thought that social exclusion plays a larger role in bullying-like phenomena in eastern than in western countries. Certainly in South Korea, not only *wang-ta* but other words like *ttadolim* and *jun-ta* describe various kinds of social exclusion, some very severe (such as shunning by a whole school in *jun-ta*; Chapter 5; Koo, 2004; Lee, Smith and Monks, 2012). In Japan, the importance of social exclusion was shown in case studies by Tanaka (2001) and Yokoyu (2003). Tom et al. (2010) noted that 'forms of victimization that involve social exclusion and causing harm to relationships may be particularly relevant in Chinese children's peer groups' (p. 35).

Nevertheless, the actual frequency of social exclusion reported by South Korean pupils is less than for verbal or physical forms (Table 5.2), at least for boys – for girls it is more common, although still less frequent than verbal abuse (Table 5.4). And in Chapter 8, Kanetsuna suggests that it is more perceptions of what are bullying-like phenomena that vary between Japan and England, than actual frequencies of behaviour. Perhaps too it is the nature of social exclusion that varies. As Kanetsuna argues, the more class-based nature of social relations in Japanese compared to English secondary schools may mean that class-based shunning is effective in Japan in a way that it would not be so much in England. Certainly some of the findings from the cartoon studies described in Chapter 14 suggest that eastern cultures may emphasise these kinds of social exclusion; by contrast, in some western countries, exclusion due to gender may be emphasised more strongly. Thus it may be the nature of social exclusion, and perhaps its severity, rather than simple frequency, that distinguishes some eastern from western countries.

Some other differences may also be noted. For example, extortion has not featured as a type of bullying much in western contexts, but it does in South Korea (Table 5.2) and Hong Kong (Table 7.1).

In his comparison of pupils in Japan and England, Kanetsuna (Chapter 8) found that Japanese students perceive *ijime* as more often from same-age peers often previously seen as 'friends'; whereas English students see *bullying* as direct physical or verbal in nature, more often by older pupils whom they had not considered as friends.

In western countries, bullying often happens in the playground. In Japan and South Korea, the classroom appears to be the place where a lot of *ijime* or *wang-ta* occurs. This is explicitly documented by Kanetsuna (Chapter 8) in comparing pupils in Japan and England.

Prevalence rates and cross-national surveys

Taking the main countries surveyed in our book as being Japan, South Korea, mainland China and Hong Kong (eastern) and USA, Canada, United Kingdom, Australia and New Zealand (western), we searched for any comparative data on bullying rates. In comparing rates of bullying across different countries, a number of data sets are available. The Health Behavior in School-aged Children (HBSC) surveys collect data from 11, 13 and 15 years olds from nationally representative samples, every 4 years (e.g., Currie et al., 2012), but do not feature the eastern countries. Similarly, the EU Kids Online survey (Livingstone et al., 2011) only reported data from European countries. Conversely, the Global School Health Survey (GSHS) only includes mainland China from our eastern countries, and no developed western countries (GSHS, 2007). However, the Trends in International Mathematics and Science Study (TIMSS) surveys (http://timssandpirls.bc.edu/timss2011/inter national-results-mathematics.html), which began in 1995 and are given every 4 years with some 5,000–6,000 eighth grade students in each country, do cover all our main countries except mainland China. The surveys include a section on school safety, and the most relevant part here is based on student reports. The 2011 survey included a Students Bullied at School scale, based on frequency of experiencing six types of behaviour (verbal, exclusion, rumour spreading, belongings stolen, physical, coercion). No definition of bullying was given, so the question may be tapping some aggressive acts as well as bullying more strictly defined.

Mullis et al. (2012)provide tables with an average scale score, available for both 4th grade and 8th grade students, and the scores for 3 eastern and 5 western countries are given in Table 20.1 (high scores reflect *less* bullying). It can be seen that at 4th grade, the three eastern countries have better scores than four of the five western countries; although at 8th grade, this remains clearly so only for South Korea and Japan. New Zealand comes out worst in these figures, as also remarked on in Chapter 3 by Slee, Sullivan, Green, Harcourt and Lynch.

There are reservations about the validity of these kinds of cross-national comparisons, including issues around language (as discussed

Table 20.1 *TIMSS scores for students perceptions of being bullied at school, 2011 data. Average scale score (higher score means less often bullied). Adapted from Mullis et al. (2012).*

Country	4th grade	8th grade
Japan	10.1	10.3
South Korea	10.3	10.3
China	na	na
Hong Kong	10.1	9.7
USA	10.1	10.1
Canada*	9.7	10.0
England	9.8	10.4
Australia	9.5	9.9
New Zealand	9.3	9.8

*average of Quebec, Alberta and Ontario

in Chapter 14) and possible response bias and acquiescence (Chapter 11; Hofstede et al., 2010). Nevertheless, they provide an initial basis for discussion. There are a few other more limited cross-national comparisons available, usually on smaller samples and comparing just two countries (but with similar methodology). For example, Aoyama, Utsumi and Hasegawa (2011) assessed cyberbullying in Japanese and US high school samples and found both cyber perpetration and victim rates lower in Japan. Similarly, Barlett et al. (2014) compared cyberbullying in college-aged participants in Japan and the USA, and found that cyberbullying perpetration was lower in Japan than in the USA. In this book, Li, Zhang and Jones (Chapter 9) report lower levels of bullying in a Chinese compared to an English sample.

Ratio of bullies to victims

Prevalence rates typically report rates for both victims, and bullies or perpetrators. It is then possible to calculate a ratio of bullies to victims, a B/V ratio. This ratio is considered in Chapter 16, in terms of changes over time at a class process level. Here, we consider it at a macro level, from large-scale surveys. From surveys using Olweus-type questionnaires, Koo, Kwak and Smith (2008; and see Chapter 4) noted that the ratio of bullies to victims in South Korea was 10.2% (bullies) to 5.8% (victims) – a ratio of. 1.76. Koo et al. (2008) used the term *wang-ta* in their survey; the FPYV surveys reported in Chapter 5 used the term *hakkyo-pokryuk*, a more general term for aggressive or violent behaviour;

here the perpetrator victim ratios are not so high, but still are greater than the value of one in the last 4 years of data reported (Table 5.1), and seem to increase with grade level (Table 5.3). In Japanese schools, Morita et al. (1999) reported a ratio of 1.33. However, in many western countries the ratio is typically less than one: 0.78 in Norway (Olweus, 1999); 0.77 in Italy (Fonzi et al., 1999); 0.70 in Belgium (Vettenburg, 1999); 0.46 and 0.80 in the Republic of Ireland, in primary and post-primary school respectively (O'Moore, Kirkham and Smith, 1997); similarly 0.44 and 0.60 in England (Whitney and Smith, 1993); and 0.23 and 0.31 in Northern Ireland (RSM McClure Watters, 2011; and see Table 1.1 in Chapter 1, taking '2 or 3 times a month' or more frequently). Strohmeier, Yanagida and Toda (Chapter 13) provide a direct comparison of pupils in Japan and Austria; Japan being moderately lower on individualism vs. collectivism (IDV) (score 46, rank 36; Austria has IDV score 55, rank 29; Hofstede et al., 2010). The findings in Table 13.2 are complex, but the authors conclude that relational bullying is more group based in Japan than Austria, although this was not true for physical bullying.

However, on bully/victim ratio, mainland China and Hong Kong seem more similar to western countries than to South Korea and Japan. As regards mainland China, all the studies cited in Chapter 6 (see Table 6.1) clearly show a bully/victim ratio much less than one, whichever study or frequency criterion is taken. Also, the direct comparison of China and England reported in Chapter 9 (see Table 9.1) shows a greater bully/victim ration in England than in China, although both well below one (the comparison cited in the text gives a ratio of 0.17 in China, 0.36 in England).

A similar generalisation appears to hold for Hong Kong (see Chapter 7). The survey by the Democratic Alliance for the Betterment (2004) found a ratio of 0.63. The survey by Wong et al. (2008), taking a '6 times or more' criterion, gives ratios of 0.61 (physical), 0.62 (verbal), 0.75 (exclusion) and 0.74 (extortion).

Coping strategies

What victims do if they experience bullying does vary by culture. Telling or seeking help is one strategy, but this appears to be less frequent in eastern countries. In his comparison of pupils in Japan and England, Kanetsuna (Chapter 8) found Japanese pupils more reluctant to tell someone about experiencing *ijime* than English pupils did about being bullied. Japanese pupils recommended taking direct action against bullies, while English pupils more often recommended seeking help from others. Aoyama et al., (2011), in their assessment of cyberbullying in Japanese and US high school samples, found that US students discussed what they were doing online much more with their parents, than did Japanese students. In South Korea, very few pupils appear to seek help for *wang-ta* (Chapter 5).

Attitudes and awareness

Western studies have documented that attitudes to victims are generally sympathetic from most pupils, but that a substantial minority is less sympathetic, and that these negative attitudes are more pronounced in boys, and in adolescence up to around 14–15 years (Chapter 1; Menesini et al., 1997; Rigby, 1997). Although direct comparisons are lacking, in South Korea it is reported that 'Korean pupils often viewed a victim as an abnormal, inept, or maladjusted person' (Chapter 5; Lee et al., 2011). However, there may be considerable variation here amongst eastern countries. In mainland China, Zhang and colleagues (Chapters 6 and 9) found that Chinese children had higher levels of anti-bullying attitudes than English children and showed greater willingness to act to help victims. Similarly Barlett et al. (2014) found that in college-aged participants, favourable attitudes to cyberbullying and perceptions of approval by friends or family, were lower in Japan than in the USA.

In addition, attitudes to bullying interventions can be assessed. In Japan, attitudes to bullying interventions in schools have been found to be more pessimistic than in England (Chapter 8; Kanetsuna, Smith and Morita, 2006).

Summary

In summary, definitions of bullying-like phenomena show linguistic variation. Studies of bullying in eastern countries suggest that there may be important differences from western countries in terms of who does the bullying (friends in the same class, or relative strangers), where it happens (classroom, playground) and types of bullying (severity of social exclusion, prevalence of extortion). However, prevalence rates appear to be lower in eastern than western countries. The ratio of bullies to victims is notably higher (above one) in South Korea and Japan, compared to western countries but also to mainland China and Hong Kong. Coping strategies vary by country, with pupils in eastern countries perhaps less willing to seek help. Attitudes to bullying also vary, but for this, there is a lack of comparative data or of any clear east/west differentiation.

Explaining cultural differences

Linguistic issues and measurement issues

As discussed earlier, and shown also by the cartoon methodology in Chapter 14, the words used to describe or measure bullying-like phenomena can have meanings that vary in the types of bullying or criteria that they emphasise, and this can clearly be one factor in bringing out or influencing apparent differences between cultures. Indeed, when relying on verbal reports – that is, without getting actual behavioural observations, which are rare in this area – it can be very difficult to distinguish between differences brought about by terminology and differences in actual behaviours.

Furthermore, actual measurement comparison across cultures is a far from easy or straightforward task. Firstly, sometimes studies make statements about national or cultural differences when sample sizes are really inadequate for such generalisations. But even if samples are sufficient, then as documented in Chapter 11, there are issues around how respondents understand and respond to survey questions. As one example, respondents in some eastern cultures may adopt a more compliant or socially desirable response set to questions. Konishi et al. (2009) gave the same measure of bullying to pupils in Japan, South Korea, Australia, Canada and the USA; despite a similar factor structure (of types of bullying), they found some degree of lack of construct equivalence across countries, indicating that some items were interpreted differently; they concluded that their findings 'suggest considerable caution in understanding simple cross-national or cross-cultural comparisons across groups based on such bullying self-report indices' (Konishi et al., 2009, p. 91).

School system differences

Countries vary in their various educational systems, as thoroughly documented by Jessel in Chapter 12. Important factors particularly likely to affect the prevalence and nature of bullying rates include use of homeroom classes, break times and their supervision and extent of grade retention. For example, prevalence of homeroom class teaching in secondary schools is higher in Japan than many western countries. Kanetsuna (Chapter 8) invoked use of homeroom classes, and supervision of break times, in explaining characteristic differences he found between *ijime* in Japan and *bullying* in England. Grade retention, whereby some pupil's performing less well academically are held back in a grade for as years or more, has also been linked to rates of bullying (Pereira et al., 2004).

Societal factors – economic level and social inequality

The HBSC surveys have provided cross-national data on bully and victim rates in western countries, which have been used to see if economic level and social inequality predict levels of bullying. This research has yielded modest significance in terms of country wealth or overall socioeconomic status levels as a negative predictor of bullying rates (Chaux, Molano and Podlesky, 2009; Elgar et al., 2009). Income inequality, as a measure of power differentials between those who have access to resources and those who do not, was also studied by Elgar et al. (2009). They found strong relations of income inequality to bullying rates (a correlation of around 0.6), independently of country wealth; these researchers (Elgar et al., 2009, p. 357) suggested that 'feelings of shame, humiliation and distrust intensify with greater income inequality and create a harsh social environment where violent acts such as school bullying may be condoned or ignored'.

Societal factors - Hofstede and other dimensions

One approach to explaining cultural differences is to use the six dimensions proposed by Hofstede (1980), as elaborated by Hofstede, Hofstede and Minkov (2010). A number of prior studies have examined the Hofstede categories in relation to aggression. Bergeron and Schneider (2005) examined thirty-six studies that compared usually two countries on prevalence of aggression, and related this to the four Hofstede dimensions available at the time: IDV, PDI, UAI and MAS (see later). All four dimensions were correlated with higher rates of aggression, with uncertainty avoidance (UAI) being the most strongly associated. However, most attention has been given to the individualism-collectivism dimension (IDV).

Forbes et al. (2009)compared rates of direct and indirect aggression in college students in the USA (a highly IDV society), Poland (moderately IDV) and China (least IDV). These researchers argued that direct or physical aggression should be predicted as lower in collectivist societies, but the prediction was less clear as regarded indirect aggression: they contrasted a parallel forms hypothesis (that since direct and indirect aggression generally correlate together, they would show the same direction of effect), and a differential reinforcement hypothesis, that indirect aggression would be used more in collectivist societies because direct aggression was heavily sanctioned. They actually found that rates of both direct and indirect aggression were highest in the USA and lowest in China, supporting the parallel forms hypothesis. Also, Li et al. (2010) examined intracultural variation in Chinese adolescents, linking endorsement of collectivism with less use of both overt (direct) and relational (mainly indirect) aggression. Nevertheless, other studies present a more complicated picture. Lansford et al. (2012) compared rates of physical and relational aggression in nine countries, including the USA and China. Physical aggression was higher in the USA than China, but relational aggression was higher in China (these differences holding for both boys and girls). In another study of 62 countries, using the TIMSS 2007 data, Bergmüller (2013) found that while head teacher's reports of physical and verbal aggression in school were higher in individualist societies, this did not hold true for student reports of physical, verbal or relational aggression.

Below we consider the Hofstede dimension in relation to bullying, examining not only IDV but the other dimensions, which may be of interest in relation to different aspects of bullying beyond prevalence. There are now six such dimensions, and scores are available for the main countries featured in our book: Japan, South Korea, mainland China and Hong Kong as eastern countries; the United States, Canada, Great Britain, Australia and New Zealand as western countries. Scores and ranks of these countries on the six Hofstede dimensions are given in Table 20.2. The definitions of the dimensions, and some hypotheses about them in relation to aggressive behaviours, are adapted from Hofstede et al. (2010). We take this as an exploratory venture, acknowledging that Hofstede's original work was on business culture, some decades ago. However, the model has been used widely and Hofstede et al. (2010) explicitly discuss applications to school environments.

***Individualism-collectivism (IDV)*:** Individualism refers to societies with loose ties, where individuals are expected to look after themselves and immediate family; whereas in collectivism, people are integrated from birth onward into strong cohesive in-groups which protect them in exchange for loyalty to the group. Thus collectivism would imply less conflict within the ingroup; however, if there is conflict, then shaming and social exclusion would be powerful weapons to hurt someone or make them conform. A more collectivistic culture implies a greater possibility of concerted whole-group (e.g., whole-class) norms emerging, which could at times be aggressive – thus the possibility of severe whole-class aggression and shunning of a victim. Thus, higher collectivism scores might predict lower bullying scores, but more emphasis on social exclusion when bullying occurs.

Table 20.2 *Scores (and ranks out of 76 in brackets) of 4 eastern countries and 5 western countries on dimensions of cultural difference, from Hofstede et al. (2010) and Gelfand et al. (2011).*

Country/ Dimension	IDV	PDI	MAS	UAI	LTO*	IVR	TIGHT**
Japan	46	54	95	92	80	42	8.6
	(35–37)	(49–50)	(2)	(11–13)	(4)	(49–51)	(8)
South Korea	18	60	39	85	75	29	10.0
	(65)	(41–42)	(59)	(23–25)	(5)	(67–69)	(5)
China	20	80	66	30	118	24	7.9
	(58–63)	(12–14)	(11–13)	(70–71)	(1)	(75)	(9)
Hong Kong	25	68	57	29	96	17	6.3
	(55–56)	(27–29)	(25–27)	(72–73)	(2)	(83–84)	(18–19)
USA	91	40	62	46	29	68	5.1
	(1)	(59–61)	(19)	(64)	(17)	(15–17)	(23)
Canada	80	39	52	48	23	68	na
	(4–6)	(62)	(33)	(62–63)	(20)	(15–17)	
Great Britain	89	35	66	35	25	69	6.9
	(3)	(65–67)	(11–13)	(68–69)	(18)	(14)	(13)
Australia	90	38	61	51	31	71	4.4
	(2)	(64)	(20)	(57–58)	(14)	(11)	(24)
New Zealand	79	22	58	49	30	75	3.9
	(7)	(73)	(22–24)	(60–61)	(16)	(9)	(25.5)

IDV = Individualism Index; PDI = Power Distance Index; MAS = Masculinity Index; UAI = Uncertainty Avoidance Index; LTO = Long-Term Orientation; IVR = Indulgence versus Restraint, TIGHT = Tightness score.
*LTO ranks out of 23 countries.
**TIGHT ranks out of 33 countries (no data for Canada).

Table 20.2 shows that the five western countries score very highly on the individualism dimension, while the four eastern cultures are much more collectivist (although Japan less so than South Korea, China and Hong Kong).

As discussed above, the IDV dimension has been invoked in previous studies of aggression. In Chapter 9 of this book, Ji, Zhang and Jones invoke the collectivist nature of Chinese society, compared to England, to predict that 'Chinese children are less likely to take part in behaviors such as aggression and bullying' – a prediction confirmed in their study. A lower prevalence of bullying does indeed appear to be found in more collectivist societies in our nine countries (Tables 20.1 and 20.2).

Koo et al. (2008) also argued that greater collectivism may explain the emphasis on class-based exclusion found in South Korea and Japan, as in a collectivist society, social exclusion is a more potent form of attack – in effect, the differential reinforcement hypothesis of Forbes et al. (2009). Koo et al. also argued that a greater ratio of bullies to victims, found in South Korea and Japan as compared to western countries, could be explained in terms of collectivism. A problem for this explanation is the low bully/victim ratio found in mainland China and Hong Kong, which are both higher on IDV than Japan. Zhang and colleagues (Chapter 9) suggest that the high bully/victim ratios in South Korea and Japan reflect the emphasis on social exclusion as a main form of bullying in those societies; this might be influenced by the terms used to describe the phenomena, as discussed above.

Power distance index (PDI): This assesses the extent to which less powerful members (e.g., in a school) expect and accept that power is distributed unequally. There is more respect for older persons, including older pupils. This acceptance of hierarchy can mean that actions by a more powerful person – such as a child in a higher year group, directed to a lower one – would be accepted as the legitimate use of power, not the abuse of power. This was found to be the case for Japanese and South Korean pupils for some cartoon scenarios described in Chapter 14.

Thus, bullying, at least as reported by students, might be more same-age and less perpetrated by older pupils, in high PDI societies. This is certainly true of *ijime* in Japan and *wang-ta* in South Korea (Chapters 4 and 5); however, these countries are intermediate on their PDI scores. The western countries are lowest, but mainland China and Hong Kong are highest (Table 20.2). It is not clear (Chapters 6 and 7) whether same-age bullying is relatively more frequent in these latter countries.

In relation to the high scores of mainland China and Hong Kong on the PDI index, it is noteworthy that the relevant terms closest to bullying in these countries have strong connotations of power. This was noted above for *qifu* (Chapter 6) and is also true for *heiling* in Cantonese, described as 'overbearing' (Chapter 7).

Masculinity index (MAS): A more masculine society is one where gender roles are distinct (less overlapping) and men are more assertive, tough and focused on material success, while women are more modest and tender. Thus, higher bullying rates could be predicted in high MAS societies, but especially for males, with a greater male-female difference in bullying rates.

From Table 20.2, Japan scores most highly on MAS, followed by the other countries with similar intermediate scores but with South Korea lowest. This would lead to the prediction that gender differences (with boys bullying more) would be high in Japan, but low in South Korea.

Another difference between Japan, compared to South Korea and England, is documented by Cowie and James (Chapter 10) in discussing peer support systems. They write that 'Peer counselling classes in South Korean schools are very similar to the face-to-face listening approach that may be used in England. The emphasis in South Korea, as in the United Kingdom, is on supporting victims and enhancing school climate rather than on directly challenging perpetrators'. However, each practice of Japanese peer support is arguably much influenced by various standpoints of practitioners and researchers, rather than by Japanese culture itself.

Uncertainty avoidance index (UAI): Uncertainty avoidance is defined as the extent to which people feel threatened by ambiguous or unknown situations. Hofstede et al. (2010) argued that high uncertainty avoidance is associated with stress and anxiety, and venting of emotions including aggression; this argument was supported by the analyses of Bergeron and Schneider (2005) who found this dimension to be the strongest predictor of levels of aggression.

From Table 20.2, Japan and South Korea come out as highest on UAI, well ahead of all the other countries. But these countries appear to have the lowest prevalence of bullying, judging by Table 20.1. Here, the distinction between aggression and bullying may be important. Hofstede et al. (2010, p. 203) suggest that 'Aggression and emotion may at proper times and places be vented' in high UAI societies. Thus, socially sanctioned aggression might be higher, but bullying is generally not socially sanctioned and it is not obvious that the findings for aggression generally are applicable to it.

Another characteristic of high UAI societies is that 'what is different is dangerous' (Hofstede et al., 2010, p. 203). This could lead to another prediction, that bias bullying (for example racist, faith or homophobic bullying, or bullying based on disability) would be relatively more common in high UAI societies. Again, the available data are not sufficient to test this.

Long-term orientation (LTO): Long-term orientation is defined as fostering virtues oriented towards future rewards, for example perseverance and thrift; whereas short-term orientation implies respect for tradition, preservation of 'face', and fulfilling societal obligations. It is not clear what implications this dimension might have for bullying, but a possible hypothesis, based on 'face' saving in low LTO societies, is that seeking help if bullied would be less likely. On this basis, one would predict less help-seeking in mainland China and Hong Kong, and then Japan and South Korea, and most help-seeking in western societies (Table 20.2). This is in part born out by empirical data from Japan, compared to England (Chapter 8).

Indulgence versus restraint (IVR): With this more recently pro-posed dimension, indulgence is defined as relatively free gratification of human desires, whereas restraint relates to curbs on this and regulation by strict social norms. This might imply lower rates of bullying; however, no obvious predictions regarding aggression are found in Hofstede et al. (2010). A related construct to this dimension is the construct of tight and loose cultures, considered next.

Gelfand: tight and loose cultures

Gelfand et al. (2011) have defined a tightness-looseness dimension of cultures, with tight cultures having strong norms and low tolerance of deviant behaviour, while loose societies have weak norms and high tolerance of deviant behaviour. Tighter countries have narrow socialisa-tion that restricts the range of permissible behaviour, while looser coun-tries have a broader range of permissible behaviour. As shown in Table 20.2, eastern cultures generally are tighter than western societies (although Great Britain – the United Kingdom in Gelfand et al.'s data – scores slightly tighter than Hong Kong). It might be expected that bullying rates would be less in tighter societies, and this does seem to be broadly compatible with the rates shown in Table 20.1.

A reservation about using national scores for these kinds of compari-sons is raised in Chapter 13. Here it is argued that it is more useful to examine individual differences rather than societal differences in these dimensions (as was done also in Li et al., 2010). Nevertheless, at present it is only the societal scores that are readily available from a range of different countries.

How do these similarities/differences impact on intervention, and how should they?

Ever since the first Norwegian National Anti-Bullying campaign in 1983 (see Chapters 1 and 15), a range of anti-bullying interventions have taken place, in many countries. Many of these are mentioned in Chapters 15, 16, 17, 18 and 19. However, those which have been systematically evaluated are much fewer in number; for example, Kwak (Chapter 17) points out that of many programs in South Korea, only two have received any evaluation. In a survey of the effectiveness of anti-bullying programs, Ttofi, Farrington and Baldry (2008) analysed findings from thirty programs that reached certain quality criteria. These studies came from a number of European countries, the USA, Canada, Australia and New Zealand; no studies in eastern cultures were represented. Ttofi and Farrington (2011) relaxed their criteria slightly and searched for 'international evaluations ... in languages other than English' (p. 29), obtaining a total of fifty-three evaluations; but again, no studies in eastern countries are featured.

As shown in Chapters 16, 17 and 19, there are many anti-bullying initiatives in Japan, South Korea and Hong Kong. Some of these have been taken or adapted from western versions. Indeed, in mainland China, the Olweus program was used and assessed (Chapter 18), and initiatives in Hong Kong have often shown some influence from western ideas, such as Pikas method and restorative approaches (Chapter 19). However many initiatives appear quite indigenous, notably in Japan and in South Korea, but perhaps surprisingly they often take an individualistic approach. As Kwak writes for South Korea (Chapter 17), 'such prevention programs have focused on curriculum work that raises awareness of school violence, and works on psychological attributes of perpetrators, victims and bystanders'. Many of the programs in Japan and in Hong Kong also seem to be of this kind.

We use the word 'surprising' here, as these eastern cultures have been seen as more collectivist, and bullying as to some extent more group-based – with at least in Japan and South Korea, more class-based bullying and a greater ratio of bullies to victims, perhaps related to whole-class exclusion or shunning. It is not clear that interventions in eastern countries have tackled these aspects of *ijime* or *wang-ta* in their countries, in optimal ways. Arguably, the KiVa program in Finland responds most adequately to the group nature of bullying, with an emphasis on encouraging defenders who have a high status in the peer group, to actively help victims.

In Japan, as discussed in Chapter 16, there are various intervention approaches, but many were implemented rather sporadically, and not systematically evaluated but reported or published as single case studies. However, many of these case studies aimed for *kurasu zukuri*, meaning nurturing better relationships and mutual supporting and collaborative motivation among classmates. In other words, *kurasu zukuri* is a classic Japanese collectivistic approach. There are also some imported individualistic approaches, and efforts are now being made to integrate this Japanese classic collectivistic approach and the imported more individualistic approaches to make more systematic, effective and long-lasting practices suited for the systems and climates of schools and classes in Japan.

Much work remains to be done in designing effective anti-bullying programs, but there are likely to be two main limitations to curriculum-based approaches. One, learnt at the time of the Sheffield Project in the

1990s, is that such awareness-raising efforts often have short-term effects but that these disappear after some months if they lack a broader, continuing context (Smith and Sharp, 1994). The other is that attempts to increase empathy and social skills may have effects on ordinary pupils but may not have much if any effect on those pupils, especially in secondary school, who have become 'hardened bullies' and find bullying behaviour may bring some rewards. Indeed this is a challenge for all anti-bullying interventions. Analysing the KiVa program effects, Garandeau, Lee and Salmivalli (2014) found that it reduced bullying amongst bullies of low and medium popularity, but had no significant effect on bullies who were high in popularity.

An important aspect of KiVa, and also of the Olweus OBPP program, is that they are multi-facetted. Their components are at individual, class and school level; and they (to some extent) target bystanders, victims and bullies with different components. Such multi-facetted programs are likely to be necessary, and these two programs do seem able to reduce bullying by some 30–50% in many cases (Ttofi and Farrington, 2011; Smith, 2014). We suggest that interventions in eastern countries also need to be multi-facetted, but the particular components might well be developed indigenously, taking account of the nature of bullying-like phenomena in that country. In other words, take the concept of a multi-facetted approach, but do not necessarily take the components as developed elsewhere.

What probably can be adapted from elsewhere is techniques of evaluation. It is vital that interventions are evaluated, and well beyond just informal feedback from those giving the intervention. The evaluations of OBPP and KiVa provide excellent exemplars of sophisticated quantitative evaluations, looking at a range of effects, on types of pupil and on teachers as well. However, we would suggest – wherever the evaluation is conducted – that advanced quantitative methods are combined with more qualitative approaches. These latter might include interviews with bullies or victims, focus groups, diary records or blogs; such material can enrich understanding and give more insight into the processes going on, and why interventions succeed or fail.

Summary and prospects for the future

The study of bullying-like phenomena has become a truly international endeavour. In child development and developmental psychology, it features prominently in conferences, and journals, including often journal special issues – a trend reinforced by the growth of interest and concern about cyberbullying in the last decade (Kowalski et al., 2014). Indeed 'bullying' seems to have grabbed attention to an extent that other kinds of victimisation may be seen to be relatively neglected (Finkelhor, Turner and Hamby, 2012). However, the imbalance of power in bullying-like phenomena has provided a powerful impetus for those concerned with human rights and specifically the right not to be bullied (Greene, 2006). This should not and need not preclude a concern for other kinds of victimisation and abuse (Smith, 2014).

Although international, we feel that the field has been rather dominated by western studies. As pointed out in our Preface, only 2 out of 41 chapters in Jimerson, Swearer and Espelage (2010) *Handbook of Bullying in Schools: An International Perspective* feature authors/perspectives from eastern countries; and meta-analyses of interventions have not included eastern work (Ttofi and Farrington, 2011). We have attempted some redress of this imbalance with this book, and also hoped to give readers some insight into the richness of cultural variation in bullying-like phenomena and how they have been tackled, in a range of the most economically developed eastern and western countries. Being able to learn from each other's experiences, but also value and respect cultural difference, are surely important aspects of progressing our field further and improving the lives of children, wherever they live.

REFERENCES

Aoyama, I., Utsumi, S. and Hasegawa, M. (2011). Cyberbullying in Japan. In Q. Li, D. Cross and P. K. Smith (Eds.), *Cyberbullying in the global playground: Research from international perspectives* (pp. 183–201). Chichester, England: Wiley-Blackwell.

Barlett, C. P., Gentile, D. A., Anderson, C. A., Suzuki, K., Sakamoto, A., Yamaoka, A. and Katsura, R. (2014). Cross-cultural differences in cyberbullying behavior: A short-term longitudinal study. *Journal of Cross-Cultural Psychology*, 45, 300–313.

Bergeron, N. and Schneider, B. H. (2005). Explaining cross-national differences in peer-directed aggression: A quantitative synthesis. *Aggressive Behavior*, 31, 116–137.

Bergmüller, S. (2013). The relationship between cultural individualism-collectivism and student aggression across 62 countries. *Aggressive Behavior*, 39, 182–200.

Chaux, E., Molano, A. and Podlesky, P. (2009). Socio-economic, socio-political and socio-emotional variables explaining school bullying: A country-wide multilevel analysis. *Aggressive Behavior*, 35, 520–529.

Currie, C. et al. (Eds.). (2012). *Social determinants of health and well-being among young people. Health Behaviour in School-aged Children (HBSC) study: International report from the 2009/23010 survey*. Copenhagen: WHO Regional Office for Europe.

Democratic Alliance for the Betterment (2004). 'Bullies in our Schools', a survey conducted by Legislative Council Member Chan Kam Lam, in affiliation with Ngau Tau Kok Kai Fong Welfare Association; *Ming Pao*, Feb 16th.

Elgar, F. J., Craig, W., Boyce, W., Morgan, A. and Vella-Zarb, R. (2009). Income inequality and school bullying: Multilevel study of adolescents in 37 countries. *Journal of Adolescent Health*, 45, 351–359.

Eslea, M., Menesini, E., Morita, Y., O'Moore, M., Mora-Merchan, J. A., Pereira, B., Smith, P. K. and Zhang, W. (2003). Friendship and loneliness among bullies and victims: Data from seven countries. *Aggressive Behavior*, 30, 71–83.

Finkelhor, D., Turner, H. A. and Hamby, S. (2012). Let's prevent peer victimization, not just bullying. *Child Abuse and Neglect*, 36, 271–274.

Fonzi, A., Genta, M. L., Menesini, E., Bacchini, D., Bonino, S. and Costabile, A. (1999). Italy. In P. K. Smith, Y. Morita, J. Junger-Tas, D. Olweus, R. Catalano and P. Slee (Eds.), *The nature of school bullying: A cross-national perspective* (pp. 140–156). London and New York: Routledge.

Forbes, G., Zhang, X., Doroszewicz, K. and Haas, K. (2009). Relationships between individualism-collectivism, gender, and direct or indirect aggression: A study in China, Poland and the US. *Aggressive Behavior*, 35, 24–30.

Garandeau, C., Lee, I. A. and Salmivalli, C. (2014). Differential effects of the KiVa anti-bullying program on popular and unpopular bullies. *Journal of Applied Developmental Psychology*, 35, 44–50.

Gelfand, M. J., Raver, J. L., Nishii, L., Leslie, L. M., Lun, J., Lim, B. C., Duan, L., Almaliach, A., Ang, S., Arnadottir, J., Aycan, Z., Boehnke, K., Boski, P., Cabecinhas, R., Chan, D., Chhokar, J., D'Amato, A., Ferrer, M., Fischlmayr, I. C., Fischer, R., Fülöp, M., Georgas, J., Kashima, E. S., Kashima, Y., Kim, K., Lempereur, A., Marquez, P., Othman, R., Overlaet, B., Panagiotopoulou, P., Peltzer, K., Florizno-Perez, L. R., Ponomarenko, L., Realo, A., Schei, V., Schmitt, M., Smith, P. B., Soomro, N., Szabo, E., Taveesin, N., Toyama, M., Van de Vliert, E., Vohra, N., Ward, C. (2011). Differences between tight and loose cultures: A 33-nation study. *Science*, 332, 1100–1104.

GSHS survey results (2007). www.who.int/chp/gshs/datasets/en/index.html Retrieved Nov. 8, 2015.

Greene, M. B. (2006). Bullying in schools: A plea for a measure of human rights. *Journal of Social Issues*, 62, 63–79.

Hofstede, G. (1980). *Culture's consequences: International differences in work-related values*. Newbury Park, CA: Sage.

Hofstede, G., Hofstede, G. J. and Minkov, M. (2010). *Cultures and organizations: Software of the mind*. New York: McGraw-Hill.

Jimerson, S. R., Swearer, S. M. and Espelage, D. L. (Eds.). (2010). *Handbook of bullying in schools: An international perspective*. New York and London: Routledge.

Kanetsuna, T., Smith, P. K. and Morita, Y. (2006). Coping with bullying at school: Children's recommended strategies and attitudes to school-based interventions in Japan and England. *Aggressive Behavior*, 32, 570–580.

Konishi, C., Hymel, S., Zumbo, B. D., Li, Z., Taki, M., Slee, P., Pepler, D., Sim, H., Craig, W., Swearer, S. and Kwak, K. (2009). Investigating the comparability of a self-report measure of childhood bullying across countries. *Canadian Journal of School Psychology*, 24, 82–93.

Koo, H. (2004). *The nature of school bullying in South Korea.* Unpublished PhD thesis, London: Goldsmiths, University of London.

Koo, H., Kwak, K. and Smith, P. K. (2008). Victimization in Korean schools: The nature, incidence and distinctive features of Korean bullying or wang-ta. *Journal of School Violence*, 7, 119–139.

Kowalski, R. M., Giumetti, G. W., Schroeder, A. N. and Lattanner, M. R. (2014). Bullying in the digital age: A critical review and meta-analysis of cyberbullying research among youth. *Psychological Bulletin*, 140, 1073–1137.

Lansford, J. E. and 17 other authors (2012). Boys' and girls' relational and physical aggression in nine countries. *Aggressive Behavior*, 38, 298–308.

Lee, S-H., Smith, P. K. and Monks. C. P. (2011). Perceptions of bullying-like phenomena in South Korea: a qualitative approach from a lifespan perspective. *Journal of Aggression, Conflict, and Peace Research*, 3, 209–221.

    (2012). Meaning and usage of a term for bullying-like phenomena in South Korea: a lifespan perspective. *Journal of Language and Social Psychology*, 31, 342–349.

Li, Y., Wang, M., Wang, C. and Shi, J. (2010). Individualism, collectivism, and Chinese adolescents' aggression: Intracultural variations. *Aggressive Behavior*, 36, 187–194.

Livingstone, S., Haddon, L., Görzig, A. and Ólafsson, K. (2011). *Risks and safety on the internet: The perspective of European children. Full findings.* LSE, London: EU Kids Online.

Menesini, E., Eslea, M., Smith, P. K., Genta, M. L., Giannetti, E., Fonzi, A. and Costabile, A. (1997). A cross-national comparison of children's attitudes towards bully/victim problems in school. *Aggressive Behavior*, 23, 245–257.

Morita, Y. (1985). *Ijime shuudan no kouzo ni kansuru shakaigakuteki kenkyu* [Sociological study on the structure of bullying group]. Osaka: Department of Sociology, Osaka City University.

Morita, Y., Soeda, H., Soeda, K. and Taki, M. (1999). Japan. In P. K. Smith, Y. Morita, J. Junger-Tas, D. Olweus, R. Catalano and P. Slee (Eds.), *The nature of school bullying: A cross-national perspective* (pp. 309–323). London and New York: Routledge.

Mullis, L. V. S., Martin, M. O., Foy, P. and Arora, A. (2012). *TIMSS 2011 International Results in Mathematics.* TIMSS and PIRLS International Study Center, Boston College.

Olweus, D. (1999). Norway. In P. K. Smith, Y. Morita, J. Junger-Tas, D. Olweus, R. Catalano and P. Slee (Eds.), *The nature of school bullying: A cross-national perspective* (pp. 28–48). London and New York: Routledge.

O'Moore, A. M., Kirkham, C. and Smith, M. (1997). Bullying behaviour in Irish schools: A nationwide study. *Irish Journal of Psychology*, 18, 141–169.

Pereira, B., Mendonça, D., Neto, C., Valente, L. and Smith, P. K. (2004). Bullying in Portuguese schools. *School Psychology International*, 25, 241–254.

Printed in the United States
By Bookmasters